Southern Living.

Secrets of the South's Best
BARBECUE

Tabb's Barbecue
Pork, page 110

Southern Living®

Secrets of the South's Best
BARBECUE

Compiled and Edited by
Jane E. Gentry and Rebecca Brennan

Oxmoor
House®

©2006 by Oxmoor House, Inc.
Book Division of Southern Progress Corporation
P. O. Box 2262, Birmingham, Alabama 35201-2262

Southern Living® is a federally registered trademark
belonging to Southern Living, Inc.

Hardcover ISBN-13: 978-0-8487-3119-9
Hardcover ISBN-10: 0-8487-3119-0
Softcover ISBN-13: 978-0-8487-3153-3
Softcover ISBN-10: 0-8487-3153-0
Library of Congress Control Number: 2006930813
Printed in the United States of America
First Printing 2006

Editor in Chief: Nancy Fitzpatrick Wyatt
Executive Editor: Susan Carlisle Payne
Copy Chief: Allison Long Lowery

SouthernLiving®
Secrets of the South's Best Barbecue

Foods Editor: Jane E. Gentry
Editor: Rebecca Brennan
Senior Copy Editor: L. Amanda Owens
Editorial Assistant: Rachel Quinlivan, R.D.
Photography Director: Jim Bathie
Senior Photographers: Ralph Anderson, Van Chaplin,
    Joseph De Sciose, Art Meripol, John O'Hagan,
    Mark Sandlin, Charles Walton IV
Photographers: Jean Allsopp, Mary Margaret Chambliss,
    Gary Clark, Tina Cornett, William Dickey, Beth Dreiling,
    Laurey W. Glenn, Meg McKinney, Becky Luigart-Stayner
Senior Photo Stylists: Kay E. Clarke, Buffy Hargett
Associate Photo Stylist: Alan Henderson
Photo Stylists: Lisa Powell Bailey, Cindy Manning Barr,
    Katherine Eckert, Sarah Jernigan, Rose Nguyen,
    Mindi Shapiro, Cari South, Amy P. Wilson
Director, Test Kitchens: Elizabeth Tyler Austin
Assistant Director, Test Kitchens: Julie Christopher
Food Stylists: Vanessa McNeil Rocchio, Angela Sellers,
    Kelley Self Wilton
Test Kitchens Staff: Nicole Lee Faber, Kathleen Royal Phillips
Director of Production: Laura Lockhart
Senior Production Manager: Greg A. Amason
Production Assistant: Faye Porter Bonner

Contributors
Designer: Nancy Johnson
Indexer: Mary Ann Laurens
Editorial Assistant: Brigette Gaucher
Interns: Jill Baughman, Ashley Leath, Mary Katherine Pappas,
    Vanessa Rusch Thomas, Lucas Whittington

Cover: Maple Spareribs, page 115
Back Cover: Bacon Potato Salad, page 233; Mocha Fudge
    Pie, page 296; Asian Barbecue Chicken, page 126;
    Smoked Brisket Sandwiches, page 99

To order additional publications, call 1-800-765-6400.

For more books to enrich your life, visit **oxmoorhouse.com**

Contents

Our Best Backyard Barbecues **8**
Barbecue Basics 10
Braggin' Rights 18
Pit Stops. 19
Barbecue Cook-offs and Festivals. 26

Outdoor Living **28**
Setting the Scene. 30
Secrets to Great Get-Togethers. 36

Barbecue Bounty **40**
Thirst Quenchers and Nibbles. 42
Great Outdoor Cooking. 94
Rainy-Day Barbecue Options 146
Sauces, Marinades, and More 178
On the Side 214
Sweet Tooth. 262

Appendices **322**
Great Barbecue Menus 322
Food Safety 324
Metric Equivalents. 325
Index 326

Welcome

Barbecue is one of those topics that's as vast and deep as the Mississippi River. Just deciding whether the term refers to a cooking method rather than a meat is cause for lengthy discussion. Go down that path, and you'll quickly find as many opinions about the ways in which barbecue should be cooked—er smoked—as there are leaves on an oak tree. Then there's the question of whether it refers to pork, beef, ribs, or chicken. And don't even think about venturing into the sauce debate (or for fans of "dry" barbecue, the lack thereof). Fact is, however you define it, barbecue is a personal, uniquely regional subject that varies from state to state and, in some cases, county to county.

That's why I'm so excited about *Southern Living® Secrets of the South's Best Barbecue*. It's your ultimate guide packed with all the recipes and ideas you'll need to host truly unforgettable gatherings. Or, if you prefer to order up 'cue rather than cook it yourself, hit the road and check out our recommendations for nearly 100 don't-miss pig stands, rib shacks, smokehouses, and smoke pits.

Whether you're new to barbecue or an old pro, there's something here for you. From equipment and gadgets to sides and sauces (and everything in between), this indispensable cookbook gives you all the confidence you need. We even tell you how to create a little slow-cooked indoor magic using an oven or slow cooker.

So fire up your favorite grill or smoker, and get ready to enjoy some of the South's finest food— and one of our favorite ways to entertain.

Fire up the Smoker!

Scott Jones
Executive Editor

Smoky Barbecue
Brisket, page 156

Our Best
Backyard
Barbecues

Barbecue Basics

On these pages, you'll get the inside scoop on choosing a grill, selecting the best barbecue gear, and mastering the fire.

Comparing Charcoal and Gas Grills

Charcoal or gas? It's a heated debate with die-hard fans in both camps. If you're serious about your barbecue, why not go for one of each? Consider the following when choosing grills.

Charcoal Grills

Some avid grillers think there's no substitute for the hands-on experience of building a fire with charcoal and controlling the heat during the cooking. Consider these features when choosing a charcoal grill.

■ **Construction**
Choose a grill made of high-grade steel. A baked-on porcelain-enamel finish is more durable than a sprayed-on paint finish. Preassembled and/or welded parts provide strength and stability.

■ **Basic Features**
The grates on charcoal grills are either stainless steel or nickel plated, which makes them easy to clean and rust resistant. Wooden or plastic handles stay cool. Choose a grill that is large enough to cook with both direct and indirect heat—you need to be able to place coals on opposite sides of the charcoal grate, leaving an empty space in the middle.

■ **Added Conveniences**
A hinged food grate makes it easy to add more charcoal when necessary. Some grills include a thermometer, which lets you effortlessly regulate the internal temperature of the grill.

■ **Advantages**
Low cost and portable; charcoal gives food an authentic smoky flavor.

■ **Disadvantages**
Coals can be difficult to light and take a while to warm up; heat can be tricky to regulate. Cleanup is not as easy as with gas.

Gas Grills

Gas grills give you greater control over heat and are easier to light than charcoal grills. Here are some points to ponder when selecting a gas grill.

■ **Construction**
Select a gas grill made of high-grade steel with a baked-on finish. For a strong and stable grill, the cart should have welded legs.

■ **Basic Features**
A basic gas grill has burners for heat; angled metal bars, lava rocks, or ceramic briquettes to distribute the heat; and a food grate. For the best heat control, purchase a grill that has two or more separate burners and angled metal bars over the burners. A lava rock system is the least preferable; collected grease can cause flare-ups.

■ **Added Conveniences**
Gas gives you greater control over the heat and is easier to light than charcoal. Side burners, an option on some grills, make it easy to cook sauces and side dishes along with the meat. Many models also have convenient side tables and condiment holders.

■ **Advantages**
Easily started with a push-button or rotary igniter. Optional accessories include smokers, steamers, and electric rotisseries. Cleanup is simple.

■ **Disadvantages**
Significantly more expensive than charcoal grills. Food cooked on a gas grill doesn't have the smoky intensity or charcoal-grilled flavor.

Before you fire up the grill, assemble the proper tools to help you get maximum flavor from your food with minimal effort from you. Here is some gear you'll want to have on hand.

■ **Chimney Starter:** Every charcoal grill owner should have one of these. Place charcoal in the top. Wad newspaper in the bottom of the starter, place the chimney on the food grate or a fireproof surface, and ignite. When the coals are ready, pour them into the grill.

■ **Butane Lighter:** No more looking for matches. A butane lighter has a long handle, which makes it safer and easier to use than matches—and easier to find!

■ **Meat Thermometer:** Repeatedly checking the temperature of any meat can cool the oven or pit and tack on extra cooking time. A digital roasting thermometer with probe can stay in the meat during cooking, allowing the oven door or grill lid to remain closed.

■ **Timer:** A standard kitchen timer paired with a meat thermometer helps you turn out perfectly grilled food every time.

■ **Skewers:** Placing small foods on skewers makes cooking easy. Soak wooden or bamboo skewers in water for 30 minutes before using them to prevent burning.

■ **Metal Spatula:** A long-handled spatula with a stainless-steel blade is an essential grilling tool. Choose a wide spatula for easy turning.

■ **Long-Handled Fork:** To lift large roasts and whole birds from the grill after cooking, use a meat fork. To avoid losing tasty juices, don't pierce meat during cooking.

■ **Grill Tongs:** These are useful for turning most foods. Look for tongs with long handles and a spring hinge.

■ **Basting Mop:** Using a good basting mop offers an efficient way to mop meats with sauces without keeping the grill lid open for long periods.

■ **Basting Brush:** Use a basting brush to apply thick sauces to meats. Most labeled as "barbecue brushes" are for small jobs. For big jobs, look for a large paintbrush with natural bristles; synthetic bristles can melt if they touch a hot grate.

■ **Barbecue Gloves:** Flame-retardant gloves protect your hands when working with hot grills and coals.

■ **Grill Brush:** A stiff wire brush makes cleanup fast. Use a grill brush to scrub down food grates before they cool.

Cooking with a Grill

With a few helpful hints and a little practice, you'll be a grillmaster in no time.

Grilling 101

Here's a review of the finer points of using a grill.

■ Start with a clean grill. Dip a paper towel in oil and rub it over the food grate before preheating or lighting charcoal. Use a light touch because dripping oil causes flare-ups.

■ Start cooking with a hot surface. Preheat the grill before adding food to ensure even cooking and to reduce sticking.

■ For a charcoal grill, use a chimney-type starter to help coals heat quickly with a match and a few pieces of newspaper. Or use an electric charcoal lighter with a heating element.

■ Fire needs oxygen to burn, so be sure vents are open enough to keep it burning; the wider the vent, the hotter the fire. Cleaning out old ashes also allows better air flow, which equals more oxygen.

■ Cook whole fish, fish steaks, or fish fillets in a grill basket to ease turning. Coat the hinged wire basket with vegetable cooking spray before placing the seafood inside. If a grill basket isn't available, place seafood pieces on aluminum foil or directly on the food grate perpendicular to the grill bars to minimize sticking and to keep pieces from falling through the grate.

■ Basting brushes made of natural bristles (rather than synthetic) are handy for dabbing on marinades and sauces.

■ Long-handled tongs and spatulas are great for turning hot foods on the grill. Tongs won't pierce the flesh and will keep juices inside.

■ Keep a spray bottle filled with water nearby to control flare-ups or stray sparks. Be careful not to douse the fire.

■ Test for doneness. Instant-read and digital thermometers with forklike prongs are available at kitchen and home-improvement stores. Best used on cuts at least 1 inch thick, they should be inserted into the thickest portion of the food.

■ Clean the food grate with a wire brush after every use. A hot grate is easier to scrape than a cold one.

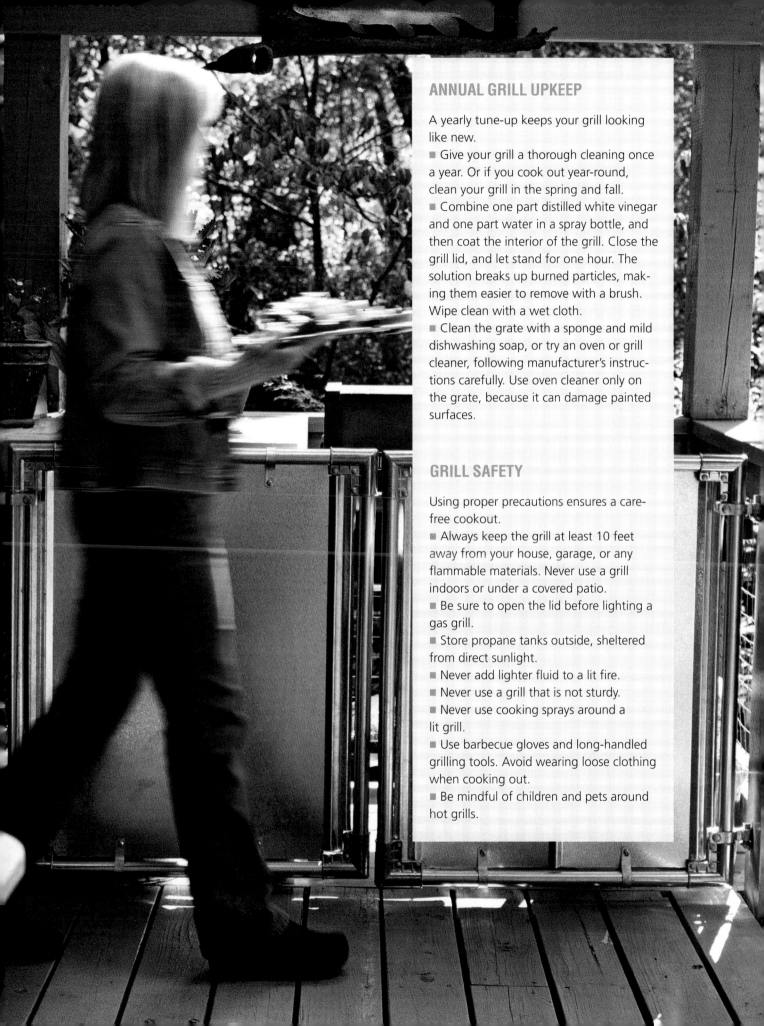

ANNUAL GRILL UPKEEP

A yearly tune-up keeps your grill looking like new.

■ Give your grill a thorough cleaning once a year. Or if you cook out year-round, clean your grill in the spring and fall.

■ Combine one part distilled white vinegar and one part water in a spray bottle, and then coat the interior of the grill. Close the grill lid, and let stand for one hour. The solution breaks up burned particles, making them easier to remove with a brush. Wipe clean with a wet cloth.

■ Clean the grate with a sponge and mild dishwashing soap, or try an oven or grill cleaner, following manufacturer's instructions carefully. Use oven cleaner only on the grate, because it can damage painted surfaces.

GRILL SAFETY

Using proper precautions ensures a care-free cookout.

■ Always keep the grill at least 10 feet away from your house, garage, or any flammable materials. Never use a grill indoors or under a covered patio.

■ Be sure to open the lid before lighting a gas grill.

■ Store propane tanks outside, sheltered from direct sunlight.

■ Never add lighter fluid to a lit fire.

■ Never use a grill that is not sturdy.

■ Never use cooking sprays around a lit grill.

■ Use barbecue gloves and long-handled grilling tools. Avoid wearing loose clothing when cooking out.

■ Be mindful of children and pets around hot grills.

Mastering the Fire

Choosing between direct and indirect heat is easy: Direct heat works best on foods that cook in no more than 30 minutes; consider using indirect heat if something needs to cook longer than 30 minutes.

Direct Heat

With direct-heat grilling, food cooks directly over the heat source. Quick-cooking foods suitable for direct heat include hamburgers, steaks, chops, boneless chicken pieces, fish fillets, and vegetables. To ensure even cooking, turn foods once. Direct heat is also used to sear meat and to get appealing grill marks.

Direct-Heat Cooking with a Charcoal Grill
■ Distribute hot coals evenly across the charcoal grate. Place the food grate over the coals, close the grill lid, and let the grate heat for 10 minutes.
■ Place food on the food grate. Close the grill lid, lifting it only to turn food or to test for doneness at the end of the recommended cooking time.

Direct-Heat Cooking with a Gas Grill
■ Turn all burners on High, close the grill lid, and pre-heat for 10 minutes.
■ Adjust the burners to the temperature recommended

in the recipe. Place food on the food grate. Close the grill lid, lifting it only to turn food or to test for doneness at the end of the recommended cooking time.

Indirect Heat

Indirect-heat grilling means the fire is off to one side of the grill. The heat circulates around the food and cooks it slowly and evenly on all sides. Foods that are fit for indirect heat include roasts, ribs, whole chickens, turkeys, and other large cuts.

Indirect-Heat Cooking with a Charcoal Grill
■ Distribute hot coals evenly on opposite sides of the charcoal grate. Center a drip pan between the coals to catch drippings. Add water to the pan for longer cooking times to keep the drippings from burning.
■ Place the food grate over the coals, close the grill lid, and let the grate heat for 10 minutes.
■ Place food on the food grate. Close the grill lid, lifting it only to turn food or to test for doneness at the end of the recommended cooking time.

Indirect-Heat Cooking with a Gas Grill
■ Turn all burners on High, close the grill lid, and pre-heat for 10 minutes.
■ Adjust the outside burners to the temperature recommended in the recipe. Place food on the food grate, and turn off the burners directly below the food. Close the grill lid, lifting it only to turn food or to test for doneness at the end of the recommended cooking time.

LIGHT YOUR COALS WITH EASE

If the thought of grilling over charcoal sends you running indoors, fear no more. Lighting the coals is easier than you think. Consider purchasing a charcoal chimney, available at any home-improvement store for about $20. It eliminates the need for lighter fluid or treated charcoal, which can affect the flavor of your food. Just follow these simple steps, and you'll have hot coals in no time.

1. Pack the bottom of the charcoal chimney with newspaper, and then fill the canister with untreated charcoal.

2. Place the chimney upright on the food grate. Light the newspaper through the holes at the bottom of the chimney.

3. Let the coals smolder in the canister until they turn completely ashy in color. Remove the food grate, and carefully pour the hot coals onto the bottom of the grill. Replace the food grate—and start grilling!

Smoking, Planking, and Rotisserie Cooking

Once you've mastered the differences between direct and indirect heat, you may want to expand your repertoire to include more advanced grilling techniques.

Smoking

The enticing aroma and flavor of smoked foods evoke the very nature of the grill; you can almost taste the fire in these dishes. Any grill can be used for smoke cooking with a few hardwood chunks.

■ To fuel a smoker, use either all-natural lump charcoal or regular charcoal briquettes.

■ Use only untreated, seasoned hardwood, such as apple, hickory, mesquite, or pecan. You'll be able to detect subtle differences in flavor depending on the type of wood used. Wood chunks are generally used for smoking; soak them at least one hour or even overnight. Wood chips are smaller than chunks and burn faster. They're generally used for foods that smoke in 30 minutes or less.

■ The amount of charcoal needed depends on the size of the smoker, its heat retention, and the weather. You'll need to add charcoal during cooking to maintain the right temperature. Your smoker should have a built-in thermometer that gives you an exact temperature reading.

■ Resist the temptation to lift the lid to check meat before the recommended cooking time has elapsed; doing so allows heat and moisture to escape and adds to the cooking time.

Planking

Unlike grilled foods, which can dry out quickly when left too long on the grill, foods cooked on a plank stay moist and tender because of the damp smoke that wafts from the wooden plank. The smoldering plank adds a smoky essence that complements other flavors without overpowering them.

■ Planks for grilling, sized to fit standard grills, are available seasonally from barbecue and gourmet stores (such as Williams-Sonoma) and year-round from seafood markets.

■ After placing the plank on the grill, immediately cover the grill so that the smoke quickly surrounds the food.

■ Cedar planks burn easier than other woods, so keep a spray bottle handy to douse flare-ups.

■ Use oven mitts to remove the plank, and place it on a heatproof serving platter or baking sheet.

Rotisserie

When you want to showcase the meat and all its natural flavors, rotisserie cooking is the way to go.

■ This method uses a meat's natural juices to baste, rather than allowing those juices to drip into the flames. Meats cooked in this manner are exceptionally succulent and have an enticing crispy skin.

■ Whether you use a charcoal or gas grill, you'll need a rotisserie attachment, which is easy to use and basically involves setting the timer. No hands-on action needed.

◀ A lot of wood isn't necessary to gain good flavor. Three or four wood chunks or a couple handfuls of chips should be plenty, but experiment by using more wood to get a stronger smoke flavor or less for milder results.

▶ Start your fire, and let coals burn down until they're covered with gray ash. Cover coals with soaked wood chunks, and set the smoker vents to produce a smooth, even draft. Add herbs, citrus peel, or spices to the fire for more complex flavor.

▲ Always soak the plank before using. A soaked plank produces maximum smoke and is less likely to burn. Submerge it in water at least an hour. Weigh it down with a can.

▲ Food that touches the wood takes on more flavor, so arrange it on the wooden plank in a single layer.

▲ A rotisserie slowly rotates food impaled on a spit over a heat source. This process allows heat to circulate evenly around meat or poultry while it self-bastes with its own juices. Most rotisseries are motorized. Extra-large rotisseries accommodate whole carcasses as shown above. Smaller rotisseries are made to fit family-size grills.

Braggin' Rights

As long as there's been a South, we've loved barbecue—the one food that defines us most as a region. From the nation's capital, south to Florida, across the Gulf states, to the Oklahoma plains, barbecue scents nearly all Southern breezes.

"There are four barbecue meccas," says Carolyn Wells, executive director of the Kansas City Barbeque Society. "The Carolinas form the cradle of American barbecue. Memphis is the undisputed pork barbecue capital of the world. The entire state of Texas considers itself a capital. Kansas City is the melting pot, where all regional styles come together."

The definition of **SOUTH CAROLINA** barbecue is as hard to nail down as hickory smoke. Folks along the coast and up toward Columbia prefer the state's trademark mustard sauce, while the people of the Pee Dee region are passionate about **vinegar-and-pepper sauce.** Upstate, they favor **red sauce.** In some establishments, you'll find all three flavors on the table; in others, serving them together is an act of heresy. And then, depending on to whom you're talking, the

geographic boundaries of these preferences can vary widely. Though a few restaurants outside the state may serve **mustard sauce,** its true home is mid- to lower-South Carolina.

In **NORTH CAROLINA,** barbecue means pork—cooked slowly, finely chopped, and seasoned with controversy. A culinary rift (some say battle line) cleaves the state into two deeply held barbecue traditions. These two traditions are **Eastern-style and Lexington-style** sometimes called Piedmont-style. Each elevates pork into a distinctively delicious offering that is aromatic, tender, and succulent. The fuss is part pride, part preference. **EASTERN-STYLE** barbecue is **prepared from the whole hog;** the cooked meat is finely chopped and seasoned with a sauce of **vinegar, salt, black pepper, and red pepper. LEXINGTON-STYLE** barbecue cooks only **pork shoulders,** which are chopped (also sliced) and seasoned with **ketchup, brown or white sugar, salt, pepper,** and other seasonings that impart a sweet flavor. Each tradition offers preferred sides and sweet tea, but coleslaw—**barbecue slaw**—reinforces the regional schism. Made from finely shredded or coarsely chopped cabbage, it's never creamy and comes in three colors: white, yellow, or red. **Eastern slaw** is dressed with

Pit Stops

From pig stands and rib shacks to smokehouses and smoke pits, here's a listing of joints we visited on our search for the best Southern barbecue.

Alabama
■ **Archibald's BBQ**
1211 Martin Luther King Blvd.
Northport, AL 35476
(205) 345-6861
other locations in Alabama
■ **Big Bob Gibson Bar-B-Q**
1715 Sixth Avenue SE
Decatur, AL 35601
(256) 350-6969
www.bigbobgibsonbbq.com
other locations in Decatur
■ **Bob Sykes BarB-Q**
1724 Ninth Avenue North
Bessemer, AL 35020
(205) 426-1400
ordering info: 1-800-447-9537
www.bobsykes.com
■ **Chuck's Bar-B-Que**
905 Short Avenue
Opelika, AL 36801
(334) 749-4043
■ **Dreamland Bar-B-Que**
5535 15th Avenue East
Tuscaloosa, AL 35405
(205) 758-8135
ordering info: 1-800-752-0544
www.dreamlandbbq.com
other locations in Alabama
and in Atlanta
■ **Whitt's Barbecue**
1397 East Elm Street
Athens, AL 35611
(256) 232-7928

Arkansas
■ **McClard's Bar-B-Q**
505 Albert Pike
Hot Springs, AR 71901
(501) 623-9665 or toll free
1-866-622-5273
www.mcclards.com

■ **Sim's Bar-B-Que**
716 West 33rd Street
Little Rock, AR 72206
(501) 372-6868
other locations in
Little Rock

Delaware
■ **Where Pigs Fly**
617 East Lockerman Street
Dover, DE 19901
(302) 678-0586
www.wherepigsflyrestaurant.com

Florida
■ **B.C.'s General Store**
8730 County Road 48
Yalaha, FL 34797
(352) 324-3730
■ **Brodus' Bar-B-Que**
103 Taylor Avenue
Groveland, FL 34736
(352) 429-4707
■ **Bubbalou's Bodacious Bar-B-Que**
12100 Challenger Parkway
Orlando, FL 32826
(407) 423-1212
www.bubbalous.com
other locations in Florida
■ **Choctaw Willy's**
214 West Broad Street
Groveland, FL 34736
(352) 429-4188
other locations in Florida
■ **Jack's Barbeque**
100 South U.S. 27
Minneola, FL 34711
(352) 394-2673
■ **King's Taste Barbecue**
503 Palmetto Street
Eustis, FL 32726
(352) 589-0404

mayonnaise (white) or mustard (yellow) and sweetened with sugar and even chopped sweet pickles, giving a mellow taste. **Lexington slaw** is red because it is dressed with vinegar, sugar, and barbecue dip—a sweet-flavored vinegar-based sauce—or ketchup, giving a sweet-tart, peppy flavor. Slaw is indispensable, whether served alongside or on the sandwich.

For some purists, the border of the barbecue belt goes no further than North Carolina's state line. But if you are 'cue hopping across the **DELMARVA PENINSULA,** you're in for a surprise. Here, you'll find plates piled with meat from **pulled pork to chicken** and sauces that range from **Texas-style to South Carolina mustard-based.**

In **DELAWARE AND MARYLAND,** where broilers, roosters, and hens outnumber people, **slow-roasted chicken halves and quarters** are the barbecue of choice. In **VIRGINIA,** there's a barbecue joint every few miles, and, not surprisingly, **pork is king.** Still, the sauces vary from South Carolina mustard-style to Memphis-style reds, depending on who started the restaurant. **Red sauce** tends to rule in central Virginia. **Vinegar-style** eastern North Carolina barbecue is found in southernmost spots.

The heart of barbecue beats in **MEMPHIS,** a city of 1.1 million people, where more than one hundred restaurants specialize in **pork and ribs** traditionally slow-cooked over coals. A Memphis native and amateur cook who competes in the Memphis in May World Championship Barbecue Cooking Contest says it best when asked where good barbecue is prepared elsewhere in Tennessee. "Nowhere," he states. "Our worst is better than the best anywhere else."

In **TEXAS,** African-Americans, Anglos, Germans, and Mexicans have tossed their flavors onto the grills and pits. **German smoked sausages** (often in hot links) and **Mexican** *cabrito* (goat) join **chicken, pork ribs, slaw, beans, and potato salad** on plates. **Beef brisket** stars, however, with a sweet, hot sauce (properly served on the side) in a color between Texas burnt orange and Aggie maroon.

Georgia
■ **Colonel Poole's Bar-B-Q**
164 Craig Street
East Ellijay, GA 30539
(706) 635-4100
www.poolesbarbq.com
■ **Fresh Air Barbecue**
1164 Highway 42 South
Jackson, GA 30233
(770) 775-3182
www.freshairbarbecue.com
other locations in Georgia
■ **Johnny Harris Restaurant & Lounge**
1651 East Victory Drive
Savannah, GA 31404
(912) 354-7810
ordering info: 1-888-547-2823
www.johnnyharris.com
■ **Old Clinton Barbecue House**
4214 Gray Highway
Gray, GA 31032
(478) 986-3225
■ **Pink Pig**
824 Cherrylog Street
Cherrylog, GA 30522
(706) 276-3311
■ **Sprayberry's Barbecue**
229 Jackson Street
Newnan, GA 30263
(770) 253-4421
www.sprayberrysbbq.com

Kentucky
■ **Carr's Barn**
216 West Broadway Street
Mayfield, KY 42066
(270) 247-8959
■ **George's Bar-B-Q**
1362 East Fourth Street
Owensboro, KY 42303
(270) 926-9276
■ **Hill's Bar-B-Que**
1002 Cuba Road
Mayfield, KY 42066
(270) 247-9121
■ **Moonlite Bar-B-Q Inn**
2840 West Parrish Avenue
Owensboro, KY 42301
(270) 684-8143 or
1-800-322-8989
www.moonlite.com
■ **Old Hickory Pit Bar-B-Que**
338 Washington Avenue
Owensboro, KY 42301
(270) 926-9000
■ **Ole South BBQ**
3523 State 54 East
Owensboro, KY 42303
(270) 926-6464

■ **Shady Rest Barbecue Inn**
3955 East Fourth Street
Owensboro, KY 42303
(270) 926-8234
■ **Starnes Bar-B-Q**
1008 Joe Clifton Drive
Paducah, KY 42001
(270) 444-9555

Louisiana
■ **Grayson's Barbeque**
5849 State 71
Clarence, LA 71414
(318) 357-0166
■ **Pig Stand Restaurant**
318 East Main Street
Ville Platte, LA 70586
(337) 363-2883

Maryland
■ **Em-Ing's**
9811 Whaleyville Road
Bishopville, MD 21813
(410) 352-5711 or toll free
1-888-458-7436
www.em-ings.com
other locations in Delaware

Mississippi
■ **Goldie's Trail Bar-B-Q**
4127 Washington Street
Vicksburg, MS 39180
(601) 636-9839
■ **Leatha's Bar-B-Que Inn**
6374 U.S. 98 West
Hattiesburg, MS 39402
(601) 271-6003
www.leathas.com
■ **Westside Bar-B-Que**
Highway 30 West
New Albany, MS 38652
(662) 534-7276

Missouri
■ **Arthur Bryant's BBQ**
1727 Brooklyn Avenue
Kansas City, MO 64127
(816) 231-1123
www.arthurbryantsbbq.com
other locations in Kansas City
■ **Danny Edwards Famous Kansas City Barbecue**
1227 Grand Blvd.
Kansas City, MO 64106
(816) 283-0880
■ **Fiorella's Jack Stack Barbecue**
101 West 22nd Street
Suite 300
Kansas City, MO 64108
(816) 472-7427
www.jackstackbbq.com
other locations in Missouri and Kansas
■ **Gates Bar-B-Q**
1325 East Emmanuel Cleaver Blvd.
Kansas City, MO 64110
(816) 531-7522
www.gatesbbq.com
other locations in Missouri and Kansas

States west of the Mississippi and east of the Red River blend Eastern and Texas traditions with their own unique styles. **ARKANSAS** feels the tug of Southeast and Southwest. It's a state divided between **beef and pork** and colored with **clear, yellow, and dark red sauces**. **OKLAHOMA** welcomes barbecued **bologna** to the plate. It accompanies beef and pork, and also forms one layer of a sandwich, the "Badwich," which is served in **TULSA** piled high with sausage, beef, ham, and chopped pork.

KANSAS CITY is no place for a vegetarian. If it runs, flies, walks, swims, or crawls, chances are it's smoked on a barbecue pit somewhere in Kansas City. In this town, nearly everyone is a "barbecutioner." October's American Royal Barbecue competition draws around 400 teams, while residents can dine at some 85 restaurants in the metropolitan area. The aromas of roasting pork and beef waft under many a visitor's nose before he or she steps off the plane at Kansas City International. Stroll into a local grocery store, and you'll find 75-plus brands of barbecue sauce sitting on the shelves. College professors debate the finer points of **tomato- versus vinegar-based sauces,** and on certain windless days, Kansas City seems to linger under a smoky haze. While the rest of the South squabbles over how and what to barbecue, Kansas City has simply adopted every conceivable style. **Hot sauces vie with sweet. Pork rubs up against brisket. Turkey, ham, and chicken share plates with spareribs, lamb ribs, baby back ribs, and beef ribs.** Kansas City sauces tend not to be as vinegary as in Memphis or as spicy as in Texas.

In **KENTUCKY,** a once-plentiful but now-vanished local resource—**sheep**—has given **OWENSBORO** a special place in the world of barbecue. Why mutton? Simple: It was available. In the late 1800s, Dutch settlers raised lots of sheep in Daviess County. When it came time to contribute to the church picnic, local farmers would often butcher a sheep that was past its prime as a breeder or wool producer. The meat of mature sheep can be tough, so the slow, tenderizing process of barbecuing became the cooking method of choice. Today, most of the mutton comes from the sheep belt running from Texas into Canada, but the folks in Owensboro still favor mutton's distinctive taste.

Drive 50 miles in any direction in **GEORGIA,** and you'll find barbecue **pulled here, chopped there, and soaked in sauces of all kinds.** While much of Georgia runs red with ketchup, **COLUMBUS** favors mustard. As one restaurant owner surmises, "It goes back to the African-American cooks here. All the old barbecue places used mustard."

BARBECUE RESTAURANT, JOINT, OR DIVE?

In the upside-down world of barbecue, many think the food is better if it's served in a joint or in a dive. Here's a handy field guide of definitions.

▪ **Restaurant:** Matching furniture, taped music, printed menus. Accepts credit cards. Member of the chamber of commerce.

▪ **Joint:** Screened door, jukebox, beer, chalkboard menu. The cook is nicknamed Bubba. Cash only.

▪ **Dive:** Torn screened door, tattoos, beer, whiskey, flies. No menu. The cook's real name is Bubba, and she has a prison record. You don't tell your mama you go there.

more Pit Stops

North Carolina

▪ **Allen & Son Pit-Cooked Bar-B-Q**
6203 Millhouse Road
Chapel Hill, NC 27516
(919) 942-7576
other locations in North Carolina

▪ **Barbecue Center**
900 North Main Street
Lexington, NC 27292
(336) 248-4633
www.barbecuecenter.com

▪ **Bill's Barbecue & Chicken**
3007 Downing Street SW
Wilson, NC 27893
(252) 237-4372 or
1-800-682-4557
www.bills-bbq.com

▪ **Jimmy's BBQ**
1703 Cotton Grove Road
Lexington, NC 27292
(336) 357-2311

▪ **Lexington Barbecue**
10 U.S. 29/70 South
Lexington, NC 27295
(336) 249-9814

▪ **Rick and Tina Sauls' Café**
8627 Caratoke Highway
Harbinger, NC 27941
(252) 491-5000

▪ **Skylight Inn**
4617 Lee Street
Ayden, NC 28513
(252) 746-4113

▪ **Speedy's Barbecue**
1317 Winston Road
Lexington, NC 27292
(336) 248-2410

▪ **Stamey's Barbecue**
2206 High Point Road
Greensboro, NC 27403
(336) 299-9888
www.stameys.com
other locations in
Greensboro

▪ **Whitley's Barbecue**
Route 11 South
Murfreesboro, NC 27855
(252) 398-4884

▪ **Wilber's Barbecue**
4172 U.S. 70 East
Goldsboro, NC 27534
(919) 778-5218 or
1-888-778-0838
other locations in Goldsboro

Oklahoma

▪ **Bad Brad's Bar-B-Q**
1215 West Main Street
Pawhuska, OK 74056
(918) 287-1212
www.badbrads.com

▪ **Earl's Rib Palace**
6816 North Western Avenue
Oklahoma City, OK 73116
(405) 843-9922
www.earlsribpalace.com
other locations in Oklahoma City

▪ **Elmer's B.B.Q.**
4130 South Peoria Avenue
Tulsa, OK 74105
(918) 742-6702
www.elmersbbq.net

South Carolina

▪ **Bessinger's Bar-B-Que House**
1602 Savannah Highway
Charleston, SC 29407
(843) 556-1354
www.bessingersbbq.com

▪ **Big T Barbecue**
7535-C Garners Ferry Road
Columbia, SC 29209
(803) 776-7132
other locations in
South Carolina

▪ **Bryan's The Pink Pig Bar-B-Que**
Highway 170-A
Hardeeville, SC 29927
(843) 784-3635

▪ **Dukes Bar-B-Que**
789 Chestnut Street
Orangeburg, SC 29115
(803) 534-9418
other locations in
South Carolina

▪ **Jackie Hite's Barbecue**
Highway 23
Leesville, SC 29070
(803) 532-3354

▪ **McCabe's BBQ**
480 North Brooks Street
Manning, SC 29102
(803) 435-2833

▪ **Shuler's Bar-B-Que**
419 Highway 38 West
Latta, SC 29565
(843) 752-4700

Tennessee

▪ **Bar-B-Q Shop**
1782 Madison Avenue
Memphis, TN 38104
(901) 272-1277
www.dancingpigs.com

▪ **Buddy's Bar-B-Q**
5806 Kingston Pike
Knoxville, TN 37919
(865) 588-0051
www.buddysbarbq.com
other locations in Tennessee

▪ **Corky's Ribs & BBQ**
5259 Poplar Avenue
Memphis, TN 38119
(901) 685-9744 or
1-800-926-7597
www.corkysbbq.com
other locations in the U.S.

▪ **Hog Heaven**
115 27th Avenue North
Nashville, TN 37203
(615) 329-1234
www.hogheavenbbq.com
other locations in Tennessee

In **ALABAMA,** sauces coat meat in many colors. A **light vinegar** soaks the chopped pork in **ATHENS.** In **DECATUR,** a **tangy mayonnaise sauce** flavors chicken, but diners may also select a **mild red sauce or a fiery vinegar** and then douse the flames with cool cream pies. As one *Southern Living* editor explains, "Sometimes the pie is as important as the pig."

Smoking is a popular method of outdoor cooking in **FLORIDA.** Just about any meat, foul, or fish that can be smoked is smoked, including mullet, snapper, shellfish, game, pork, beef, and turkey. From the tip of the Keys to the top of the Panhandle, Floridians savor barbecue today just as they have done through the ages. Each bite taken here has been seasoned by natives, immigrants, retirees, and folks just passing through.

In the gumbo and jambalaya provinces of **LOUISIANA,** what is considered traditional Southern barbecue often takes a backseat to the pot dishes of New Orleans and Cajun Country. However, contrary to popular opinion, for those bent on barbecue, all is not lost. In **VILLE PLATTE,** on the northern cusp of Cajun Country, locals dote on turtle stew and tasso and, yes, **smoked pork ribs** smothered in an **onion-and-garlic barbecue sauce.** Then there's **NATCHITOCHES,** the first European settlement in what is now the state of Louisiana. In this Central Louisiana town, you can see that French influences endure. Order a barbecue sandwich in nearby **CLARENCE,** and you have your choice of smoked ham or beef served on homemade French bread, or **"frog bun"** as some locals—in a jab at the French—sometimes call it.

Not surprisingly, barbecue tastes develop close to home. Despite the regional preferences, most Southerners agree that barbecue is the food of home that feeds the heart.

more **Pit Stops**

Tennessee *(continued)*
■ **Jim Neely's Interstate Bar-B-Que**
2265 South Third Street
Memphis, TN 38109
(901) 775-2304
www.jimneelysinterstate
barbecue.com
■ **Neely's Bar-B-Que**
670 Jefferson Avenue
Memphis, TN 38103
(901) 521-9798 or
1-888-780-7427
other locations in Tennessee
■ **Rib & Loin**
5946 Brainerd Road
Chattanooga, TN 37421
(423) 499-6465
other location in Tennessee
■ **Shuford's Smokehouse**
924 Signal Mountain Road
Chattanooga, TN 37405
(423) 267-0080
■ **The Rendezvous**
52 South Second Street
Memphis, TN 38103
(901) 523-2746

Texas
■ **Black's BBQ**
215 North Main Street
Lockhart, TX 78644
(512) 398-2712
www.blacksbbq.com
■ **Cooper's Old Time Pit Bar-B-Que**
505 West Dallas
Llano, Texas 78643
(325) 247-5713
www.coopersbbq.com
■ **Country Tavern**
Highway 31, west of Kilgore
Kilgore, TX 75663
(903) 984-9954
■ **Kreuz Market**
619 North Colorado Street
Lockhart, TX 78644
(512) 398-2361
www.kreuzmarket.com
■ **Lone Star BBQ**
2010 South Bridge Street
Brady, TX 76825
(915) 597-1936
■ **Louie Mueller BBQ**
206 West Second Street
Taylor, TX 76574
(512) 352-6206
■ **Meyer's Elgin Smokehouse**
188 Highway 290
Elgin, TX 78621
(512) 281-3331
www.meyerselginsausage.com

■ **The Salt Lick**
18001 FM 1826
Driftwood, TX 78619
(512) 894-3117
www.saltlickbbq.net
■ **Stubb's Bar-B-Q**
801 Red River
Austin, TX 78701
(512) 480-8341
www.stubbsbbq.com

Virginia
■ **Allman's Bar-B-Que**
1299 Jeff Davis Highway
Fredericksburg, VA 22401
(540) 373-9881
■ **King's Barbecue No.1**
3221 West Washington Street
Petersburg, VA 23803
(804) 732-5861
■ **Olde Virginia Barbecue**
35 Meadow View Avenue
Rocky Mount, VA 24151
(540) 489-1788
■ **Pierce's Pitt Bar-B-Que**
447 East Rochambeau Drive
Williamsburg, VA 23185
(757) 565-2955
■ **Short Sugar's**
2215 Riverside Drive
Danville, VA 24540
(434) 793-4800
■ **The Smokey Pig**
212 South Washington Hwy.
Ashland, VA 23005
(804) 798-4590

Washington, D.C.
■ **Capital Q**
707 H Street NW
Washington, DC 20001
(202) 347-8396
■ **Old Glory All-American Bar-B-Que**
3139 M Street NW
Washington, DC 20007
(202) 337-3406
www.oldglorybbq.com
■ **Rocklands Barbeque and Grilling Company**
2418 Wisconsin Avenue NW
Washington, DC 20007
(202) 333-2558
www.rocklands.com

West Virginia
■ **Big Frank's Bar-B-Que**
1629 West Virginia Avenue
Clarksburg, WV 26301
(304) 623-1009
■ **Dirty Ernie's Rib Pit**
310 Keller Avenue
Fayetteville, WV 25840
(304) 574-4822
www.dirtyernies.com
■ **The Teays House Family Restaurant**
120 Carl's Lane
Scott Depot, WV 25560
(304) 757-5265
■ **Three Little Pigs, Inc.**
HC 37 Box 220
Lewisburg, WV 24901
(304) 645-3270

Barbecue Cook-offs and Festivals

These barbecue cook-offs and festivals, held from Memorial Day weekend to Labor Day weekend, are sanctioned by the International Barbeque Cookers Association, Kansas City Barbeque Society, and Memphis in May.

International Barbeque Cookers Association

■ Colorado County Fair BBQ Cook-off, Columbus, TX
Contact Fausta Kaiser at (979) 732-5030, or e-mail coloradocountybbq@yahoo.com

■ Annual American Legion Barbeque Cook-off, Clifton, TX
Contact American Legion at (254) 675-8782.

■ Annual Itasca Chamber of Commerce BBQ Cook-off, Itasca, TX
Contact Bob Wilson at (254) 687-2331, or e-mail bwilson@hilcozap.net

Kansas City Barbeque Society

■ American Royal Barbecue Contest, Kansas City, MO
Contact Sharon Brown at (816) 569-4030, or email BBQ@americanroyal.com

■ Annual Blue Ridge BBQ Festival, Tryon, NC
Contact Peggy Bolen at (828) 859-7427, e-mail bobbolen@alltel.net, or visit www.blueridgebbqfestival.com

■ Platte City Barbecue Fest Missouri State Championship, Platte City, MO
Contact Karen Wagoner at (816) 858-5270, or e-mail karenwagoner@earthlink.net

■ Wild Turkey Bourbon & Lawrenceburg Kiwanis Club Tennessee State Championship BBQ Cook-off, Lawrenceburg, TN
Contact Carl Counce at (931) 762-3399, or e-mail ccounce@bellsouth.net

■ Annual Pawnee Bill Smoke-off, Pawnee, OK
Contact Sandy Beaudoin at (918) 762-3205, or e-mail pawneetrader@sbcglobal.net

■ Tennessee Amazin' Blazin BBQ Cook-off, Lebanon, TN
Contact Kristina McKee or Wanda Bates at (615) 444-5730, or e-mail tnamazinblazin@aol.com

■ Whistle Stop Festival & Rocket City BBQ Cook-off, Huntsville, AL
Contact Dorothy Havens at (256) 564-8116, e-mail dorothy.havens@hsvcity.com, or visit www.rocketcitybbq.com

■ Florence Labor Day BBQ Cook-off, Florence, KS
Contact Les Allison at (620) 878-4310, or e-mail lesallison@kans.com

■ Benton County Fair & BBQ Cook-off, Ashland, MS
Contact Cathy McMullen at (662) 224-6330, or e-mail cathym@ext.msstate.edu

■ Smoke on the Water BBQ & Music Festival, Pine Bluff, AR
Contact Ron Cates at (870) 537-8175, or e-mail ronnie@catesandcompany.com

Memphis in May

■ Safeway's National Capital Barbecue Battle, Pennsylvania Avenue, Washington, D.C.
Contact Allen Tubis at (301) 860-0630, e-mail barbecue1@aol.com, or visit www.bbq-usa.com

■ Memphis in May World Championship Barbecue Cooking Contest, Memphis, TN
Contact www.memphisinmay.org

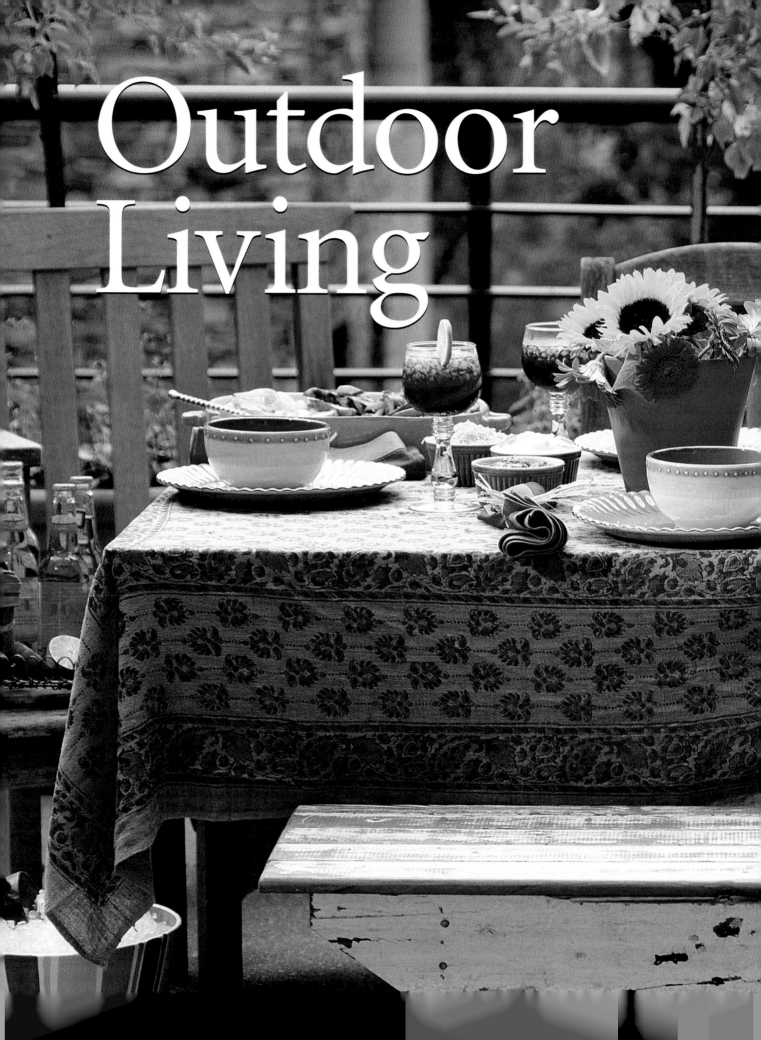

Outdoor Living

Setting the Scene

A little ingenuity ensures that your outdoor dining experience is comfortable, relaxed, and stylish.

A Handy Sideboard

A simple deck bench is the inspiration for this multiuse outdoor table.

■ To create a buffet from a standard bench design, double the height of the bench from 18 to 36 inches.
■ Include a shelf underneath to store such items as an ice chest, which is especially useful when entertaining.
■ Craft a skirt from outdoor fabric, and attach it to the buffet with a tension rod. It hides the storage shelf and gives the buffet indoor style.
■ For entertaining at night, add lamps to the table.

Table to Go

If you don't have an outdoor dining table, create one on the spot.

■ Start with a 7-foot-long folding table.
■ To accommodate eight guests, place three 40- x 30-inch plywood rectangles over the top of the table to form one extended 40- x 90-inch top. Using three sections instead of one makes the top more convenient to transport and store.
■ Install latch hooks and eyes underneath each corner to lock the pieces together when placed side by side. Fit small wooden pegs into adjacent drilled holes for a tight fit.
■ When the party is over, lift off the plywood, stack the pieces, and fold up the table. The parts can be stored easily under a bed, in a closet, or in a garage.

Gather the Goods

Having everything you need on hand in advance of the party means a more relaxed prep time.

■ Stock up on baskets. They're great for serving breads, chips, and cookies.

■ Before a party, bring some of your indoor pillows outside and place them on chairs to add color and comfort.

■ If you're short on outdoor furniture, carry ottomans outside for extra seating, use a tea cart as a bar, and clean up a potting bench to serve as a buffet.

■ String white Christmas lights on deck rails for sparkle.

▲ Colorful kitchen towels make perfect napkins. Wrap flatware in the napkins, and use whimsical shower curtain rings as napkin holders.

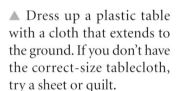 ▲ Dress up a plastic table with a cloth that extends to the ground. If you don't have the correct-size tablecloth, try a sheet or quilt.

▶ Paint the inside of terra-cotta pot saucers with acrylic paint to coordinate with your table setting. When the paint dries, the saucers serve as colorful coasters. Stack additional sets of coasters and tie with ribbon to give as party favors to guests.

CASUAL CARD HOLDERS

Terra-cotta pot feet (normally used to elevate planters) make perfect place-card holders at a barbecue. Use them as easels to hold cards in place.

Tips for the Table

A few decorative touches at the table make your barbecue seem even more special.

■ Lay out serving pieces and utensils ahead so they'll be handy when the food comes off the grill.

■ Pair patterned dishes with solid-colored napkins and vice versa. Mix and match different-colored napkins, and then embellish each place setting with a fresh flower or herb sprig.

■ Turn place mats vertically for a creative twist and to make room for more guests at the table.

■ When guests bring food to the barbecue, use a sticky note or tape to label each dish on the underside with the name of the person who brought it.

■ For candlelight, use votive holders, lanterns, or glass vases to avoid open flames.

▼ For colorful accents, fill vases with aquarium sand; set pillar candles securely in the sand.

▲ Use a multi-plant stand to organize condiments and tableware. Toy bugs are a fun addition to the table decorations.

Add Flair with Flowers

Flowers needn't be fussy. Keep a few key containers on hand for a head start on quick-and-easy arrangements. Here's advice for freshening the scene with blooms.

■ Don't hesitate to use items not traditionally used for floral arranging. If a container won't hold water or is too large, place a jar or cup inside to hold the flowers.

■ Pick up fresh flowers the day before your cookout. Prepare them by stripping the leaves, cutting each stem at an angle under cool running water, and then soaking the stems overnight in a cool place.

■ Arrange the tallest stems first so they set an outline for the bouquet. Insert taller flowers in the center, and fill in with flowers that become progressively shorter as you near the edges of the container.

■ Feel free to supplement garden flowers with blooms purchased from the florist for variety.

■ To keep an arrangement from wilting, place it away from direct sunlight.

■ Keep centerpieces at a height that allows good eye contact among guests.

■ For a long table, use several small arrangements, placing a few blooms in small vases spaced along the length of the table.

▼ Arrange on a coordinating dinner plate small bud vases filled with flowers for an instant centerpiece.

◄ Simple vases, bottles, and canning jars are suitable containers for instant flower arranging. Use a platter to corral a few bedding plants from a garden shop.

▲ Search your kitchen cabinets for an eclectic mix of teapots to compose an interesting—and easy—centerpiece. To arrange long-stemmed flowers, fit a block of water-soaked florist foam in the teapot opening. Insert the flower stems at slight angles to create the appearance of a lush bouquet.

A HINT OF FRAGRANCE

Garnish stemmed glasses with fresh sprigs of rosemary woven around the base. The day before, run cut sprigs under cool water; wrap sprigs in damp paper towels and store in the refrigerator until you're ready to decorate.

Secrets to Great Get-Togethers

Planning ahead is the key to a relaxing party. Here are ways to make the day fun for everyone—even the host and hostess!

Family Reunions

Warm weather and sizzling barbecue signal the season of family gatherings. Follow these suggestions for a carefree event.

Invitations

Clever invitations set the mood for a great party and convey all the essential information so everyone knows "what, when, and where." Here are some pointers.

■ Add a personal touch with handwritten invitations. Use standard wording, or show your poetic side with a rhyming verse. Keep the tone and design casual to match the barbecue mood.

■ Include the necessary facts—who, what, when, where, why—and the how-tos: how to respond, how to get there, and perhaps how to help (what to bring).

■ Use unexpected materials in creative ways. For example, for an outdoor barbecue write party facts on paper fans using a paint pen or permanent marker.

■ Include "RSVP" or "please reply" instead of "regrets only." You need to know how many people will be attending.

■ "Save-the-date" notices are popular for family reunions and other large parties, where people will be traveling to attend. Make these compatible with the invitations to follow.

■ Package your invitations to make a statement. The appearance, the handwriting, and the stamps all factor in having your envelopes grab attention. Visit your post office, or go to www.usps.com to order designer stamps online.

REUNION SURVIVAL TIPS

A good time had by all is the goal of every reunion. Here are a few considerations that can make things run smoothly.

■ Simplify bookkeeping by choosing one person to pay deposits in advance for any rentals—location, cooking equipment, seating—and the balances upon arrival.

■ Spread the fun around: Ask each family to prepare a meal and bring a snack and dessert to share.

■ Find out about special events in the area, consider having a family talent show or sing-along to help pass the time, and don't forget to bring the equipment for outdoor games.

■ A group that arrives early can call others to request last-minute or forgotten items.

Tips for Take-Alongs

Transporting food and other amenities to an outdoor event takes planning. These suggestions make organizing easy.

■ Shop for lightweight, sealable serving containers. Shallow containers provide more surface area to keep food cold and make packing easier.

■ Arrange heavier items on the bottom of your basket and lighter, more fragile items on top. Begin by packing items that you'll need last, ending with the tablecloth.

■ Pack a cooler for perishable food. Use frozen gel packs or ice sealed in zip-top freezer bags to avoid soggy food. Also, freeze water or fruit juice in plastic bottles to help keep food cold; you can have the drinks later with your meal.

■ Know your perishables. Milk products, eggs, poultry, meats, fish, shellfish, cream pies, custards, and creamy salads should be kept at 40° or below. Chill the food before placing it in the cooler.

■ Use a thermos designed to keep hot foods hot.

Don't forget to rinse the thermos with boiling water just before filling it, and heat the food to a high temperature before pouring it into the thermos.

■ On warm days, don't leave food out for more than an hour. Be safe: When in doubt, throw it out.

■ Take along folding chairs for extra seating.

■ Plan entertainment, such as games, and bring a portable CD player and a beach ball, soccer ball, or Frisbee. Add a telescope for stargazing.

■ Tuck in disposable cameras and a small journal to record the memories.

■ For evening gatherings, pack breezeproof torches, hurricane lanterns, or citronella candles, which provide light and repel bugs. To create luminarias, fill paper bags with sand and place a votive holder and candle inside each bag.

■ Bring bug spray, and keep insects away from food with mesh domes.

■ Prepare for cleanup by bringing wet wipes and paper towels. Include two garbage bags: one for trash and one for dirty dishes.

Backyard Buffets

Buffets are a blessing. You can invite more friends than you have seating and set up ahead so guests can dine at their leisure. Consider these ways to make buffet entertaining a breeze.

Strategy

▪ Let guests eat with plates on their laps at large, casual parties, but be sure to serve food that doesn't require a knife. (It's awkward, if not dangerous, to cut while balancing a plate on two knees.)

▪ When dining alfresco, consider setting up the buffet table inside to keep bugs at bay. Use citronella candles to keep bugs away outdoors.

▪ Have a separate table for desserts. Also, put out extra forks and napkins, as guests may not have kept their first set after the main course.

Hardware

▪ Use separate dinner, salad, and dessert plates for small seated gatherings. At large barbecues, guests should be able to put all their food on one plate.

▪ Use a metal bucket or wall pocket to organize bundles of napkins and flatware.

▪ Help traffic flow by placing beverage glasses on a separate table. Offer a variety of sizes, but reserve the largest ones for water. (A 16-ounce cup for wine is just as awkward as a 4-ounce glass for water.)

▪ Designate a tray for dirty plates and glasses, and frequently move dirty dishware out of sight.

Table

▪ Go with the flow. For large parties, set out a double-sided buffet to avoid bottlenecks. Circular tables are fine for small parties. Ask a friend to be first in line in case other guests are hesitant to begin.

▪ Set up the buffet table in logical order. Keep flatware and napkins together at the end for guests to pick up after getting their food.

▪ Use varying heights for visual appeal. Place food on pedestals or over sturdy cloth-covered containers. Fill vertical space with flowers or breadsticks.

▪ Have additional trays of food ready so that you can replenish by exchanging a full tray for an empty one.

▪ Fill serving bowls at least three-fourths full for a sumptuous spread. Bread and buns can spill over to give the look of abundance. Use simple garnishes.

Drink Details

▪ A gracious host offers each guest upon arrival something to drink: iced tea, soft drink, wine, or spirited beverage. However, an elaborate bar setup is not necessary. Place the bar out of the main traffic flow to give room for guests to mingle while getting their drinks.

RAISE THE BAR

Before the crowd gathers, check your supply of bar equipment. Here's a list to get you started.

▪ Bar glasses
▪ Jiggers
▪ Blender (Purchase an extra canister to handle a large party.)
▪ Mixing/serving pitcher
▪ Ice bucket and scoop
▪ Corkscrews
▪ Bottle opener, stoppers
▪ Sharp knife and small cutting board
▪ Party tub
▪ Cocktail napkins

■ For a small barbecue, offer a limited selection of beverages, such as wine or beer, lemonade, and one special mixed drink. For a large party, offer a wider variety of mixed drinks.

■ Have a supply of sparkling and mineral waters, fruit juices, and nonalcoholic beer on hand.

■ To make the bar area look inviting, set beverage supplies on an attractive cart, tray, table, or counter.

■ A wheelbarrow makes a handy ice chest for beverages. If your wheelbarrow is used, line it with a plastic tablecloth.

Do the Math

Plan on approximately two drinks per hour per guest. To help in planning, count on these figures:

■ There are four 6-ounce servings in each 750-milliliter bottle of wine.

■ There are about 17 drinks per 750-milliliter bottle of liquor when $1\frac{1}{2}$ ounces are used per drink.

■ One 10-ounce bottle of mixer per person is usually sufficient.

■ For large parties, consider a keg of beer. It makes for easy serving and serves 30 to 40 guests.

Barbecue Bounty

Blackberry Iced Tea,
page 50

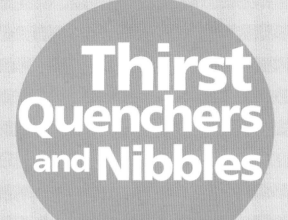

Thirst Quenchers and Nibbles

It sure gets hot on long summer days—especially when the smoker's fired up. Cool off with refreshing tea, fresh-squeezed lemonade, or a spirited beverage. Keep cravings satisfied with a smorgasbord of snacks.

Watermelon-Lemonade
Coolers

Watermelon-Lemonade Coolers
Prep: 25 min., Cook: 10 min., Other: 8 hrs.

15 cups seeded and cubed watermelon
2 (12-oz.) cans frozen lemonade concentrate, thawed
    and undiluted
2 mint sprigs
Garnishes: watermelon wedges, fresh mint sprigs

Process watermelon, in batches, in a blender or food processor until smooth.
Combine lemonade concentrate and 2 mint sprigs, and cook in a saucepan over medium-high heat 10 minutes. Stir together watermelon puree and lemonade mixture; cover and chill 8 hours. Remove and discard mint. Stir and serve over ice. Garnish, if desired. **Makes** 14 cups.

Lemonade Ice Cubes
Prep: 10 min., Other: 8 hrs.

1 (6-oz.) can frozen lemonade concentrate
Red liquid food coloring

Prepare lemonade according to package directions. Stir 4 drops of red food coloring into lemonade; pour into ice cube trays, and freeze 8 hours. **Makes** 2 trays.

Quick Tip: *Lemonade's just the thing to cool off from an all-day barbecue. Add pizzazz to ice cubes by placing lemon rind curls in ice cube trays, filling with water, and freezing.*

Kiwi-Lemonade Spritzer
Prep: 10 min.

4 kiwifruit, peeled
1 (12-oz.) can frozen lemonade concentrate, thawed
    and undiluted
3 cups lemon-lime soft drink, chilled

Cut kiwifruit into chunks. Process fruit chunks and lemonade concentrate in a food processor until smooth, stopping to scrape down sides.
Pour mixture through a wire-mesh strainer into a pitcher, discarding solids. Stir in lemon-lime soft drink just before serving. **Makes** 5 cups.

Strawberry-Kiwi-Lemonade Spritzer: Process 2 cups fresh strawberries; 4 kiwifruit, peeled and cut into chunks; and 1 (12-oz.) can frozen lemonade concentrate, thawed and undiluted, in a food processor until smooth, stopping to scrape down sides. Proceed as directed.

Strawberry-Lemonade Slush
Prep: 20 min., Other: 30 min.

Fresh lemon juice offers a tart tang to this beverage.

2 (16-oz.) containers fresh strawberries, sliced
1½ cups sugar
2 cups water
1½ cups fresh lemon juice (about 6 to 9 medium lemons)
4 cups ice cubes

Stir together sliced strawberries and sugar; let stand 30 minutes.
Process half of strawberry mixture, 1 cup water, ¾ cup lemon juice, and 2 cups ice in a blender until smooth. Repeat procedure with remaining ingredients. Serve immediately. **Makes** about 8 cups.

Fizzy Raspberry Lemonade
Prep: 10 min.

1 (12-oz.) can frozen lemonade concentrate, thawed
  and undiluted
1 (10-oz.) package frozen raspberries, partially thawed
3 Tbsp. sugar
1 (1-liter) bottle club soda, chilled

Process first 3 ingredients in a blender until smooth, stopping to scrape down sides.
Pour raspberry mixture through a wire-mesh strainer into a large pitcher, discarding seeds; stir in club soda. Serve over ice. **Makes** about 7 cups.

Fizzy Strawberry Lemonade: Substitute 1 (10-oz.) package frozen strawberries, partially thawed, for frozen raspberries. Proceed as directed.

make ahead
Cranberry Lemonade
Prep: 10 min.

5 cups water, divided
½ cup sugar
1 (6-oz.) can frozen lemonade concentrate, thawed and
  undiluted
3 cups cranberry juice

Stir together 2 cups water and sugar in a small saucepan over medium heat, stirring until sugar dissolves.
Stir together sugar mixture, lemonade concentrate, cranberry juice, and remaining 3 cups water. Chill until ready to serve. **Makes** 8 cups.

make ahead
Blackberry Lemonade
Prep: 20 min.

3 cups fresh blackberries
7 cups water
¼ cup sugar
¼ cup sugar-free pink lemonade drink mix (we tested
  with part of a 1.9-oz. package of Crystal Light)
Garnishes: fresh mint sprigs, lemon slices

Process blackberries in a blender until smooth, stopping to scrape down sides. Pour through a fine wire-mesh strainer into a 2-qt. pitcher, discarding solids.
Stir in 7 cups water, sugar, and drink mix. Serve over ice. Garnish, if desired. **Makes** 8 cups.

Homemade Lemonade
Prep: 20 min., Other: 8 hrs.

1½ cups sugar
½ cup boiling water
2 tsp. grated lemon rind
1½ cups fresh lemon juice
5 cups cold water
Garnish: lemon slices

Stir together sugar and ½ cup boiling water until sugar dissolves.
Stir in lemon rind, lemon juice, and 5 cups cold water. Chill 8 hours. Garnish, if desired. **Makes** 8 cups.

Homemade Limeade: Substitute 2 tsp. grated lime rind for lemon rind and 1½ cups fresh lime juice for lemon juice. Proceed as directed.

Quick Tip: *About 2 lb. lemons equals 2 cups juice.*

Blackberry Lemonade

Sweet-Tart Lemonade

Sweet-Tart Lemonade
Prep: 20 min.

3 cups cold water
2 cups Sugar Syrup
1¾ to 2 cups fresh lemon juice
Garnish: lemon slices

Stir together all ingredients until well blended; serve over ice. Garnish, if desired. **Makes** 7 cups.

Sugar Syrup
Prep: 5 min., Cook: 5 min.

2 cups sugar
1 cup water
¼ tsp. fresh lemon juice

Stir together all ingredients in a small saucepan. Bring to a boil over medium heat, stirring often. Reduce heat, and simmer 1 minute or until sugar dissolves. Remove from heat; cool. **Makes** 2 cups.

Ginger Tea
Prep: 20 min., Cook: 10 min., Other: 5 min.

2 qt. water
½ cup grated fresh ginger
⅓ cup fresh lemon juice
¼ cup honey
4 regular size green tea bags
1½ cups sugar

Combine 2 qt. water and next 3 ingredients in a large Dutch oven; bring mixture to a boil. Reduce heat to low, and simmer 5 minutes, stirring occasionally. Remove mixture from heat.
Add tea bags; cover and steep 5 minutes. Remove tea bags; stir in sugar, and cool.
Pour tea through a wire-mesh strainer into a pitcher; serve over ice. **Makes** 8 cups.

Iced Hibiscus Tea
Prep: 5 min., Cook: 7 min.

7 cups water, divided
1 cup firmly packed hibiscus flowers*
1 cup sugar

Bring 6 cups water and hibiscus flowers to a boil in a large saucepan. Reduce heat to low, and simmer 5 minutes. Remove from heat, and stir in sugar.
Pour mixture through a wire-mesh strainer into a pitcher, discarding hibiscus flowers. Stir in remaining 1 cup water. Serve over ice. **Makes** 8 cups.

*Substitute 6 regular size red tea bags for 1 cup hibiscus flowers, if desired.

Note: Hibiscus flowers can be found in supermarkets featuring Mexican or Latin foods.

Fruity Mint Tea
Prep: 5 min., Cook: 5 min., Other: 5 min.

1 qt. water
1 cup loosely packed fresh mint leaves
8 regular size tea bags
1 (6-oz.) can frozen lemonade concentrate, thawed and undiluted
1 (6-oz.) can frozen orange juice concentrate, thawed and undiluted
2 cups cold water

Heat 1 qt. water and 1 cup mint leaves in a small saucepan just until water begins to boil. Remove from heat; add tea bags. Cover and steep 5 minutes. Remove tea bags, squeezing gently.
Pour mixture through a fine wire-mesh strainer into a pitcher. Add concentrates and 2 cups cold water, stirring until concentrates dissolve. Cover and chill until ready to serve. Serve over ice. **Makes** about 8 cups.

> **"In the vernacular of the South of not so long ago, there was no such thing as sweet tea. There was just tea, always sweetened in a jug or pitcher with cane sugar, always poured over ice."**
>
> —Rick Bragg, author and Alabama native

Passion Tea

Prep: 10 min.; Other: 1 hr., 3 min.

6¼ cups boiling water
3 family size orange pekoe tea bags
⅓ cup sugar
1 cup cranberry juice cocktail
1 cup frozen passion-fruit juice concentrate, thawed and undiluted

Pour 6¼ cups boiling water over tea bags. Cover and steep 3 minutes. Remove and discard tea bags. Stir in sugar until dissolved. Chill 1 hour.

Stir together chilled tea, cranberry juice, and juice concentrate. Serve over ice. **Makes** 8 cups.

make ahead

Blackberry Iced Tea

Prep: 10 min.; Other: 1 hr., 3 min.

3 cups fresh or frozen blackberries, thawed
1¼ cups sugar
1 Tbsp. chopped fresh mint
Pinch of baking soda
4 cups boiling water
2 family size tea bags
2½ cups cold water
Garnishes: fresh blackberries, fresh mint sprigs

Combine blackberries and sugar in large container. Crush blackberries with wooden spoon. Add mint and baking soda. Set aside.

Pour 4 cups boiling water over tea bags in a large saucepan; cover and steep 3 minutes. Remove and discard tea bags.

Pour tea over blackberry mixture; let stand at room temperature 1 hour.

Pour tea through a wire-mesh strainer into a large pitcher, discarding solids. Add 2½ cups cold water, stirring until sugar dissolves. Cover and chill until ready to serve. Garnish, if desired. **Makes** about 7½ cups.

Simple Southern Iced Tea

Prep: 10 min., Cook: 5 min., Other: 30 min.

4 regular size tea bags (we tested with Luzianne)
5 cups water, divided
½ cup sugar
Garnishes: lemon slices, fresh mint sprigs

Bring tea bags and 2 cups water to a boil in a saucepan; turn off heat. Cover and steep 30 minutes. Remove and discard tea bags.

Pour into a ½-gal. pitcher, and add remaining 3 cups water and sugar, stirring well. Serve over ice. Garnish, if desired. **Makes** 5 cups.

**Simple Southern
Iced Tea**

Iced Red Tea
Prep: 15 min., Other: 5 min.

4 cups boiling water
8 regular size red tea bags (we tested with Kalahari Red
   Tea or Celestial Seasonings Red Zinger)
2 cups cold water
½ cup sugar

Pour 4 cups boiling water over tea bags; cover and steep 5 minutes. Remove tea bags from water, squeezing gently. Add 2 cups cold water and sugar, stirring until sugar dissolves. Serve over ice. **Makes** 8 cups.

make ahead
Cranberry Tea
Prep: 5 min.; Other: 1 hr., 3 min.

1 qt. water
12 whole cloves
2 (3-inch) cinnamon sticks
⅓ cup sugar
4 regular size tea bags
1 (12-oz.) can frozen cranberry juice concentrate,
   thawed and undiluted

Bring first 4 ingredients to a boil in a large saucepan. Pour boiling mixture over tea bags; cover and steep 3 minutes. Remove and discard tea bags. Pour tea through a fine wire-mesh strainer into a pitcher, discarding spices. Stir in juice concentrate. Chill at least 1 hour. Serve over ice. **Makes** about 8 cups.

Speedy Spring Coolers
Prep: 5 min.

1 (6-oz.) can frozen orange juice concentrate, thawed
   and undiluted
1 (12-oz.) can frozen unsweetened apple juice
   concentrate, thawed and undiluted
1 (33.8-oz.) bottle club soda, chilled

Combine all ingredients, and serve over ice. **Makes** 6 cups.

make ahead
Fresh Mint-Citrus Sippers
Prep: 15 min., Cook: 5 min.

This refreshing drink starts out with a simple syrup. You can store the syrup in an airtight container in the refrigerator up to two weeks—making party planning a cinch!

1½ cups fresh lemon juice
1 cup fresh lime juice
1 cup fresh orange juice
2 cups Fresh Mint Sugar Syrup
1 (25-oz.) bottle lemon-flavored sparkling water, chilled
   (about 3 cups)

Combine first 4 ingredients in a large pitcher, stirring well. Stir in sparkling water just before serving. Serve over ice. **Makes** 8 cups.

Fresh Mint Sugar Syrup
Prep: 5 min., Cook: 5 min.

2 cups sugar
1 cup water
1 cup loosely packed fresh mint leaves

Bring all ingredients to a boil in a saucepan, stirring until sugar dissolves; boil 1 minute. Remove from heat; cool.
Pour mixture through a wire-mesh strainer into a pitcher, discarding mint. **Makes** 2 cups.

Iced Apple Quencher
Prep: 10 min., Other: 5 min.

3 cups boiling water
4 cinnamon-apple tea bags
1 Tbsp. sugar
1 (6-oz.) can frozen apple juice concentrate, thawed
   and undiluted
2 cups cold water
Garnishes: green apple slices, cinnamon sticks

Pour 3 cups boiling water over tea bags; cover and steep 5 minutes. Remove and discard tea bags. Stir in sugar, juice concentrate, and 2 cups cold water. Serve over ice; garnish, if desired. **Makes** 5½ cups.

Homemade Orange Soda
Prep: 5 min.

Kids will request this delightful drink time and time again. Stir this refreshing beverage occasionally to keep the ingredients thoroughly mixed.

1 (12-oz.) can frozen, pulp-free orange juice
    concentrate, thawed and undiluted
2 (2-liter) bottles lemon-lime soft drink, chilled
1 to 2 oranges, thinly sliced

Stir together orange juice concentrate and lemon-lime soft drink when ready to serve.
Serve over ice in individual glasses with an orange slice. **Makes** about 10 cups.

Tangy Limeade
Prep: 5 min., Cook: 5 min.

1 cup sugar
6½ cups water, divided
¼ tsp. lemon juice
1¼ cups fresh lime juice (about 6 to 8 large limes)

Cook sugar, ½ cup water, and lemon juice in a small saucepan over medium heat, stirring constantly, 2 minutes or until sugar dissolves. Bring to a boil over medium-high heat; cook, stirring occasionally, 3 minutes. Cool.
Stir together sugar mixture, remaining 6 cups water, and lime juice in a large pitcher; chill. Serve over ice, if desired. **Makes** 8 cups.

Southern Breeze
Prep: 10 min., Other: 8 hrs.

The raspberry ice cubes can be made in advance and stored in zip-top freezer bags in the freezer until ready to serve.

1 cup sugar
1 (0.22-oz.) envelope unsweetened blue raspberry lemonade mix (we tested with Kool-Aid Island Twists Ice Blue Raspberry Lemonade Unsweetened Soft Drink Mix)
7 cups water
1 (6-oz.) can frozen lemonade concentrate, thawed and undiluted
1 (46-oz.) can unsweetened pineapple juice, chilled
1 (2-liter) bottle ginger ale, chilled

Stir together first 4 ingredients in a 2-qt. pitcher; pour evenly into 5 ice cube trays, and freeze at least 8 hours.
Combine pineapple juice and ginger ale; serve over raspberry ice cubes. **Makes** 21 cups.

Berry Blue Fizz
Prep: 10 min.

Kids love this thick, brightly colored drink. Serve it with vivid-colored straws for extra fun.

3 cups water
4 (3-oz.) packages blueberry gelatin (we tested with Jell-O Berry Blue)
5 (12-oz.) cans lemon-lime soft drink
6 cups pineapple sherbet

Microwave 3 cups water in an 8-cup glass measuring cup at HIGH 5 minutes or until it boils. Stir in blueberry gelatin until dissolved. Cool slightly, and stir in lemon-lime soft drink.
Scoop ¾ cup sherbet into each of 8 (16-oz.) glasses. Pour gelatin mixture over sherbet. Serve immediately. **Makes** 8 servings.

Brunch Punch
Prep: 5 min., Other: 2 hrs.

1 (46-oz.) can pineapple juice
3 cups orange juice
2 cups cranberry juice
¾ cup powdered sugar
¼ cup lime juice
Garnishes: fresh mint sprigs, lime slices, orange slices, cranberries

Stir together first 5 ingredients. Cover and chill at least 2 hours. Stir before serving. Garnish, if desired. **Makes** about 12 cups.

Tropical Shakes
Prep: 10 min.; Other: 1 hr., 30 min.

You can make this drink at a moment's notice when you have a handy supply of banana slices in your freezer. Simply toss fresh banana slices in lemon juice, and freeze up to six months in zip-top freezer bags.

1 medium-size ripe banana, cut into 1-inch slices
2 tsp. lemon juice
1 medium mango, peeled and cut into pieces
1½ cups pineapple-orange juice, chilled
1 (8-oz.) container fat-free vanilla yogurt

Toss banana with lemon juice; drain, reserving lemon juice. Place banana slices on a baking sheet, and freeze 1½ hours.
Process frozen banana slices, reserved lemon juice, mango, 1½ cups pineapple-orange juice, and yogurt in a blender until smooth, stopping to scrape down sides. Pour into chilled glasses; serve immediately. **Makes** 4 cups.

Tropical Shake

Peach Melba Shakes
Prep: 15 min.

The original peach Melba dessert was created for Australian opera singer Dame Nellie Melba. It consists of poached peach halves topped with vanilla ice cream, raspberry sauce, whipped cream, and sliced almonds. But don't let the origin of this recipe keep you from making use of the South's most beloved fruit. Create shakes that are out of this world.

2 cups peeled, sliced fresh peaches (about 2 medium-size ripe peaches)
2 cups vanilla ice cream
¾ cup milk
3 Tbsp. sugar
¼ tsp. almond extract
½ cup fresh raspberries*
½ cup sugar

Process first 5 ingredients in a food processor or blender until smooth, stopping to scrape down sides. Pour mixture into glasses.
Process raspberries and ½ cup sugar until smooth; swirl evenly into shakes. Serve immediately. **Makes** 4½ cups.

*Substitute ½ cup fresh strawberries, if desired.

quick & easy
Blackberry Smoothies
Prep: 5 min.

Use any of your favorite berries in this simple smoothie, or mix it up with a combination of fruits.

1 cup fat-free milk
1 pt. low-fat frozen vanilla yogurt, softened
1 medium banana, coarsely chopped
½ cup fresh blackberries

Process all ingredients in a blender until smooth, stopping to scrape down sides. Serve immediately. **Makes** about 4 cups.

Banana-Berry Smoothies
Prep: 5 min.

Freeze leftover fruit in zip-top freezer bags to use in shakes, smoothies, or any blended treat.

1 cup low-fat plain yogurt
3 cups frozen strawberries
2 bananas, coarsely chopped
¾ cup fat-free milk
¼ cup crushed ice
¼ cup honey

Process all ingredients in a blender until smooth, stopping to scrape down sides. Serve immediately. **Makes** about 5 cups.

make ahead
Mango Smoothies
Prep: 20 min., Other: 2 hrs.

A large peeled, seeded, and chopped mango yields about 2 cups fruit.

2 cups chopped mango (1 large mango)*
½ cup cold water
2 Tbsp. lemon juice
1 (8-oz.) container vanilla yogurt
¼ cup sugar

Process first 3 ingredients in a blender until smooth, stopping to scrape down sides. Add yogurt and sugar; process until smooth. Cover and chill 2 hours. **Makes** 3 cups.

*Substitute 2 cups chopped refrigerated mango slices, drained, if desired.

Banana-Berry
Smoothie

Caffé Latte Smoothies

Prep: 15 min., Other: 8 hrs.

½ cup sugar
2 cups hot brewed coffee or espresso
2 cups fat-free milk or fat-free half-and-half, divided

Combine sugar and coffee in a large bowl, stirring until sugar dissolves; stir in 1 cup milk. Cover and freeze 8 hours.
Thaw slightly in refrigerator; add remaining 1 cup milk. Break into pieces with a fork; beat at medium speed with an electric mixer until smooth. Serve immediately. **Makes** 5 cups.

Orange Jubilee

Prep: 5 min.

1 (6-oz.) can frozen orange juice concentrate, thawed
    and undiluted
2¼ cups milk
½ tsp. vanilla extract
¼ cup powdered sugar
1 cup ice cubes

Process all ingredients in a blender until smooth, stopping to scrape down sides. Serve immediately. **Makes** 4½ cups.

Quick Tip: *Blender beverages are at their best when the ice is finely ground. Starting with small ice cubes or crushed ice simplifies the process.*

Peach Slush

Prep: 5 min., Other: 10 min.

2 cups fresh peach slices*
¼ cup sugar
1⅓ cups unsweetened pineapple juice
1 Tbsp. lemon juice
3 cups ice cubes

Toss together peaches and sugar in a small bowl. Cover mixture, and chill 10 minutes.
Process peach mixture, juices, and ice cubes in a blender until ice is finely ground. Serve immediately, or freeze for later use. **Makes** 3¾ cups.

*Substitute 2 cups frozen peaches, partially thawed, if desired.

Watermelon Daiquiris

Prep: 20 min., Other: 8 hrs.

4 cups seeded and cubed watermelon
⅓ cup light rum
¼ to ½ cup orange juice
2 Tbsp. orange liqueur (we tested with Cointreau)
4 tsp. powdered sugar
2 tsp. fresh lime juice

Place watermelon in a zip-top freezer bag. Seal bag; freeze 8 hours.
Process watermelon, rum, and remaining ingredients in a blender or food processor until smooth, stopping to scrape down sides. Serve immediately. **Makes** 3 cups.

Margaritas from Scratch
Prep: 5 min., Other: 30 min.

2 cups sugar
2 cups water
2 cups orange liqueur (we tested with Cointreau)
2 cups tequila
2 cups fresh lime juice
Margarita salt
Garnish: lime wedges

Bring sugar and water to a boil over medium heat; cook, stirring constantly, 1 to 2 minutes or until sugar dissolves. Remove from heat; cool.

Stir together sugar mixture, liqueur, tequila, and juice. Cover; chill at least 30 minutes. Dip glass rims in water; dip rims in salt. Serve margaritas over crushed ice. Garnish, if desired. **Makes** 8 cups.

Frozen Margaritas: Freeze margaritas 8 hours. Let stand 5 minutes before serving.

Strawberry Margaritas
Prep: 10 min.

This Southwestern beverage uses sweet strawberries and sugar to smooth out the tartness of the limeade.

1 (8-oz.) package frozen strawberries, partially thawed
5 cups ice
¾ cup tequila
½ cup frozen limeade concentrate
⅓ cup powdered sugar
3 Tbsp. orange liqueur (we tested with Grand Marnier)
Lime juice
Red decorator sugar crystals
Garnishes: lime slices, fresh strawberries

Process first 6 ingredients in a blender until smooth. Dip margarita glass rims in lime juice; dip rims in red sugar crystals, coating well. Pour margarita mixture into glasses. Serve immediately. Garnish, if desired. **Makes** about 5½ cups.

freezer friendly • make ahead
Watermelon Margaritas
Prep: 10 min.

Lime juice
Sugar
⅓ cup tequila
2 cups crushed ice
2 cups seeded and cubed watermelon
¼ cup sugar
¼ cup lime juice (about 1½ limes)
1 Tbsp. vodka
1 Tbsp. orange liqueur

Coat rims of cocktail glasses with lime juice; dip in sugar.
Process remaining 7 ingredients in a blender until slushy. Pour into prepared glasses. **Makes** 5 cups.

To Make Ahead: Place mixture into a large zip-top freezer bag; freeze up to 1 month. Let stand about 30 minutes before serving.

Blue Margaritas
Prep: 5 min.

For an even coating around the rim of each glass, dip first in lime juice and then in salt.

1 (10-oz.) can frozen margarita mix
¾ cup tequila
¼ cup blue curaçao liqueur
2 Tbsp. lime juice
Ice

Combine first 4 ingredients in a blender. Fill with ice to 5-cup level, and process until smooth. Serve immediately. **Makes** about 5 cups.

make ahead
Texas White Sangría
Prep: 15 min., Other: 8 hrs.

1⅓ cups water
½ cup sugar
4 (3-inch) cinnamon sticks
1 cup fresh mint leaves, divided
1 (750-milliliter) bottle dry white wine
2 lemons, sliced
2 oranges, sliced
2 peaches, peeled and sliced
2 cups club soda, chilled

Bring first 3 ingredients and ½ cup mint leaves to a boil in a saucepan over medium heat. Reduce heat, and simmer 5 minutes. Remove from heat, and cool. **Cover** and let stand 8 hours, if desired. Remove cinnamon sticks and mint leaves with a slotted spoon. **Combine** sugar mixture, remaining ½ cup mint leaves, wine, and next 3 ingredients in a large pitcher; chill overnight, if desired. Stir in club soda just before serving. Serve over ice. **Makes** 7½ cups.

Blue Margaritas

Bellinis
Prep: 10 min.

1 (16-oz.) bottle peach nectar, chilled
1 (750-milliliter) bottle sparkling wine, chilled (we tested
   with Prosecco)
Garnish: fresh raspberries

Fill each of 6 champagne flutes with 2 oz. peach
nectar and 4 oz. sparkling wine. Garnish, if desired.
Serve immediately. **Makes** 6 servings.

Mimosas
Prep: 5 min.

1 (64-oz.) carton orange juice (not from concentrate),
   chilled
2 (750-milliliter) bottles Champagne, chilled
Garnishes: orange slices, fresh orange blossom sprigs

Fill each of 6 champagne flutes with 4 oz. orange juice
and 4 oz. Champagne. Garnish, if desired. **Makes**
12 servings.

Mint Bellinis
Prep: 10 min., Cook: 20 min.

4 (12-oz.) cans peach nectar
2 cups sugar
1 lemon, halved
¼ cup firmly packed fresh mint leaves
1 (750-milliliter) bottle Champagne or 2½ cups
   sparkling water
Garnish: lemon slices

Bring first 4 ingredients to a boil, and cook 20 minutes. Remove from heat and cool.
Remove and discard lemon and mint; store mixture
in an airtight container in refrigerator until ready to
serve. Stir in Champagne just before serving. Serve
over ice; garnish, if desired. **Makes** 9½ cups.

freezer friendly
Lemon-Rum Slush
Prep: 5 min., Other: 6 hrs.

¼ cup sugar
2 (6-oz.) cans frozen lemonade concentrate, thawed
   and undiluted
2 cups water
1½ cups pineapple juice
2 cups rum

Combine all ingredients, and freeze 6 hours, stirring
occasionally. Remove lemonade mixture from freezer,
and stir until slushy. Serve immediately. **Makes**
7 cups.

Quick Tip: *If you're looking
for kid-friendly beverages to serve
at your next barbecue, sparkling
water may be substituted in
recipes calling for Champagne.*

Citrus-Wine Punch
Prep: 15 min.

2 cups cranberry juice cocktail, chilled
2 cups orange juice, chilled
½ cup frozen lemonade concentrate, thawed
   and undiluted
1 (1-liter) bottle club soda, chilled
1 (750-milliliter) bottle dry red wine, chilled
1 (750-milliliter) bottle pink Champagne, chilled

Stir together all ingredients. Serve immediately over
ice or with an ice ring. **Makes** 16 cups.

Champagne Punch
Prep: 10 min.

Chilling ingredients ahead of time makes this beverage ready to serve immediately. If you prefer a less-sweet punch, just add sparkling water to taste until you get the perfect blend.

1 (11.5-oz.) can frozen pineapple-orange juice
   concentrate, thawed and undiluted
1 (6-oz.) can frozen lemonade concentrate, thawed
   and undiluted
1 (12-oz.) can or 1½ cups ginger ale, chilled
1 (750-milliliter) bottle Champagne or sparkling white
   grape juice, chilled
2 cups bottled sparkling water, chilled

Stir together concentrates in a punch bowl. Add remaining ingredients, stirring gently. Serve immediately. **Makes** about 8 cups.

Bloody Mary Punch
Prep: 10 min.

Here's a spicy spin on this classic tomato cocktail—just right for a barbecue brunch.

1 (46-oz.) can vegetable juice, chilled
¾ cup vodka, chilled
1 Tbsp. freshly ground pepper
3 Tbsp. lime juice
1 to 2 Tbsp. hot sauce
2 Tbsp. Worcestershire sauce
1 tsp. Old Bay seasoning
Celery sticks (optional)
Cooked shrimp (optional)

Combine first 7 ingredients in a punch bowl or a pitcher. Serve over ice in glasses. Serve with celery and shrimp, if desired. **Makes** about 6 cups.

Mint Julep Martini
Prep: 5 min.

¼ cup bourbon
¼ cup orange liqueur (we tested with Grand Marnier)
1 tsp. vanilla vodka* (we tested with Smirnoff Vanilla
   Twist)
1 tsp. clear crème de menthe
6 ice cubes
Garnishes: fresh mint sprig, orange rind curl

Combine first 5 ingredients in a martini shaker. Cover with lid, and shake until thoroughly chilled. **Remove** lid, and strain mixture into a chilled martini glass. Serve immediately. Garnish, if desired. **Makes** 1 serving.

*Substitute ½ tsp. vanilla extract, if desired.

Mint Julep Martini

Sunset Vodka-
Orange Sippers

Sunset Vodka-Orange Sippers
Prep: 5 min.

For the best flavor, use orange juice labeled "not from concentrate."

2 to 3 cups vodka
3 cups orange juice
2 (12-oz.) cans lemon-lime soft drink
Ice cubes
⅓ cup maraschino cherry juice
Garnishes: lime slices, maraschino cherries

Stir together first 3 ingredients in a pitcher. Fill 8 glasses with ice cubes, filling three-quarters full. Pour vodka mixture evenly over ice. Spoon 2 tsp. cherry juice into each glass (do not stir). Garnish, if desired, and serve immediately. **Makes** 8 servings.

Pineapple-Grapefruit Spritzers
Prep: 5 min., Other: 1 hr.

For a refreshing alcohol-free drink, make these spritzers with ginger ale instead of wine.

2 cups pineapple juice
1 cup pink grapefruit juice
2 Tbsp. honey
1 Tbsp. minced fresh ginger
1 (750-milliliter) bottle sparkling white wine, chilled
Garnish: pink grapefruit slices

Stir together first 4 ingredients in a large container; cover and chill at least 1 hour. Pour mixture through a fine wire-mesh strainer into a pitcher, discarding ginger. Add wine just before serving. Serve over ice. Garnish, if desired. **Makes** about 7 cups.

Pomegranate-Champagne Cocktail
Prep: 5 min.

Pomegranate juice is available in the refrigerated juice section or produce section of the grocery store. Turbinado is a raw, very coarse sugar with a mild brown sugar flavor.

1 turbinado sugar cube*
2 Tbsp. pomegranate juice
½ cup Champagne or sparkling wine, chilled

Place sugar cube in a Champagne flute; add 2 Tbsp. pomegranate juice and ½ cup Champagne. Serve immediately. **Makes** 1 serving.

*Substitute 1 rock candy stirrer or granulated sugar cube, if desired. We found rock candy stirrers at an import store that carries wines and specialty food items.

make ahead
Mojitos
Prep: 5 min.

2 cups light rum
1 cup Mint Syrup
1 cup lime juice
Ice cubes
Garnish: fresh mint leaves, rinsed

Combine rum, Mint Syrup, and lime juice in a 2-qt. pitcher; add about 2 cups ice cubes. Pour into ice-filled glasses; garnish, if desired. **Makes** 4 cups.

Mint Syrup
Cook: 10 min., Other: 30 min.

1¼ cups lightly packed fresh mint leaves, rinsed
1 cup water
½ cup sugar

Combine all ingredients in a 1- to 2-qt. pan. Stir over medium heat until sugar is dissolved and mixture is simmering. Remove from heat, cover, and let stand 30 minutes. Pour mixture through a fine wire-mesh strainer into a small pitcher or bowl; discard mint leaves. Use syrup immediately; or cover and chill up to 1 week. **Makes** about 1 cup.

Citrus Batidas
Prep: 5 min.

2 cups orange juice
2 cups Ruby Red grapefruit juice
⅔ cup fresh lemon juice
¾ cup superfine sugar
1 cup rum

Process all ingredients in a blender until frothy. Serve over ice. **Makes** 5 cups.

Sazerac
Prep: 10 min., Cook: 5 min.

This New Orleans original is made using sugar syrup, whiskey, and bitters.

1 cup sugar
1 cup water
Ice cubes
¼ cup rye whiskey or bourbon (we tested with Jim Beam Straight Rye Whiskey)
¼ tsp. bitters (we tested with Peychaud's Bitters)
¼ tsp. anise liqueur (we tested with Herbsaint)
Lemon rind twist

Cook 1 cup sugar and 1 cup water in a small saucepan over medium-high heat 5 minutes, stirring until sugar dissolves. Remove from heat, and cool.
Pack a 3½-oz. cocktail glass with ice cubes, and set glass aside.
Combine whiskey, bitters, sugar syrup, and a few ice cubes in a cocktail shaker; shake to chill.
Discard ice cubes in cocktail glass. Coat inside of glass with liqueur, shaking out excess liqueur. (For stronger licorice flavor, leave excess liqueur in glass.) Rub lemon rind over rim of glass, and discard rind.
Strain whiskey mixture into prepared glass. Serve drink immediately. **Makes** 1 serving.

Whiskey Sours
Prep: 5 min.

1 (6-oz.) can frozen orange juice concentrate, thawed and undiluted
1 (6-oz.) can frozen limeade concentrate, thawed and undiluted
1 (6-oz.) can frozen lemonade concentrate, thawed and undiluted
4⅓ cups water
2 cups bourbon
1 (33.8-oz.) bottle club soda, chilled
Garnishes: orange, lime, and lemon slices

Stir together concentrates, 4⅓ cups water, and bourbon. Stir in club soda just before serving. Serve over ice, and garnish, if desired. **Makes** about 12½ cups.

Slushy Whiskey Sours: Stir together first 5 ingredients. Pour into a large zip-top freezer bag; seal. Freeze 2 hours. Spoon into a pitcher. Stir in club soda, and serve immediately.

Creamy Coconut Sipper
Prep: 5 min.

2½ cups ice cubes
1 cup half-and-half
½ cup cream of coconut
½ cup creme de cacao
½ cup coffee liqueur (we tested with Kahlúa)
½ cup rum

Process all ingredients in a blender until smooth. Serve immediately. **Makes** 5 cups.

Whiskey Sours

Bourbon-Barrel Coffee
Prep: 5 min.

This recipe was inspired by a coffee drink served by The Oakroom restaurant at The Seelbach Hilton Hotel in Louisville. For a gentler brew, omit the ¾ cup bourbon.

¾ cup bourbon
½ cup Bourbon Syrup
3 cups hot brewed coffee
Whipped cream

Place 3 Tbsp. bourbon and 2 Tbsp. Bourbon Syrup in each of 4 coffee cups. Stir ¾ cup hot brewed coffee into each mug. Top with whipped cream. **Makes** 4 servings.

Bourbon Syrup
Prep: 5 min., Cook: 10 min.

Use leftover syrup on waffles, pancakes, roasted bananas, or ice cream. Or add to iced tea along with fresh mint for a refreshing tea julep. You can purchase superfine sugar at the supermarket, or make your own by processing granulated sugar in a food processor until powdery.

1 cup superfine sugar
1 cup firmly packed light brown sugar
1 cup water
1 cup bourbon (we tested with Maker's Mark Bourbon)

Bring superfine sugar, brown sugar, and 1 cup water to a boil in a small saucepan over medium-high heat; cook 10 minutes until reduced by half. Remove from heat, and stir in bourbon. **Makes** 2 cups.

Fireside Coffee
Prep: 5 min., Cook: 2 min., Other: 1 min.

1 cup half-and-half
1 (1-oz.) unsweetened chocolate baking square, chopped
1 cup hot brewed coffee
6 Tbsp. bourbon
¼ to ½ cup sugar
⅓ cup whipping cream
½ tsp. vanilla extract
Whipped cream (optional)

Microwave half-and-half in a 2-cup glass measuring cup on HIGH 1 to 2 minutes or until steamy. Pour over chocolate in a 2-qt. pan; let stand 1 minute, and whisk until smooth. Stir in coffee and next 4 ingredients. Serve immediately. Top with whipped cream, if desired. **Makes** 4 servings.

Easy Chut-Nut Ball
Prep: 10 min., Other: 30 min.

2 (8-oz.) packages cream cheese, softened
1 (9-oz.) jar hot mango chutney (we tested with Major Grey's Hot Mango Chutney)
½ tsp. curry powder
½ tsp. dry mustard
⅔ cup sliced blanched almonds

Stir together first 4 ingredients until blended. Shape into a ball, and chill 30 minutes. Roll in almonds. Serve with crackers. **Makes** 10 appetizer servings.

Quick Tip: *Cheese balls are a hit at any barbecue. Stir things up a bit by serving with unusual dippers, such as asparagus, whole pecans, or graham crackers.*

Party Cheese Ball

Party Cheese Ball

Prep: 10 min., Other: 1 hr.

1 (2¼-oz.) jar dried beef, finely chopped, or
   1 (2½-oz.) package thinly sliced ham, chopped
1 (8-oz.) package cream cheese, softened
1 cup finely chopped mixed vegetables of your choice
   (such as green onions, pimiento, and ripe olives)
¼ tsp. garlic powder
¼ tsp. hot sauce
¾ cup chopped pecans or walnuts, toasted
Garnish: fresh parsley sprigs

Combine first 5 ingredients; stir well. Cover and chill at least 1 hour.
Shape cheese mixture into a ball; roll in pecans. Wrap cheese ball in heavy-duty plastic wrap; refrigerate up to 3 days. Garnish, if desired. Serve with unsalted crackers. **Makes** 10 appetizer servings.

Pecan Cheese Ball

Prep: 10 min., Other: 30 min.

2 (8-oz.) packages cream cheese, softened
1 (8-oz.) can crushed pineapple, drained
¼ cup chopped green bell pepper
2 Tbsp. finely chopped onion
1 Tbsp. seasoned salt
2 cups chopped pecans, toasted and divided
Garnishes: pineapple slices, maraschino cherries,
   fresh parsley sprigs

Combine first 5 ingredients; stir in 1 cup pecans. Cover and chill 30 minutes or until firm.
Shape mixture into a ball; roll in remaining 1 cup chopped pecans.
Place cheese ball on a serving platter; garnish, if desired. Serve with crackers, green bell pepper squares, and celery sticks. **Makes** 10 appetizer servings.

Roasted Corn and Avocado Dip
Prep: 10 min., Cook: 15 min., Other: 8 hrs.

If your guests like maximum heat from their jalapeños, chop the peppers—seeds and all.

1 cup frozen whole kernel corn, thawed
2 tsp. olive oil
1 ripe avocado, peeled and mashed
1 ripe avocado, peeled and chopped
¾ cup seeded, diced tomato
3 Tbsp. lime juice
3 Tbsp. chopped fresh cilantro
2 Tbsp. minced onion
2 small canned jalapeño peppers, seeded and diced
2 garlic cloves, minced
½ tsp. salt
¼ tsp. ground cumin

Combine corn and oil in a shallow pan. Bake at 400° for 15 minutes or until corn is lightly browned, stirring occasionally. Cool.
Combine corn, mashed avocado, chopped avocado, and remaining ingredients, stirring well. Cover and chill at least 8 hours before serving. Serve with tortilla chips. **Makes** 2¾ cups.

Guacamole
Prep: 10 min.

5 ripe avocados
½ to ¾ cup reduced-fat sour cream
¼ cup chopped fresh cilantro
3 Tbsp. fresh lime juice
2 Tbsp. Italian dressing
½ tsp. garlic salt
¼ tsp. hot sauce (we tested with Cholula Hot Sauce)

Cut avocados in half. Scoop pulp into a bowl; mash with a potato masher or fork just until slightly chunky. Stir in sour cream and next 5 ingredients. Serve with tortilla chips. **Makes** 4 cups.

Tomato-Basil Dip
Prep: 10 min., Other: 1 hr.

1 cup mayonnaise
½ cup sour cream
½ cup chopped fresh basil
1 Tbsp. tomato paste
1 Tbsp. grated lemon rind

Stir together all ingredients. Cover and chill at least 1 hour or up to 2 days. Serve with fresh vegetables. **Makes** 1½ cups.

Roasted Poblano Guacamole with Garlic and Parsley
Prep: 5 min., Cook: 12 min., Other: 10 min.

Roasted poblanos add spark to the creamy, almost nutty flavor of avocados, especially when bolstered with a little roasted tomato and flat-leaf parsley.

2 poblano chile peppers (about 6 oz.)
2 plum tomatoes (about 6 oz.)
2 garlic cloves, unpeeled
1⅓ cups ripe peeled avocado, seeded and coarsely mashed (about 3 avocados)
3 Tbsp. chopped fresh flat-leaf parsley
2 Tbsp. fresh lime juice
¼ tsp. salt
2 Tbsp. grated queso añejo or Parmesan cheese
2 Tbsp. sliced radishes

Cut poblanos in half lengthwise, and discard seeds and membranes. Place poblano halves, skin sides up, tomatoes, and garlic on an aluminum foil-lined baking sheet.
Broil for 12 minutes or until poblanos are blackened, turning tomatoes once. Place poblanos in a zip-top freezer bag, and seal. Let stand 10 minutes. Peel poblanos, tomatoes, and garlic.
Place poblanos and garlic cloves in a food processor, and pulse until coarsely chopped. Combine poblano mixture, tomato, avocado, parsley, juice, and salt in a bowl. Sprinkle with cheese and radishes. Serve with tortilla chips. **Makes** 2 cups.

Tomato-Basil Dip

Creamy Chipotle-Black Bean Dip
Prep: 5 min.

½ cup sour cream
½ cup prepared black bean dip
1 tsp. minced canned chipotle peppers in adobo sauce
1 tsp. adobo sauce from can
¼ tsp. salt

Stir together all ingredients. Cover and chill until ready to serve. Serve with tortilla chips. **Makes** 1 cup.

White Bean Hummus
Prep: 20 min., Other: 1 hr.

2 garlic cloves
1 tsp. chopped fresh rosemary
2 (15.5-oz.) cans great Northern beans, rinsed and
   drained
3 Tbsp. lemon juice
3 Tbsp. tahini
¾ tsp. salt
¼ tsp. ground red pepper
¼ cup olive oil
Garnish: paprika

Pulse garlic and rosemary in a food processor 3 or 4 times or until minced.
Add beans and next 4 ingredients; process until smooth, stopping to scrape down sides.
Pour olive oil gradually through food chute with processor running; process until mixture is smooth. Cover and chill 1 hour. Garnish, if desired. Serve with crackers, sliced cucumber, pimiento-stuffed olives, and pitted kalamata olives. **Makes** 3 cups.

Florentine Artichoke Dip
Prep: 5 min., Cook: 25 min.

1 (10-oz.) package frozen chopped spinach, thawed
2 (6-oz.) jars marinated artichoke hearts
3 garlic cloves, minced
½ cup mayonnaise
1½ (8-oz.) packages cream cheese, softened
2 Tbsp. lemon juice
1 cup grated Parmesan cheese
1½ cups fine, dry breadcrumbs

Drain spinach; press between layers of paper towels. Drain and chop artichoke hearts.
Combine spinach, artichoke hearts, garlic, and next 4 ingredients, stirring well. Spoon into a lightly greased 11- x 7-inch baking dish; sprinkle with breadcrumbs.
Bake at 375° for 25 minutes, and serve with crackers or breadsticks. **Makes** 4 cups.

Layered Nacho Dip
Prep: 12 min.

1 (16-oz.) can refried beans
½ (1.25-oz.) package taco seasoning mix (2 Tbsp.)
1 (6-oz.) carton avocado dip or 1 cup guacamole
1 (8-oz.) container sour cream
1 (4½-oz.) can chopped black olives, drained
2 tomatoes, diced
1 small onion, finely chopped
1 (4.5-oz.) can chopped green chiles, undrained
1½ cups (6 oz.) shredded Monterey Jack or Cheddar
   Jack cheese

Combine beans and seasoning mix; spread in an 11- x 7-inch dish, a 9- or 10-inch deep-dish pieplate, or a cast-iron skillet. Layer avocado dip and remaining ingredients in order listed. Serve with corn or tortilla chips. **Makes** 8 cups.

Blue Cheese-Bacon Dip

Prep: 15 min., Cook: 15 min.

7 bacon slices, chopped
2 garlic cloves, minced
2 (8-oz.) packages cream cheese, softened
⅓ cup half-and-half
4 oz. crumbled blue cheese
2 Tbsp. chopped fresh chives
3 Tbsp. chopped walnuts, toasted

Cook chopped bacon in a skillet over medium-high heat 10 minutes or until crisp. Drain bacon; set aside. Add minced garlic to skillet, and sauté 1 minute.
Beat cream cheese at medium speed with an electric mixer until smooth. Add half-and-half, beating until combined. Stir in bacon, garlic, blue cheese, and chives. Spoon mixture evenly into 4 (1-cup) individual baking dishes.
Bake at 350° for 15 minutes or until golden and bubbly. Sprinkle evenly with chopped walnuts; serve with grape clusters and flatbread or assorted crackers. **Makes** 12 to 15 appetizer servings.

Baked Vidalia Onion Dip
Prep: 15 min., Cook: 25 min., Other: 10 min.

2 Tbsp. butter or margarine
3 large Vidalia onions, coarsely chopped
2 cups (8 oz.) shredded Swiss cheese
2 cups mayonnaise
1 (8-oz.) can sliced water chestnuts, drained and
 chopped
¼ cup dry white wine
1 garlic clove, minced
½ tsp. hot sauce

Melt butter in a large skillet over medium-high heat;
add onion, and sauté 10 minutes or until tender.
Stir together shredded Swiss cheese and next 5 ingredients; stir in onion, blending well. Spoon mixture
into a lightly greased 2-qt. baking dish.
Bake at 375° for 25 minutes, and let stand 10 minutes. Serve with tortilla chips or crackers. **Makes**
6 cups.

To Lighten: Substitute vegetable cooking spray for
butter; substitute reduced-fat Swiss cheese and light
mayonnaise for regular.

Quick Tip: *If you need to
keep a dip or spread warm
during a party, serve it from
a slow cooker. Just select a
cooker that is complementary
in size to the dish used for
baking, transfer the finished
dish to the slow cooker, and
set the cooker on LOW or
WARM.*

Layered Sun-Dried Tomato-and-Basil Spread
Prep: 25 min., Other: 8 hrs.

This recipe can be made up to three days before the party.

2 (8-oz.) packages cream cheese, softened
¾ cup butter, softened
1 tsp. salt, divided
¼ tsp. pepper
1⅓ cups dried tomatoes in oil, drained
2 (3-oz.) packages cream cheese, softened and divided
⅓ cup tomato paste
4 garlic cloves, chopped
1½ cups firmly packed fresh basil
¼ cup pine nuts
2 Tbsp. olive oil
2 Tbsp. fresh lemon juice
¼ cup grated Parmesan cheese
Garnishes: fresh rosemary sprigs, dried tomatoes

Beat 2 (8-oz.) packages cream cheese, butter, ½ tsp.
salt, and pepper at medium speed with an electric
mixer until creamy. Set aside.
Process dried tomatoes in a food processor until
chopped. Add 1 (3-oz.) package cream cheese, tomato
paste, and ¼ tsp. salt; process until smooth, stopping to scrape down sides. Spoon into a bowl, and
set aside. Wipe container of food processor clean.
Process garlic and next 4 ingredients in food processor until chopped. Add Parmesan cheese, remaining
3-oz. package cream cheese, and remaining ¼ tsp.
salt; pulse just until blended, stopping to scrape
down sides.
Spray a 6-inch springform pan with cooking spray.
Spread ½ cup butter mixture evenly on bottom of
springform pan. Layer with half of tomato mixture,
½ cup butter mixture, and half of basil mixture; top
with ½ cup butter mixture. Repeat layers with
remaining tomato mixture, ½ cup butter mixture,
and remaining basil mixture. Top with remaining
butter mixture. Cover with plastic wrap; chill at least
8 hours.
Run a knife gently around edge of pan to loosen sides.
Remove sides of pan; carefully remove bottom of
pan, and place layered spread on a serving tray.
Garnish, if desired. Serve with crackers or baguette
slices. **Makes** 20 appetizer servings.

Pecan-Crusted Artichoke and Cheese Spread

Prep: 10 min., Cook: 35 min.

¼ cup butter or margarine, divided

1 medium onion, diced

2 garlic cloves, minced

4 cups coarsely chopped fresh spinach

1 (14-oz.) can artichoke hearts, drained and chopped

1 (8-oz.) package cream cheese, cut up

½ cup mayonnaise

¾ cup (3 oz.) shredded Parmesan cheese (we tested with Sargento Fancy Supreme)

1 (8-oz.) package recipe blend shredded cheese (we tested with Sargento 4 Cheese Country Casserole)

⅔ cup chopped pecans

½ cup herb-seasoned stuffing mix

Melt 3 Tbsp. butter in a large skillet; add onion and garlic, and sauté until tender. Add chopped fresh spinach, and cook over medium heat, stirring often, 3 minutes.

Add artichoke hearts and next 4 ingredients, stirring until cheese melts. Spoon into a greased 2-qt. baking dish.

Bake at 350° for 20 minutes; stir gently.

Combine remaining 1 Tbsp. butter, pecans, and stuffing mix, tossing until blended. Sprinkle over top of artichoke mixture, and bake 15 more minutes. Serve spread with pita chips or French bread. **Makes** 15 to 20 appetizer servings.

Horseradish Spread
Prep: 5 min.

1 (5-oz.) package buttery garlic-and-herb spreadable
    cheese (we tested with Rondelé Garlic & Herbs
    Gourmet)
3 Tbsp. prepared horseradish, drained
½ (8-oz.) package cream cheese, softened
¼ cup sour cream
1 Tbsp. chopped fresh dill

Stir together all ingredients until blended. Cover and
chill up to 7 days. **Makes** 1¼ cups.

Chile-Cheese Spread
Prep: 20 min., Other: 2 hrs.

*Reserve your energy on barbecue day—make this zesty starter
up to three days ahead. Serve leftovers on sandwiches.*

2 (8-oz.) packages light cream cheese, softened
1 cup (4 oz.) shredded Cheddar cheese
3 green onions, finely chopped
3 chipotle peppers in adobo sauce
1 tsp. adobo sauce from can
½ tsp. Creole seasoning
½ tsp. ground cumin
½ tsp. chili powder
¼ tsp. Worcestershire sauce
⅛ tsp. hot sauce
⅓ cup pecan pieces, toasted
Garnishes: green onion curls, pecan halves

Combine cream cheese and next 9 ingredients in a
food processor, and pulse 3 times, stopping to scrape
down sides. Stir in toasted pecans, and chill 2 hours.
Garnish, if desired. Serve with assorted crackers and
vegetables. **Makes** 3 cups.

Black Bean Salsa
Prep: 30 min., Other: 8 hrs.

2 medium tomatoes
1 red bell pepper
1 green bell pepper
1½ cups fresh or frozen corn kernels (3 ears fresh)
¼ cup finely chopped red onion
1 serrano chile pepper, seeded and minced
1 (15-oz.) can black beans, rinsed and drained
⅓ cup fresh lime juice
¼ cup olive oil
⅓ cup chopped fresh cilantro
1 tsp. salt
½ tsp. ground cumin
¼ tsp. ground red pepper

Chop tomatoes and bell peppers.
Stir together tomato mixture, corn, and remaining
ingredients. Cover and chill 8 hours. Serve with
tortilla chips. **Makes** 7 cups.

Corn Salsa
Prep: 20 min., Other: 2 hrs.

3 large ears fresh corn
1 large tomato, finely chopped
1 (7-oz.) jar roasted red bell peppers, drained and
    chopped
2 green onions, finely chopped
1 jalapeño pepper, seeded and minced
3 Tbsp. minced fresh cilantro
2 Tbsp. fresh lime juice
1 Tbsp. white wine vinegar
½ tsp. salt
¼ tsp. pepper
¼ tsp. ground cumin
2 avocados, chopped (optional)

Cut corn from cobs.
Stir together corn kernels, next 10 ingredients, and,
if desired, avocado. Cover and chill at least 2 hours.
Serve with tortilla chips. **Makes** 2½ cups.

make ahead
Tomatillo Salsa
Prep: 20 min.; Cook: 8 min.; Other: 2 hrs., 10 min.

This fresh mixture is great as an appetizer with tortilla chips or as a main dish accompaniment for grilled meats and poultry.

10 fresh tomatillos, husks removed
3 medium tomatoes
1 jalapeño pepper
½ medium-size red onion, sliced
½ cup chopped fresh cilantro
1 garlic clove
2 Tbsp. lime juice
¾ tsp. salt
½ tsp. pepper
½ tsp. ground cumin

Grill first 4 ingredients, covered with grill lid, over high heat (400° to 500°) 3 to 4 minutes on each side or until tomatoes look blistered and onion is tender. Cool 10 minutes. Discard jalapeño seeds, if desired.
Pulse grilled tomatillo mixture and remaining ingredients in a blender or food processor 6 times or until mixture is coarsely chopped, stopping to scrape down sides.
Cover salsa, and chill at least 2 hours. Serve with tortilla chips. **Makes** about 5 cups.

quick & easy
Fresh Avocado Salsa
Prep: 10 min.

Don't let this treat chill too long. Offer guests this chunky salsa within four hours for best results.

4 plum tomatoes, chopped
1 small avocado, chopped
1 small sweet onion, chopped
1 small jalapeño pepper, seeded and minced
¼ cup chopped fresh cilantro
2 Tbsp. fresh lime juice
½ tsp. salt

Combine all ingredients gently. Chill until ready to serve. **Makes** about 2 cups.

Avocado-Feta Salsa
Prep: 20 min.

Make this tangy guacamole dual-purpose by serving it as an appetizer or with Tex-Mex dishes, burgers, pasta, or grilled fish or chicken.

1 large avocado
2 plum tomatoes
¼ cup chopped red onion
1 garlic clove, minced
1 Tbsp. chopped fresh parsley
½ tsp. chopped fresh oregano
1 Tbsp. olive oil
½ Tbsp. red wine vinegar
½ (4-oz.) package crumbled feta cheese

Peel and seed avocado; chop avocado and tomatoes, and place in a large bowl. Add onion and next 5 ingredients, tossing to coat. Fold in cheese. Serve immediately with tortilla chips. **Makes** 2 cups.

make ahead
Tropical Salsa
Prep: 15 min.

This exotic concoction of mango, bell pepper, and jalapeño turns a casual gathering into a spiced-up party.

1 ripe mango, peeled and chopped
½ cup chopped plum tomatoes
½ cup chopped red bell peppers
½ cup chopped red onion
1 Tbsp. minced garlic
1½ tsp. minced jalapeño pepper
1 tsp. ground cumin
1 Tbsp. olive oil
1 Tbsp. red wine vinegar
¼ cup fresh lime juice
¼ tsp. pepper
½ tsp. hot sauce
½ cup chopped fresh cilantro
¼ tsp. salt

Combine all ingredients. Serve immediately with tortilla chips, or refrigerate up to 3 days. **Makes** 2½ cups.

Parmesan-Bacon
Sticks

Parmesan-Bacon Sticks

Prep: 15 min., Cook: 1 hr.

15 bacon slices, cut in half lengthwise (about 1 lb.)
1 (3-oz.) package thin breadsticks (30 breadsticks)
   (we tested with Alessi Thin Breadsticks)
½ to ⅔ cup grated Parmesan cheese

Wrap bacon strips around breadsticks; roll in cheese, and place on baking sheets.
Bake at 250° for 1 hour. Serve immediately. **Makes** 2½ dozen.

Garlic-Pepper Parmesan Crisps

Prep: 5 min., Cook: 10 min. per batch

12 oz. freshly grated Parmigiano-Reggiano cheese
2 tsp. minced fresh garlic
1 tsp. freshly ground pepper

Combine all ingredients in a small bowl, stirring well. Sprinkle cheese mixture into a 1½-inch round cookie cutter on a nonstick baking sheet. Repeat procedure with cheese mixture, placing 16 circles on each sheet.
Bake at 350° for 9 to 10 minutes or until golden. Cool slightly on baking sheets.
Remove to wire racks to cool completely. Repeat procedure 5 times with remaining cheese mixture.
Makes about 80 appetizers.

Parmesan Cheese Straws
Prep: 10 min., Cook: 7 or 10 min.

Choose a robust red wine as an alternative barbecue beverage to beer. These elegant appetizers are great paired with your favorite vino.

⅔ cup refrigerated shredded Parmesan cheese*
½ cup butter or margarine, softened
1 cup all-purpose flour
¼ tsp. salt
¼ tsp. ground red pepper
¼ cup milk
Pecan halves (optional)

Position knife blade in food processor bowl; add cheese and butter. Process until blended. Add flour, salt, and ground red pepper; process about 30 seconds or until mixture forms a ball, stopping often to scrape down sides.
Divide dough in half. Roll each portion into an ⅛-inch-thick rectangle, and cut into 2- x ½-inch strips; or shape dough into ¾-inch balls, and flatten each ball to about ⅛-inch thickness. Place on ungreased baking sheets; brush with milk. Top with pecan halves, if desired.
Bake at 350° for 7 minutes for strips and 10 minutes for rounds or until lightly browned. Transfer to wire racks to cool. **Makes** 5 dozen straws or 3 dozen wafers.

*Substitute ⅔ cup freshly grated Parmesan cheese plus an additional ¼ cup all-purpose flour for refrigerated shredded Parmesan cheese, if desired.

quick & easy
Garlic Pita Chips
Prep: 5 min., Cook: 6 min.

6 (6-inch) pitas
Butter-flavored cooking spray
¼ tsp. garlic powder

Coat 1 side of each pita with cooking spray; sprinkle with garlic powder. Cut each pita into 8 wedges; arrange wedges in a single layer on baking sheets.
Bake at 425° for 6 minutes or until golden. **Makes** 4 dozen.

freezer friendly • make ahead
Cream Cheese-and-Olive Biscuits with Olive-Parsley Spread
Prep: 30 min., Cook: 10 min.

2¼ cups all-purpose baking mix
1 (3-oz.) package cream cheese, softened
⅓ cup buttermilk
½ cup green olives, chopped
1 (6-oz.) jar pitted kalamata olives
1 Tbsp. capers, drained
1 garlic clove, pressed
1 Tbsp. chopped fresh parsley
2 Tbsp. balsamic vinegar
2 Tbsp. olive oil
¼ tsp. pepper
1 (3-oz.) log goat cheese or package cream cheese, softened

Pulse first 4 ingredients in a food processor 3 to 4 times or until combined.
Turn dough out onto a lightly floured surface. Pat dough to a ½-inch thickness; cut with a 2-inch fluted cutter. Place on ungreased baking sheets.
Bake biscuits at 425° for 10 minutes or until golden.
Pulse kalamata olives and next 6 ingredients in a food processor until combined.
Split biscuits in half, and spread cut sides evenly with goat cheese; top with olive mixture. **Makes** 30 appetizer servings.

To Make Ahead: Bake biscuits as directed. Cool completely on baking sheets on wire racks. Cover and freeze until firm. Place biscuits into zip-top freezer bags; freeze up to 2 weeks. Remove from freezer; place on baking sheets, and let stand 30 minutes. Bake at 325° for 7 to 10 minutes. Prepare olive-parsley mixture as directed. Place in an airtight container; freeze up to 2 weeks. Thaw in refrigerator 24 hours. Stir before serving.

Spicy Cheese-Walnut Wafers

Prep: 20 min., Cook: 15 min. per batch, Other: 8 hrs.

2 (4-oz.) packages crumbled blue cheese
½ (8-oz.) package cream cheese, softened
½ cup butter, softened
1½ cups all-purpose flour
¼ tsp. salt
1 to 1½ tsp. ground red pepper
1 cup finely chopped walnuts
2 egg yolks, lightly beaten

Beat first 3 ingredients at medium speed with an electric mixer until blended; add flour and remaining ingredients, beating until blended.
Shape dough into 2 (10-inch) logs. Wrap in plastic wrap; chill 8 hours.
Cut cold dough into ¼-inch slices; place on ungreased baking sheets.
Bake, in batches, at 350° for 12 to 15 minutes or until lightly browned. Remove to wire racks to cool. Store wafers in an airtight container up to 1 week. **Makes** 80 wafers.

Smoky Pecans

Prep: 30 min., Cook: 1 hr.

Hickory chips
2 lb. pecan halves
½ cup butter or margarine, melted
1 tsp. salt

Soak wood chips in water for at least 30 minutes.
Prepare charcoal fire in smoker; let burn 15 to 20 minutes.
Drain chips, and place on coals. Place water pan in smoker; add water to depth of fill line.
Stir together pecan halves, butter, and salt in a 24- x 12-inch pan. Place on upper food grate; cover with smoker lid.
Cook 1 hour or until golden, stirring once after 30 minutes. **Makes** 2 lb.

Note: Use a baking pan that fits your grill if the 24- x 12-inch pan is too large.

Smoky Pecans

Spicy Pecans
Prep: 5 min., Cook: 8 min.

2 Tbsp. brown sugar
2 Tbsp. orange juice concentrate
1½ Tbsp. butter or margarine
½ tsp. salt
½ tsp. chili powder
¼ tsp. pepper
1½ cups coarsely chopped pecans

Cook first 6 ingredients in a skillet over medium-high heat, stirring until brown sugar dissolves. Remove from heat, and stir in pecans. Transfer to a lightly greased baking sheet.
Bake at 350° for 8 minutes or until toasted. Cool and store in an airtight container. **Makes** 1½ cups.

Mexico Nuts
Prep: 10 min.; Cook: 1 hr., 30 min.

¾ cup powdered sugar
1 Tbsp. cornstarch
1 tsp. ground cinnamon
¼ tsp. salt
¼ tsp. ground cloves
¼ tsp. ground red pepper
¼ tsp. ground allspice
1 egg white
2 Tbsp. cold water
1 cup pecan halves

Combine first 7 ingredients in a small bowl.
Whisk egg white lightly; add 2 Tbsp. water, whisking mixture until blended.
Dip pecan halves into egg white mixture. Drain well with a slotted spoon. Dredge in sugar mixture. Place nuts in a single layer on a baking sheet coated with cooking spray. Bake at 250° for 1½ hours. **Makes** 1 cup.

Savory Kalamata Cheesecake Squares
Prep: 20 min., Cook: 32 min.

Purplish black olives scatter specks of color into each savory bite. Garnish your serving platter with herbs and olives so that your guests know this dish is not a dessert.

1¼ cups Italian-seasoned breadcrumbs
½ cup very finely chopped pecans
⅓ cup butter or margarine, melted
1 (8-oz.) package cream cheese, softened
1 (3-oz.) package cream cheese, softened
1 (8-oz.) container sour cream
1 Tbsp. all-purpose flour
¼ tsp. salt
¼ tsp. pepper
1 large egg
1 egg yolk
½ cup kalamata olives, pitted and sliced or chopped
1 Tbsp. chopped fresh rosemary
Garnishes: fresh rosemary sprigs, kalamata olives

Combine first 3 ingredients; stir well. Press crumb mixture firmly into a lightly greased aluminum foil-lined 9-inch square pan. Bake at 350° for 12 minutes. Set aside to cool.
Beat cream cheese, sour cream, flour, and seasonings at medium speed with an electric mixer until smooth. Add egg and egg yolk, 1 at a time, beating just until blended. Stir in sliced or chopped olives and chopped rosemary; pour filling into baked crust. Bake at 350° for 20 minutes or just until firm. Cool to room temperature on a wire rack. Cover and chill.
To serve, lift foil out of pan, and cut cheesecake into squares. Garnish serving platter, if desired. **Makes** 3 dozen.

Three-Layer Cheesecake
Prep: 20 min., Other: 3 hrs.

3 (8-oz.) packages cream cheese, softened and divided
3 Tbsp. chopped pimiento-stuffed olives
2 tsp. olive juice
1 Tbsp. mayonnaise
1 cup (4 oz.) shredded sharp Cheddar cheese
1 (2-oz.) jar diced pimiento, drained
1 tsp. grated onion
¼ cup butter or margarine, softened
2 garlic cloves, pressed
1 tsp. dried Italian seasoning

Beat 1 package cream cheese at medium speed with an electric mixer until creamy; stir in olives and olive juice. Spread olive mixture into bottom of a plastic wrap-lined 8- x 4-inch loafpan.

Beat 1 package cream cheese at medium speed until creamy; add mayonnaise and Cheddar cheese, beating until blended. Stir in pimiento and onion; spread over olive mixture.

Beat remaining package cream cheese and butter at medium speed until creamy; add garlic and Italian seasoning, beating until blended. Spread garlic mixture over pimiento mixture. Cover and chill at least 3 hours or until firm. Serve with crackers. **Makes** 8 appetizer servings.

> **Quick Tip:** *If you're making a cheesecake ahead, simply leave it in the pan after it has cooled; then cover and chill until serving time. Remove the sides of the pan just before serving.*

Sun-Dried Tomato Cheesecake
Prep: 15 min.; Cook: 47 min.; Other: 8 hrs., 35 min.

Find edible flowers for garnish next to the fresh herbs in the produce section of large grocery stores. We chose pansies, marigolds, and nasturtiums, but you can use your favorite edible flower.

¾ cup minced dried tomatoes in oil
1 (15-oz.) package refrigerated piecrusts
2 (8-oz.) packages cream cheese, softened
3 large eggs
1 (5-oz.) package shredded Swiss cheese
3 green onions, chopped (about ¼ cup)
1 tsp. salt
½ tsp. black pepper
¼ tsp. ground red pepper
1¾ cups sour cream
Garnishes: edible pansies, marigolds, and nasturtiums; fresh chives; green onion stems; fresh mint leaves

Drain tomatoes well, pressing between paper towels. Set aside.

Unfold piecrusts; place 1 piecrust on a lightly floured surface, and brush with water. Top with remaining crust. Roll into 1 (12½-inch) circle.

Press piecrust on bottom and 2½ inches up sides of a 9-inch springform pan. Press out folds in piecrust on sides of pan. Crimp with a fork. Freeze piecrust 30 minutes.

Bake at 450° for 9 minutes. Remove piecrust from oven, and reduce oven temperature to 350°.

Beat cream cheese at medium speed with an electric mixer 2 minutes. Add eggs, 1 at a time, beating well after each addition. Stir in tomatoes, Swiss cheese, and next 4 ingredients, mixing well. Pour into baked piecrust.

Bake on lower rack at 350° for 32 minutes or until golden brown and set. Cool 5 minutes. Spread sour cream evenly over top. Cool completely on wire rack; cover and chill 8 hours.

Release and remove sides of pan. Transfer cheesecake to a serving plate. If desired, garnish and serve with crackers. **Makes** 20 appetizer servings.

Note: Use a springform pan without a nonstick coating; otherwise the crust may fall away from the sides of the pan during the first baking.

Sun-Dried Tomato
Cheesecake

Cinco de Mayo Shrimp Cocktail
Prep: 35 min., Cook: 5 min.

4 plum tomatoes, coarsely chopped
½ red onion, sliced
¼ cup chopped fresh cilantro
1 jalapeño pepper, seeded
2 garlic cloves
¼ cup fresh lime juice
2 tsp. sugar
¼ tsp. chili powder
¼ tsp. pepper
½ tsp. salt (optional)
6 cups water
30 unpeeled, large fresh shrimp
1 large avocado, diced
Garnish: lime slices

Process first 9 ingredients and, if desired, salt in a blender or food processor until smooth, stopping to scrape down sides. Cover and chill sauce up to 1 week.
Bring 6 cups water to a boil; add shrimp, and cook 2 to 3 minutes or just until shrimp turn pink. Drain and rinse with cold water. Chill up to 24 hours.
Peel shrimp, leaving tails intact; devein, if desired.
Stir avocado into sauce; spoon sauce evenly into 6 chilled martini glasses or small bowls. Arrange 5 shrimp around edge of each glass; garnish, if desired. Serve with tortilla chips. **Makes** 6 servings.

make ahead
Olives Scaciati
Prep: 20 min., Other: 8 hrs.

Double the recipe for a dramatic presentation that feeds a large group.

2 lb. large, unpitted green olives
2 cups ½-inch celery pieces with leaves
¾ cup extra-virgin olive oil
¼ cup red wine vinegar
2 Tbsp. dried oregano
1 tsp. black pepper
¾ tsp. dried crushed red pepper
6 garlic cloves, coarsely chopped

Wash olives, and drain. Gently pound each olive with a wooden mallet to open. (Don't mash, and don't remove pit.) Place olives and celery in a large bowl.
Whisk together olive oil and next 5 ingredients until blended; pour over olive mixture, tossing to coat. Cover and chill 8 hours. Refrigerate up to 1 month. Serve at room temperature. **Makes** 6 cups.

make ahead
Marinated Spanish Olives
Prep: 5 min., Other: 8 hrs.

You can make and refrigerate this dish up to a week before your party; the flavors improve as the olives marinate. Use a mortar and pestle, meat mallet, or rolling pin to crush the coriander seeds and rosemary.

24 large unpitted Spanish olives
2 Tbsp. sherry vinegar
1 Tbsp. extra-virgin olive oil
2 tsp. coriander seeds, crushed
1 tsp. dried thyme
1 tsp. dried rosemary, crushed
½ tsp. dried crushed red pepper
2 garlic cloves, thinly sliced
Garnish: fresh rosemary sprigs

Combine first 8 ingredients in a bowl. Cover and marinate in refrigerator at least 8 hours. Serve at room temperature. Garnish, if desired. **Makes** 6 servings.

Olives Scaciati

Southwestern Cheese Appetizer

Prep: 30 min., Other: 8 hrs.

½ cup olive oil

½ cup white wine vinegar

¼ cup fresh lime juice

½ (7-oz.) jar roasted red bell peppers, drained and diced

3 green onions, minced

3 Tbsp. chopped fresh parsley

3 Tbsp. chopped fresh cilantro

1 tsp. sugar

½ tsp. salt

½ tsp. freshly ground pepper

1 (8-oz.) block sharp Cheddar cheese, chilled

1 (8-oz.) block Monterey Jack cheese with peppers, chilled

1 (8-oz.) package cream cheese, chilled

Whisk together first 3 ingredients until mixture is blended; stir in diced bell peppers and next 6 ingredients. Set marinade aside.

Cut block of Cheddar cheese in half lengthwise. Cut halves crosswise into ¼-inch-thick slices. Repeat procedure with Monterey Jack cheese and cream cheese.

Arrange cheese slices alternately in a shallow baking dish, standing slices on edge. Pour marinade over cheeses. Cover and chill at least 8 hours.

Transfer cheese to a serving plate, and spoon remaining marinade over top. Serve with assorted crackers.

Makes 16 appetizer servings.

Southwestern Cheese Appetizer

Baby Hot Browns
Prep: 35 min., Cook: 6 min.

24 pumpernickel party rye bread slices
3 Tbsp. butter or margarine
3 Tbsp. all-purpose flour
½ cup (2 oz.) shredded sharp Cheddar cheese
1 cup milk
1½ cups diced cooked turkey
¼ tsp. salt
¼ tsp. ground red pepper
½ cup freshly grated Parmesan cheese
6 bacon slices, cooked and crumbled

Arrange bread slices on a lightly greased baking sheet. Bake at 500° for 3 to 4 minutes.
Melt butter in a saucepan over low heat. Add flour; cook, whisking constantly, until smooth. Add Cheddar cheese, whisking until cheese melts. Gradually whisk in milk; cook over medium heat, whisking constantly, until mixture is thickened and bubbly. Stir in turkey, salt, and pepper. Chill, if desired.
Top bread slices evenly with cheese mixture. Sprinkle evenly with Parmesan cheese and bacon.
Bake at 500° for 2 minutes or until Parmesan is melted. **Makes** 2 dozen.

---

freezer friendly
Sausage Balls
Prep: 10 min., Cook: 18 min.

Freshly shredded cheese is a must because it's moister than preshredded cheese, which helps the mixture hold together better. Use a food processor to shred cheese; then process half of sausage mixture at a time.

3 cups biscuit mix
1 lb. hot ground pork sausage
1 (10-oz.) package sharp Cheddar cheese, shredded

Combine all ingredients in a large bowl, pressing mixture together with hands. Shape into ¾-inch balls, and place on lightly greased baking sheets.
Bake at 400° for 15 to 18 minutes or until lightly browned. **Makes** about 8 dozen.

Note: Sausage Balls may be frozen uncooked. Bake frozen balls at 400° for 18 to 20 minutes.

Spicy Party Meatballs
Prep: 5 min., Cook: 45 min.

1 (12-oz.) jar cocktail sauce
1 (10.5-oz.) jar jalapeño jelly
½ small sweet onion, minced
½ (3-lb.) package frozen cooked meatballs

Cook first 3 ingredients in a Dutch oven over medium heat, stirring until jelly melts and mixture is smooth. **Stir** in meatballs. Reduce heat, and simmer, stirring occasionally, 35 to 40 minutes or until thoroughly heated. **Makes** 8 dozen.

Mini Pork Sandwiches
Prep: 10 min., Cook: 30 min., Other: 5 min.

2 Tbsp. chopped fresh rosemary
1½ Tbsp. black peppercorns, crushed
1 tsp. salt
3 lb. pork tenderloins
2 Tbsp. olive oil
½ cup mayonnaise
2 Tbsp. prepared horseradish
1 Tbsp. brandy
1 garlic clove, minced
½ cup Dijon mustard
3 Tbsp. capers, chopped
Several bunches arugula
Sweet gherkin pickles, thinly sliced
40 party rolls or small square dinner rolls (we tested with Pepperidge Farm country-style soft dinner rolls)

Combine rosemary, crushed peppercorns, and salt. Rub mixture over tenderloins. Fold thin end under each tenderloin; secure with wooden picks.
Place tenderloins on a lightly greased rack in a broiler pan. Drizzle with olive oil.
Bake at 375° for 25 to 30 minutes or until a meat thermometer inserted in thickest part registers 160° (medium). Let stand 5 minutes. Thinly slice tenderloins.
Combine mayonnaise and next 3 ingredients. Combine mustard and capers. Spoon sauces into separate serving bowls.
Serve pork with sauces, arugula, gherkin pickles, and rolls for do-it-yourself sandwiches. **Makes** 40 appetizers.

Pesto-Chicken Cheesecakes
Prep: 15 min., Cook: 30 min., Other: 10 min.

2 (8-oz.) packages cream cheese, softened

2 large eggs

3 Tbsp. all-purpose flour, divided

3 Tbsp. Pesto*

1 cup chopped cooked chicken

1 (8-oz.) container sour cream

Mixed salad greens

Garnish: chopped fresh chives

Beat cream cheese at medium speed with an electric mixer until smooth. Add eggs, 2 Tbsp. flour, and Pesto, beating until blended. Stir in chicken. Pour into 4 (4-inch) springform pans.
Bake at 325° for 20 minutes.
Stir together remaining 1 Tbsp. flour and sour cream. Spread over cheesecakes; bake 10 more minutes.
Cool on a wire rack 10 minutes. Gently run a knife around edges of cheesecakes, and release sides. Serve hot or cold atop salad greens or with crackers. Garnish, if desired. **Makes** 4 servings.

*Substitute 1 cup prepared pesto, if desired.

Note: Cheesecake mixture can be baked in a 9-inch springform pan. Add 5 minutes to the initial baking time and an additional 5 minutes after adding the flour and sour cream.

Pesto
Prep: 6 min.

1½ cups firmly packed fresh basil leaves

½ cup pecan pieces, toasted

½ cup olive oil

3 garlic cloves

2 Tbsp. lemon juice

½ tsp. salt

Process all ingredients in a food processor until smooth. Refrigerate leftover Pesto up to 5 days, or freeze up to 3 months. **Makes** 1 cup.

Roasted Red Pepper Bruschetta

Prep: 10 min., Cook: 7 min.

Top these toasts with a sweet-tangy roasted red pepper mix and feta cheese. They make colorful hors d'oeuvres for a 4th of July barbecue.

1 (12-oz.) jar roasted red bell peppers, drained well and finely chopped
½ cup finely chopped plum tomato
¼ cup finely chopped red onion
2 Tbsp. balsamic vinegar
2 Tbsp. olive oil
½ tsp. salt
½ tsp. freshly ground pepper
Dash of sugar
1 baguette, cut into 28 slices
¼ cup olive oil
Salt and pepper
½ cup crumbled garlic and herb-flavored feta cheese

Combine first 3 ingredients in a bowl. Combine vinegar, 2 Tbsp. olive oil, ½ tsp. salt, ½ tsp. pepper, and sugar; pour over bell pepper mixture. Toss. Cover and chill until ready to serve.

Arrange baguette slices on a large ungreased baking sheet. Brush or drizzle slices with ¼ cup oil. Sprinkle with salt and pepper. Bake at 400° for 4 minutes or until barely toasted.

Spoon about 1 Tbsp. pepper mixture onto each toast; top each with crumbled feta. Broil 5½ inches from heat 3 minutes or until bubbly and barely browned. Serve warm. **Makes** 28 appetizers.

Phyllo Potato Tarts

Prep: 25 min., Cook: 45 min.

12 frozen phyllo pastry sheets, thawed
½ cup butter or margarine, melted
2 medium-size baking potatoes, peeled and thinly sliced
1 medium onion, quartered and thinly sliced
8 bacon slices, cooked and crumbled
½ cup freshly grated Parmesan cheese
1 tsp. dried thyme
1 tsp. salt
1 tsp. pepper
¾ cup whipping cream
4 fresh chives

Unfold phyllo, and cut into 14-inch squares. Cover squares with a slightly damp towel to prevent pastry from drying out.

Place 1 phyllo square on a flat surface covered with wax paper; brush with butter. Top with 2 more squares, brushing each with butter. Place in a 5-inch baking dish or tart pan. Repeat procedure with remaining phyllo squares and butter.

Layer potato, onion, bacon, and cheese in each tart. Sprinkle evenly with thyme, salt, and pepper. Pour 3 Tbsp. whipping cream over filling in each tart. Bring corners of phyllo to center, and twist to seal; tie with a chive.

Bake at 350° for 45 minutes, shielding with aluminum foil, if necessary. Serve immediately. **Makes** 4 servings.

freezer friendly • make ahead

Raspberry-Brie Tartlets

Prep: 40 min.; Cook: 10 min.

20 white bread slices
Melted butter
1 (8-oz.) wedge Brie, cut up
1 (13-oz.) jar raspberry jam

Remove crusts from bread with a serrated knife. Roll and flatten each bread slice with a rolling pin. Cut 3 circles out of each bread slice with a 1¾-inch fluted or round cookie cutter.

Brush mini muffin pans with melted butter. Press bread circles into bottom and up sides of muffin cups; brush bread cups with melted butter.

Bake at 350° for 7 minutes or until lightly toasted.

Remove bread cups from muffin pans, and place on ungreased baking sheets. Fill cups evenly with cheese pieces; top each with ¼ tsp. jam.

Bake at 300° for 10 minutes or until cheese is melted. **Makes** 5 dozen.

To Make Ahead: Freeze toasted bread shells up to 1 month in advance. Thaw at room temperature about 30 minutes. Assemble tartlets, and bake as directed.

Goat Cheese Wrapped in Phyllo
Prep: 1 hr., 10 min.; Cook: 12 min.

1 Tbsp. light butter
4 small white onions, chopped
1 tsp. sugar
½ cup balsamic vinegar
⅓ cup honey
1 tsp. chopped fresh thyme
4 frozen phyllo pastry sheets, thawed
Butter-flavored vegetable cooking spray
1 (3-oz.) log goat cheese, crumbled
Garnish: fresh thyme sprigs

Melt butter in a large nonstick skillet over medium heat; add onion and sugar, and cook, stirring often, 30 minutes or until caramel colored. Add vinegar and honey, and cook over medium heat, stirring occasionally, 15 to 20 minutes or until thickened. Stir in thyme.
Stack phyllo, coating each layer with cooking spray. Cut into 6 (5-inch) squares. Spoon onion mixture evenly onto center of phyllo squares. Top evenly with goat cheese. Lift corners, and twist together. Place packets on a lightly greased baking sheet; coat each with cooking spray.
Bake at 375° for 12 minutes or until golden. Garnish, if desired. **Makes** 6 servings.

Mini Mexican Quiches
Prep: 25 min., Cook: 35 min., Other: 20 min.

½ cup butter or margarine, softened
1 (3-oz.) package cream cheese, softened
1 cup all-purpose flour
1 cup (4 oz.) shredded Monterey Jack cheese
1 (4.5-oz.) can chopped green chiles, undrained
2 large eggs
½ cup whipping cream
¼ tsp. salt
⅛ tsp. pepper

Beat butter and cream cheese at medium speed with an electric mixer until smooth. Add flour, and beat well. Shape dough into a ball; cover and chill 20 minutes.

Shape dough into 36 (¾-inch) balls. Place in ungreased miniature (1¾-inch) muffin pans, and shape each ball into a shell. Divide shredded cheese and green chiles evenly among shells.
Whisk together eggs and remaining 3 ingredients. Spoon mixture evenly into shells. Bake at 350° for 35 minutes or until set. Serve warm. **Makes** 3 dozen.

freezer friendly • make ahead
Mini Spinach Quiches
Prep: 15 min., Cook: 35 min.

1 (15-oz.) package refrigerated piecrusts
2 Tbsp. butter or margarine
1 small onion, chopped
2 green onions, chopped
¼ cup chopped fresh parsley
1 (10-oz.) package frozen chopped spinach, thawed
    and well drained
1 Tbsp. Worcestershire sauce
1 tsp. salt
½ tsp. pepper
3 large eggs
¼ cup milk
1 cup (4 oz.) shredded Swiss cheese

Roll each piecrust into a 12-inch square; cut each square into 24 pieces. Shape into balls, and press into lightly greased miniature muffin pans.
Melt butter in a large skillet over medium heat. Add onions and parsley; sauté until onions are tender. Add spinach; cook 2 minutes. Stir in Worcestershire sauce, salt, and pepper. Remove from heat.
Whisk together eggs and milk until blended; stir in cheese. Add egg mixture to spinach mixture; spoon evenly into prepared pans.
Bake at 350° for 30 to 35 minutes. Remove immediately from pans, and cool on wire racks. Freeze quiches up to 2 months. **Makes** 4 dozen.

Note: Thaw frozen quiches in refrigerator; bake at 300° for 10 minutes or until thoroughly heated.

Texas Firecrackers

Prep: 45 min., Cook: 25 min.

2 skinned and boned chicken breasts
24 pepperoncini salad peppers
6 oz. Monterey Jack cheese with peppers, cut into
    24 strips
12 frozen phyllo pastry sheets, thawed
½ cup butter or margarine, melted

Cook chicken in boiling water to cover 20 minutes or until done; drain. Cut into 2- x ½-inch pieces.
Cut tops from peppers; remove seeds. Stuff each pepper with 1 piece of chicken and 1 cheese strip.

Stack 3 phyllo sheets on a large cutting board, brushing each with melted butter. Keep remaining sheets covered with a slightly damp towel. Cut phyllo crosswise into thirds; cut in half lengthwise.
Place a stuffed pepper 1 inch from short edge; roll up, and twist ends of phyllo. Repeat procedure with remaining phyllo, butter, and stuffed peppers. Place peppers on baking sheets coated with cooking spray.
Bake at 375° for 20 to 25 minutes or until golden.
Makes 2 dozen.

Crab Fritters

Prep: 20 min., Cook: 30 sec. per batch

½ lb. fresh crabmeat
1 cup biscuit mix
¾ tsp. salt
⅛ tsp. garlic powder
½ tsp. ground red pepper
1 Tbsp. chopped fresh parsley
½ tsp. grated lemon rind
¼ cup milk
1 large egg
2 Tbsp. fresh lemon juice
¼ tsp. Worcestershire sauce
Vegetable oil
Creole Sauce

Drain and flake crabmeat, removing any bits of shell. Set aside.

Stir together biscuit mix and next 5 ingredients; make a well in center of mixture.

Combine milk and next 3 ingredients. Add to dry ingredients; stir just until moistened.

Add crabmeat, and stir to combine.

Pour vegetable oil to a depth of 2 inches in a Dutch oven; heat to 375°.

Drop batter by teaspoonfuls into hot oil, and fry, a few at a time, 30 seconds or until golden brown, turning once.

Serve fritters immediately with Creole Sauce. **Makes** about 40 fritters.

Creole Sauce

Prep: 5 min.

½ cup Creole mustard
¼ cup mayonnaise
1 tsp. lemon juice
½ tsp. hot sauce
¼ tsp. pepper

Stir together mustard and remaining ingredients. **Makes** about ¾ cup.

Crab-Stuffed Mushrooms
Prep: 20 min., Cook: 20 min.

1½ lb. very large fresh mushrooms (about 18 mushrooms)
3 Tbsp. butter or margarine
½ cup chopped onion
1 garlic clove, minced
½ cup soft breadcrumbs
¼ cup chopped fresh parsley
2 Tbsp. dry sherry
½ tsp. Worcestershire sauce
½ tsp. salt
¼ tsp. ground red pepper
¼ cup mayonnaise
2 to 3 Tbsp. grated Parmesan cheese
8 oz. fresh lump crabmeat, drained
2 Tbsp. butter or margarine, melted

Remove and chop mushroom stems; set mushroom caps aside.

Melt 3 Tbsp. butter in a large skillet. Add chopped mushroom stems, onion, and garlic; sauté 3 to 5 minutes or until tender. Stir in breadcrumbs and next 7 ingredients until well blended; gently stir in crabmeat.

Spoon crabmeat mixture evenly into mushroom caps, and place on a rack in a broiler pan. Drizzle with 2 Tbsp. melted butter.

Bake at 350° for 20 minutes. **Makes** about 1½ dozen.

Grilled Zucchini-Wrapped Shrimp
Prep: 20 min., Cook: 6 min., Other: 15 min.

1 lb. unpeeled, large fresh shrimp
½ cup fresh lime juice
8 Tbsp. vegetable oil, divided
2 garlic cloves, pressed
¾ tsp. salt
½ tsp. ground red pepper
2 large zucchini

Peel shrimp; devein, if desired.

Combine lime juice, 3 Tbsp. vegetable oil, and next 3 ingredients in a zip-top freezer bag, gently squeezing to blend; add shrimp. Seal and chill 15 minutes.

Remove shrimp from marinade, reserving marinade.

Bring reserved marinade to a boil in a small saucepan; remove from heat.

Cut zucchini lengthwise into thin slices with a vegetable peeler. Wrap each shrimp with a zucchini slice, and secure with a wooden pick. Brush rolls with remaining 5 Tbsp. vegetable oil.

Grill rolls, without grill lid, over medium-high heat (350° to 400°) about 4 minutes.

Brush with reserved marinade; turn and brush again. Grill 2 more minutes or just until shrimp turn pink. Serve shrimp hot or at room temperature. **Makes** 6 appetizer servings.

Coconut Shrimp with Mustard Sauce
Prep: 30 min., Cook: 2 min. per batch

1½ lb. unpeeled, jumbo fresh shrimp
2 cups all-purpose baking mix, divided
1 cup beer
½ tsp. salt
⅛ to ¼ tsp. ground red pepper
3 cups sweetened flaked coconut
Vegetable oil
Mustard Sauce

Peel shrimp, leaving tails intact; devein, if desired. Set aside. Stir together 1 cup baking mix and 1 cup beer until smooth. Stir together remaining 1 cup baking mix, salt, and ground red pepper.

Dredge shrimp in dry mixture, and dip in beer mixture, allowing excess coating to drip.

Gently roll shrimp in flaked coconut.

Pour vegetable oil to a depth of 3 inches into a Dutch oven or heavy saucepan, and heat to 350°. Cook shrimp, in batches, 1 to 2 minutes or until golden; remove shrimp, and drain on paper towels. Serve immediately with Mustard Sauce. **Makes** 10 to 12 appetizer servings.

Mustard Sauce
Prep: 5 min.

½ cup Dijon mustard
2 Tbsp. light brown sugar
2 Tbsp. beer
⅛ to ¼ tsp. ground red pepper

Stir together all ingredients. **Makes** ⅔ cup.

Tabb's Barbecue
Pork, page 110

Great
Outdoor
Cooking

Get ready to wow family and friends

with restaurant-style barbecue

from your own backyard!

Barbecued and slow-smoked

briskets, ribs, pork shoulders,

chicken, and more have endless

possibilities when firing up the pit.

Barbecue Beef Brisket
Prep: 10 min.; Cook: 4 hrs., 30 min.; Other: 1 hr., 10 min.

The slow cooking of the meat makes this barbecue melt in your mouth—we gave it our best rating.

1 (5- to 6-lb.) boneless beef brisket, trimmed
2 tsp. paprika
½ tsp. pepper
1 (11- x 9-inch) disposable aluminum roasting pan
1 cup water
Hickory chunks
Smoky Barbecue Sauce

Sprinkle brisket with paprika and pepper; rub over surface of roast. Place roast in disposable pan; add 1 cup water, and cover with aluminum foil.
Soak hickory chunks in water to cover 1 hour; drain. Wrap chunks in heavy-duty aluminum foil, and make several holes in foil. Light gas grill on one side; place foil-wrapped chunks directly on hot coals. Let grill preheat 10 to 15 minutes. Place pan with brisket on grate opposite hot coals; cover and grill 3½ to 4 hours or until tender. Turn brisket every hour, adding water as needed. Remove brisket from pan, reserving 1 cup pan drippings for sauce.
Coat food grate with cooking spray; place grate over hot coals. Place brisket on grate; cover and grill 10 to 15 minutes on each side. Let stand 10 minutes before slicing. Slice against grain into thin slices. Serve with Smoky Barbecue Sauce. **Makes** 12 servings.

Smoky Barbecue Sauce
Prep: 5 min., Cook: 18 min.

1 small onion, finely chopped
1 Tbsp. butter or margarine, melted
1 cup reserved pan drippings
½ tsp. pepper
1½ cups ketchup
1 Tbsp. lemon juice
1 Tbsp. Worcestershire sauce
1 tsp. hot sauce

Sauté onion in butter in a large skillet over medium-high heat until tender. Stir in drippings and remaining ingredients. Bring to a boil; reduce heat, and simmer 15 minutes, stirring occasionally. **Makes** 3 cups.

Texas-Smoked Beer-Marinated Brisket
Prep: 10 min.; Cook: 8 hrs.; Other: 8 hrs., 10 min.

1 (8-lb.) boneless beef brisket, untrimmed
1 garlic bulb, peeled
1 Tbsp. salt
1 Tbsp. pepper
2 (12-oz.) cans dark beer
1 (8-oz.) bottle Italian dressing
Mesquite chunks
6 bacon slices

Cut 1-inch-deep slits into brisket with a paring knife; insert garlic cloves into each slit. Rub brisket with salt and pepper, and place in a shallow dish or large zip-top freezer bag. Pour beer and dressing over brisket. Cover or seal, and chill, turning occasionally, 8 hours.
Soak wood chunks in water at least 1 hour.
Remove brisket from marinade, discarding marinade.
Prepare charcoal fire in smoker; let burn 15 to 20 minutes.
Drain chunks, and place on coals. Place water pan in smoker; add water to depth of fill line.
Place brisket on lower food grate; arrange bacon on top of brisket, and close smoker.
Smoke 4 hours; remove bacon, and cook 4 more hours or until a meat thermometer registers 155°. Let stand 10 minutes before slicing. **Makes** 8 servings.

> "Texas likes to bill itself as 'a whole other country.' So is its barbecue—smoky blends of beef and pork from the Anglo and African-American traditions by way of the Deep South and seasoned with accents from Mexico and Germany."

—Gary D. Ford, *Southern Living* Staff

Traditional Red-Sauced Brisket
Prep: 40 min.; Cook: 7 hrs.; Other: 9 hrs., 30 min.

1 (5¾-lb.) boneless beef brisket, trimmed
Brisket Rub
Hickory chunks
Brisket Mopping Sauce
Mop
Brisket Red Sauce (optional)

Sprinkle each side of beef with ¼ cup Brisket Rub; rub thoroughly into meat. Wrap brisket in plastic wrap, and chill 8 hours.

Soak hickory chunks in water for 8 hours. Drain.

Prepare smoker according to manufacturer's directions, regulating temperature with a thermometer to 225°; allow it to maintain that temperature for 1 hour before adding beef.

Remove beef from refrigerator, and let stand 30 minutes.

Place brisket, fat side up, on food grate. Insert heat-proof thermometer horizontally into thickest portion of beef. Maintain smoker temperature between 225° and 250°.

Add a handful (about ¼ cup) of hickory chunks about every hour.

Brush beef liberally with Brisket Mopping Sauce when beef starts to look dry (internal temperature will be about 156°). Mop top of brisket every hour. When internal temperature reaches 170°, place brisket on a sheet of heavy-duty aluminum foil; mop liberally with Brisket Mopping Sauce. Wrap tightly, and return to smoker.

Remove brisket from smoker when internal temperature reaches 190° with an instant-read thermometer. Let stand 1 hour. Cut into very thin (⅛- to ¼-inch thick) slices. Serve with Brisket Red Sauce, if desired. **Makes** 8 servings.

Brisket Rub
Prep: 5 min.

¼ cup kosher salt
¼ cup sugar
¼ cup black pepper
¾ cup paprika
2 Tbsp. garlic powder
2 Tbsp. garlic salt
2 Tbsp. onion powder
2 Tbsp. chili powder
2 tsp. ground red pepper

Combine all ingredients. Store in an airtight container up to 6 months. **Makes** 2 cups.

Brisket Mopping Sauce
Prep: 10 min.

This makes enough sauce for about two briskets, so make half the recipe if you're preparing just one brisket.

1 (12-oz.) bottle beer
1 cup apple cider vinegar
1 onion, minced
4 garlic cloves, minced
½ cup water
½ cup Worcestershire sauce
¼ cup vegetable oil
2 Tbsp. Brisket Rub

Stir together all ingredients until blended. **Makes** 4 cups.

Brisket Red Sauce
Prep: 10 min.

1½ cups cider vinegar
1 cup ketchup
½ tsp. ground red pepper
¼ cup Worcestershire sauce
1 tsp. salt
½ tsp. black pepper
½ tsp. onion powder
½ Tbsp. garlic powder
½ Tbsp. ground cumin
2 Tbsp. unsalted butter, melted
½ cup firmly packed brown sugar

Stir together all ingredients until blended. Serve sauce heated or at room temperature. **Makes** 3½ cups.

Smoked Brisket Sandwiches

Prep: 5 min.; Cook: 3 hrs., 30 min.; Other: 1 hr.

Hickory chunks
2 Tbsp. dried rosemary
2 Tbsp. paprika
2 Tbsp. pepper
2 Tbsp. dried garlic flakes
1 tsp. salt
1 (7-lb.) boneless beef brisket, untrimmed
Favorite barbecue sauce
Hamburger buns
Pickles
Garnish: fresh rosemary sprigs

Soak wood chunks in water for at least 1 hour.
Prepare charcoal fire in smoker; let burn 15 to 20 minutes.
Combine rosemary and next 4 ingredients; rub on brisket.
Drain wood chunks, and place on coals. Place water pan in smoker; add water to depth of fill line. Place brisket on lower food grate; cover with smoker lid.
Smoke 3½ hours or until meat thermometer inserted into thickest portion registers 155°. Slice and serve with barbecue sauce, buns, and pickles. Garnish, if desired. **Makes** 8 servings.

GRILLING TIPS

■ Keep a spray bottle full of water handy to extinguish flare-ups that can char food.

■ When turning meats, use a pair of tongs rather than a meat fork, which pierces food and allows valuable juices to escape.

■ Always place grilled food on a clean platter or cutting board.

Smoked Garlic Prime Rib

Prep: 5 min.; Cook: 6 hrs.; Other: 8 hrs., 10 min.

1 (10-lb.) beef rib roast
2 Tbsp. kosher salt
3 Tbsp. freshly ground pepper
6 garlic cloves, minced
Hickory chunks

Rub rib roast with salt, pepper, and garlic; cover and chill at least 8 hours.
Soak wood chunks in water 1 hour.
Prepare charcoal fire in smoker; let burn 15 to 20 minutes.
Drain chunks, and place on coals. Place water pan in smoker; add water to depth of fill line.
Place rib roast in center on the lower food grate, and cover with smoker lid.
Smoke, covered, 6 hours or until a meat thermometer inserted into thickest portion of roast registers 145° (medium-rare), refilling water pan and adding charcoal and wood chunks as needed. Let stand 10 minutes before slicing. **Makes** 12 servings.

Smoked Herbed Prime Rib

Prep: 10 min.; Cook: 5 hrs.; Other: 1 hr., 10 min.

Red wine bathes the roast and drips into the water pan, infusing the smoke with fruity essence.

Hickory chunks
4 garlic cloves, minced
1 Tbsp. salt
2 Tbsp. coarsely ground pepper
1 Tbsp. dried rosemary
1 tsp. dried thyme
1 (6-lb.) beef rib roast
1½ cups dry red wine
1½ cups red wine vinegar
½ cup olive oil

Soak wood chunks in water 1 hour.
Combine minced garlic and next 4 ingredients, and rub garlic mixture evenly over rib roast.
Stir together wine, vinegar, and olive oil; set wine mixture aside.
Prepare charcoal fire in smoker; let burn 15 to 20 minutes.
Drain wood chunks, and place on coals. Place water pan in smoker, and add water to just below fill line.
Place rib roast in center on lower food grate. Gradually pour wine mixture over rib roast.
Smoke roast, covered, 5 hours or until a meat thermometer inserted into thickest portion of roast registers 145° (medium-rare), refilling water pan and adding charcoal and wood chunks as needed. Let stand 10 minutes before slicing. **Makes** 8 to 10 servings.

"Two things fundamental to great barbecue are the right temperature and smoke. Long, slow cooking allows the meat to tenderize, while the smoke gives the meat flavor."

—Troy Black, *Southern Living* Contributor

Smoked Marinated Eye of Round

Prep: 6 min.; Cook: 6 hrs.; Other: 12 hrs., 10 min.

½ cup Worcestershire sauce
½ cup teriyaki sauce
⅓ cup lemon juice
¼ cup white wine vinegar
2 Tbsp. seasoned salt
1 (4- to 5-lb.) eye of round roast
Hickory or mesquite chunks

Combine first 5 ingredients; stir well. Place roast in a zip-top freezer bag or large shallow dish; pour marinade over roast. Seal or cover, and marinate in refrigerator 12 to 24 hours, turning occasionally.
Remove roast from marinade, discarding marinade.
Soak wood chunks in water 1 hour.
Prepare charcoal fire in smoker, and let burn 15 to 20 minutes. Drain chunks and place on hot coals. Place water pan in smoker, and fill with water.
Place roast on lower food grate; cover with smoker lid.
Cook, covered, 5 to 6 hours or until tender, refilling water pan and adding charcoal and wood chunks as needed.
Let stand 10 minutes. Slice roast thinly to serve.
Makes 12 servings.

THE LOWDOWN ON SMOKING

■ The amount of charcoal or logs you start out with when smoking depends on the size of your smoker, its heat retention, and the weather.
■ Remember, you'll need to add charcoal and/or logs regularly during smoking to maintain the right temperature (generally between 225° and 250°—any hotter and you're grilling).
■ Your smoker should have a built-in thermometer that gives you an exact temperature reading. If it doesn't, purchase a heatproof one.

Smoked Strip Steaks

Prep: 10 min.; Cook: 1 hr., 18 min.; Other: 1 hr., 5 min.

Strip steaks offer a lot of surface area relative to their total size, which allows them to absorb a maximum amount of smoke. Serve thin slices of the steak over rice pilaf.

2 cups hickory or mesquite chunks
2 tsp. freshly ground pepper
1 tsp. garlic powder
½ tsp. salt
¼ tsp. dry mustard
2 (12-oz.) New York strip or sirloin strip steaks, trimmed
2 tsp. Worcestershire sauce

Soak wood chunks in water 1 hour; drain.
Combine pepper, garlic powder, salt, and mustard, and rub evenly over both sides of steaks. Place coated steaks in a large zip-top freezer bag; add Worcestershire sauce. Seal and shake to coat. Marinate in refrigerator 30 minutes.
Prepare grill for indirect grilling, heating one side to low and leaving one side with no heat. Maintain temperature at 200° to 225°.
Heat a large, heavy skillet over high heat. Remove steaks from bag, and discard marinade. Coat pan with cooking spray. Add steaks to pan; cook 1½ minutes on each side or until browned. Remove from pan.
Place wood chunks on hot coals. Place a disposable aluminum foil pan on unheated side of grill. Pour 2 cups water in pan. Coat the food grate with cooking spray, and place on grill.
Place steaks on food grate over aluminum foil pan on unheated side. Close lid; smoke 1 hour and 15 minutes or until a thermometer inserted into steak registers 145° (medium-rare) or until desired degree of doneness. Let stand 5 minutes. Cut steaks across grain into thin slices. **Makes** 4 to 6 servings.

Beef Fajitas with Pico de Gallo

Prep: 5 min.; Cook: 13 min.; Other: 8 hrs., 5 min.

1 (8-oz.) bottle zesty Italian dressing
3 Tbsp. fajita seasoning
2 (1-lb.) flank steaks
12 (6-inch) flour tortillas, warmed
Shredded Cheddar cheese
Pico de Gallo
Garnishes: lime wedges, fresh cilantro sprigs

Combine Italian dressing and fajita seasoning in a shallow dish or zip-top freezer bag; add steak. Cover or seal, and chill 8 hours, turning occasionally. Remove steak from marinade, discarding marinade.
Grill steaks, covered with grill lid, over medium-high heat (350° to 400°) for 8 minutes. Turn and grill 5 more minutes or to desired degree of doneness. Let stand 5 minutes before slicing.
Cut steaks diagonally across the grain into very thin slices, and serve with tortillas, cheese, and Pico de Gallo. Garnish, if desired. **Makes** 6 servings.

Pico de Gallo
Prep: 25 min., Other: 1 hr.

1 pt. grape tomatoes, chopped*
1 green bell pepper, chopped
1 red bell pepper, chopped
1 avocado, peeled and chopped
½ medium-size red onion, chopped
½ cup chopped fresh cilantro
1 garlic clove, pressed
¾ tsp. salt
½ tsp. ground cumin
½ tsp. grated lime rind
¼ cup fresh lime juice

Stir together all ingredients; cover and chill 1 hour.
Makes about 3 cups.

*Substitute 2 large tomatoes, chopped, if desired.

Beef-and-Chicken Fajitas
with Peppers and Onions

Beef-and-Chicken Fajitas with Peppers and Onions
Prep: 30 min., Cook: 16 min., Other: 4 hrs.

¼ cup olive oil
1 tsp. grated lime rind
2½ Tbsp. fresh lime juice
2 Tbsp. Worcestershire sauce
1½ tsp. ground cumin
1 tsp. salt
½ tsp. dried oregano
½ tsp. coarsely ground pepper
2 garlic cloves, minced
1 (14-oz.) can beef broth
1 (1-lb.) flank steak
1 lb. skinned and boned chicken breasts
2 red bell peppers, each cut into 12 wedges
2 green bell peppers, each cut into 12 wedges
1 large Vidalia or other sweet onion, cut into
    16 wedges
16 (6-inch) flour tortillas
1 cup bottled salsa
¼ cup sour cream
½ cup chopped fresh cilantro
Garnish: fresh cilantro sprigs

Combine first 10 ingredients in a large bowl; set marinade aside.
Trim fat from steak. Score a diamond pattern on both sides of the steak using a sharp knife. Combine 1½ cups marinade, steak, and chicken in a large zip-top freezer bag. Seal and marinate in refrigerator 4 hours or overnight, turning occasionally. Combine remaining marinade, bell peppers, and onion in a large zip-top freezer bag. Seal and marinate in refrigerator for 4 hours or overnight, turning occasionally.
Remove steak and chicken from bag; discard marinade. Remove vegetables from bag; reserve marinade. Place reserved marinade in a small saucepan; set aside. Place steak, chicken, and vegetables on food grate coated with cooking spray; grill 8 minutes on each side or until desired degree of doneness.
Wrap tortillas tightly in foil; place tortilla packet on food grate during the last 2 minutes of grilling time. Bring reserved marinade to a boil. Cut steak and chicken diagonally across grain into thin slices. Place steak, chicken, and vegetables on a serving platter; drizzle with reserved marinade. Serve with tortillas, salsa, sour cream, and cilantro. Garnish, if desired. Serve immediately. **Makes** 8 servings.

Java Fajitas
Prep: 10 min., Cook: 27 min., Other: 8 hrs.

⅓ cup tomato paste
1¼ cups strong brewed coffee
½ cup Worcestershire sauce
1 Tbsp. sugar
2 tsp. ground red pepper
1 tsp. ground black pepper
3 Tbsp. fresh lime juice
1 Tbsp. vegetable oil
2 (1½-lb.) flank steaks
24 (10-inch) flour tortillas
Pico de Gallo (page 103)
Garnishes: fresh cilantro, lime wedges, avocado slices

Combine tomato paste and next 7 ingredients in a shallow dish or large zip-top freezer bag; add steaks. Cover or seal; chill 8 hours. Turn steaks occasionally.
Remove steaks from marinade, reserving marinade.
Grill steaks, covered with grill lid, over high heat (400° to 500°) about 6 minutes on each side or to desired degree of doneness.
Cut steaks diagonally across grain into thin slices; keep warm. Bring reserved marinade to a boil in a skillet; boil 10 to 15 minutes or until reduced to 1 cup.
Serve steak with tortillas, reduced marinade, and Pico de Gallo. Garnish, if desired. **Makes** 12 servings.

Barbecue Chopped Steaks
Prep: 9 min., Cook: 10 min.

1 lb. ground round
¼ cup barbecue sauce, divided
2 Tbsp. Italian-seasoned breadcrumbs
2 Tbsp. minced onion
¼ tsp. freshly ground pepper
1 egg white, lightly beaten

Combine ground round, 2 Tbsp. barbecue sauce, and remaining 4 ingredients, stirring well. Shape into 4 (¾-inch-thick) oval patties.
Coat food grate with cooking spray; place on grill over medium-high heat (350° to 400°). Place patties on grate; grill, covered, 5 minutes. Turn patties, and brush with remaining 2 Tbsp. barbecue sauce. Grill, covered, 5 more minutes or until juices run clear. **Makes** 4 servings.

North Carolina Smoked
Pork Shoulder

North Carolina
Smoked Pork Shoulder

Prep: 30 min.; Cook: 5 hrs., 30 min.; Other: 1 hr.

Pair this Carolina favorite with Cider Vinegar Barbecue Sauce (page 186) or Peppery Barbecue Sauce (page 185).

Hickory chunks
1 (5- to 6-lb.) bone-in pork shoulder or Boston butt
    pork roast
2 tsp. salt
10 lb. hardwood charcoal, divided
Cider Vinegar Barbecue Sauce (page 186) or Peppery
    Barbecue Sauce (page 185)

Soak hickory chunks in water 1 hour. Drain well.
Sprinkle pork with salt; cover and chill 30 minutes.
Prepare charcoal fire with half of charcoal in grill; let burn 15 to 20 minutes or until covered with gray ash. Push coals evenly into piles on both sides of grill. Carefully place 2 hickory chunks on top of each pile, and place food grate on grill.
Place pork, meaty side down, on grate directly in center of grill. Cover with lid, leaving ventilation holes completely open.
Prepare an additional charcoal fire with 12 briquettes in an auxiliary grill or fire bucket; let burn 30 minutes or until covered with gray ash. Carefully add 6 briquettes to each pile in smoker; place 2 more hickory chunks on each pile. Repeat procedure every 30 minutes.
Smoke, covered, 5½ hours or until meat thermometer inserted into thickest portion registers at least 165°, turning once during the last 2 hours. (Cooking the pork to 165° makes the meat easier to remove from bone.)
Remove pork; cool slightly. Chop and serve with Cider Vinegar Barbecue Sauce or Peppery Vinegar Sauce. **Makes** 6 servings.

Smoked Teriyaki-Marinated
Boston Butt

Prep: 15 min.; Cook: 6 hrs.; Other: 8 hrs., 10 min.

1 (10-oz.) bottle teriyaki sauce
1 cup honey
½ cup cider vinegar
2 Tbsp. black pepper
2 Tbsp. garlic powder
1 tsp. dried crushed red pepper
1 (6-lb.) Boston butt pork roast
 Hickory chunks

Combine first 6 ingredients in a shallow dish or large zip-top freezer bag. Cut deep slits in roast using a paring knife; add roast to marinade. Cover or seal, and chill 8 hours, turning occasionally.
Soak wood chunks in water 1 hour.
Prepare charcoal fire in smoker; let burn 15 to 20 minutes.
Drain wood chunks, and place on coals. Place water pan in smoker; add water to depth of fill line. Drain roast, discarding marinade. Place roast in center of lower food grate.
Smoke, covered, 6 hours or until a meat thermometer inserted into thickest portion registers 165°, adding additional water, if necessary. Let stand 10 minutes. Chop or shred; serve with barbecue sauce, if desired. **Makes** 6 to 8 servings.

66 Eastern North Carolina goes whole hog for vinegar sauce, while western North Carolina shoulders the demand for a little ketchup. 99

—Glenn Morris, *Southern Living* Contributor

Smoked Mustard-Sauced Pork

Prep: 10 min.; Cook: 6 hrs.; Other: 1 hr., 10 min.

Hickory chunks
2 cups prepared mustard
1½ cups ketchup
¾ cup cider vinegar
2 Tbsp. sugar
2 Tbsp. Worcestershire sauce
1 Tbsp. hot sauce
2 Tbsp. butter or margarine
1 (5- to 6-lb.) Boston butt pork roast
5 garlic cloves, chopped
2 Tbsp. salt
1 Tbsp. pepper

Soak hickory chunks in water 1 hour.

Cook mustard and next 6 ingredients in a saucepan over low heat, stirring often, 20 minutes; set aside.

Cut deep slits in roast using a paring knife. Stir together garlic, salt, and pepper; rub on all sides of roast.

Prepare charcoal fire in smoker; let burn 15 to 20 minutes.

Drain wood chunks, and place on coals. Place water pan in smoker; add water to depth of fill line.

Place roast on lower food grate, and top with 1 cup mustard mixture.

Smoke, covered, 5 to 6 hours or until a meat thermometer inserted into thickest portion registers 165°. Let stand 10 minutes; chop and serve with remaining mustard sauce. **Makes** 8 to 10 servings.

Mesquite-Smoked Pork with Texas Caviar

Prep: 20 min.; Cook: 2 hrs., 5 min.; Other: 2 hrs., 15 min.

Texas Caviar is a mixture of black-eyed peas, fresh vegetables, and seasonings.

1 cup frozen black-eyed peas
1 cup water
⅓ cup seeded, chopped tomato
¼ cup chopped yellow bell pepper
¼ cup chopped green bell pepper
¼ cup chopped onion
¼ cup oil-free Italian dressing
1 Tbsp. chopped fresh parsley
2 tsp. seeded, minced jalapeño pepper
¼ tsp. minced garlic
⅛ tsp. black pepper
⅛ tsp. ground cumin
Mesquite chunks
1 (8-rib) center rib pork roast (about 4 lb.)
8 garlic cloves, minced
½ tsp. salt
½ tsp. coarsely ground pepper

Combine peas and 1 cup water. Bring to a boil. Cover, reduce heat, and simmer 35 minutes or until tender. Drain; cool.

Combine peas, tomato, and next 9 ingredients in a medium bowl, stirring well. Cover; chill at least 2 hours.

Soak mesquite chunks in water at least 1 hour; drain. Wrap chunks in heavy-duty aluminum foil, and make several holes in foil.

Light gas grill on one side; place foil-wrapped chunks directly on hot lava rocks. Coat food grate on opposite side of grill with cooking spray. Place grate over cool lava rocks; preheat grill to medium-high (350° to 400°) 10 to 15 minutes.

Trim fat from roast. Mash 8 minced garlic cloves, salt, and ½ tsp. pepper to a paste. Rub surface of roast with garlic paste. Coat roast with cooking spray. Insert meat thermometer into thickest part of roast, making sure it does not touch the bone. Place roast on grate opposite hot lava rocks.

Smoke, covered, 1½ hours or until meat thermometer registers 150°. Remove roast from grill. Cover with aluminum foil; let stand 15 minutes or until thermometer registers 160°.

Carve roast into 8 chops, and serve with black-eyed pea mixture. **Makes** 8 servings.

Three-Alarm BBQ

Prep: 10 min.; Cook: 5 hrs., 5 min.; Other: 8 hrs., 10 min.

Choose your own fate of 1, 2, or 3 tsp. of hot sauce in this barbecue with a kick.

2 to 4 cups hickory chunks
1 (2½-lb.) lean, bone-in pork loin roast
1 cup cider vinegar
2 Tbsp. grated fresh onion
2 Tbsp. ketchup
1 tsp. salt
1 tsp. black pepper
1 to 3 tsp. hot sauce
2 tsp. Worcestershire sauce
½ tsp. ground red pepper
4 garlic cloves, minced
12 white bread slices
12 hamburger dill pickle slices
Garnish: red onion slices

Soak hickory chunks in water 1 to 24 hours. Drain well.

Trim fat from roast. Combine vinegar and next 8 ingredients in a large zip-top freezer bag. Add roast; seal bag. Marinate in refrigerator 8 hours, turning bag occasionally.

Remove roast from bag, reserving marinade. Place reserved marinade in refrigerator.

Prepare charcoal fire in smoker; let burn 20 minutes or until coals are gray. Place hickory chunks on top of coals. Place water pan in smoker; add hot water to fill pan.

Coat food grate with cooking spray, and place in smoker. Place roast on grate; cover with lid.

Smoke 5 hours or until meat thermometer inserted into thickest part of roast registers 160°. Refill pan with water, and add charcoal and hickory chunks to fire as needed.

Remove roast from smoker; let stand 10 minutes. Cut roast from bone. Separate into bite-size pieces using 2 forks. Place in a bowl; set aside, and keep warm.

Bring reserved marinade to a boil over medium heat; cook 1 minute. Pour over roast; toss well. Serve with bread and pickles. Garnish, if desired. **Makes** 6 servings.

Note: If you prefer your barbecue with only one alarm, use 1 tsp. hot sauce and decrease the ground red pepper to ¼ tsp.

Barbecue Pork Shoulder

Prep: 15 min.; Cook: 7 hrs.; Other: 1 hr., 10 min.

1 (2-lb.) package hickory chunks, divided
2 qt. white vinegar
½ cup ground red pepper, divided
5 oranges, quartered and divided
5 lemons, quartered and divided
½ cup firmly packed brown sugar
¼ cup ground black pepper
2 Tbsp. lemon juice
¼ cup liquid smoke
1 (7- to 8-lb.) bone-in pork shoulder roast (Boston butt)

Soak 1 lb. of wood chunks in water 1 hour.

Bring vinegar, ¼ cup ground red pepper, 3 oranges, and 3 lemons to a boil in a Dutch oven over medium heat; cook 10 minutes. Remove vinegar mixture from heat, and cool.

Combine remaining ¼ cup ground red pepper, brown sugar, and next 3 ingredients. Rub evenly over pork. Drizzle 1 cup vinegar mixture over pork; set aside 2 cups vinegar mixture for basting, and reserve remaining mixture to fill the water pan.

Prepare charcoal fire in smoker; let burn 15 to 20 minutes.

Drain wood chunks, and place on coals. Place water pan in smoker; add vinegar mixture and remaining 2 oranges and 2 lemons to depth of fill line. Place pork on lower food grate; cover with smoker lid.

Smoke pork roast 6 to 7 hours or until a meat thermometer inserted into the thickest part of roast registers 170°. Baste with reserved 2 cups vinegar mixture every hour after pork roast has cooked 3 hours. Add more charcoal, remaining 1 lb. wood chunks, and vinegar mixture to smoker as needed. Let stand 10 minutes before slicing. **Makes** 10 servings.

■ Push the marinade injector needle straight into the meat. Don't try to move the needle to a new position without removing it from the meat and reinserting it in another place—otherwise, the needle could break off.

■ Inject marinade randomly around all sides of meat until it starts coming back out of holes.

kids love it
Slow-Smoked Pork with Ranch-Barbecue Sauce
Prep: 15 min.; Cook: 4 hrs., 30 min.; Other: 8 hrs., 40 min.

A Creole sauce injected into the pork tenderizes and flavors the roast.

1 (5-lb.) bone-in pork shoulder roast (Boston butt)
1 (1-oz.) envelope Ranch dressing mix
½ (16-oz.) bottle Creole butter injector sauce (with injector) (we tested with Cajun Injector Creole Butter Injectable Marinade)
Ranch-Barbecue Sauce (page 188)
Garnish: bread-and-butter pickle slices

Rub roast with dressing mix. Inject butter sauce evenly into roast. Wrap tightly with plastic wrap, and place in a shallow dish or large zip-top freezer bag; cover or seal, and chill 8 hours. Let stand at room temperature 30 minutes before grilling. Remove plastic wrap.
Light one side of grill, heating to high heat (400° to 500°); leave other side unlit. Place roast, fat side up, over unlit side of grill.
Smoke, covered with grill lid, 3½ to 4½ hours or until meat thermometer inserted into thickest portion registers 185°. (Meat will easily pull away from bone.) Let stand 10 minutes. Coarsely chop, and serve with Ranch-Barbecue Sauce. Garnish, if desired. **Makes 6 servings.**

Tabb's Barbecue Pork
Prep: 5 min.; Cook: 8 hrs.; Other: 9 hrs., 10 min.

The sweet, not-too-spicy rub on Tabb's Barbecue Pork is the perfect complement to the lip-smacking tanginess of Honey-Mustard Barbecue Sauce (page 187).

1 (6-lb.) bone-in pork shoulder roast (Boston butt)
1 cup Sweet 'n' Spicy Barbecue Rub (page 192)
Hickory chunks
Apple juice

Trim fat on pork shoulder roast to about ⅛ inch thick.
Sprinkle pork evenly with Sweet 'n' Spicy Barbecue Rub; rub thoroughly into meat. Wrap pork tightly with plastic wrap, and chill 8 hours.
Discard plastic wrap. Let pork stand at room temperature 1 hour.
Soak hickory chunks in water 1 hour.
Prepare smoker according to manufacturer's instructions, bringing internal temperature to 225° to 250°; maintain temperature for 15 to 20 minutes.
Drain wood chunks, and place on coals. Place pork, fat side up, on lower food grate.
Spritz pork with apple juice each time charcoal or wood chunks are added to the smoker.
Smoke pork roast, maintaining the temperature inside smoker between 225° and 250°, for 6 hours or until a meat thermometer inserted horizontally into thickest portion of pork registers 170°.
Remove pork from smoker, and place on a sheet of heavy-duty aluminum foil; spritz with apple juice. Wrap tightly, and return to smoker; smoke 2 hours or until thermometer inserted horizontally into the thickest portion of pork registers 190°. Let stand 10 minutes. Remove bone, and chop pork. **Makes 8 servings.**

Pork Tenderloin with Molasses Barbecue Sauce and Mango Salsa
Prep: 10 min.; Cook: 2 hrs., 30 min.; Other: 3 hrs., 10 min.

1 small onion, finely chopped
1 jalapeño pepper, seeded and minced
1 garlic clove, minced
2 tsp. olive oil
½ cup molasses
½ cup cider vinegar
¼ cup Dijon mustard
1 Tbsp. soy sauce
1 (1½-lb.) package pork tenderloin
Hickory chunks
Fresh Mango Salsa (page 207)

Cook first 3 ingredients in olive oil in a saucepan over medium-high heat, stirring constantly, until tender. Stir in molasses and next 3 ingredients. Bring to a boil; reduce heat, and simmer, uncovered, 5 minutes, stirring occasionally. Cool.

Place tenderloins in a large zip-top freezer bag. Pour marinade over tenderloins. Seal bag; marinate in refrigerator 3 hours, turning occasionally.

Soak hickory chunks in water to cover at least 1 hour.

Prepare charcoal fire in smoker; let burn 15 to 20 minutes. Place hickory chunks on coals. Remove tenderloins from marinade, reserving marinade. Place water pan in smoker; add reserved marinade and water to pan to fill line. Coat food grate with cooking spray. Place grate in smoker. Place tenderloins on food grate; cover with smoker lid.

Smoke 2½ hours or until meat thermometer inserted in thickest portion of tenderloin registers 160° (medium). (Add additional charcoal and wood chunks to maintain an internal smoker temperature of 200° to 225°.) Let stand 10 minutes before serving. Serve with Fresh Mango Salsa. **Makes** 6 servings.

Fiery-Barbecued Pork Tenderloin
Prep: 10 min., Cook: 59 min., Other: 10 min.

3 cups apple cider vinegar
¼ cup ketchup
1 Tbsp. dried crushed red pepper
1 Tbsp. hot sauce (we tested with Texas Pete Hot Sauce)
1 Tbsp. Worcestershire sauce
¼ tsp. black pepper
2 (2-lb.) packages pork tenderloin

Bring first 6 ingredients to a boil in large saucepan over medium-high heat. Reduce heat to low, and simmer 30 minutes. Reserve 1 cup mixture.

Grill pork, without grill lid, over medium-high heat (350° to 400°) 10 to 12 minutes on each side or until a meat thermometer inserted in thickest portion of tenderloin registers 155°, basting often with remaining vinegar mixture. Remove from grill, and let stand 10 minutes or until temperature registers 160°. Serve with reserved 1 cup vinegar mixture. **Makes** 12 servings.

Pork Chops with Tangy Barbecue Sauce
Prep: 5 min., Cook: 14 min.

8 (4-oz.) boneless pork loin chops (½ inch thick)
Sweet-and-Tangy Barbecue Sauce (page 183)

Grill pork chops, covered with grill lid, over medium-high heat (350° to 400°) 7 minutes on each side, basting often with 1 cup Sweet-and-Tangy Barbecue Sauce. Serve with remaining 1 cup sauce. **Makes** 8 servings.

66In North Carolina, barbecue means pork—cooked slowly, finely chopped, and seasoned with controversy.99

—Glenn Morris, *Southern Living* Contributor

Smoky Chipotle Baby Back Ribs

Prep: 10 min.; Cook: 2 hrs., 30 min.; Other: 8 hrs., 40 min.

3 slabs baby back pork ribs (about 5½ lb.)
2 oranges, halved
Chipotle Rub (page 192)
Chipotle Barbecue Sauce (page 186)

Rinse and pat ribs dry. If desired, remove thin membrane from back of ribs by slicing into it with a knife and then pulling it off (this makes ribs more tender).
Rub meat with cut sides of oranges, squeezing as you rub. Massage Chipotle Rub into meat, covering all sides. Wrap tightly with plastic wrap, and place in a zip-top freezer bag or 13- x 9-inch baking dish; chill 8 hours. Let ribs stand at room temperature 30 minutes before grilling. Remove plastic wrap.

Prepare hot fire by piling charcoal on one side of grill, leaving the other side empty. If using a gas grill, light only one side. Place food grate on grill; position rib rack on grate over unlit side. Place slabs in rack.
Grill, covered with grill lid, over medium-high heat (350° to 400°) 1 hour. Reposition rib slabs, placing the one closest to the heat source away from heat, moving other slabs closer.
Grill 1 more hour or until meat is tender. Grill 30 more minutes over medium heat (300° to 350°), basting with half of Chipotle Barbecue Sauce. Remove ribs from grill, and let stand 10 minutes. Cut ribs, slicing between bones. Serve with remaining sauce.
Makes 6 servings.

BARBECUE SMOKY CHIPOTLE BABY BACK RIBS LIKE A PRO

Follow these easy steps to get the most flavor out of your rib-smoking experience.

1. Don't skip rubbing the ribs with citrus fruit halves; the juice adds a perky zip to the flavor. You'll find the canned chipotle peppers at the grocery store alongside other ethnic ingredients. Remove the thin membrane on the back, or bone side, of each rib rack if you want the meat to almost fall off the bone; leave it on if you like a crispy texture.

2. For best flavor, wrap seasoned ribs in plastic wrap to hold rub mixture close to the meat. Place each slab in a separate 2-gal. zip-top freezer bag, and refrigerate overnight. Slide ribs into rib rack as you remove them from the bag; then discard bag.

3. When the meat is tender and done, bones should wiggle easily when moved, and the meat will be shrunk down from the bones. Slow the fire by partially or fully closing vents before basting. Pour sauce over ribs, guiding it to cover with a grill brush.

Sweet-and-Sour Baby Back Ribs

Prep: 10 min.; Cook: 2 hrs., 30 min.; Other: 8 hrs., 40 min.

3 slabs baby back pork ribs (about 5½ lb.)
2 limes, halved
Ginger Rub
Sweet-and-Sour 'Cue Sauce

Rinse and pat ribs dry. If desired, remove thin membrane from back of ribs by slicing into it with a knife and then pulling it off (this makes ribs more tender). **Rub** meat with cut sides of limes, squeezing as you rub. Massage Ginger Rub into meat, covering all sides. Wrap tightly with plastic wrap, and place in a zip-top freezer bag or 13- x 9-inch baking dish; chill 8 hours. Let ribs stand at room temperature 30 minutes before grilling. Remove plastic wrap.

Prepare hot fire by piling charcoal on one side of grill, leaving the other side empty. If using a gas grill, light only one side. Place food grate on grill; position rib rack on grate over unlit side. Place slabs in rack.

Grill, covered with grill lid, over medium-high heat (350° to 400°) 1 hour. Reposition rib slabs, placing the one closest to the heat source away from heat, moving other slabs closer.

Grill 1 more hour or until meat is tender.

Grill 30 more minutes over medium heat (300° to 350°); baste with half of Sweet-and-Sour 'Cue Sauce.

Remove ribs from grill, and let stand 10 minutes.

Cut ribs, slicing between bones. Serve with remaining sauce. **Makes** 6 servings.

Ginger Rub

Prep: 5 min.

2 Tbsp. ground ginger
½ tsp. dried crushed red pepper
1 tsp. salt
1 tsp. black pepper

Combine all ingredients. **Makes** about 3 Tbsp.

Sweet-and-Sour 'Cue Sauce

Prep: 5 min., Cook: 35 min.

2 (10-oz.) bottles sweet-and-sour sauce (we tested with
    Ty Ling Sweet & Sour Sauce)
2 cups ketchup
½ cup cider vinegar
½ tsp. ground ginger
2 tsp. hot sauce

Stir together all ingredients. Bring to a boil over medium-high heat. Reduce heat; simmer 30 minutes. **Makes** 3½ cups.

Beer-Smoked Baby Back Ribs
Prep: 30 min., Cook: 5 hrs., Other: 1 hr.

3 slabs baby back pork ribs (about 6 lb.)
¼ cup lemon juice
¼ cup olive oil
6 Tbsp. Pork Ribs Rub
Hickory chunks
4 to 6 (12-oz.) bottles dark beer
2 cups Sweet Jalapeño Barbecue Sauce (page 125)

Rinse and pat ribs dry. If desired, remove thin membrane from back of ribs by slicing into it with a knife and then pulling it off (this makes ribs more tender).
Place lemon juice in a small bowl; add oil in a slow, steady stream, whisking constantly. Coat ribs evenly with lemon juice mixture. Sprinkle meat evenly with Pork Ribs Rub, and rub into meat. Let stand at room temperature 30 minutes.
Soak wood chunks in water for at least 1 hour.
Prepare smoker according to manufacturer's directions, substituting beer for water in water pan. Bring internal temperature to 225° to 250°, and maintain temperature for 15 to 20 minutes.
Drain wood chunks, and place on coals. Place rib slabs in a rib rack on upper food grate; cover with smoker lid.
Smoke ribs, maintaining the temperature inside smoker between 225° and 250°, for 4½ hours. Remove lid, baste with half of Sweet Jalapeño Barbecue Sauce, and, if necessary, add more beer to water pan. Cover with smoker lid, and smoke 30 more minutes. Cut meat into 3-rib sections, slicing between bones, and serve with remaining half of Sweet Jalapeño Barbecue Sauce. **Makes** 6 servings.

Pork Ribs Rub
Prep: 5 min.

1 cup Greek seasoning (we tested with Cavender's
    All-Purpose Greek Seasoning)
¼ cup garlic powder
¼ cup paprika
¼ cup firmly packed brown sugar

Combine all ingredients. Store in an airtight container. **Makes** about 1¾ cups.

Barbecued Country-Style Ribs
Prep: 10 min.; Cook: 2 hrs., 30 min.

1 small onion
1 cup finely chopped celery
1½ Tbsp. bacon drippings
1 (15-oz.) can tomato sauce
¾ cup honey
½ cup water
¼ cup dry red wine
2 Tbsp. lemon juice
2 Tbsp. Worcestershire sauce
1 tsp. salt
½ tsp. pepper
¼ tsp. garlic powder
1 cup water
2 Tbsp. white vinegar
4 lb. bone-in or boneless country-style ribs, cut apart

Sauté onion and celery in hot bacon drippings in a saucepan over medium-high heat until tender. Add tomato sauce and next 8 ingredients. Bring to a boil. Reduce heat; simmer, stirring occasionally, 1 hour. Remove from heat.
Combine 1 cup water and vinegar in a spray bottle.
Grill ribs, covered with grill lid, over medium heat (300° to 350°) 1 to 1½ hours, spraying with vinegar solution, turning ribs occasionally, and basting with 1 cup tomato sauce mixture every 30 minutes. Serve with remaining tomato sauce mixture. **Makes** 8 servings.

> "Having been swept up in a few rib-induced feeding frenzies over the years, there have been times when I thought I could never eat the stuff again. But I always rally and recover."
>
> —Richard Banks, *Southern Living* Staff

Maple Spareribs

Prep: 45 min.; Cook: 1 hr., 30 min.

3 to 4 lb. pork spareribs
1 cup maple syrup
⅓ cup soy sauce
1 Tbsp. garlic powder
3 Tbsp. sweet rice wine (we tested with Kikkoman
   Aji-Mirin Sweet Cooking Rice Wine)
2 tsp. salt
½ tsp. sugar

Bring ribs and water to cover to a boil in a large Dutch oven; reduce heat, and simmer 30 minutes. Drain. Place ribs in a lightly greased 13- x 9-inch pan.

Stir together maple syrup and remaining 5 ingredients; pour half of marinade over ribs, reserving other half of marinade for basting.

Prepare a hot fire by piling charcoal on 1 side of grill, leaving other side empty. Coat rack with cooking spray, and place on grill. Arrange ribs over unlit side, and grill, covered with grill lid, 1½ hours, basting occasionally with reserved marinade. **Makes** 2 to 3 servings.

Peach-Glazed Barbecue Pork Chops and Peaches
Prep: 20 min., Cook: 40 min., Other: 35 min.

The cooking time for your peaches varies depending on their ripeness. This glaze also works well on chicken.

3 cups chopped peeled peaches (about 1½ lb.)
1 cup dry white wine
¼ cup sugar
1 tsp. salt, divided
¼ tsp. black pepper, divided
2 Tbsp. white wine vinegar
2 Tbsp. molasses
1 tsp. chili powder
½ tsp. paprika
¼ tsp. ground red pepper
6 (6-oz.) bone-in center-cut pork chops
    (about ½ inch thick), trimmed
6 peaches, halved and pitted

Combine first 3 ingredients in a small saucepan; bring to a boil. Cover, reduce heat, and simmer 25 minutes. Uncover and simmer 5 minutes. Place peach mixture in a food processor; process until smooth. Add ¾ tsp. salt, ⅛ tsp. black pepper, vinegar, and next 4 ingredients; pulse to combine. Let stand 5 minutes. Place half of peach mixture in a large zip-top freezer bag; reserve other half for basting. Add chops to bag; seal bag and refrigerate 30 minutes to 4 hours.

Remove pork from bag; discard marinade. Sprinkle pork with remaining ¼ tsp. salt and remaining ⅛ tsp. black pepper. Place pork and peach halves on food grate coated with cooking spray.

Grill pork, without grill lid, over medium-high heat (350° to 400°) 10 minutes or until pork is done and peaches are tender, turning once. Baste pork and peach halves with reserved peach mixture every 2 minutes during first 6 minutes of cooking. **Makes** 6 servings.

Barbecue Pork Chops with Grilled Corn Salsa

Prep: 5 min., Cook: 8 min., Other: 8 hrs.

Pork needs to cook to an internal temperature of 160° and to be still slightly pink in the center. An instant-read thermometer is perfect for quickly testing for doneness.

½ cup ketchup
⅓ cup cola soft drink
1 Tbsp. minced fresh onion
½ tsp. dry mustard
½ tsp. garlic powder
¼ tsp. ground red pepper
4 (4-oz.) lean, boneless center-cut loin pork chops
   (about ½ inch thick)
Grilled Corn Salsa

Stir together first 6 ingredients in a small bowl. Combine one half marinade and chops in a large zip-top freezer bag; seal bag, and marinate in refrigerator 8 hours, turning bag occasionally. Reserve remaining one-half marinade for basting.

Remove chops from bag; discard marinade. Place chops on food grate coated with cooking spray; grill 4 minutes on each side or until chops are done, basting frequently with reserved marinade. Serve with Grilled Corn Salsa. **Makes** 4 servings.

Grilled Corn Salsa

Prep: 20 min., Cook: 10 min., Other: 2 hrs.

3 ears fresh corn
1 large sweet onion, cut into ½-inch-thick slices
1 red bell pepper, halved
2 large tomatoes, seeded and chopped
2 jalapeño peppers, seeded and minced
2 garlic cloves, minced
¼ cup chopped fresh cilantro
½ tsp. salt
¼ tsp. ground cumin
1 Tbsp. olive oil
1 Tbsp. lime juice

Grill first 3 ingredients, covered with grill lid, over medium-high heat (350° to 400°) 8 to 10 minutes or until tender, turning occasionally.

Cut corn kernels from cobs. Coarsely chop onion and red bell pepper halves. Combine grilled vegetables, tomato, and next 7 ingredients in a large bowl; cover and chill 2 hours or up to 2 days. **Makes** 5 cups.

Sage-Smoked Maple Quail

Prep: 1 hr., Cook: 2 hrs., Other: 1 hr.

The combination of ingredients that are stuffed in, wrapped around, and brushed on these quail is flavor blending at its best.

4 Golden Delicious apples, diced
½ cup chopped pecans
½ tsp. salt
1 (0.4-oz.) jar dried sage, divided
12 quail, dressed
12 pepper-cured bacon slices
Hickory chunks
1 qt. apple cider
⅓ cup pure maple syrup

Combine apple, pecans, salt, and 2 tsp. sage; stuff each quail with apple mixture, and wrap a bacon slice around each quail, securing ends with a wooden pick. Cover and chill 30 minutes.

Soak chunks in water 1 hour; moisten remaining sage with water.

Prepare charcoal fire in smoker; let burn 15 to 20 minutes. Drain chunks; place chunks and one-third of remaining sage on hot coals. Place water pan in smoker; add 1 qt. cider.

Place quail, breast sides up, on food grate; brush quail with maple syrup.

Smoke, covered with smoker lid, 2 hours or until done, adding remaining sage at 30-minute intervals. **Makes** 6 servings.

❞During hunting season, game hunters thrive in the South. And when the prize reaches the table, it's time for the hunter's feast.❟

—Julie Gunter, *Southern Living* Books

Asian Grilled Quail

Asian Grilled Quail
Prep: 20 min., Cook: 30 min., Other: 30 min.

¼ cup hoisin sauce
2 Tbsp. sesame seeds
3 Tbsp. garlic-chili sauce
3 Tbsp. dark sesame oil
3 Tbsp. honey
1 tsp. ground ginger
8 quail, dressed
1 (14-oz.) can chicken broth
2 tsp. cornstarch
Garnish: sliced green onions or green onion curls

Combine first 6 ingredients in a shallow dish or large zip-top freezer bag, gently squeezing to blend; add quail. Cover or seal, and chill 30 minutes, turning occasionally.

Remove quail from marinade, reserving marinade. Prepare fire by piling charcoal or lava rocks on one side of grill, leaving the other side empty. Place food grate on grill. Arrange quail over empty side; grill, covered with grill lid, 30 minutes or until done.

Pour reserved marinade into a small saucepan. Reserve ¼ cup chicken broth, and add remaining chicken broth to marinade. Bring mixture to a boil over medium-high heat; boil, stirring occasionally, 5 minutes.

Whisk together cornstarch and reserved ¼ cup chicken broth until smooth. Whisk into marinade mixture; boil, whisking constantly, 1 minute. Serve with quail. Garnish, if desired. **Makes** 4 servings.

Asian Grilled Cornish Hens: Substitute 4 (1- to 1½-lb.) Cornish hens for quail. Grill as directed 45 to 50 minutes or until done.

editor's favorite
Mesquite-Grilled Quail
Prep: 20 min., Cook: 25 min., Other: 30 min.

Jalapeño peppers are a simple but not-so-subtle seasoning for this quail. For a tamer flavor, cut off stem ends of the peppers and remove the seeds with a grapefruit knife.

8 bacon slices
8 quail, dressed
8 jalapeño peppers
Mesquite chips

Place bacon on a food grate in a 13- x 9-inch baking dish; cover with paper towels.

Microwave at HIGH 3 to 4 minutes or until bacon is partially cooked. Drain bacon; set aside.

Rinse quail thoroughly with cold water; pat dry with paper towels. Place a jalapeño pepper into body cavity of each quail; tie ends of legs together with string. Wrap 1 bacon slice around each quail, and secure with wooden picks.

Soak mesquite chips in water 30 minutes; drain. Wrap chips in heavy-duty aluminum foil, and make several holes in foil. Light gas grill on one side; place foil-wrapped chips directly on hot coals. Coat food grate on opposite side with cooking spray. Place grate over cool lava rocks; let grill preheat 10 to 15 minutes or until chips smoke. Arrange quail on grate opposite hot coals; cover and grill 25 minutes or until done. **Makes** 4 servings.

QUAIL 101

■ Quail are lean game birds—the most commonly eaten in the United States. Domestic quail are mildly flavored, but the wild variety have a subtle gamey taste.

■ When serving quail as an entrée, allow two birds per person. Look for domestic quail in the frozen meats section at the supermarket or special-order them from your grocer.

■ Quail are really too small to check for doneness using a thermometer. Whether slow-smoked for a long period of time or grilled more quickly, you'll know they're done when you can easily wiggle the legs in their joints and no pink juices remain.

Grilled Wild Duck Breasts
Prep: 10 min., Cook: 20 min., Other: 1 hr.

12 skinned and boned wild duck breasts
2 Tbsp. Dijon mustard
½ cup dry sherry
½ cup Italian dressing
1 tsp. Worcestershire sauce
12 bacon slices
¼ tsp. pepper

Rinse duck breasts with cold water; pat dry with paper towels. Brush mustard evenly over both sides of duck; place in a 13- x 9-inch baking dish.
Combine sherry, dressing, and Worcestershire sauce; pour over duck. Cover and marinate in refrigerator 1 hour.
Remove duck from marinade, discarding marinade. Wrap each duck with 1 slice bacon; secure with wooden picks. Sprinkle with pepper.
Grill duck breasts, uncovered, over medium-hot coals (350° to 400°) 10 minutes on each side or until bacon is crisp and meat thermometer registers 170° (well done). Remove wooden picks. **Makes** 6 servings.

Grilled Venison Steaks
Prep: 5 min., Cook: 10 min., Other: 4 hrs.

4 (4-oz.) lean, boneless venison loin steaks (1 inch thick)
1 cup cranberry-orange crushed fruit for chicken, divided (we tested with Ocean Spray)
½ cup dry red wine
2 Tbsp. Dijon mustard
2 tsp. minced garlic (about 4 cloves)
2 tsp. dried rosemary, crushed
½ tsp. ground pepper

Trim fat from steaks. Place steaks in a large zip-top freezer bag. Combine ½ cup cranberry-orange sauce, red wine, and remaining 4 ingredients; pour over steaks. Seal bag; turn to coat steaks. Marinate in refrigerator 4 to 8 hours, turning bag occasionally.
Coat food grate with cooking spray; place on grill over medium-hot coals (350° to 400°). Remove steaks from marinade, discarding marinade. Place steaks on grate; grill, covered, 5 minutes on each side or to desired degree of doneness. Serve with remaining ½ cup cranberry-orange sauce. **Makes** 4 servings.

Grilled Venison with Apricot and Green Peppercorn Glaze
Prep: 10 min., Cook: 45 min., Other: 8 hrs.

Yes, this recipe really calls for ¼ cup minced garlic in the glaze and six more cloves in the marinade. Garlic sweetens as it cooks and, in this recipe, enhances the piquant peppercorn glaze.

¼ cup olive oil
2 tsp. chopped fresh marjoram
2 tsp. chopped fresh rosemary
2 tsp. chopped fresh thyme
6 garlic cloves, cut in half
1 (1½-lb.) boneless venison loin
¼ cup minced garlic
½ cup minced shallot
2 Tbsp. olive oil
2 cups marsala
¼ cup balsamic vinegar
¼ cup canned green peppercorns, drained
1 (6-oz.) package dried apricot halves, cut into thin strips
1½ to 2 qt. canned beef broth, undiluted
Salt and pepper to taste

Combine first 5 ingredients in a large shallow dish; stir well. Add venison, turning to coat meat. Cover and marinate in refrigerator 8 to 24 hours, turning once.
Cook ¼ cup garlic and shallot in 2 Tbsp. hot oil in a large skillet over medium heat, stirring constantly, until browned. Add wine and next 3 ingredients; bring to a boil. Reduce heat, and simmer 2 minutes. Add broth; bring to a boil. Reduce heat, and simmer 45 minutes or until thickened. Add salt and pepper to taste; set aside, and keep warm.
Drain venison, discarding marinade. Grill, covered, over medium-hot coals (350° to 400°) 25 minutes or until meat thermometer inserted in thickest part registers 160° (medium), turning once.
To serve, slice venison across grain into thin slices. Serve with warm glaze. **Makes** 4 servings.

Grilled Venison Roast
Prep: 10 min.; Cook: 3 hrs.; Other: 2 hrs., 15 min.

1 (5-lb.) venison chuck roast, trimmed
2 large garlic cloves, halved
½ cup Worcestershire sauce
2 Tbsp. soy sauce
2 tsp. garlic powder
2 tsp. lemon pepper
Hickory chunks
4 (14-oz.) cans chicken broth
1 (10-oz.) jar red currant jelly
½ cup bourbon
2 Tbsp. black peppercorns
1 Tbsp. gin
¼ tsp. dried thyme

Make 4 small slits in top of roast. Insert a garlic half into each slit. Combine Worcestershire sauce and next 3 ingredients. Place in a large shallow dish or a large zip-top freezer bag; add roast. Cover or seal, and chill 2 hours, turning occasionally. Remove roast from marinade, discarding marinade.

Soak hickory chunks in water at least 1 hour. Prepare charcoal fire by piling charcoal on each side of grill, leaving center empty. Place a drip pan between coals and fill with water. Prepare fire; let burn 15 to 20 minutes. Drain chunks, and place on hot coals.

Coat food grate with cooking spray, and place on grill over coals. Arrange roast on grate over drip pan; grill, covered with grill lid, 3 hours or until a meat thermometer inserted into thickest part of meat registers 160° (medium). Refill water pan, and add charcoal as needed.

Transfer roast to a serving platter, reserving 2 Tbsp. pan drippings. Cover roast with aluminum foil, and let stand 10 to 15 minutes before slicing.

While venison cooks, combine chicken broth and remaining 5 ingredients in a large saucepan. Bring to a boil; reduce heat, and simmer, uncovered, 1 hour or until liquid is reduced to 4 cups. Stir in reserved pan drippings. Serve venison with sauce. **Makes** 15 to 18 servings.

quick & easy
Grilled Marinated Venison Tenderloin
Prep: 5 min.; Cook: 10 min.; Other: 4 hrs., 10 min.

Classic barbecue sauce ingredients blended well with fresh blueberries result in a tangy-sweet topping you'll want to ladle generously over this oh-so-tender venison.

1½ lb. venison tenderloin
¾ cup vegetable oil
⅓ cup soy sauce
¼ cup red wine vinegar
3 Tbsp. fresh lemon juice
2 Tbsp. Worcestershire sauce
1 Tbsp. dry mustard
1 Tbsp. chopped fresh parsley
1½ tsp. freshly ground pepper
1 tsp. salt
1 garlic clove, minced
Blueberry Barbecue Sauce (page 189)

Place tenderloins in a large zip-top freezer bag. Combine oil and next 9 ingredients; pour over tenderloins. Seal bag securely; marinate in refrigerator 4 to 5 hours, turning bag occasionally.

Remove tenderloins from marinade, discarding marinade. Grill, covered, over medium-hot coals (350° to 400°) 10 minutes or until meat thermometer registers 160° (medium), turning once. Let stand 10 minutes before slicing. Slice tenderloins, and serve with Blueberry Barbecue Sauce. **Makes** 4 servings.

GAME ACCOMPANIMENTS

■ Classic game accompaniments include cabbage, turnips, chestnuts, mushrooms, and onions, as well as hot buttered grits or rice.

■ A tangy relish or chutney also pairs well with game. Try Grandma's Pepper Relish (page 206) with any of our venison recipes or Cranberry-Ginger Chutney (page 208) with such wild poultry as quail.

■ Choose an appropriate bread to escort platters of game, such as hot buttered biscuits, French bread, garlic bread, cornbread, muffins, or homemade rolls.

Jerk Smoked Chicken
Prep: 15 min.; Cook: 3 hrs.; Other: 2 hrs., 10 min.

Serve dinner in style with Roasted Asparagus (page 243) and Glazed Carrots with Bacon and Onion (page 245).

2 medium limes
1 medium orange
⅔ cup sliced green onions
¼ cup habanero pepper sauce (we tested with Yucatan)
1½ Tbsp. dried thyme
1½ tsp. ground allspice
1 tsp. freshly ground pepper
½ tsp. salt
¼ tsp. ground cloves
3 garlic cloves, peeled
2 (3-lb.) whole chickens
4 (3-inch) hickory chunks

Squeeze juice from limes and orange; set citrus rinds aside. Combine citrus juice, green onions, and next 7 ingredients in a blender or food processor; process until well blended.

Remove and discard giblets and neck from chickens. Rinse chickens under cold water; pat dry. Trim excess fat. Starting at neck cavities, loosen skin from breasts and drumsticks by gently pushing fingers between skin and meat. Place citrus rinds in body cavities. Tie legs together with string; lift wings up and over backs and tuck under chickens.

Place chickens in a large zip-top freezer bag. Pour juice mixture under loosened skin of chickens. Seal bag, and marinate in refrigerator at least 2 hours, turning bag occasionally.

Soak hickory wood chunks in water for 1 hour. Drain well.

Prepare charcoal fire in meat smoker; let burn 15 to 20 minutes or until center coals are covered with gray ash. Place soaked hickory chunks on top of coals. Remove chickens from bag, reserving marinade. Place water pan in smoker; add reserved marinade and hot water to pan to within 1 inch of rim.

Place chickens, breast sides up, on food grate in smoker, allowing enough room between chickens for air to circulate.

Cover with lid; smoke 3 hours or until meat thermometer inserted in thickest part of thigh registers 180°. Refill water pan, and add additional charcoal to fire as needed.

Remove chickens from smoker; let stand 10 minutes. Remove and discard skin before serving. **Makes** 8 servings.

Note: If habanero pepper sauce is not available, you may substitute any red hot sauce.

66Conquistadors in the 17th century found island natives of the Caribbean smoking meat on makeshift racks set over slow-burning fires. The Spanish called the rough framework *barbacoa*, which some historians link to the modern word 'barbecue.'99

——Heather McPherson, Food Editor for the *Orlando Sentinel* in Florida

Basic Beer-Can Chicken
Prep: 10 min.; Cook: 1 hr., 15 min.; Other: 5 min.

Grill out for a crowd by easily doubling or tripling this recipe. It's adapted from Steven Raichlen's book **Beer-Can Chicken,** *so it's sure to be a five-star performer.*

2 Tbsp. All-Purpose Barbecue Rub, divided (page 192)
1 (3½- to 4-lb.) whole chicken
1 Tbsp. vegetable oil
1 (12-oz.) can beer

Sprinkle 1 tsp. All-Purpose Barbecue Rub inside body cavity and ½ tsp. inside neck cavity of chicken.
Rub oil over skin. Sprinkle with 1 Tbsp. All-Purpose Barbecue Rub, and rub over skin.
Pour out half of beer (about ¾ cup), and reserve for another use, leaving remaining beer in can.

Make 2 additional holes in top of can. Spoon remaining 1½ tsp. rub into beer can. Beer will start to foam.
Place chicken upright onto the beer can, fitting can into cavity. Pull legs forward to form a tripod, allowing chicken to stand upright.
Prepare a fire by piling charcoal on one side of grill, leaving other side empty. (For gas grills, light only one side.) Place a drip pan on unlit side, and place food grate on grill.
Place chicken upright over drip pan. Grill, covered with grill lid, 1 hour and 15 minutes or until golden and a meat thermometer inserted in thickest part of thigh registers 180°.
Remove chicken from grill, and let stand 5 minutes; carefully remove can. **Makes** 2 to 4 servings.

Chicken with White Barbecue Sauce

Prep: 5 min.; Cook: 1 hr., 5 min.; Other: 8 hrs.

If you don't have a drip pan, fashion one from a long piece of heavy-duty aluminum foil—fold in half and bend edges up.

1½ cups mayonnaise (we tested with Kraft)
⅓ cup apple cider vinegar
¼ cup lemon juice
2 Tbsp. sugar
2 Tbsp. cracked pepper
2 Tbsp. white wine Worcestershire sauce
1 (2½- to 3-lb.) whole chicken, quartered

Whisk together first 6 ingredients in a small bowl.
Arrange chicken in a shallow dish. Pour 1 cup sauce over chicken, turning to coat. Cover and chill chicken and remaining sauce 8 hours, turning chicken once.
Remove chicken from sauce, discarding sauce.
Grill chicken, covered with grill lid, over medium heat (300° to 350°) 1 hour and 5 minutes or until meat thermometer inserted in thickest part of thigh registers 180°, turning every 15 minutes. Serve with remaining sauce. **Makes** 4 servings.

Red Hot Barbecue Chicken

Prep: 15 min.; Cook: 1 hr., 15 min. or 2 hrs., 15 min.

¼ cup butter or margarine
1 cup white wine vinegar
1 cup water
4 Tbsp. dry mustard
4 tsp. brown sugar
4 tsp. Worcestershire sauce
4 tsp. red hot sauce
1 (3-lb.) whole chicken, cut into quarters

Cook first 7 ingredients in a large saucepan over medium heat, stirring occasionally, 15 minutes or until mixture is thoroughly heated.
Reserve 1 cup barbecue sauce to serve with chicken. Dip chicken in remaining sauce, and place on grill.
Grill chicken according to directions below, basting every 30 minutes by dipping in sauce and returning to grill (do not dip chicken last 5 minutes of cooking).

Place cooked chicken in reserved 1 cup sauce (not marinade), and cover to keep warm until serving. **Makes** 4 servings.

For Gas Grills
Indirect Cooking: Place 2 cups hickory, mesquite, or other wood chips in the center of a large square of heavy-duty aluminum foil; fold into a rectangle, and seal. Punch holes in top of packet. Preheat one side of grill, leaving center empty, for 20 minutes. Place wood chip packet on hot coals. Place chicken on food grate over unlit side. Grill, covered with grill lid, 2 hours and 15 minutes or until done (170°). Baste as directed.

For Charcoal Grills
Direct Cooking: Preheat grill over low heat, under 300°, for 20 minutes. Place chicken, skin side up, on food grate. Grill, covered with grill lid, over low heat 1 hour and 15 minutes or until done. (Don't turn chicken.) Baste as directed.

Marinated Chicken Quarters

Prep: 15 min., Cook: 45 min., Other: 8 hrs.

½ cup butter or margarine, melted
½ cup lemon juice
1 Tbsp. paprika
1 Tbsp. dried oregano
1 tsp. garlic salt
1 tsp. dried or 1 Tbsp. chopped fresh cilantro
1 tsp. ground cumin
1 (2½-lb.) whole chicken, quartered
½ tsp. salt
½ tsp. pepper

Combine first 7 ingredients; reserve ½ cup butter mixture.
Sprinkle chicken evenly with salt and pepper. Place in shallow dishes or zip-top freezer bags; pour remaining butter mixture evenly over chicken.
Cover or seal, and chill, along with reserved butter mixture, 8 hours.
Remove chicken from marinade; discard marinade.
Grill, covered with grill lid, over medium-high heat (350° to 400°) 40 to 45 minutes or until done, basting often with reserved butter mixture and turning once. **Makes** 4 servings.

Big "D" Smoked Chicken
Prep: 15 min.; Cook: 3 hrs., 30 min.; Other: 6 hrs.

2 (5- to 5½-lb.) whole chickens
½ cup lemon juice
½ cup olive oil
1 cup Garlic Chicken Rub
Hickory chunks
4 to 6 (12-oz.) bottles dark beer
2 cups Sweet Jalapeño Barbecue Sauce

Rinse chickens, and pat dry.
Place lemon juice in a small bowl; add oil in a slow, steady stream, whisking constantly. Coat outside skin and inside cavities of chickens evenly with lemon juice mixture; sprinkle evenly with Garlic Chicken Rub, and rub into chickens. Wrap each chicken tightly with plastic wrap, and chill at least 6 hours.
Soak wood chunks in water for at least 1 hour.
Prepare smoker according to manufacturer's directions, substituting beer for water in water pan. Bring internal temperature to 225° to 250°, and maintain temperature for 15 to 20 minutes.
Drain hickory wood chunks, and place on coals. Place chickens, breast sides up, on upper food grate, and cover with smoker lid.
Smoke chickens, maintaining the temperature inside smoker between 225° and 250°, for 2 hours. Remove lid, baste with half of Sweet Jalapeño Barbecue Sauce, and, if necessary, add more beer to water pan. Cover with smoker lid; smoke 1 to 1½ more hours or until a meat thermometer inserted into thickest part of thighs registers 180°. Serve with remaining half of Sweet Jalapeño Barbecue Sauce. **Makes** 8 servings.

POULTRY PRIMER

■ Whole chickens range from 2 to 4 lb. A 3-lb. chicken yields about 4 to 6 servings or about 3 cups chopped cooked chicken.
■ Each lb. of whole turkey averages about 1 serving.
■ Always rinse poultry before cooking.
■ A thermometer should register 180° for a whole chicken or turkey when inserted into meaty portion of the thigh. Poultry breasts should register 170°.
■ Juices from cooked poultry should run clear when meat is pierced with a fork.

Garlic Chicken Rub
Prep: 5 min.

1 cup Greek seasoning (we tested with Cavender's All-Purpose Greek Seasoning)
¼ cup garlic powder
¼ cup paprika
3 Tbsp. dried oregano

Combine all ingredients. Store in an airtight container. **Makes** about 1⅔ cups.

Sweet Jalapeño Barbecue Sauce
Prep: 20 min., Cook: 20 min.

2 Tbsp. butter
1 Tbsp. olive oil
1 medium onion, finely chopped
½ green bell pepper, finely chopped
4 garlic cloves, minced
3 medium jalapeño peppers, seeded and minced
1 cup firmly packed brown sugar
1 cup cider vinegar
1 cup chili sauce
1 cup bottled barbecue sauce
1 Tbsp. mustard powder
1 Tbsp. paprika
3 Tbsp. fresh lemon juice
2 Tbsp. Worcestershire sauce
2 Tbsp. hot sauce
2 Tbsp. molasses
¼ tsp. salt

Melt butter with oil in a large Dutch oven over medium heat. Add onion and next 3 ingredients, and sauté 5 to 6 minutes or until onion is tender.
Stir in brown sugar and remaining ingredients; bring to a boil. Reduce heat to medium-low, and simmer 10 minutes. Pour mixture through a wire-mesh strainer into a bowl, discarding solids. **Makes** about 3½ cups.

Sweet Barbecue Chicken
Prep: 8 min., Cook: 35 min.

1 cup firmly packed brown sugar
1 cup bottled barbecue sauce
2 tsp. dried thyme
1 tsp. chili powder
1 tsp. ground red pepper
1 (6-oz.) can frozen apple juice concentrate, thawed and undiluted
12 small chicken leg quarters (about 5¼ lb.), skinned
¾ tsp. salt
½ tsp. black pepper

Combine first 6 ingredients in a saucepan. Cook over medium heat 5 minutes or until thoroughly heated, stirring occasionally.

Prepare grill or broiler. Sprinkle chicken with salt and pepper. Place on a food grate or broiler pan coated with cooking spray. Grill 10 minutes on each side. Brush chicken with sauce, and cook 15 more minutes or until meat thermometer inserted in thickest part of thigh registers 180°, turning and basting frequently. **Makes** 12 servings.

66 Pork may be king in Virginia, but in Maryland and Delaware, folks prefer their barbecue on the wing. 99

—Deborah Garrison Lowery,
Southern Living Contributor

Asian Barbecue Chicken
Prep: 5 min., Cook: 20 min., Other: 4 hrs.

Southern grilling gets ethnic flavor from soy sauce and curry powder. Serve this spicy chicken with Bacon-Mandarin Salad (page 224).

¼ cup firmly packed brown sugar
¼ cup low-sodium soy sauce
1 Tbsp. fresh lime juice
½ tsp. dried crushed red pepper
¼ tsp. curry powder
3 garlic cloves, minced
8 chicken thighs, skinned
Garnishes: lime wedges, green onion tops

Combine first 6 ingredients in a large zip-top freezer bag; add chicken. Seal and marinate in refrigerator 4 hours, turning occasionally.

Prepare grill.

Remove chicken from bag, reserving marinade. Place marinade in a small saucepan. Bring to a boil; cook 1 minute.

Place chicken on food grate coated with cooking spray; grill 20 minutes or until done, turning and basting frequently with the marinade. Garnish, if desired. **Makes** 4 servings.

Honey-Barbecue Chicken
Prep: 5 min.; Cook: 1 hr., 10 min.

Make delicious Honey-Barbecue Sauce (page 180) up to a week in advance and refrigerate it until you're ready to grill.

6 bone-in chicken breasts
8 chicken drumsticks
2 cups Honey-Barbecue Sauce (page 180)

Coat food grate with cooking spray; place on grill over medium-high heat (350° to 400°). Place chicken on grate, and grill, covered, 5 to 10 minutes on each side. Reduce heat to low (under 300°); grill, covered, 40 to 50 minutes for breasts and 30 to 40 minutes for drumsticks or until done. Brush with 1 cup Honey Barbecue Sauce during last 10 minutes of grilling. Serve with remaining 1 cup sauce. **Makes** 8 to 10 servings.

Asian Barbecue
Chicken

Chicken-and-Beef Fajitas

Prep: 20 min., Cook: 30 min., Other: 2 hrs.

2 Tbsp. chili powder

2 tsp. ground cumin

1 tsp. brown sugar

1 tsp. pepper

¼ tsp. salt

¼ tsp. garlic powder

¼ tsp. chipotle seasoning (optional)

1 cup Italian dressing

6 skinned and boned chicken breasts

4 lb. flank steak

20 (8-inch) flour tortillas, warmed

Toppings: sour cream, shredded lettuce, chopped
     tomato, shredded Cheddar cheese

Combine first 6 ingredients and, if desired, chipotle seasoning.

Stir together chili powder mixture and dressing. Pour half of marinade in a shallow dish or large zip-top freezer bag; add chicken. Cover or seal. Pour remaining marinade in a separate shallow dish or large zip-top freezer bag; add beef. Cover or seal; chill chicken and beef 2 hours.

Remove chicken and beef from marinade, discarding marinade.

Grill, covered with grill lid, over medium heat (300° to 350°) about 15 minutes on each side or until chicken is done and beef is at desired degree of doneness. Cut chicken and beef into strips. Serve in tortillas with desired toppings. **Makes** 10 servings.

Tangy Chicken Fajitas
Prep: 10 min., Cook: 15 min., Other: 4 hrs.

2 lb. skinned and boned chicken breasts
¼ cup white wine vinegar
¼ cup lime juice
2 Tbsp. low-sodium Worcestershire sauce
2 Tbsp. chopped onion
¼ tsp. ground cumin
2 garlic cloves, minced
8 (8-inch) flour tortillas
½ cup salsa
½ cup plain low-fat yogurt
¼ cup chopped green chiles

Place chicken between 2 sheets of heavy-duty plastic wrap; flatten to ¼-inch thickness, using a meat mallet or rolling pin. Place chicken in a 13- x 9-inch baking dish.
Combine vinegar and next 5 ingredients; pour over chicken. Cover and refrigerate 4 hours.
Remove chicken from marinade; discard marinade. Coat food grate with cooking spray; grill chicken, covered, over medium-high heat (350° to 400°) 4 minutes on each side or until done. Remove chicken from grill; slice into strips.
Wrap tortillas in aluminum foil; bake at 325° for 15 minutes. Arrange chicken strips evenly in centers of tortillas; top with salsa, yogurt, and chiles. Roll up tortillas, and serve immediately. **Makes** 8 servings.

FAJITA FIESTA

Pick any combination of these toppings to make your next fajita cookout the best in the neighborhood.

- Shredded iceberg lettuce
- Chopped plum tomatoes
- Sour cream
- Shredded Cheddar or Monterey Jack cheese
- Guacamole
- Mild or spicy tomato-based salsa
- Tomatillo salsa

kids love it
Raspberry-Barbecue Chicken
Prep: 5 min., Cook: 14 min.

4 skinned and boned chicken breasts
1 tsp. Creole seasoning (we tested with Tony Chachere's Original Creole Seasoning)
Raspberry Barbecue Sauce (page 189)
Garnish: fresh flat-leaf parsley sprigs

Sprinkle chicken evenly with Creole seasoning.
Place chicken on food grate coated with cooking spray.
Grill chicken, covered with grill lid, over medium-high heat (350° to 400°) 7 minutes on each side or until done, brushing Raspberry Barbecue Sauce evenly on 1 side of chicken during the last 2 minutes of grilling. Serve with remaining sauce. Garnish, if desired. **Makes** 4 servings.

editor's favorite
Best BBQ Chicken Ever
Prep: 5 min., Cook: 27 min.

2 Tbsp. butter
½ cup ketchup
¼ cup fresh lemon juice
¼ cup low-sodium soy sauce
¼ tsp. pepper
¼ tsp. hot sauce
6 skinned and boned chicken breasts

Melt butter in a medium saucepan over medium-low heat. Add ketchup and next 4 ingredients; bring to a boil. Partially cover, and cook until reduced to ⅔ cup (about 15 minutes), stirring often.
Place chicken on food grate coated with cooking spray. Grill 12 minutes or until done, turning and basting with ⅓ cup sauce after 8 minutes; serve with remaining ⅓ cup sauce. **Makes** 6 servings.

Seasoned Smoked Turkey

Prep: 10 min., Cook: 8 hrs., Other: 1 hr.

Creole Deviled Eggs (page 240), Spinach Soufflé (page 247), and Lemon-Scented Sugar Snap Peas (page 251) make a delightful holiday cookout with this hickory-smoked turkey.

Hickory chunks
1 (9- to 10-lb.) whole turkey
2 tsp. salt
6 fresh sage sprigs or 2 Tbsp. rubbed sage
2 Tbsp. Creole seasoning
1 tsp. ground black pepper
1 tsp. ground red pepper
2 garlic cloves, minced

Soak wood chunks in water at least 1 hour.

Remove giblets and neck from turkey, and reserve for another use. Rinse turkey with cold water; pat dry. Sprinkle cavity with salt; place fresh sage or sprinkle rubbed sage in cavity.

Combine Creole seasoning and remaining 3 ingredients, and rub over sides of turkey.

Prepare charcoal fire in smoker; let burn 15 to 20 minutes.

Drain wood chunks; place on coals. Place water pan in smoker; add water to pan to depth of fill line. Place turkey on lower food grate; cover with smoker lid.

Cook 8 hours or until a meat thermometer inserted into thickest part of thigh registers 180°. Add more charcoal, wood chunks, and water to smoker as needed. **Makes** 6 to 8 servings.

Note: Don't rely on the turkey's built-in ready button that should pop out when it's done. These are rarely accurate in slow-cooking methods. Use a meat thermometer to be sure.

SMOKED TURKEY TIP

Any time you're grilling a large piece of meat, such as a turkey, be sure to let it stand at room temperature 10 to 15 minutes before slicing. This lets the juices evenly distribute and makes the meat more tender.

Hickory-Smoked Bourbon Turkey

Prep: 20 min.; Cook: 6 hrs.; Other: 2 days, 15 min.

1 (11-lb.) whole turkey
2 cups maple syrup
1 cup bourbon
1 Tbsp. pickling spice
Hickory chunks
1 large carrot, scraped
1 celery rib
1 medium onion, peeled and halved
1 lemon
1 Tbsp. salt
2 tsp. pepper
Garnishes: mixed greens, lemon wedges

Remove giblets and neck from turkey; reserve for other uses, if desired. Rinse turkey thoroughly with cold water, and pat dry.

Add water to a large stockpot, filling half full; stir in maple syrup, bourbon, and pickling spice. Add turkey and, if needed, additional water to cover. Cover and chill turkey 2 days.

Soak hickory wood chunks in fresh water at least 1 hour. Prepare charcoal fire in smoker; let fire burn 20 to 30 minutes.

Remove turkey from water, discarding water mixture; pat dry. Cut carrot and celery in half crosswise. Stuff cavity with carrot, celery, and onion. Pierce lemon with a fork; place in neck cavity.

Combine salt and pepper; rub mixture over turkey. Fold wings under, and tie legs together with string, if desired.

Drain wood chunks, and place on coals. Place water pan in smoker, and add water to depth of fill line. Place turkey in center of lower food grate; cover with smoker lid.

Cook 6 hours or until a meat thermometer inserted into thickest portion of thigh registers 180°, adding additional water, charcoal, and wood chunks as needed. Remove from smoker, and let stand 15 minutes before slicing. Garnish, if desired. **Makes** 12 to 14 servings.

Spicy-Sweet Smoked Turkey Breast

Prep: 8 min.; Cook: 6 hrs.; Other: 1 hr., 10 min.

Hickory chunks
2 Tbsp. coarsely ground pepper
2 (6-lb.) bone-in turkey breasts*
2 (5-oz.) bottles sweet pepper sauce

Soak wood chunks in water 1 hour. Prepare charcoal fire in smoker; let burn 20 to 25 minutes.

Rub pepper evenly over turkey breasts. Pour sauce evenly over breasts.

Drain wood chunks, and place on coals. Place water pan in smoker; add water to depth of fill line. Place turkey breasts, side by side, on upper food grate; cover with smoker lid.

Smoke 5 to 6 hours or until a meat thermometer inserted into thickest portion registers 170°, adding additional water to depth of fill line, if necessary. Remove from smoker; let stand 10 minutes before slicing. **Makes** 16 servings.

*Substitute 2 (6-lb.) fully cooked or fully cooked smoked bone-in turkey breasts, if desired. Proceed as directed, reducing smoking time to 1 hour or until thoroughly heated.

Mesquite-Smoked Turkey Breast

Prep: 5 min., Cook: 3 hrs., Other: 1 hr. 10 min.

Mesquite chunks
1 (6-lb.) turkey breast, skinned
¼ cup Southwestern Spice Blend (page 192)

Soak chunks in water at least 1 hour; drain.

Rinse turkey breast thoroughly under cold water, and pat dry with paper towels. Rub Southwestern Spice Blend inside and outside turkey breast.

Preheat gas grill to medium-high (350° to 400°) using both burners. After preheating, turn left burner off. Place mesquite chunks in a disposable aluminum foil pan or an aluminum foil packet poked with holes on grill over right burner. Coat food grate with cooking spray; place on grill over medium-hot coals.

Place turkey on grate over left burner. Cook, covered, 3 hours or until meat thermometer registers 170°. Let stand 10 minutes before carving. **Makes** 12 servings.

Chili-Spiced Smoked Turkey Breast

Prep: 10 min.; Cook: 1 hr., 45 min.; Other: 2 hrs., 10 min.

You don't need a smoker; any covered grill gives the same effect. Simply place the turkey breast on the cool side of the grill, and use soaked wood chips.

¼ cup fresh lime juice
2 Tbsp. olive oil
2 tsp. unsweetened cocoa
2 tsp. paprika
2 tsp. brown sugar
1 tsp. salt
1 tsp. dried oregano
1 tsp. chili powder
1 tsp. dried thyme
2 garlic cloves, minced
1 (6-lb.) turkey breast
2 cups mesquite chips

Combine first 10 ingredients in a small saucepan; bring to a boil. Remove from heat; cool. Combine lime juice mixture and turkey in a large zip-top freezer bag. Seal and marinate in refrigerator 2 hours.

Soak mesquite chips in water at least 30 minutes. Drain well.

Preheat gas grill to medium-high (350° to 400°) using both burners. Turn left burner off.

Place mesquite chips in a disposable foil pan or a foil packet pierced with holes on grill over right burner. Remove turkey from marinade; discard marinade. Place turkey, skin side up, on food grate coated with cooking spray over left burner.

Cover and cook 1½ hours. Turn turkey over; cook 15 more minutes or until meat thermometer registers 170°. Remove turkey from grill. Cover loosely with foil, and let stand at least 10 minutes before carving. Discard skin. **Makes** 16 servings.

Hickory-Smoked Barbecue Shrimp
Prep: 40 min., Cook: 20 min., Other: 30 min.

2 cups hickory chips

3 lb. unpeeled, large fresh shrimp

3 lemons, sliced

½ to ⅔ cup hickory-flavored barbecue sauce (we tested with Kraft Thick 'n' Spicy)

½ cup dry shrimp-and-crab boil seasoning (we tested with McCormick)

1 tsp. pepper

1 tsp. hot sauce

¾ cup butter or margarine, cut up

¾ cup dry white wine

Soak wood chips in water at least 30 minutes.

Prepare charcoal fire in grill; let burn 15 to 20 minutes.

Drain wood chips, and place on coals.

Place layers of shrimp and lemon slices alternately in a 13- x 9-inch baking dish; brush with barbecue sauce. Sprinkle with shrimp-and-crab boil seasoning, pepper, and hot sauce; dot with butter. Add wine to dish.

Place dish on food grate, and cook, covered with grill lid, 15 to 20 minutes or just until shrimp turn pink, stirring once. **Makes** 6 to 8 servings.

Grilled Shrimp with Bacon and Jalapeños
Prep: 20 min., Cook: 6 min., Other: 30 min.

If you're in a hurry, buy fully cooked bacon slices.

18 thick, round wooden picks

18 unpeeled, large fresh shrimp

2 jalapeño peppers

2 Tbsp. olive oil

¼ tsp. salt

⅛ tsp. pepper

9 thick bacon slices, halved

Soak wooden picks in water 30 minutes.

Peel shrimp, leaving tails on; devein, if desired. Set shrimp aside.

Cut each pepper lengthwise into 9 pieces; remove seeds.

Toss together shrimp, jalapeño peppers, olive oil, salt, and pepper in a large bowl. Set aside.

Microwave bacon slices on HIGH 30 seconds.

Wrap 1 bacon slice half around 1 shrimp and 1 piece of jalapeño pepper. Secure with a wooden pick. Repeat procedure with remaining bacon slices, shrimp, and jalapeño pepper pieces.

Grill, without grill lid, over medium-high heat (350° to 400°) for 4 to 6 minutes or until shrimp turn pink, turning once. **Makes** 3 servings.

Hickory-Smoked Barbecue Shrimp

Spicy Smoked Shrimp with Orange and Lime

Prep: 20 min., Cook: 30 min., Other: 30 min.

The deep, smoky taste from the grill complements the spicy dry rub in this easy entrée. It might be difficult to tell when the shrimp are done; they're fully cooked when opaque and slightly firm.

2 cups wood chips
1½ lb. unpeeled, large fresh shrimp
½ tsp. salt
½ tsp. ground red pepper
¼ tsp. freshly ground black pepper
⅛ tsp. garlic powder
⅛ tsp. ground coriander
Orange wedges
Lime wedges

Soak wood chips in water 30 minutes; drain.

Peel shrimp, and devein, if desired.

Combine salt, red pepper, black pepper, garlic powder, and coriander in a small bowl. Rub mixture over shrimp. Cover and chill 20 minutes.

Prepare the grill for indirect grilling, heating one side to low and leaving one side with no heat. Maintain temperature at 200° to 225°.

Place wood chips on hot coals. Place a disposable aluminum foil pan on unheated side of grill. Pour 2 cups water in pan. Coat food grate with cooking spray; place on grill.

Place shrimp on food grate over foil pan on unheated side. Close lid; cook 30 minutes or until shrimp are done. Serve with orange and lime wedges. **Makes** 4 servings.

Citrus-Marinated Smoked Shrimp

Prep: 20 min., Cook: 45 min., Other: 1 hr.

Serve this aromatic shrimp with Cucumber Salad with Roasted Red Bell Pepper Dressing (page 222) to keep supper easy.

Maple or cherry wood chips
2 lb. unpeeled, jumbo fresh shrimp
1 cup fresh orange juice
¼ cup honey
1 tsp. grated orange rind
1 Tbsp. chopped fresh basil
1 Tbsp. chopped fresh thyme
2 oranges, sliced
Garnishes: orange slices, fresh thyme sprigs

Soak wood chips in water at least 30 minutes.

Devein shrimp, if desired. Place shrimp in a shallow dish or large zip-top freezer bag. Stir together orange juice and next 4 ingredients; pour over shrimp, stirring to coat. Cover or seal, and chill 1 hour. Drain, reserving marinade.

Prepare charcoal fire in smoker; let burn 15 to 20 minutes. Drain chips, and place on coals. Place water pan in smoker; add orange slices. Add water to fill line. Coat food grate with cooking spray; place in smoker.

Place shrimp on upper grate; cover with smoker lid.

Smoke 45 minutes.

Bring marinade to a boil. Reduce heat, and simmer, uncovered, 5 to 7 minutes or until reduced by half. Serve with shrimp. Garnish, if desired. **Makes** 6 servings.

FISH AND SHELLFISH 101

■ Delicate seafood is delicious barbecued, smoked, or quickly grilled.

■ Mild flavors of fish and shellfish swiftly take on the flavors of the sauce or marinade, so marinating times can be minimal.

■ For the juiciest fish and seafood (when grilling rather than slow-smoking), grill it quickly over high or medium-high heat. This helps prevent the tender morsels from sticking to the grate.

Smoked Fish

Prep: 20 min., Cook: 4 hrs., Other: 8 hrs.

This smoky fish makes a wonderful entrée with crisp greens and your favorite salad dressing, or enjoy it as an appetizer on baguette slices smeared with cream cheese.

Hickory chunks
5 lb. trout or mackerel, cut into 1½-inch-thick steaks (leave skin on)
1½ cups water
⅓ cup firmly packed brown sugar
3 Tbsp. salt
¼ tsp. ground red pepper

Soak hickory chunks in water for 1 to 24 hours.
Place trout in a large zip-top freezer bag. Combine water and remaining 3 ingredients; pour over trout. Seal bag; marinate in refrigerator 8 hours, turning bag occasionally.
Prepare charcoal fire in smoker, and let burn 10 to 15 minutes. Cover coals with soaked hickory chunks. Place water pan in smoker; add hot water to fill pan.
Place upper food grate on appropriate shelf in smoker. Arrange trout on food grate, and discard marinade. Cover with smoker lid, and smoke 3 to 4 hours or until fish flakes easily when tested with a fork. **Makes** 10 servings.

Smoked Trout

Prep: 10 min., Cook: 1 hr., Other: 2 hrs.

Pecan shell chunks or hickory chips
1¼ cups water
⅓ cup firmly packed dark brown sugar
¼ cup lemon juice
¼ tsp. ground red pepper
3 (8-oz.) trout fillets, each halved lengthwise
¼ tsp. salt

Soak wood chips in water to cover 30 minutes. Drain well.
Combine 1¼ cups water and next 3 ingredients in a large zip-top freezer bag; add fish. Seal bag; marinate in refrigerator 2 hours, turning bag occasionally.
Remove fish from bag, reserving marinade. Set aside.

Prepare charcoal fire in smoker; let burn 15 to 20 minutes. Place soaked wood chips on top of hot coals. Place water pan in smoker; add reserved marinade. Add hot tap water to fill pan.
Coat food grate with cooking spray; place grate in smoker. Arrange fish, skin side down, on grate, allowing enough room between fish pieces for air to circulate. Cover with smoker lid, and smoke 1 hour or until fish flakes easily when tested with a fork. Sprinkle with salt. **Makes** 6 servings.

Smoked Tuna

Prep: 15 min.; Cook: 3 hrs.; Other: 3 hrs., 30 min.

Cook enough tuna to make your favorite tuna salad tomorrow. The smoky flavor transforms this lunch standby into an extraordinary treat.

Cherry wood chunks
4 (10-oz.) tuna steaks
2 qt. water
⅔ cup coarse kosher salt
½ cup firmly packed brown sugar
5 bay leaves, crumbled
2 Tbsp. fresh lemon juice
Vegetable oil
2 Tbsp. coarsely ground black peppercorns
4 cups dry white wine

Soak wood chunks in water to cover at least 1 hour.
Place tuna steaks in a large zip-top freezer bag. Stir together 2 qt. water and next 4 ingredients; pour over steaks. Seal bag; chill 3 hours, turning bag occasionally.
Remove steaks from brine; discard brine. Wash and pat dry. Place on a rack to air-dry 30 minutes.
Brush steaks with vegetable oil. Pat pepper on both sides of steaks.
Prepare charcoal fire in smoker; let burn 15 to 20 minutes.
Drain wood chunks, and place on coals. Place water pan in smoker; add wine. Coat food grate with cooking spray; place in smoker. Place steaks on upper grate; cover with smoker lid. Smoke 2 to 3 hours or until fish flakes easily when tested with a fork. **Makes** 4 servings.

BBQ Grilled Salmon

Prep: 5 min., Cook: 14 min., Other: 45 min.

Mesquite or hickory chips
4 (6-oz.) salmon fillets
2 Tbsp. Sweet 'n' Spicy Barbecue Rub (page 192)

Soak wood chips in water to cover at least 30 minutes; drain well. Wrap chips in heavy-duty aluminum foil; pierce several holes in foil.

Coat salmon with Sweet 'n' Spicy Barbecue Rub; cover and chill 30 minutes.

Place foil-wrapped chips on left side of food grate over medium-high heat (350° to 400°); cover with grill lid, and heat 10 to 15 minutes or until chips begin to smoke. Coat right side of food grate with cooking spray. Place salmon on grate. Grill, covered with grill lid, 5 to 7 minutes on each side or until fish flakes easily with a fork. **Makes** 4 servings.

Smoked Salmon with Sweet-Hot Mustard and Dill

Prep: 20 min., Cook: 35 min., Other: 30 min.

Rich, meaty salmon fillets are seasoned with a paste that offers more flavor than a marinade.

2 cups wood chips
1 Tbsp. minced fresh dill
1 Tbsp. fresh lemon juice
3 Tbsp. sweet-hot mustard (we tested with Inglehoffer)
½ tsp. salt
1 (1½-lb.) salmon fillet

Soak wood chips in water 30 minutes; drain.

Combine dill, juice, mustard, and salt, stirring well. Place salmon, skin side down, in a shallow baking dish; brush mustard mixture over salmon. Cover and refrigerate 20 minutes.

Prepare grill for indirect grilling, heating one side to low and leaving one side with no heat. Maintain temperature at 200° to 225°. Place wood chips on hot coals. Place a disposable aluminum foil pan on unheated side of grill. Pour 2 cups water in pan. Coat food grate with cooking spray; place on grill. Place salmon, skin side down, on grate over foil pan on unheated side. Close lid; smoke 35 minutes or until fish flakes easily when tested with a fork. **Makes** 4 servings.

Smoked Dilled Salmon

Prep: 10 min., Cook: 25 min., Other: 2 hrs.

The fish in this recipe is extra-moist because it soaks in a brine (salt-water solution). Start soaking the wood chunks while the salmon brines.

3½ cups water
½ cup kosher salt (we tested with Diamond Crystal)
¼ cup sugar
2 Tbsp. dried dill
2 Tbsp. low-sodium soy sauce
1 cup ice cubes
1 (1½-lb.) salmon fillet (about 1 inch thick)
Hickory chips
Freshly cracked black pepper
Garnish: fresh dill sprigs

Combine water, salt, sugar, dill, and soy sauce in a large bowl, stirring until salt and sugar dissolve. Pour salt mixture into a large zip-top freezer bag. Add ice and salmon; seal. Refrigerate 2 hours, turning bag occasionally.

Soak the wood chips in water for 30 minutes. Drain well.

Prepare the grill for indirect grilling, heating one side to medium and leaving one side with no heat.

Place half of wood chips on hot coals. Remove salmon from bag, and discard brine. Pat salmon dry with paper towels. Place salmon on food grate coated with cooking spray over unheated side. Close lid; smoke 10 minutes. Place remaining wood chips on hot coals; close lid, and smoke 15 more minutes or until fish flakes easily when tested with a fork. Sprinkle with black pepper; garnish, if desired. **Makes** 4 servings.

"Versatile shrimp and fish swimmingly take on the bold flavors of barbecue and slow smoking."

—Joy Zacharia, *Southern Living* Contributor

Smoked Rosemary-Scented Salmon

Prep: 10 min., Cook: 50 min., Other: 3 hrs.

Hickory or alder chunks
1 (3-lb.) salmon fillet, halved crosswise
¾ cup fresh lime juice
3 Tbsp. minced fresh rosemary
2 Tbsp. olive oil
1½ tsp. prepared horseradish
1½ tsp. cracked pepper
¾ tsp. salt
Garnishes: fresh rosemary sprig, lime wedges

Soak wood chunks in water to cover 1 to 24 hours. Drain well.

Place fish in a large zip-top freezer bag. Combine lime juice and next 3 ingredients. Pour over fish; seal bag, and shake gently until fish is well coated. Marinate in refrigerator 3 hours, turning bag occasionally. Remove fish from bag, reserving marinade. Sprinkle fish with pepper and salt; set aside.

Prepare charcoal fire in smoker; let burn 15 to 20 minutes. Place soaked wood chunks on top of coals. Place water pan in smoker; add reserved marinade. Add hot tap water to fill pan.

Coat food grate with cooking spray; place grate in smoker. Arrange fish, skin side down, on grate, allowing enough room between fish pieces for air to circulate. Cover with smoker lid, and smoke 50 minutes or until fish flakes easily when tested with a fork. Garnish, if desired. **Makes** 12 servings.

Smoked King Crab Legs and Lobster Tails

Prep: 30 min.; Cook: 1 hr., 20 min.; Other: 1 hr.

Apple or alder wood chunks
1 cup butter or margarine, melted
¼ cup fresh lemon juice
1 Tbsp. minced fresh parsley
½ tsp. grated lemon rind
Pinch of salt
5 lb. frozen king crab legs, thawed
4 frozen lobster tails, thawed (about 2 lb.)

Soak wood chunks in water to cover at least 1 hour.

Prepare charcoal fire in smoker; let burn 15 to 20 minutes.

Drain chunks, and place on coals. Place water pan in smoker; add water to fill line.

Stir together butter and next 4 ingredients. Divide lemon-butter mixture in half. Crack crab legs, and split lobster tails. Brush lobster and crab with half of mixture; set aside remaining mixture.

Coat food grate with cooking spray; place in smoker. Arrange crab legs and lobster tails on grate; cover with grill lid. Smoke crab about 20 minutes and lobster about 45 minutes to 1 hour or until flesh is white and firm.

Serve with reserved lemon-butter mixture. **Makes** 4 servings.

editor's favorite
Smoked Sea Scallops

Prep: 20 min., Cook: 20 min., Other: 2 hrs.

Mesquite chips
6 cups water
⅓ cup kosher salt
¼ cup sugar
36 sea scallops
⅔ lb. thinly sliced prosciutto
6 green onions, sliced

Soak wood chips in water to cover at least 30 minutes.

Combine 6 cups water, salt, and sugar in a bowl, stirring to dissolve. Rinse scallops, and stir into brine. Cover and chill 1 hour; drain.

Arrange scallops in a single layer on a wire rack; chill 1 hour.

Prepare charcoal fire in smoker; let burn 15 to 20 minutes. Drain chips, and place on coals. Place water pan in smoker; add water to fill line.

Wrap strips of prosciutto around scallops, securing with wooden picks. Place scallops on upper food grate. Place grate in smoker. Sprinkle green onions over scallops (most will drop into water); cover with smoker lid. Smoke 20 minutes or until done. **Makes** 6 servings.

Grilled Corn with
Jalapeño-Lime Butter
Prep: 25 min., Cook: 15 min., Other: 1 hr.
(pictured on page 139)

To make the butter a bit more kid-friendly, make a second batch and omit the jalapeño peppers.

¾ cup butter, softened
2 large jalapeño peppers, seeded and minced
2 Tbsp. grated lime rind
1 tsp. fresh lime juice
10 ears fresh corn, husks removed
2 Tbsp. olive oil
1 Tbsp. kosher salt
1 tsp. freshly ground pepper

Combine first 4 ingredients, and shape into a 6-inch log; wrap in wax paper or plastic wrap, and chill 1 hour.
Rub corn with olive oil; sprinkle evenly with salt and pepper.
Grill, covered with grill lid, over high heat (400° to 500°), turning often, 10 to 15 minutes or until tender. Serve with flavored butter. **Makes** 10 servings.

quick & easy
Grilled Corn with
Creamy Chipotle Sauce
Prep: 15 min., Cook: 15 min.

Instead of using butter, try this smoky, spicy sauce—it's a savory complement to the sweet corn. Though the corn needs to be grilled at the last minute, the sauce can be prepared a day ahead. To remove the silks from an ear of corn, rub with a damp paper towel or a damp soft-bristled toothbrush.

¼ tsp. salt
1 drained canned chipotle pepper, seeded
1 garlic clove
½ cup 2% reduced-fat cottage cheese
2 Tbsp. light mayonnaise
2 Tbsp. plain fat-free yogurt
6 ears fresh corn, husks removed

Place first 3 ingredients in a food processor; process until minced. Add cottage cheese; process until smooth, scraping sides of bowl occasionally. Add mayonnaise and yogurt; process until blended. Spoon sauce into a bowl; cover and chill.
Place corn on food grate coated with cooking spray. Grill, covered with grill lid, over high heat (400° to 500°), turning often, 10 to 15 minutes or until tender. Serve corn with sauce. **Makes** 6 servings.

Sage-Grilled Eggplant
Prep: 10 min., Cook: 15 min., Other: 1 hr.

1 large eggplant, unpeeled
1½ tsp. salt
⅓ cup Sage Butter
¼ tsp. pepper

Cut eggplant crosswise into ½-inch slices; sprinkle cut sides with salt. Place in a single layer on paper towels; let stand 1 hour.
Rinse eggplant with water, and pat dry. Arrange in a single layer in a lightly greased grill basket.
Melt Sage Butter in a small saucepan over low heat; stir in pepper. Brush on eggplant.
Grill, covered with grill lid, over medium-high heat (350° to 400°) 12 to 15 minutes or until lightly browned, turning and brushing with melted butter mixture. **Makes** 4 servings.

Sage Butter
Prep: 10 min.

Try this butter on grilled chicken or fish, or toss with steamed vegetables.

½ cup fresh sage leaves, loosely packed
1 large shallot
½ cup butter, softened
1 tsp. grated lemon rind
½ tsp. fresh lemon juice
¼ tsp. freshly ground pepper

Process sage and shallot in a food processor until chopped.
Add butter and remaining ingredients; process until mixture is thoroughly blended, stopping occasionally to scrape down sides. **Makes** ½ cup.

Grilled Red Onions
Prep: 20 min., Cook: 10 min., Other: 8 hrs.

If you've tried to grill onions only to have the rings separate and end up in the fire, then we have a solution. Insert a skewer through an onion slice to hold the rings together.

12 (8-inch) wooden skewers
3 medium-size red or sweet onions
1½ cups dry white wine
2 to 4 Tbsp. butter or margarine, melted
1 tsp. chopped fresh thyme
⅛ tsp. pepper

Insert 4 wooden skewers (1 at a time) through each onion about ½-inch apart to create horizontal segments. Cut onions into slices between skewers. (Leave skewers in place to hold onion slices together during marinating and cooking.)
Place slices in a shallow container; add wine. Cover and chill 8 hours, turning occasionally. Drain.
Melt butter in small saucepan; stir in thyme and pepper. Brush onion slices with butter mixture, reserving some for basting.
Grill onions, covered with grill lid, over medium-high heat (350° to 400°) 6 to 10 minutes, turning and basting often with reserved butter mixture. **Makes** 6 servings.

Grilled Yellow Squash Halves
Prep: 2 min., Cook: 2 min., Other: 20 min.

This is the best two-ingredient side dish you can make. It's easy, delicious, and healthy.

6 yellow squash
½ cup Italian dressing

Cut yellow squash in half lengthwise. Place squash in a large zip-top freezer bag; add dressing. Seal and chill 20 minutes. Remove squash from marinade, discarding marinade.
Grill, cut sides down, covered with grill lid, over medium-high heat (350° to 400°) 2 minutes or until tender. **Makes** 6 servings.

Grilled Summer Squash
Prep: 10 min., Cook: 10 min., Other: 15 min.

¼ cup fresh lemon juice
¼ cup plain fat-free yogurt
1 Tbsp. olive oil
2 tsp. chopped fresh rosemary
½ tsp. freshly ground pepper
2 garlic cloves, minced
¾ tsp. salt, divided
3 small yellow squash, halved lengthwise (about 1 lb.)
3 small zucchini, halved lengthwise (about 1 lb.)

Combine first 6 ingredients in a 13- x 9-inch baking dish. Add ½ tsp. salt. Make 3 diagonal cuts, ¼-inch deep, across cut side of each squash and zucchini half. Place squash and zucchini halves, cut sides down, in baking dish. Marinate squash and zucchini at room temperature 15 minutes.
Remove squash and zucchini from marinade, and discard marinade. Place squash and zucchini on food grate coated with cooking spray. Grill over medium-high heat (350° to 400°) 5 minutes on each side or until tender. Sprinkle evenly with remaining ¼ tsp. salt. **Makes** 6 servings.

Grilled Asparagus
Prep: 10 min., Cook: 4 min.

This grilling time is for pencil-thin asparagus; increase the time for thicker spears.

1 lb. fresh asparagus
1 Tbsp. olive oil
1 tsp. balsamic vinegar
¼ tsp. salt
¼ tsp. pepper
1 tsp. grated lemon rind

Snap off and discard tough ends of asparagus.
Combine olive oil, balsamic vinegar, salt, and pepper in a shallow dish or large zip-top freezer bag; add asparagus, turning to coat.
Remove asparagus from oil mixture. Grill asparagus, covered with grill lid, over medium-high heat (350° to 400°) 2 to 4 minutes or until tender, turning once. Remove asparagus, and sprinkle evenly with grated lemon rind; serve immediately. **Makes** 4 servings.

Grilled Tomatoes
Prep: 5 min., Cook: 4 min.

Serve these savory tomatoes with your favorite burgers, Grilled Corn with Jalapeño-Lime Butter (page 137), and dill pickle spears.

2 garlic cloves, minced
2 Tbsp. olive oil
5 large tomatoes, cut in half crosswise
½ tsp. salt
½ tsp. pepper
½ cup chopped fresh basil

Stir together garlic and oil. Brush cut sides of tomato halves evenly with garlic mixture; sprinkle evenly with salt and pepper.

Grill tomato halves, covered with grill lid, over medium-high heat (350° to 400°) about 2 minutes on each side. Sprinkle evenly with basil. **Makes** 10 servings.

Grilled Vegetables
with Cilantro Butter

Grilled Vegetables with Cilantro Butter

Prep: 10 min., Cook: 25 min., Other: 1 hr.

4 ears fresh corn with husks
Cilantro Butter
4 medium tomatoes, halved
4 medium zucchini, cut into 1-inch-thick slices
½ tsp. salt
½ tsp. freshly ground pepper
Garnish: fresh cilantro sprigs

Soak corn in water to cover 1 hour. Peel back corn husks, leaving husks attached. Remove silks.
Spread Cilantro Butter evenly over corn, tomato, and zucchini; sprinkle with salt and pepper. Pull husks over corn, and twist ends tightly. Place corn on food grate. Place tomato and zucchini in a grill basket.
Grill vegetables, covered, over medium-high heat (350° to 400°) 10 to 15 minutes or until zucchini and tomato are tender, turning corn often. Grill corn 5 to 10 more minutes or until tender. (Husks will blacken.) Remove husks, or pull them back and knot ends to make a "handle" for corn. Serve with beef fajitas. Garnish, if desired. **Makes** 4 servings.

Cilantro Butter

Prep: 5 min.

½ cup butter or margarine, softened
¼ cup minced fresh cilantro
4 garlic cloves, pressed

Stir together all ingredients. **Makes** ½ cup.

Grilled Sweet Potatoes with Orange-Chipotle Glaze

Prep: 10 min., Cook: 13 min.

4 large sweet potatoes (about 2 lb.)
1 (7-oz.) can chipotle peppers in adobo sauce
2 Tbsp. butter or margarine, melted
1 Tbsp. chopped fresh cilantro
½ tsp. salt
1 (6-oz.) can orange juice concentrate, thawed and undiluted

Cut potatoes in half lengthwise. Cook potato halves in boiling water 5 minutes or until crisp-tender; drain. Rinse with cold water; drain well.
Meanwhile, remove 3 Tbsp. adobo sauce from canned chiles. Place remaining sauce and chiles in a zip-top freezer bag; freeze for another use.
Combine 3 Tbsp. adobo sauce, butter, cilantro, salt, and juice in a small bowl.
Place potatoes on food grate coated with cooking spray; grill over medium-high heat (350° to 400°) 4 minutes on each side or until potatoes are done, basting frequently with juice mixture. **Makes** 8 servings.

Grilled Portobello Mushrooms and Asparagus

Prep: 5 min., Cook: 14 min.

For a hearty veggie burger, place whole mushrooms caps on buns after grilling, add condiments, and serve asparagus on the side.

4 portobello mushroom caps
2 Tbsp. Rosemary Oil
1 lb. fresh asparagus

Remove brown gills from undersides of portobello mushroom caps using a spoon, discarding gills. Brush mushrooms with 1 Tbsp. Rosemary Oil. Snap off tough ends of asparagus; brush asparagus with remaining 1 Tbsp. Rosemary Oil.
Grill mushrooms, covered with grill lid, over high heat (400° to 500°) 5 minutes on each side. Cut mushrooms into strips. Grill asparagus, covered with grill lid, over high heat 2 minutes on each side. **Makes** 6 servings.

Rosemary Oil

Prep: 5 min., Cook: 3 min.

⅓ cup olive oil
2 fresh rosemary sprigs
1 tsp. pepper

Bring all ingredients to a boil over high heat, and cook, stirring occasionally, 3 minutes. Remove from heat; cool. Discard rosemary sprigs. **Makes** ⅓ cup.

Grilled Balsamic-Glazed Peaches

Prep: 10 min., Cook: 15 min., Other: 10 min.

Serve these tangy peaches with barbecue entrées or scoop homemade ice cream on top of a half peach for a luscious hot-and-cold dessert

½ cup balsamic vinegar
3 Tbsp. brown sugar
1 tsp. cracked pepper
⅛ tsp. salt
6 firm, ripe peaches, halved
¼ cup vegetable oil

Combine first 4 ingredients in a saucepan. Bring to a boil; reduce heat, and simmer 2 to 3 minutes.
Place peaches in a shallow dish. Pour vinegar mixture over peaches, tossing gently to coat. Let stand 10 minutes.
Remove peaches from vinegar mixture, reserving 2 Tbsp. mixture. Set aside remaining vinegar mixture.
Whisk together reserved 2 Tbsp. vinegar mixture and oil, blending well. Set vinaigrette aside.
Place peach halves, cut sides down, on a lightly greased food grate. Grill, covered with grill lid, over medium heat (300° to 350°) 5 minutes on each side or until firm and golden, basting with remaining vinegar mixture. Serve peaches with vinaigrette.
Makes 6 servings.

Goat Cheese-and-Grilled Pepper Pizza

Prep: 10 min., Cook: 20 min. per pizza

Any combination of bell peppers can be used for this dynamic veggie pizza.

2 tsp. olive oil
¼ tsp. salt
¼ tsp. pepper
1 cup yellow bell pepper rings
1 cup green bell pepper rings
1 cup red bell pepper rings
1 cup sliced red onion, separated into rings
2 (10-inch) Quick-and-Easy Pizza Crusts (page 143)
½ cup crumbled herbed goat cheese, at room
    temperature

Combine first 3 ingredients in a small bowl; set aside.
Prepare grill. Place bell peppers and onion on food grate coated with cooking spray; grill 10 to 12 minutes or until tender. Set aside.
Place 1 crust on food grate coated with cooking spray; grill 3 minutes or until puffy and golden. Turn crust, grill mark side up; brush with half of oil mixture. Top with half of grilled vegetables and half of goat cheese. Grill, covered, over medium heat (300° to 350°) 4 to 5 minutes or until cheese melts and crust is lightly browned. Repeat with remaining crust and toppings. **Makes** 6 servings.

PIZZA GRILLING 101

■ A little preparation goes a long way. Be sure you have all of your topping ingredients ready and nearby before you start to grill the pizza dough.
■ To give your pizza a more pronounced smoky flavor, soak a couple of handfuls of aromatic wood chips in water for about 30 minutes. Sprinkle them over the hot coals, and close the grill lid. Wait a few minutes before you place the pizza crust on the food grate.
■ Always remember to coat the pizza dough or food grate with cooking spray unless the recipe calls to do otherwise.
■ Don't fret when your crust has irregular, puffy circles and grill marks—they're part of the rustic attraction.

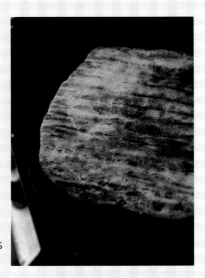

Quick-and-Easy Pizza Crusts

Prep: 30 min.; Other: 1 hr., 5 min.

We call for bread flour because it's higher in protein than all-purpose flour and makes a firmer, denser crust. You can, however, substitute all-purpose flour.

2 cups bread flour
½ tsp. salt
½ tsp. sugar
1 (¼-oz.) envelope rapid-rise yeast
¾ cup warm water (120° to 130°)
1 Tbsp. olive oil
2 Tbsp. cornmeal

Combine first 4 ingredients in a large bowl; make a well in center of mixture. Combine water and oil; add to flour mixture. Stir until mixture forms a ball. Turn dough out onto a lightly floured surface; knead until smooth and elastic (about 10 minutes).

Place the dough in a large bowl coated with cooking spray, turning to coat top. Cover and let rise in a warm place (85°), free from drafts, 45 minutes or until doubled in bulk. Punch dough down; divide in half. Cover and let dough rest 10 minutes.

Working with 1 portion at a time (cover remaining dough to keep from drying), roll each portion into a 10-inch circle on a lightly floured surface. Place dough on 2 baking sheets, each sprinkled with 1 Tbsp. cornmeal. **Makes** 2 (10-inch) pizza crusts.

Food Processor Variation: Place the first 4 ingredients in a food processor, and pulse 2 times or until well blended. With processor on, slowly add water and oil through food chute; process until dough forms a ball. Process 1 more minute. Turn out onto a lightly floured counter; knead 9 to 10 times. Proceed with recipe as directed.

Bread Machine Variation: Follow manufacturer's instructions for placing all ingredients except cornmeal into bread pan. Select dough cycle; start bread machine. Remove dough from machine. (Do not bake.) Proceed with recipe as directed.

Grilled Vegetable Pizza with Feta and Spinach

Prep: 10 min., Cook: 11 min. per pizza

Any flavor of feta cheese works on this pizza. The tangy, fresh spinach mixture is a nice contrast to the grilled veggies and cheese.

3 Tbsp. balsamic vinegar
1 garlic clove, crushed
1 (1¼-lb.) eggplant, cut crosswise into ¼-inch-thick slices
½ tsp. pepper
¼ tsp. salt
2 (10-inch) Quick-and-Easy Pizza Crusts (at left)
2 tsp. olive oil, divided
2 cups chopped plum tomato (about 8 tomatoes)
1 cup crumbled feta cheese with basil and tomato
2 Tbsp. chopped fresh or 1 tsp. dried oregano
2 cups thinly sliced spinach leaves
2 Tbsp. balsamic vinegar

Combine 3 Tbsp. vinegar and garlic in a small bowl; brush over both sides of eggplant slices. Sprinkle both sides of eggplant with pepper and salt. Place eggplant on food grate coated with cooking spray; grill 2 minutes on each side or until tender. Remove from grill; set aside.

Place 1 crust on food grate coated with cooking spray; grill, covered, over medium heat (300° to 350°) 3 minutes or until puffy and golden.

Turn crust, grill mark side up; brush with 1 tsp. oil. Arrange half of eggplant slices over crust, overlapping slightly. Top with half of tomato, cheese, and oregano. Cover and grill 3 to 4 minutes or until thoroughly heated; remove from heat.

Combine spinach and 2 Tbsp. vinegar in a small bowl. Top pizza with half of spinach mixture. Repeat with remaining crust and toppings. **Makes** 6 servings.

Grilled Pizza with Smoked Tofu and Roasted Red Peppers

Prep: 35 min.; Cook: 19 min.; Other: 1 hr., 35 min.

With its firm texture, smoked tofu shreds easily and replaces some of the cheese that traditionally tops pizza.

1 tsp. sugar
1 (¼-oz.) envelope active dry yeast
1 cup warm water (100° to 110°)
2¾ cups all-purpose flour, divided
2 Tbsp. olive oil, divided
1¼ tsp. salt, divided
1 garlic clove, minced
1 (28-oz.) can plum tomatoes, undrained and chopped
¼ tsp. pepper
2 red bell peppers
2 cups shredded smoked tofu (about 6 oz.)
1½ cups (6 oz.) shredded fresh mozzarella cheese

Dissolve sugar and yeast in warm water in a large bowl; let stand 5 minutes. Lightly spoon flour into dry measuring cups; level with a knife.

Add 2½ cups flour, 1 Tbsp. oil, and 1 tsp. salt; stir well to form a stiff dough. Turn dough out onto a lightly floured surface. Knead until smooth and elastic (about 10 minutes); add enough of remaining flour, 1 Tbsp. at a time, to prevent dough from sticking to hands. (The dough will feel tacky.)

Place dough in a large bowl coated with cooking spray, turning to coat top.

Cover and let rise in a warm place (85°), free from drafts, 45 minutes or until dough is doubled in size. (Gently press two fingers into dough. If indentation remains, the dough has risen enough.)

Heat remaining 1 Tbsp. olive oil in a medium non-stick skillet over medium-high heat. Add garlic, and sauté 1 minute. Add tomatoes; bring to a boil. Reduce heat; simmer 30 minutes or until sauce is thick. Stir in remaining ¼ tsp. salt and ¼ tsp. black pepper.

Punch the dough down. Cover and let rest 5 minutes. Divide dough into 6 equal portions; working with 1 portion at a time, shape each into a ball. (Cover remaining dough to prevent drying.)

Roll each ball into a 6-inch circle. Place on baking sheets coated with cooking spray. Lightly coat dough with cooking spray; cover with plastic wrap. Let rest 15 minutes.

Cut bell peppers in half lengthwise; discard seeds and membranes. Place pepper halves, skin sides down, on food grate coated with cooking spray; grill 15 minutes or until blackened. Place in a zip-top freezer bag; seal. Let stand 15 minutes. Peel and cut into strips.

Place dough rounds on food grate coated with cooking spray; grill, covered, over medium heat (300° to 350°) 2 minutes or until lightly browned. Turn dough over.

Spread ⅓ cup tomato sauce over each dough round, leaving a ½-inch border. Sprinkle ⅓ cup tofu and ¼ cup cheese evenly over each pizza. Divide pepper strips evenly among pizzas.

Close grill lid; grill 2 minutes or until cheese melts. Serve immediately. **Makes** 6 servings.

quick & easy
Grilled Onion Pizzas

Prep: 5 min., Cook: 19 min.

Grilling caramelizes the natural sugars in onions; the flavor is unbeatable.

2 large red onions
3 Tbsp. olive oil, divided
1½ Tbsp. minced fresh rosemary
½ tsp. ground cinnamon
¼ tsp. salt
¼ tsp. ground red pepper
4 (6-inch) Italian bread shells
1 (4-oz.) package crumbled blue cheese
½ cup chopped walnuts, toasted

Cut each onion into 4 (½-inch-thick) slices. Combine 2 Tbsp. oil, rosemary, and next 3 ingredients; brush over both sides of onion slices.

Cook onion, covered with grill lid, 4 to 5 minutes on each side or until browned and tender.

Brush tops of bread shells with remaining 1 Tbsp. oil; cook, without grill lid, 1 to 2 minutes. Sprinkle with crumbled cheese; top with onion, and sprinkle with chopped walnuts.

Grill, covered with grill lid, over medium heat (300° to 350°) 5 to 7 minutes or until cheese melts and bread shells are golden. Cut into wedges, and serve immediately. **Makes** 4 servings.

Grilled Veggie Pizzas

Prep: 20 min.; Cook: 21 min.; Other: 1 hr., 20 min.

Homemade pizza on the grill tastes like wood-fired restaurant pizza. Personalize the recipe by using your favorite vegetable or cheese combinations. Mushrooms, asparagus, squash, or eggplant also works well for the following vegetable toppings.

1 (¼-oz.) envelope active dry yeast
1½ cups warm water (100° to 110°)
2 Tbsp. extra-virgin olive oil
4 cups all-purpose flour, divided
½ tsp. salt
2 large zucchini, cut lengthwise into ¼-inch strips
2 red bell peppers, cut into ¼-inch rings
1 large onion, halved and cut into ½-inch slices
1 Tbsp. extra-virgin olive oil
¼ tsp. freshly ground pepper
2 garlic cloves, minced
6 Tbsp. (about 1½ oz.) shredded part-skim mozzarella
6 Tbsp. (about 1½ oz.) shredded Gruyère cheese

Dissolve yeast in warm water in a large bowl. Stir in 2 Tbsp. oil, and let stand 5 minutes.

Lightly spoon all-purpose flour into dry measuring cups; level with a knife. Add 3½ cups flour and salt to yeast mixture; stir until a dough forms.

Turn dough out onto a lightly floured surface. Knead until smooth and elastic (about 10 minutes); add enough of remaining flour, 1 Tbsp. at a time, to prevent dough from sticking to hands.

Place dough in a large bowl coated with cooking spray, turning to coat top. Cover and let rise in a warm place (85°), free from drafts, 1 hour or until doubled in size. (Gently press two fingers into dough. If indentation remains, dough has risen enough.) Punch dough down; cover and let rest 5 minutes.

Place zucchini, bell pepper, and onion in a large bowl; stir in 1 Tbsp. oil and pepper, tossing well. Place on food grate coated with cooking spray; grill 5 minutes on each side or until tender. Remove from grill; stir in garlic.

Divide dough into 6 equal portions, pressing each portion into a 7-inch round. Coat both sides of dough rounds with cooking spray. Place 3 dough rounds on food grate. Grill, covered, over medium heat (300° to 350°) 4 minutes or until puffed and golden. Remove from grill.

Turn rounds over; top each round with 1 Tbsp. mozzarella, about one-sixth of vegetables, and 1 Tbsp. Gruyère cheese. Place topped rounds on grill.

Cover and cook 1½ minutes or until bottoms are browned. Repeat procedure with remaining 3 dough rounds, vegetables, and cheeses. **Makes** 6 servings.

Grilled Andouille Grits

Prep: 5 min., Cook: 23 min., Other: 8 hrs.

Once chilled, these sturdy wedges of grits hold their shape; just make sure the grill is good and hot to keep them from sticking. These are especially tasty with smoked pork.

½ large Vidalia onion, chopped
½ cup chopped andouille or spicy smoked sausage
2 Tbsp. vegetable oil
1 (14-oz.) can chicken broth
¾ cup half-and-half
1 cup quick-cooking grits, uncooked
½ tsp. salt
2 Tbsp. butter or margarine, melted

Sauté onion and sausage in hot oil in a 3-qt. saucepan over medium-high heat until tender. Add chicken broth and half-and-half; bring to a boil. Gradually stir in grits and salt. Cover, reduce heat, and simmer, stirring occasionally, 10 minutes or until thickened.

Pour grits onto a lightly greased baking sheet into a 10½-inch circle (should be about ⅓-inch thick); cover and chill 8 hours.

Invert grits circle onto a flat surface; cut into 8 wedges. Brush top and bottom of each wedge with melted butter.

Grill, uncovered, over medium heat (300° to 350°) 3 to 4 minutes on each side. Remove and keep warm. **Makes** 6 servings.

Note: Grits may be broiled, if desired. Prepare as directed, and arrange buttered wedges on baking sheet. Broil 6 inches from heat 2 minutes on each side or until golden.

Barbecue Meat Loaf
Sandwiches, page 157

Rainy-Day Barbecue Options

Never mind the grill if it's
rainy or cold outside.
You can slow-simmer tender
and tasty 'cue indoors on the
cooktop, in the oven, or in the
slow cooker. Those familiar flavors
come through just the same—the
secret's in the sauce.

Barbecue
Beefwiches

Barbecue Beefwiches

Prep: 20 min., Cook: 4 hrs.

1 (3-lb.) lean beef rump roast
1½ cups ketchup
¼ cup plus 2 Tbsp. red wine vinegar
⅓ cup firmly packed dark brown sugar
1 Tbsp. dried onion flakes
1 tsp. liquid smoke
½ tsp. salt
½ tsp. pepper
⅛ tsp. garlic powder
2½ cups finely shredded cabbage
½ cup finely shredded carrot
2 Tbsp. white vinegar
2 Tbsp. minced sweet pickle
1½ Tbsp. sugar
1½ tsp. vegetable oil
⅛ tsp. celery seeds
12 hamburger buns, split and toasted

Trim fat from roast. Coat a Dutch oven with cooking spray; place over medium heat until hot. Add roast; cook until browned on all sides, turning frequently. Remove roast from pan; wipe drippings from pan with a paper towel.

Combine ketchup and next 7 ingredients, stirring well. Return roast to pan, and pour ketchup mixture over roast. Bring to a boil. Cover, reduce heat, and simmer 4 hours or until meat is tender. Remove roast from pan, reserving sauce in pan. Cool slightly. Shred meat with 2 forks, and return to pan. Cover and cook over medium heat until thoroughly heated, stirring occasionally.

Combine cabbage and carrot. Combine vinegar and next 4 ingredients in a saucepan; bring to a boil, stirring occasionally. Boil 1 minute. Pour over cabbage mixture, and toss gently. Spoon about ½ cup meat mixture on bottom half of each bun; top each with ¼ cup cabbage mixture and a remaining bun half. **Makes** 12 servings.

Barbecue Roast

Prep: 15 min.; Cook: 2 hrs., 15 min.

This roast has a sweet side due to brown sugar, ketchup, and cola in the recipe. Pair it with Simple Southern Iced Tea, page 50, with a squirt of lemon.

1 (3-lb.) boneless chuck roast
1 tsp. salt
½ tsp. pepper
¼ cup firmly packed brown sugar, divided
2 cups water
2 cups ketchup
¾ cup cola soft drink
¼ cup liquid smoke
2 Tbsp. white vinegar
2 Tbsp. Worcestershire sauce
1 Tbsp. prepared mustard
½ tsp. hot sauce
8 to 10 hamburger buns

Sprinkle roast with salt and pepper, and rub with 2 Tbsp. brown sugar. Place in a Dutch oven, and add 2 cups water. Cook, partially covered, over low heat 2 hours or until tender. Remove roast, and shred with 2 forks.

Bring remaining 2 Tbsp. brown sugar, ketchup, and next 6 ingredients to a boil in a large heavy saucepan. Reduce heat, and simmer 15 minutes or until thickened. Stir in shredded roast. Serve on hamburger buns. **Makes** 8 to 10 servings.

Four-Hour Barbecue

Prep: 15 min.; Cook: 4 hrs., 10 min.

The longer and slower you cook this roast the more tender it will be. Four hours for this roast makes it melt in your mouth and leaves you lots of free time for other activities.

1 (3-lb.) boneless chuck roast, trimmed
2 Tbsp. vegetable oil
2 cups water
1 cup ketchup
2 small onions, chopped
1 garlic clove, minced
¼ cup white vinegar
¼ cup Worcestershire sauce
1 Tbsp. chili powder
2 tsp. salt
1 tsp. pepper

Brown roast on all sides in hot oil in a Dutch oven over medium-high heat. Stir together 2 cups water and next 8 ingredients. Pour over roast.
Bake, covered, at 325° for 4 hours. Cool meat, and shred with 2 forks. Stir together shredded meat and sauce. **Makes** 6 to 8 servings.

Savory Onion Brisket

Prep: 15 min., Cook: 3 hrs.

1 (4½-lb.) beef brisket, untrimmed
3 Tbsp. olive oil
¼ cup white wine vinegar
2 Tbsp. vegetable oil
2 Tbsp. ketchup
1 tsp. salt
2 tsp. garlic powder
2 tsp. pepper
1 (1.4-oz.) envelope dry onion soup mix
1 cup water

Brown brisket in hot oil over high heat 5 minutes on each side. Place in a lightly greased 13- x 9-inch pan.
Stir together vinegar and next 6 ingredients; pour over brisket. Add 1 cup water to pan.
Bake, covered, at 350° for 2 hours, basting every hour. Reduce oven temperature to 300°, and bake 1 more hour. Skim fat from drippings, discarding fat; serve drippings with brisket. **Makes** 6 to 8 servings.

Quickest Brisket Sandwiches

Prep: 15 min.; Cook: 1 hr., 20 min.

Cooking this brisket in the pressure cooker speeds up the process so you can have barbecue in record time.

1 cup sliced onion, separated into rings
¾ cup bottled chili sauce
½ cup beer
1 Tbsp. Worcestershire sauce
1 (2½-lb.) beef brisket
1 tsp. pepper
4 garlic cloves, minced
¼ cup packed brown sugar
8 (2½-oz.) submarine rolls

Combine first 4 ingredients in a 6-qt. pressure cooker. Bring to a boil; reduce heat, and simmer 5 minutes. Remove ½ cup mixture from cooker.
Trim fat from brisket. Cut brisket in half crosswise. Rub brisket with pepper and garlic. Place in cooker. Spoon ½ cup chili sauce mixture over brisket. Close lid securely; bring to high pressure over high heat (about 5 minutes). Adjust the heat to medium or level needed to maintain high pressure; cook 1 hour.
Remove from heat; place cooker under cold running water. Remove lid. Remove brisket from cooker, and set aside. Add brown sugar to chili sauce mixture in cooker; bring to a boil. Reduce heat, and simmer, uncovered, 5 minutes, stirring frequently.
Shred brisket with 2 forks. Return meat to sauce in pressure cooker; cook until thoroughly heated. Spoon 1 cup meat with sauce over bottom of each roll, and cover with a remaining roll half. **Makes** 8 servings.

Quick Tip: *Brisket is an essential cut of beef because it adapts easily to many different styles and flavors of barbecue. If you like sweet barbecue, try Ketchup 'n' Cola Brisket (page 154); if you like spicy, try Chili-Spiced Brisket (page 153). You can find interesting flavors paired with brisket such as Coffee-Baked Brisket (page 154) and Lone Star Brisket in Chili Sauce and Beer (page 152). Some of our recipes call for untrimmed brisket—the fat helps keep the meat from drying out when cooking.*

Quickest Brisket
Sandwiches

Saucy Brisket and Potatoes
Prep: 10 min., Cook: 3 hrs.

1 (4- to 5-lb.) beef brisket
2 Tbsp. vegetable oil
1 (8-oz.) package sliced fresh mushrooms
½ cup firmly packed brown sugar
½ cup barbecue sauce
½ cup ketchup
½ cup cider vinegar
½ cup duck sauce
1 (1.0-oz.) envelope dry onion soup mix
1 cup water
4 bay leaves
4 large baking potatoes, each cut into 8 wedges
   (optional)

Brown brisket on both sides in hot oil in a Dutch oven over medium-high heat; place in a large roasting pan. Stir together mushrooms and next 6 ingredients; spread over brisket.
Bake, covered, at 350° for 1 hour. Add 1 cup water and bay leaves, and bake, covered, 1½ hours. Add potato, if desired, and bake, uncovered, 30 minutes or until potato is tender. Remove and discard bay leaves. Cut brisket diagonally across the grain into thin slices. Serve with sauce and potato. **Makes** 8 servings.

Lone Star Brisket in Chili Sauce and Beer
Prep: 15 min.; Cook: 5 hrs., 30 min.

1 (5- to 7-lb.) beef brisket, trimmed
2½ tsp. seasoned salt
1 tsp. pepper
2 garlic cloves, minced
2 medium-size red onions, thinly sliced and
   separated into rings
2 celery ribs, chopped
1 (12-oz.) bottle chili sauce
¼ cup water
1 (12-oz.) can beer

Sprinkle brisket with salt, pepper, and garlic. Place half each of onion rings and celery in bottom of a lightly greased roasting pan.
Place brisket, fat side up, over vegetables. Top with remaining onion rings and celery. Pour chili sauce and ¼ cup water over top.
Bake at 300° for 1½ hours, basting every 30 minutes. Pour beer over brisket. Tightly cover pan with double-layered heavy-duty aluminum foil, and bake 3 to 4 more hours. **Makes** 10 to 14 servings.

66 Most of the South considers barbecue to be all about pork, but in the Lone Star State, barbecue means one thing—brisket. If you've never tried this Southern favorite, you're missing a real treat. 99

—Troy Black, *Southern Living* Contributor

Brisket with Veggies

Prep: 10 min., Cook: 4 hrs.

1 (5-lb.) beef brisket
½ tsp. salt
½ tsp. pepper
1 lb. carrots, cut into chunks
4 lb. small new potatoes
2 cups water
¼ cup Worcestershire sauce
1 (1.0-oz.) envelope dry onion soup mix

Trim fat from brisket; place brisket in a large Dutch oven. Sprinkle with salt and pepper. Add carrot chunks and next 3 ingredients; sprinkle with soup mix.
Bake, covered, at 350° for 4 hours. **Makes** 10 to 12 servings.

freezer friendly
Baked Brisket Au Jus

Prep: 10 min., Cook: 5 hrs., Other: 20 min.

1 (5-lb.) beef brisket
2 tsp. salt
¼ tsp. pepper
1 large onion, sliced
4 celery ribs
½ cup tomato paste
½ cup tomato sauce
1 Tbsp. Worcestershire sauce
1 cup brewed coffee
¼ cup water (optional)

Place brisket, fat side up, in a roasting pan. Sprinkle with salt and pepper. Top with onion and celery.
Stir together tomato paste, tomato sauce, and Worcestershire sauce; pour over beef.
Bake brisket at 325° for 1 hour. Cover and bake 2 more hours, basting with pan juices occasionally. Add coffee; cover and bake 2 more hours, checking every 30 minutes for dryness. Add ¼ cup water, if necessary.
Remove brisket from pan; let stand 20 minutes. Cut brisket across grain into thin slices using a sharp knife.
Strain pan drippings, and serve with sliced brisket.
Makes 8 to 10 servings.

Chili-Spiced Brisket

Prep: 10 min., Cook: 4 hrs.

The pan juices from this brisket provide a flavorful topping for mashed potatoes.

1 (4-lb.) beef brisket
1 Tbsp. vegetable oil
¼ tsp. salt
¼ tsp. ground pepper
4 black peppercorns, crushed
1 bay leaf
1 cup chili sauce
1½ cups chopped onion
1 (10½-oz.) can beef broth
1½ Tbsp. brown sugar
1 Tbsp. Worcestershire sauce
⅛ tsp. garlic salt

Trim excess fat from brisket. Brown brisket in hot oil in a large Dutch oven on all sides. Add salt and next 5 ingredients to Dutch oven. Combine beef broth and remaining 3 ingredients; stir well. Pour over brisket. Cover and bake at 350° for 4 hours or until tender. Remove meat to a serving platter; keep warm.
Pour pan juices through a wire-mesh strainer into a bowl, discarding solids. Slice meat across grain into thin slices, and serve with pan juices. **Makes** 8 to 10 servings.

5-Ingredient Brisket

Prep: 15 min., Cook: 3 hrs., Other: 20 min.

2 cups ketchup
1¼ cups cola soft drink
1 cup chili sauce
1 (1.4-oz.) envelope dry onion soup mix
1 (3- to 4-lb.) beef brisket, trimmed

Stir together first 4 ingredients in a small bowl.
Place brisket, fat side up, in an aluminum foil-lined 13- x 9-inch baking dish. Pour chili sauce mixture over brisket. Cover with foil, and seal.
Bake at 350° for 3 hours. Remove from oven; let stand 20 minutes. Slice meat, and pour sauce over slices.
Makes 6 to 8 servings.

Ketchup 'n' Cola Brisket
Prep: 10 min.; Cook: 5 hrs., 30 min.; Other: 8 hrs.

1 (4-lb.) beef brisket
2 gal. water
3 Tbsp. pickling spice
1 cup ketchup
1 cup cola soft drink
½ cup firmly packed light brown sugar
2 Tbsp. prepared mustard

Bring brisket, 2 gal. water, and 3 Tbsp. pickling spice to a boil in a stockpot; reduce heat, and simmer for 2½ hours. Drain; cover and chill brisket 8 hours.
Place brisket in a lightly greased shallow roasting pan. Stir together 1 cup ketchup and next 3 ingredients. Drizzle one-third of sauce over brisket.
Bake brisket at 350° for 3 hours, basting every hour with remaining sauce. **Makes** 8 servings.

Beer-Baked Brisket
Prep: 10 min., Cook: 4 hrs.

1 (3- to 4-lb.) beef brisket
¼ tsp. salt
¼ tsp. pepper
1 medium onion, sliced
1 (12-oz.) can beer
¼ cup chili sauce
3 Tbsp. brown sugar
1 garlic clove, minced
½ cup water
3 Tbsp. all-purpose flour

Trim excess fat from brisket. Place brisket in a 13- x 9-inch baking dish; sprinkle with salt and pepper. Cover with onion slices.
Combine beer and next 3 ingredients; pour over meat. Cover with aluminum foil, and bake at 350° for 3½ hours. Remove foil; bake 30 more minutes, basting occasionally with pan juices. Remove meat to a platter; keep warm.
Skim fat from pan juices; drain, reserving 1½ cups. Combine water and flour in a saucepan, stirring until smooth. Gradually add reserved 1½ cups juices; cook over medium heat until thickened. Thinly slice meat across grain; serve with gravy. **Makes** 6 to 8 servings.

German-Style Beef Brisket
Prep: 10 min.; Cook: 3 hrs., 30 min.

1 (2½-lb.) beef brisket
4½ cups sliced baking apple (about 2 large)
2¾ cups sauerkraut, drained
1 tsp. caraway seeds
1 (14-oz.) can low-sodium chicken broth
10 medium-size round red potatoes, quartered

Trim fat from brisket. Place meat on a rack in a roasting pan coated with cooking spray.
Arrange apple slices over meat; spoon sauerkraut over apple, and sprinkle with caraway seeds. Drizzle broth over and around brisket. Cover and bake at 325° for 1½ hours.
Arrange potato around meat; baste potato and meat with pan juices. Cover and bake 2 more hours or until potato is tender.
Transfer meat to a serving platter. Arrange apple, sauerkraut, and potato around meat; drizzle with 1 cup pan juices. **Makes** 8 servings.

Coffee-Baked Brisket
Prep: 15 min., Cook: 4 hrs.

1 (4-lb.) beef brisket
2 tsp. kosher salt
2 tsp. pepper
All-purpose flour
2 Tbsp. butter or margarine
2 cups strong brewed coffee
2 cups dry white wine
2 cups ketchup

Trim fat from brisket, and discard; sprinkle brisket evenly with salt and pepper, and dredge in flour.
Melt butter in a large skillet over medium-high heat; add brisket to butter, and brown on both sides. Transfer to a roasting pan. Whisk together coffee, wine, and ketchup; pour over brisket.
Bake, covered, at 350° for 4 hours or until tender, basting occasionally with pan juices. Remove brisket, reserving drippings; cut brisket with a sharp knife across grain into thin slices.
Strain drippings using a gravy strainer, discarding fat. Serve hot drippings with brisket. **Makes** 8 servings.

Beef Brisket with Sweet Potato Mélange
Prep: 15 min.; Cook: 2 hrs., 15 min.

Making sure that carrots and potatoes are sliced to the same thickness ensures that they cook evenly.

1 (3-lb.) lean beef brisket
2 cups thinly sliced onion
1 orange, thinly sliced
1 cup orange juice
2 Tbsp. brown sugar
2 Tbsp. tomato paste
2 tsp. dried thyme
½ tsp. ground cloves
2 (14-oz.) cans chicken broth
2 (3-inch) cinnamon sticks, broken in half
1 lb. carrots, scraped and cut into ½-inch-thick slices
1 lb. sweet potatoes, peeled and cut crosswise into
   ½-inch-thick slices
1 medium Granny Smith apple, peeled and cut into
   1-inch pieces
8 oz. dried pitted prunes
¼ cup all-purpose flour

Trim fat from brisket. Place onion in a large Dutch oven; top with meat. Arrange orange slices over meat. Combine juice and next 6 ingredients, stirring well. Pour mixture over meat. Bring to a boil; cover, reduce heat, and simmer 1½ hours.

Add carrot, potato, and apple to Dutch oven; cover and cook 30 minutes or until carrot and potato are tender. Add prunes; cook 15 more minutes.

Transfer meat and vegetable mixture to a serving platter, using a slotted spoon. Set aside; keep warm.

Skim fat from broth in Dutch oven. Add flour to broth, stirring until smooth. Cook over medium heat, stirring constantly, until thickened.

Cut meat diagonally across grain into ¼-inch-thick slices. Serve meat and vegetable mixture with gravy. **Makes** 12 servings.

Spicy Apricot Brisket
Prep: 20 min.; Cook: 3 hrs., 30 min.; Other: 20 min.

1 (5½-lb.) beef brisket, trimmed
2 tsp. garlic salt
¼ tsp. pepper
2 (10-oz.) cans shredded sauerkraut, drained
2 (10-oz.) jars apricot preserves
2 (12-oz.) bottles chili sauce

Place brisket, fat side up, in a roasting pan. Sprinkle evenly with garlic salt and pepper.

Stir together sauerkraut, preserves, and chili sauce; pour over beef.

Bake, covered, at 350° for 3½ hours or until tender. Remove brisket from pan, reserving sauce mixture in pan; let stand 20 minutes. Cut brisket across the grain into thin slices using a sharp knife.

Pour sauce mixture from roasting pan through a wire-mesh strainer into a bowl; reserve, if desired. Serve strained sauce and, if desired, sauerkraut with sliced brisket. **Makes** 10 servings.

Make Ahead: Prepare and bake as directed. Remove brisket from pan, reserving sauce mixture in pan; let stand 1 hour. Cut brisket across the grain into thin slices using a sharp knife. Place brisket slices in a 13- x 9-inch baking dish. Pour sauce mixture through a wire-mesh strainer into a bowl, reserving sauerkraut mixture, if desired. Pour strained sauce over brisket slices; cover and chill up to 24 hours. Reheat as directed.

Freeze up to 3 Months: Place brisket slices and strained sauce evenly into large zip-top freezer bags; freeze. Thaw in refrigerator overnight. Place brisket and sauce in a 13- x 9-inch baking dish. Reheat as directed.

Reheat: Let stand at room temperature 30 minutes. Bake, covered, at 325° for 45 minutes or until hot.

Smoky Barbecue Brisket

Prep: 10 min., Cook: 6 hrs., Other: 8 hrs.

This brisket is even better if kept in the refrigerator a day after cooking—it allows the flavors to absorb into the meat and also makes a great make-ahead solution for a barbecue gathering. Slice and reheat in the oven or microwave.

1 (4- to 6-lb.) beef brisket, trimmed
1 (5-oz.) bottle liquid smoke
1 onion, chopped
2 tsp. garlic salt
1 to 2 tsp. salt
1/3 cup Worcestershire sauce
1 (12- to 18-oz.) bottle barbecue sauce

Place brisket in a large shallow dish or extralarge zip-top freezer bag; pour liquid smoke over brisket. Sprinkle evenly with onion, garlic salt, and salt. Cover or seal, and chill 8 hours, turning occasionally.

Remove brisket, and place on a large piece of heavy-duty aluminum foil, discarding liquid smoke mixture. Pour Worcestershire sauce evenly over brisket, and fold foil to seal; place wrapped brisket in a roasting pan.

Bake at 275° for 5 hours. Unfold foil; pour barbecue sauce evenly over brisket. Bake 1 more hour, uncovered. **Makes** 8 to 12 servings.

Barbecue Burritos
Prep: 10 min., Cook: 10 min.

½ lb. ground round
¼ cup chopped onion
½ cup no-salt-added whole kernel corn
¼ cup barbecue sauce
2 cups thinly sliced cabbage
2 Tbsp. mayonnaise
⅛ tsp. pepper
3 (8-inch) flour tortillas
¼ cup (1 oz.) shredded reduced-fat Cheddar cheese

Cook ground round and onion in a large nonstick skillet over medium heat until meat is browned, stirring until it crumbles.
Add corn and barbecue sauce to skillet. Cook over medium heat until thoroughly heated, stirring occasionally.
Meanwhile, combine cabbage, mayonnaise, and pepper, stirring mixture well.
Place tortillas on 3 individual serving plates. Top evenly with beef mixture, cabbage mixture, and cheese; roll up. **Makes** 3 servings.

kids love it
Barbecue Meat Loaf
Prep: 13 min.; Cook: 1 hr., 20 min.

2 whole wheat bread slices, torn into pieces
1 cup frozen seasoning blend, thawed
1½ lb. ground round
½ cup 1% low-fat milk
½ cup egg substitute
1 tsp. minced garlic
¼ tsp. salt
¼ tsp. pepper
½ cup barbecue sauce

Position knife blade in food processor bowl. Add bread and seasoning blend to processor bowl; process until chopped. Add meat and next 5 ingredients. Pulse until combined.
Shape meat mixture into an 8- x 4-inch loaf; place on a rack in a roasting pan coated with cooking spray. Bake at 350° for 1 hour and 10 minutes. Spread barbecue sauce over meat loaf; bake 10 more minutes.
Makes 8 servings.

editor's favorite
Barbecue Meat Loaf Sandwiches
Prep: 30 min., Cook: 10 min.

These hearty sandwiches are almost a meal in themselves. Cook extra onion rings to serve on the side. Feel free to use any type of bread as long as it is thickly sliced. A sturdy bread that's close to 1 inch thick works best to hold a hefty slice of meat loaf in place.

1 (9.5-oz.) box frozen five-cheese Texas toast (we tested with Pepperidge Farm)
1 (8-oz.) box frozen onion rings (we tested with Ore-Ida Vidalia O's)
6 (1-inch-thick) cold meat loaf slices
½ cup barbecue sauce
1 cup prepared coleslaw

Prepare Texas toast according to package directions.
Prepare onion rings according to package directions. Spray a large nonstick skillet with cooking spray, and heat over medium-high heat.
Add meat loaf slices, and cook 5 minutes. Turn, brush evenly with barbecue sauce, and cook 5 more minutes or until thoroughly heated.
Top each slice of toast evenly with meat loaf slices, coleslaw, and onion rings. Serve immediately. **Makes** 6 servings.

Individual Barbecue
Pizzas

Individual Barbecue Pizzas
Prep: 13 min., Cook: 12 min.

½ lb. ground round
½ cup chopped onion
½ cup chopped carrot
⅓ cup barbecue sauce
3 Tbsp. brown sugar
¼ tsp. salt
Dash of pepper
4 (4-oz.) prebaked Italian pizza crusts (we tested with Boboli)
¼ cup (1 oz.) finely shredded provolone or part-skim mozzarella cheese
2 Tbsp. chopped fresh cilantro

Cook beef, onion, and carrot in a large nonstick skillet over medium-high heat until browned, stirring to crumble. Drain well; return meat mixture to pan. Stir in barbecue sauce, sugar, salt, and pepper; reduce heat, and simmer 5 minutes.

Place pizza crusts on a baking sheet. Divide beef mixture evenly among crusts, and sprinkle with cheese. Bake pizzas at 450° for 12 minutes or until cheese melts. Sprinkle pizzas with cilantro. Cut each pizza into wedges. **Makes** 4 servings.

Barbecue Ribs
Prep: 10 min.; Cook: 1 hr., 15 min.

Barbecue Ribs may be messy to eat with your fingers, but there's no mess in the oven because these are baked in a foil baking bag.

2½ to 3 lb. spareribs, cut in half
1½ tsp. seasoned salt
½ tsp. pepper
1 large aluminum-foil baking bag
1½ cups barbecue sauce
1 Tbsp. all-purpose flour

Sprinkle spareribs with salt and pepper; place in a single layer in foil bag. Stir together barbecue sauce and flour; spread over ribs. Seal bag, and place in a 15- x 10-inch jelly-roll pan.

Bake ribs at 450° for 1 hour and 15 minutes or until tender. **Makes** 6 servings.

Barbecue 'n' Slaw Sandwiches
Prep: 25 min.; Cook: 4 hrs., 45 min.

1 cup finely chopped onion
3 Tbsp. butter, melted
2 cups ketchup
½ cup firmly packed brown sugar
½ cup cider vinegar
3 Tbsp. Worcestershire sauce
1 Tbsp. prepared mustard
2 tsp. chili powder
1 (5-lb.) Boston butt pork roast
1 tsp. salt
¾ tsp. pepper
2 Tbsp. vegetable oil
3 cups finely shredded cabbage
½ cup shredded carrot
2 Tbsp. chopped green onions
⅓ cup mayonnaise
1 Tbsp. sugar
1 Tbsp. white vinegar
¼ tsp. dry mustard
⅛ tsp. celery seeds
12 hamburger buns, split and toasted

Sauté 1 cup onion in butter in a large saucepan until onion is tender. Add ketchup and next 5 ingredients; bring to a boil. Reduce heat, and simmer 10 minutes.

Sprinkle roast with salt and pepper. Cook in hot oil in a Dutch oven until browned on all sides, turning occasionally. Drain. Return roast to pan; pour half of ketchup mixture over roast. Bring to a boil. Cover, reduce heat, and simmer 3 hours and 45 minutes or until meat is tender, turning occasionally. Drain and cool slightly. Shred meat with 2 forks; return to pan. Add remaining ketchup mixture. Bring to a boil; cover, reduce heat, and simmer 1 hour, stirring occasionally.

Combine cabbage, carrot, and green onions. Combine mayonnaise and next 4 ingredients; add to cabbage mixture. Spoon about ½ cup meat mixture on bottom half of each bun; top each with ¼ cup cabbage mixture and a remaining bun half. **Makes** 12 servings.

Barbecue Pork-and-Coleslaw Hoagies

Prep: 10 min., Cook: 15 min., Other: 10 min.

1 (1-lb.) pork tenderloin
½ cup spicy barbecue sauce (we tested with Kraft
    Spicy Cajun), divided
2½ cups packaged cabbage-and-carrot coleslaw
2½ Tbsp. sour cream
1½ Tbsp. mayonnaise
1½ tsp. sugar
2½ tsp. prepared horseradish
4 (2½-oz.) hoagie rolls with sesame seeds
Dill pickle slices (optional)

Trim fat from pork; cut pork in half lengthwise. Brush the pork with 3 Tbsp. barbecue sauce. Place pork on a broiler pan coated with cooking spray, and broil for 15 minutes or until a thermometer registers 155° (slightly pink); turn pork occasionally.

Remove pork from oven, and let stand 10 minutes for temperature to rise to 160°. Cut into ¼-inch-thick slices.

While pork is cooking, combine coleslaw and next 4 ingredients in a medium bowl; set aside.

Combine pork and 3 Tbsp. barbecue sauce. Brush cut sides of bread with 2 Tbsp. barbecue sauce. Divide pork evenly among bottom halves of rolls. Top each roll half with about ½ cup coleslaw and, if desired, pickles; cover with remaining roll tops. **Makes** 4 servings.

Note: The pork can also be grilled. Place pork on a food grate coated with cooking spray, and grill 15 minutes or until thermometer registers 155°, turning pork occasionally.

Chipotle Pulled-Pork Barbecue Sandwiches

Prep: 10 min.; Cook: 1 hr., 25 min.

Bread-and-butter pickles are a tasty foil to the smoky barbecue sauce in this updated Southern-style sandwich. Serve with coleslaw.

1 (7-oz.) can chipotle peppers in adobo sauce

¼ cup barbecue sauce

1 tsp. garlic powder

1½ tsp. ground cumin

1 (1-lb.) pork tenderloin, trimmed and cut into ½-inch cubes

1 (14.5-oz.) can diced tomatoes, undrained

1 Tbsp. olive oil

3 cups thinly sliced onion

2 tsp. chopped fresh thyme

1 tsp. sugar

6 slices provolone cheese

12 sandwich-cut bread-and-butter pickles

6 Kaiser rolls

Remove 1 pepper from can; reserve remaining peppers and sauce for another use. Finely chop pepper.

Place chopped pepper, barbecue sauce, and next 4 ingredients in a medium saucepan; bring to a boil over medium-high heat. Cover, reduce heat, and simmer 45 minutes, stirring occasionally. Uncover and cook 10 more minutes or until sauce thickens and pork is very tender. Remove from heat. Remove pork from sauce; shred pork with 2 forks. Return pork to sauce in pan.

Heat oil in a large nonstick skillet over medium-high heat. Add onion, thyme, and sugar; cook 10 minutes or until golden, stirring occasionally.

Heat a large nonstick skillet over medium heat. Place 1 cheese slice, ½ cup pork mixture, about 2 Tbsp. onions, and 2 pickle slices on bottom half of each roll; cover with remaining top of roll. Add 3 sandwiches to pan. Place a cast-iron or heavy skillet on top of sandwiches, and press gently to flatten.

Cook 2 minutes on each side or until cheese melts and bread is toasted. (Leave cast-iron skillet on sandwiches while they cook.) Repeat procedure with remaining sandwiches. **Makes** 6 servings.

Double-Stuffed
Barbecue Potatoes

quick & easy

Asian Barbecue Pork Sandwiches

Prep: 15 min., Cook: 30 min.

1 (1½-lb.) package pork tenderloins
3 cups hot water
⅔ cup ketchup
3 Tbsp. soy sauce
2 Tbsp. hoisin sauce
2 Tbsp. honey
2 Tbsp. chili-garlic paste
6 hamburger buns

Place pork on a lightly greased rack in a broiler pan; add 3 cups hot water to pan (to prevent drippings from burning).
Stir together ketchup and next 4 ingredients; divide sauce in half. Reserve half of sauce to toss with cooked pork.
Bake at 475° for 15 minutes. Turn pork, and brush with remaining half of sauce; bake 15 more minutes or until a meat thermometer inserted into thickest portion registers 160°. Cool slightly. Coarsely chop pork, and toss with reserved half of sauce. Serve on buns. **Makes** 6 servings.

Double-Stuffed Barbecue Potatoes

Prep: 55 min., Bake: 25 min.

8 large baking potatoes
1 (8-oz.) container cream cheese, softened
½ cup mayonnaise
1 Tbsp. white wine vinegar
1 tsp. seasoned pepper
2 tsp. fresh lemon juice
¾ tsp. salt
3 cups chopped barbecued pork, warmed
1 cup (4 oz.) shredded Cheddar cheese
¼ cup chopped fresh chives

Wrap each potato in a piece of aluminum foil; place potatoes on a baking sheet.
Bake potatoes at 425° for 45 minutes or until tender. Cut a 4- x 2-inch strip from top of each baked potato. Carefully scoop out pulp into a large bowl, leaving 8 shells intact; set aside about 2 cups pulp for another use.
Mash together remaining potato pulp, cream cheese, and next 5 ingredients; stir in pork. Spoon mixture evenly into shells; top evenly with Cheddar cheese and chives. Place on a lightly greased baking sheet. Bake at 375° for 20 to 25 minutes or until thoroughly heated. **Makes** 8 servings.

3 Tbsp. butter
1 small onion, chopped
1 lb. shredded barbecue pork
3½ cups barbecue sauce
12 oz. hot cooked spaghetti

Melt butter in a 3-qt. saucepan over medium heat; add onion, and sauté until tender. Add pork and barbecue sauce; cook 10 minutes or until thoroughly heated. Serve over hot cooked spaghetti. **Makes** 4 servings.

quick & easy
Barbecue Quesadillas
Prep: 5 min., Cook: 6 min. per batch

½ lb. shredded barbecue pork
8 (6-inch) flour tortillas
1 cup shredded Mexican four-cheese blend or Monterey
   Jack cheese
Salsa
Guacamole

Divide ½ lb. shredded barbecued pork evenly among 8 flour tortillas; sprinkle each with 2 Tbsp. shredded cheese. Fold tortillas in half. Cook quesadillas in a large nonstick skillet over medium heat 3 minutes on each side or until tortillas are crisp and cheese melts. Serve with salsa and guacamole. **Makes** 4 servings.

Quick Tip: *If you don't have time to make barbecued pork from scratch for these recipes, purchase shredded pork or beef from your favorite restaurant.*

Barbecue Pot Pie with Cheese Grits Crust
Prep: 20 min., Cook: 25 min.

1 large sweet onion, diced
1 Tbsp. vegetable oil
2 Tbsp. all-purpose flour
1½ cups thick barbecue sauce
1½ cups beef broth
1 lb. shredded barbecued pork*
Cheese Grits Crust Batter

Sauté onion in hot oil in a large skillet over medium-high heat 5 minutes or until golden brown. Stir in flour, and cook, stirring constantly, 1 minute. Gradually stir in barbecue sauce and beef broth; cook, stirring constantly, 3 minutes or until mixture begins to thicken.
Stir in pork, and bring to a boil. Remove from heat, and spoon mixture into a lightly greased 13- x 9-inch baking dish.
Spoon Cheese Grits Crust Batter evenly over hot barbecue mixture.
Bake at 425° for 20 to 25 minutes or until golden brown and set. **Makes** 8 to 10 servings.

*Substitute 1 lb. shredded beef for pork, if desired.

Cheese Grits Crust Batter
Prep: 9 min., Cook: 7 min.

2 cups water
2 cups milk
1 cup quick-cooking grits
2 cups (8 oz.) shredded sharp Cheddar cheese
¾ tsp. salt
½ tsp. seasoned pepper
2 large eggs, lightly beaten

Bring water and milk to boil in a large saucepan; add grits, and cook, stirring often, 5 minutes or until thickened. Stir in cheese, salt, and pepper; remove from heat.
Stir about one-fourth of grits mixture gradually into beaten eggs; add to remaining grits mixture, stirring constantly. **Makes** 1 (13- x 9-inch) crust.

Seared Chicken with Feisty Hot Barbecue Dipping Sauce

Prep: 10 min., Cook: 12 min., Other: 3 hrs.

Serve over sticky white rice to counter the heat of the dipping sauce, which is also good with pork, shrimp, or seared tofu.

¼ cup chopped shallots
2 Tbsp. sugar
2 Tbsp. fresh lime juice
1 Tbsp. fish sauce
4 garlic cloves, minced
1½ tsp. dark sesame oil, divided
8 (2-oz.) skinned and boned chicken thighs
3 Tbsp. ketchup
1 Tbsp. Sriracha (hot chile sauce; we tested with Huy Fong)
4 tsp. rice vinegar
2 tsp. honey
1 tsp. grated peeled fresh ginger

Combine first 5 ingredients; stir in ½ tsp. oil. Place shallot mixture in a large zip-top freezer bag; add chicken to bag. Seal and marinate in refrigerator 3 hours to overnight, turning bag occasionally.

Combine ketchup and next 4 ingredients.

Heat remaining 1 tsp. oil in a large nonstick skillet over medium-high heat. Remove chicken from bag; discard marinade. Add chicken to pan; cook 2 minutes on each side or until browned.

Cover, reduce heat to medium-low, and cook 8 minutes or until done, turning twice. Serve with ketchup mixture. **Makes** 4 servings.

Oven-Baked Barbecue Chicken

Prep: 20 min., Cook: 2 hrs.

3 cups spicy tomato juice
½ cup cider vinegar
3 Tbsp. vegetable oil
2 to 3 garlic cloves, minced
1 bay leaf
2 tsp. salt
1 tsp. sugar
½ tsp. black pepper
¼ tsp. ground red pepper (optional)
4½ tsp. Worcestershire sauce
2 cups all-purpose flour
10 chicken thighs, skin removed
10 chicken legs, skin removed

Stir together first 10 ingredients in a saucepan over medium-high heat; bring to a boil. Reduce heat, and simmer 10 minutes.
Place flour in a shallow dish; dredge chicken pieces on both sides. Arrange thighs, bone side up, and legs in a roasting pan. Pour tomato juice mixture evenly over chicken.
Bake at 350° for 1½ to 2 hours, basting occasionally. **Makes** 8 to 10 servings.

quick & easy
Chicken with Cranberry Barbecue Sauce

Prep: 20 min., Cook: 4 min. per batch

Like all barbecue sauces, this sauce contains flavors ranging from sweet to spicy—cranberry sauce flavors this 'cue for holiday gatherings. Pound the chicken thinly so it cooks evenly.

1 cup whole-berry cranberry sauce
⅓ cup apricot preserves
2 Tbsp. tomato paste
2 Tbsp. balsamic vinegar
2 tsp. prepared mustard
1 tsp. chili powder
¼ tsp. ground cumin
6 (6-oz.) skinned and boned chicken breasts
¾ tsp. ground coriander
½ tsp. salt
¼ tsp. freshly ground pepper
1 Tbsp. olive oil

Combine first 7 ingredients in a small saucepan; bring to a boil. Reduce heat, and simmer 10 minutes.
Place each chicken breast between 2 sheets of plastic wrap; pound to a ¼-inch thickness using a meat mallet or rolling pin. Combine coriander, salt, and pepper in a small bowl; sprinkle evenly over chicken.
Heat 1½ tsp. oil in a large nonstick skillet over medium-high heat. Add half of chicken; cook 2 minutes on each side or until done. Repeat with remaining oil and chicken. Serve with sauce. **Makes** 6 servings.

quick & easy
Hoisin Barbecue Chicken Breasts

Prep: 15 min., Cook: 13 min.

The basting sauce for this dish is sticky. For easy cleanup, line the broiler pan with aluminum foil and coat with cooking spray. Serve with basmati rice and spinach salad with sesame seeds.

¼ cup hoisin sauce
2 Tbsp. honey
1 Tbsp. rice vinegar
1 tsp. dark sesame oil
2 tsp. cornstarch
2 tsp. water
¼ tsp. salt
¼ tsp. garlic powder
¼ tsp. ground ginger
¼ tsp. pepper
⅛ tsp. five-spice powder
4 (6-oz.) skinned and boned chicken breasts

Combine hoisin, honey, vinegar, and oil in a small saucepan; bring to a boil over medium-high heat. Combine cornstarch and water; add to hoisin mixture, stirring with a whisk. Bring to a boil; cook 1 minute, stirring constantly. Remove from heat.
Combine salt and next 4 ingredients; rub evenly over both sides of chicken. Place chicken on a broiler pan coated with cooking spray, and broil 5 minutes. Brush with hoisin mixture; broil 4 minutes. Turn chicken; brush with hoisin mixture. Broil 4 minutes or until done, basting frequently with hoisin mixture. **Makes** 4 servings.

Barbecue-Battered Chicken Fingers
Prep: 20 min., Cook: 7 min. per batch

If your little ones like to pair mustard with a sauce that's on the sweet side, let them dip their chicken fingers in Honey-Mustard Barbecue Sauce, page 187.

3 lb. skinned and boned chicken breasts
3 cups all-purpose flour
1½ tsp. seasoned salt
1½ tsp. pepper
¾ tsp. garlic powder
2 cups buttermilk
¾ cup honey smoke barbecue sauce
2 large eggs
Vegetable oil
Additional honey smoke barbecue sauce

Cut each chicken breast into 3- x 1-inch strips, and set aside.

Combine flour and next 3 ingredients in a large shallow dish.

Whisk together buttermilk, ¾ cup barbecue sauce, and eggs in a bowl. Dredge chicken pieces in flour mixture; dip in buttermilk mixture, and dredge again in flour mixture. (If flour gets gummy, just press into chicken pieces.)

Pour oil to a depth of 1½ inches in a deep skillet or Dutch oven; heat to 360°.

Fry chicken, in batches, 5 to 7 minutes or until golden. Drain on wire racks over paper towels. Serve with extra barbecue sauce. **Makes** 6 to 8 servings.

Barbecue-Battered Pork Chops: Substitute 3 lb. boneless breakfast pork chops for chicken, and proceed as directed. For a delicious serving idea, serve cooked chops in biscuits.

Barbecue Pulled Chicken with Marinated Cucumbers
Prep: 10 min., Cook: 55 min., Other: 10 min.

Instead of on buns, you can also serve this chicken on barbecue bread or Texas toast. The marinated cucumbers are so good you might want to make a double batch.

¼ cup light brown sugar
1 Tbsp. chili powder
2 tsp. ground cumin
½ tsp. salt
½ tsp. paprika
¼ tsp. pepper
1 lb. skinned and boned chicken breasts
2 tsp. olive oil
1 cup thinly sliced onion
1 cup low-sodium chicken broth
1 Tbsp. balsamic vinegar
¼ cup cider vinegar
2 Tbsp. light brown sugar
¼ tsp. salt
1 cucumber, peeled and sliced
4 hamburger buns

Combine first 6 ingredients. Rub surface of chicken breasts with brown sugar mixture. Heat oil in a large nonstick skillet over medium-high heat. Add chicken; cook 2 minutes on each side. Remove from pan. Add onion to pan; cook 2 minutes or until tender, stirring constantly.

Return chicken to pan; add broth. Bring to a boil; cover, reduce heat, and simmer 30 minutes or until chicken is done. Remove from heat. Remove chicken from pan; shred with 2 forks. Return chicken to pan. Bring to a boil; reduce heat, and simmer, uncovered, 15 minutes or until liquid is absorbed. Stir in balsamic vinegar.

Combine cider vinegar and next 3 ingredients in a large zip-top bag; seal and marinate in refrigerator 10 minutes. Remove cucumber from bag; discard marinade.

Spoon 1 cup chicken mixture onto bottom half of each bun. Top each with ¼ cup cucumber mixture and top half of bun. **Makes** 4 servings.

Carolina Blond
Open-Faced Sandwiches
Prep: 15 min., Cook: 12 min.

1 (12-oz.) bag coleslaw
⅓ cup light coleslaw dressing (we tested with Marzetti)
¼ tsp. celery seeds
1 cup ketchup
½ cup water
¼ cup cider vinegar
2 Tbsp. instant minced onion
2 Tbsp. dark brown sugar
1 Tbsp. prepared mustard
1 tsp. pepper
1 tsp. hot sauce
½ tsp. garlic powder
1½ cups (¾ lb.) skinned, shredded roasted chicken
    breast (we tested with Tyson)
4 (2-oz.) slices Texas toast, lightly toasted

Combine first 3 ingredients in a bowl; toss well to coat. Combine ketchup and next 8 ingredients in a medium saucepan; bring to a boil. Reduce heat; simmer 5 minutes or until mixture begins to thicken. Stir in chicken, and cook 4 minutes or until roasted chicken is thoroughly heated.
Top each toasted bread slice with ½ cup chicken and ½ cup coleslaw mixture. **Makes** 4 servings.

Barbecue Turkey Sandwiches
Prep: 10 min., Cook: 10 min.

¾ lb. freshly ground raw turkey breast
1 medium onion, chopped
1 (8-oz.) can tomato sauce
1 (7-oz.) jar roasted red peppers, drained and chopped
¼ tsp. salt
¼ tsp. pepper
2 tsp. liquid mesquite smoke (optional)
4 whole wheat or plain Kaiser rolls

Cook turkey and onion in a nonstick skillet over medium-high heat 4 to 5 minutes or until onion is tender and turkey is done, stirring until turkey crumbles. Stir in sauce and peppers; simmer 5 minutes.
Stir in salt, pepper, and, if desired, liquid smoke. Spoon turkey mixture evenly onto bottom halves of rolls; top with remaining halves. **Makes** 4 servings.

Warm Barbecue Chicken Salad
Prep: 40 min., Cook: 35 min.

3 cups shredded cooked chicken
Barbecue Dressing, divided
1 cup frozen whole kernel corn, thawed
2 bacon slices, cooked and crumbled
6 cups torn leaf lettuce (about 1 head)
4 plum tomatoes, chopped
⅓ large red onion, sliced and separated into rings
⅔ cup shredded mozzarella cheese

Stir together chicken and 1 cup Barbecue Dressing in a lightly greased 9-inch square pan.
Bake, covered, at 350° for 35 minutes or until warm. Cook corn in boiling water to cover 3 to 4 minutes; drain.
Toss together corn, bacon, and next 3 ingredients. Top with warm chicken mixture, and sprinkle with cheese. Serve immediately with remaining dressing.
Makes 6 servings.

Barbecue Dressing
Prep: 10 min., Cook: 15 min.

1 (18-oz.) bottle barbecue sauce
⅓ cup firmly packed light brown sugar
½ cup honey
⅓ cup ketchup
1 Tbsp. butter or margarine
1 Tbsp. Worcestershire sauce
½ tsp. seasoned salt
1 tsp. lemon pepper

Bring all ingredients to a boil; reduce heat, and simmer, stirring occasionally, 10 minutes. Store in refrigerator up to 3 months, if desired. **Makes** 3 cups.

Barbecue Chicken Pizza

Barbecue Chicken Pizza

Prep: 25 min., Cook: 10 min.

For even more flavor, sprinkle pizza with chopped cooked bacon and chopped fresh cilantro before adding the cheese.

1 small onion, chopped
½ red bell pepper, chopped
½ tsp. salt
¼ tsp. pepper
1 tsp. olive oil
1 (13.8-oz.) can refrigerated pizza crust
½ cup hickory smoke barbecue sauce
2 (6-oz.) packages grilled boneless, skinless chicken breast strips
2 cups (8 oz.) shredded Monterey Jack cheese with peppers
Garnish: chopped fresh parsley
Additional hickory smoke barbecue sauce

Sauté first 4 ingredients in hot oil in a large skillet over medium-high heat 8 to 10 minutes or until vegetables are tender. Drain well.

Unroll pizza crust; press or pat into a lightly greased 13- x 9-inch pan.

Bake crust at 400° for 12 to 14 minutes. Spread ½ cup barbecue sauce evenly over top of pizza crust in pan. Arrange chicken strips evenly over barbecue sauce, top with onion mixture, and sprinkle evenly with cheese.

Bake at 400° for 8 to 10 minutes or until cheese melts. Garnish, if desired. Serve with extra sauce for dipping. **Makes** 6 servings.

Quick 'n' Easy Barbecue Chicken Pizza

Prep: 5 min., Cook: 15 min., Other: 15 min.

2 cups chopped cooked chicken
¾ cup barbecue sauce
1 (14-oz.) package prebaked Italian pizza crust (we tested with Boboli)
1 cup (4 oz.) shredded mozzarella cheese
¼ medium-size red onion, thinly sliced
2 green onions, chopped

Combine chicken and barbecue sauce; let stand 15 minutes.

Place pizza crust on a baking sheet. Spread chicken mixture over pizza crust. Top with remaining ingredients.

Bake at 450° for 15 minutes or until cheese melts.

Makes 4 servings.

Tex-Mex Chicken-and-Bacon Pizza

Prep: 20 min., Bake: 19 min.

1 (13.8-oz.) can refrigerated pizza crust
½ tsp. ground cumin
1 cup black bean-and-corn salsa
1 cup (4 oz.) shredded sharp Cheddar cheese
1 cup diced cooked chicken
4 fully cooked bacon slices, diced
½ red onion, thinly sliced and separated into rings
½ cup diced seeded plum tomatoes
1 cup (4 oz.) shredded four-cheese blend
2 small jalapeño peppers, sliced and seeded
1 ripe avocado
1 lime, halved
Sour cream
Chopped fresh cilantro

Coat a 14-inch pizza pan lightly with cooking spray. Unroll pizza crust; press or pat onto prepared pan. Lightly coat dough with cooking spray; sprinkle with cumin.

Bake at 425° for 7 minutes or just until crust begins to brown. Remove from oven, and reduce oven temperature to 375°.

Spread salsa evenly over crust; sprinkle evenly with Cheddar cheese. Layer with chicken and next 5 ingredients in order listed.

Bake at 375° for 9 to 12 minutes or until cheese melts.

Slice avocado. Squeeze lime over slices. Arrange slices in a spoke design on pizza; dollop with sour cream, and sprinkle evenly with chopped cilantro. **Makes** 6 servings.

Barbecue Baked Catfish
Prep: 20 min., Cook: 12 min.

¾ cup ketchup
¼ cup butter or margarine
1 Tbsp. balsamic vinegar
1 Tbsp. Worcestershire sauce
1 tsp. Dijon mustard
½ tsp. Jamaican jerk seasoning
1 garlic clove, minced
10 (3- to 4-oz.) catfish fillets
⅛ tsp. pepper
Garnish: chopped fresh parsley

Stir together first 7 ingredients in a small saucepan over medium-low heat; cook mixture 10 minutes, stirring occasionally.
Sprinkle catfish with pepper; arrange in an even layer in a lightly greased aluminum foil-lined broiler pan. Pour sauce over catfish.
Bake catfish at 400° for 10 to 12 minutes or until fish flakes with a fork. Garnish, if desired. **Makes** 5 servings.

Barbecue Roasted Salmon
Prep: 10 min., Cook: 12 min., Other: 1 hr.

¼ cup pineapple juice
2 Tbsp. fresh lemon juice
4 (6-oz.) salmon fillets
2 Tbsp. brown sugar
4 tsp. chili powder
2 tsp. grated lemon rind
¾ tsp. ground cumin
½ tsp. salt
¼ tsp. ground cinnamon
Lemon wedges (optional)

Combine first 3 ingredients in a zip-top freezer bag; seal and marinate in refrigerator 1 hour, turning occasionally.
Remove fish from bag; discard marinade. Combine sugar and next 5 ingredients in a bowl. Rub over fish; place in an 11- x 7-inch baking dish coated with cooking spray. Bake at 400° for 12 minutes or until fish flakes easily when tested with a fork. Serve with lemon, if desired. **Makes** 4 servings.

Barbecue Roasted Salmon

Barbecue Shrimp and Cornbread-Stuffed Peppers
Prep: 45 min., Cook: 20 min.

This restaurant-style masterpiece was created by Chef John I. Akhile from the Waverly Grill at the Renaissance Waverly Hotel in Atlanta. He grills his shrimp over medium-high heat for 5 minutes; we broiled them indoors for simplicity while the peppers baked. The recipe is perfect for combining Southern barbecue flavors with a more formal setting, such as a bridal shower.

16 unpeeled, large fresh shrimp
½ tsp. kosher salt, divided
½ tsp. pepper, divided
1 (6-oz.) package Mexican cornbread mix
½ cup diced onion
½ cup diced celery
1 yellow bell pepper, diced
½ cup diced country ham
1 Tbsp. olive oil
½ cup milk
½ cup buttermilk
1 Tbsp. chopped fresh thyme
2 large eggs, lightly beaten
1¼ cups chopped pecans, toasted
8 medium-size red bell peppers
⅓ cup butter or margarine, cut into pieces
1 (8-oz.) bottle barbecue sauce
1 (4-oz.) jar chipotle pepper sauce
Green Bell Pepper Sauce

Peel shrimp, and devein, if desired. Sprinkle evenly with ¼ tsp. salt and ¼ tsp. pepper; cover and chill.
Prepare cornbread according to package directions; cool on a wire rack. Crumble.
Sauté onion and next 3 ingredients in hot oil in a large skillet until vegetables are tender. Reduce heat, and stir in crumbled cornbread, milk, buttermilk, and thyme. Remove from heat, and stir in eggs, pecans, remaining ¼ tsp. salt, and remaining ¼ tsp. pepper.
Cut bell peppers in half crosswise; remove and discard seeds and membranes. Stuff bell pepper shells evenly with cornbread mixture. Top each evenly with butter, and place in a 13- x 9-inch pan.
Bake at 375° for 15 to 20 minutes. Remove from oven, and keep warm.
Meanwhile, stir together barbecue sauce and chipotle pepper sauce. Toss shrimp in sauce mixture; reserve remaining sauce.

Place shrimp on rack coated with cooking spray; place rack in broiler pan. Broil shrimp 5½ inches from heat for 4 minutes or until shrimp turn pink, basting twice. Set aside.
Spoon Green Bell Pepper Sauce onto individual serving plates; place stuffed peppers in center, and top with shrimp. **Makes** 8 servings.

Green Bell Pepper Sauce
Prep: 10 min., Cook: 15 min.

2 green bell peppers, diced
½ medium onion, diced
1½ tsp. minced garlic
1 Tbsp. olive oil
2 cups chicken broth, divided
2 cups loosely packed fresh spinach leaves
1 tsp. salt
1 tsp. pepper

Sauté first 3 ingredients in hot oil in a large saucepan until tender. Add 1 cup chicken broth. Bring to a boil over medium heat; reduce heat, and simmer, stirring occasionally, 7 minutes. Add spinach leaves, and simmer 3 minutes. Remove from heat; cool slightly.
Process bell pepper mixture in a blender until very smooth. Stir in enough remaining chicken broth to reach sauce consistency, if necessary. Pour through a wire-mesh strainer into a bowl, discarding solids; stir in salt and pepper. **Makes** 4 cups.

quick & easy
Cajun-Barbecue Shrimp
Prep: 10 min., Cook: 10 min.

16 unpeeled, jumbo fresh shrimp (1¼ lb.)
½ cup unsalted butter, sliced
¼ cup Worcestershire sauce
3 garlic cloves, chopped
2 Tbsp. lemon juice
1 Tbsp. Creole seasoning
1 Tbsp. coarsely ground pepper
1 lemon, cut into 4 wedges

Stir all ingredients in an ovenproof skillet.
Bake at 450° for 10 minutes or just until shrimp turn pink. Serve with crusty bread. **Makes** 2 servings.

Chuck Roast Barbecue

Prep: 10 min., Cook: 6 hrs.

1 (2- to 2½-lb.) boneless chuck roast, trimmed
2 medium onions, chopped
¾ cup cola soft drink
¼ cup Worcestershire sauce
1 Tbsp. apple cider vinegar
1 tsp. beef bouillon granules
½ tsp. dry mustard
½ tsp. chili powder
¼ tsp. ground red pepper
2 garlic cloves, minced
½ cup ketchup
2 tsp. butter or margarine
6 hamburger buns
Potato chips (optional)
Pickle spears (optional)

Combine roast and chopped onion in a 4-qt. slow cooker.

Combine cola and next 7 ingredients; reserve ½ cup in refrigerator. Pour remaining mixture over roast and onion.

Cover and cook on HIGH 6 hours or until roast is very tender; drain and shred roast in slow cooker. Keep warm.

Combine reserved ½ cup cola mixture, ketchup, and butter in a small saucepan; cook mixture over medium heat, stirring constantly, just until thoroughly heated. Pour over shredded roast, stirring gently.

Spoon onto buns; serve with potato chips and pickle spears, if desired. **Makes** 6 servings.

make ahead
Barbecue Beef Sandwiches
Prep: 10 min., Cook: 7 hrs.

Make your favorite creamy coleslaw to serve with or on these barbecue sandwiches. Freeze leftover meat up to one month.

1 (3½-lb.) eye of round roast, cut in half vertically
2 tsp. salt, divided
2 garlic cloves, pressed
1 (10½-oz.) can condensed beef broth
1 cup ketchup
½ cup firmly packed brown sugar
½ cup lemon juice
3 Tbsp. steak sauce
1 tsp. coarse ground pepper
1 tsp. Worcestershire sauce
12 Kaiser rolls or sandwich buns
Dill pickle slices

Sprinkle beef evenly with 1 tsp. salt.
Stir together remaining 1 tsp. salt, garlic, and next 7 ingredients. Pour half of mixture into a 5½-qt. slow cooker. Place beef in slow cooker, and pour remaining mixture over beef.
Cover and cook on HIGH 7 hours.
Shred beef in slow cooker with 2 forks. Serve on rolls or buns with dill pickle slices. **Makes** 12 servings.

Guinness-Braised Beef Brisket
Prep: 5 min., Cook: 8 hrs.

Tender from gentle cooking, this entrée is a classic preparation made without the usual pot watching. Serve it with grainy, coarse-ground mustard. Use the leftovers in Reuben sandwiches.

2 cups water
1 cup chopped onion
1 cup chopped carrot
1 cup chopped celery
1 cup Guinness stout
⅔ cup packed brown sugar
¼ cup chopped fresh or 1 Tbsp. dried dill
¼ cup tomato paste
1 (14-oz.) can low-sodium beef broth
6 black peppercorns
2 whole cloves
1 (3-lb.) cured corned beef brisket, trimmed

Combine first 11 ingredients in a 5- to 6-qt. slow cooker, stirring until well blended; top with beef. Cover and cook on HIGH 8 hours or until beef is tender. Remove beef; cut diagonally across grain into ¼-inch slices. Discard broth mixture. **Makes** 6 servings.

Knife-and-Fork Barbecued Brisket Sandwiches
Prep: 10 min., Cook: 5 hrs.

2 large onions, thinly sliced
1 (3-lb.) beef brisket
1 tsp. ground pepper
¼ tsp. salt
2 Tbsp. all-purpose flour
1 (12-oz.) bottle chili sauce
½ cup light beer
2 Tbsp. brown sugar
1 Tbsp. prepared horseradish
1 Tbsp. minced garlic (about 6 cloves)
5 submarine rolls, split and toasted

Place half of onion slices in a 4-qt. slow cooker. Trim fat from meat, and cut meat into large pieces to fit in slow cooker; sprinkle with pepper and salt. Dredge meat in flour; place on top of onion, sprinkling with any remaining flour. Add remaining half of onion.
Combine chili sauce and next 4 ingredients in a medium bowl, stirring well. Pour over meat mixture. Cover and cook on HIGH 4 to 5 hours or until meat is tender. Remove brisket, and replace slow cooker cover.
Shred beef with 2 forks; return meat to hot liquid in slow cooker, stirring well. Spoon meat mixture over toasted roll halves. **Makes** 10 servings.

Quick Tip: *Meat shreds easier while it's still warm. Barbecued meat can be refrigerated up to two days; reheat in the microwave to serve.*

Spiced Beef Barbecue

Prep: 15 min., Cook: 9 hrs.

Cinnamon and cloves add an exotic spiciness to the traditional barbecue sandwich. You can freeze leftover meat for later use.

4 lb. beef stew meat, cubed
2 (8-oz.) cans tomato sauce
1 medium onion, chopped
½ cup white vinegar
¼ cup firmly packed brown sugar
2 tsp. salt
1 tsp. minced garlic
1½ tsp. ground cinnamon (optional)
¾ tsp. ground cloves (optional)
12 sandwich buns

Place beef in 5-qt. slow cooker. Combine tomato sauce, next 5 ingredients, and, if desired, cinnamon and cloves; pour over beef. Cover and cook on HIGH 1 hour; reduce heat to LOW and cook 7 to 8 hours.
Remove beef from slow cooker; shred with 2 forks. Return beef to slow cooker, and stir into sauce. Serve on buns. **Makes** 12 servings.

Beef and Pork Barbecue

Prep: 5 min., Cook: 8 hrs.

1½ lb. beef stew meat
1½ lb. lean cubed pork
1 medium-size green bell pepper, chopped
1 small onion, chopped (about 1 cup)
1 (6-oz.) can tomato paste
½ cup firmly packed brown sugar
¼ cup white vinegar
1 Tbsp. chili powder
2 tsp. salt
1 tsp. dry mustard
2 tsp. Worcestershire sauce

Combine all ingredients in a 5-qt. slow cooker. Cover and cook on HIGH 8 hours. Shred meat before serving. **Makes** 6 servings.

Saucy Chipotle Barbecue Pork

Prep: 15 min., Cook: 7 hrs.

2 tsp. dry mustard
1 tsp. salt
½ tsp. ground red pepper
1 (4- to 5-lb.) boneless pork butt roast, cut in half
2 Tbsp. butter
1 large onion, chopped (about 2½ cups)
1 (18-oz.) bottle spicy original barbecue sauce (we tested with KC Masterpiece)
1 (12-oz.) bottle Baja chipotle marinade (we tested with Lawry's)
Garnish: sliced green onions

Rub first 3 ingredients evenly over pork. Melt butter in a large nonstick skillet over medium-high heat.
Add pork; cook 10 minutes or until browned on all sides.
Place onion and pork in a 5-qt. slow cooker. Add barbecue sauce and marinade.
Cover and cook on HIGH 7 hours or until pork is tender and shreds easily.
Remove pork to a large bowl, reserving sauce; shred pork. Stir shredded pork into sauce in slow cooker. Serve as is, over a cheese-topped baked potato, in a sandwich, or over a green salad. Garnish, if desired. **Makes** 8 servings.

3-Ingredient BBQ Pork

Prep: 5 min., Cook: 8 hrs.

This supersimple recipe delivers big flavor with the addition of cola. Serve on buns with slaw or over hot toasted cornbread.

1 (3- to 4-lb.) shoulder pork roast
1 (18-oz.) bottle barbecue sauce (we tested with Kraft Original)
1 (12-oz.) can cola soft drink

Place pork roast in a 6-qt. slow cooker; pour barbecue sauce and cola over roast.
Cover and cook on HIGH 8 hours or until meat is tender and shreds easily. **Makes** 6 servings.

Easy Barbecue Pork Chops
Prep: 10 min., Cook: 4 or 8 hrs.

8 (5-oz.) center-cut pork chops (½ inch thick)
¼ tsp. pepper
½ cup thick-and-spicy honey barbecue sauce
1 (14½-oz.) can stewed tomatoes, undrained
1 (10-oz.) package frozen vegetable seasoning
    blend

Trim fat from chops; sprinkle chops with pepper. Coat a large nonstick skillet with cooking spray; place over medium-high heat until hot.

Add chops, in 2 batches, and cook until browned on both sides.
Coat a 3½- or 4-qt. slow cooker with cooking spray. Place chops in cooker.
Combine barbecue sauce, stewed tomatoes, and frozen vegetable blend, stirring well; pour mixture over chops.
Cover and cook on HIGH 4 hours; or cover and cook on HIGH 1 hour and then on LOW 7 hours. **Makes** 8 servings.

Spicy-Sweet Ribs and Beans
Prep: 30 min., Cook: 6 or 10 hrs., Other: 20 min.

Slow cookers don't brown food, so here we broil the ribs for extra flavor before adding them to the pot. Serve with cornbread and a simple green salad with creamy Italian or Ranch dressing.

2 (16-oz.) cans pinto beans, drained
4 lb. country-style pork ribs, trimmed
1 tsp. garlic powder
½ tsp. salt
½ tsp. pepper
1 medium onion, chopped
1 (10.5-oz.) jar red jalapeño jelly
1 (18-oz.) bottle hickory-flavored barbecue sauce (we tested with Kraft Thick 'n Spicy)
1 tsp. green hot sauce (we tested with Tabasco)

Place beans in a 5-qt. slow cooker; set aside.
Cut ribs apart; sprinkle with garlic powder, salt, and pepper. Place ribs on a roasting pan.
Broil 5½ inches from heat 18 to 20 minutes or until browned, turning once. Add ribs to slow cooker, and sprinkle with onion.
Combine jelly, barbecue sauce, and hot sauce in a saucepan; cook over low heat until jelly melts. Pour over ribs; stir gently.
Cover and cook on HIGH 5 to 6 hours or on LOW 9 to 10 hours.
Remove ribs. Drain bean mixture, reserving sauce. Skim fat from sauce.
Arrange ribs over bean mixture; serve with sauce.
Makes 8 servings.

So-Simple Baby Back Ribs

Prep: 15 min., Cook: 8 hrs.

4 lb. pork back ribs
1 (18-oz.) bottle honey-mustard barbecue sauce

Cut ribs to fit in a 6-qt. slow cooker. Pour sauce over ribs; cover and cook on HIGH 8 hours or until tender. **Makes** 4 to 6 servings.

editor's favorite • make ahead
Country-Style Barbecue Ribs

Prep: 15 min., Cook: 7 hrs.

Put these on to cook before you leave for work, or cook them overnight and refrigerate until dinnertime. If you reheat in the microwave, use 50% power.

4 lb. bone-in country-style pork ribs
2 tsp. salt, divided
1 medium onion, chopped
1 cup firmly packed light brown sugar
1 cup apple butter
1 cup ketchup
½ cup lemon juice
½ cup orange juice
1 Tbsp. steak sauce (we tested with A.1. Steak Sauce)
1 tsp. coarse ground pepper
1 tsp. minced garlic
½ tsp. Worcestershire sauce

Cut ribs apart, if necessary, and trim; sprinkle 1 tsp. salt evenly over ribs, and set aside.
Stir together remaining 1 tsp. salt, chopped onion, and remaining 9 ingredients until blended. Pour half of mixture into a 5-qt. slow cooker. Place ribs in slow cooker; pour remaining mixture over ribs.
Cover and cook on HIGH 6 to 7 hours. **Makes** 6 to 8 servings.

Debate Barbecue Sandwiches

Prep: 8 min., Cook: 8 hrs.

A Test Kitchen staffer reports that his mother-in-law sold these at his debate team meetings to pay for his travel.

1 (3-lb.) boneless pork loin roast, trimmed
1 cup water
1 (18-oz.) bottle barbecue sauce
¼ cup firmly packed brown sugar
2 Tbsp. Worcestershire sauce
1 to 2 Tbsp. hot sauce
1 tsp. salt
1 tsp. pepper
Hamburger buns
Coleslaw

Place roast in a 4-qt. slow cooker; add 1 cup water. **Cover** and cook on HIGH 7 hours or until tender; shred meat with a fork. Add barbecue sauce and next 5 ingredients. Reduce to LOW; cook, covered, 1 hour. Serve on buns with coleslaw. **Makes** 20 servings.

Shredded Barbecue Chicken

Prep: 22 min., Cook: 7 hrs.

1½ lb. skinned and boned chicken thighs
1 Tbsp. olive oil
1 cup ketchup
¼ cup dark brown sugar
1 Tbsp. Worcestershire sauce
1 Tbsp. cider vinegar
1 Tbsp. yellow mustard
1 tsp. ground red pepper
½ tsp. garlic salt
6 hamburger buns
Dill pickle slices

Brown chicken 4 minutes on each side in 1 Tbsp. hot oil in a large skillet over medium-high heat. Remove from heat, and place in a 4-qt. slow cooker. Combine ketchup and next 6 ingredients. Pour over chicken. **Cover** and cook on HIGH 1 hour. Reduce heat to LOW, and cook 5 to 6 hours. Remove chicken from sauce; shred chicken. Stir shredded chicken into sauce. **Spoon** mixture evenly onto buns, and top with pickle slices. **Makes** 6 servings.

Spicy Pickled Okra,
page 202

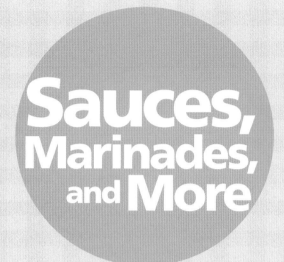

Sauces, Marinades, and More

Every barbecuer depends on a great
collection of sauces and marinades.
Whether you favor sweet or tangy
flavors for basting, marinating, and
dipping, you'll find a complement
here. Condiments, such as pickles
and relishes, continue the
play on flavors.

quick & easy
Thick 'n' Sweet Barbecue Sauce
Prep: 8 min., Cook: 20 min.

½ cup chopped onion
1 garlic clove, minced
¼ cup vegetable oil
1 (8-oz.) can tomato sauce
¼ cup firmly packed brown sugar
1½ tsp. grated lemon rind
¼ cup fresh lemon juice
2 Tbsp. Worcestershire sauce
2 Tbsp. prepared mustard
1 Tbsp. chopped fresh parsley

Cook onion and garlic in oil in a medium skillet over medium-high heat, stirring constantly, until tender. Add tomato sauce and remaining ingredients. Bring to a boil; reduce heat, and simmer 20 minutes or until thickened, stirring often. Use as a basting sauce for burgers, chicken, or ribs. **Makes** 1½ cups.

editor's favorite • quick & easy
Sweet and Simple Barbecue Sauce
Prep: 3 min., Cook: 6 min.

2 garlic cloves, crushed
2 Tbsp. butter or margarine, melted
1 cup ketchup
1 cup water
¾ cup chili sauce
¼ cup firmly packed brown sugar
2 Tbsp. prepared mustard
2 Tbsp. Worcestershire sauce
1½ tsp. celery seeds
½ tsp. salt
2 dashes of hot sauce

Sauté garlic in butter 4 to 5 minutes in a saucepan. Add ketchup and remaining ingredients; bring to a boil. Use to baste pork or chicken during cooking. **Makes** 3½ cups.

quick & easy
Honey-Barbecue Sauce
Prep: 5 min., Cook: 5 min.

Bold, distinct gallberry honey holds its own in this zesty sauce.

2 cups ketchup
½ cup white vinegar
½ cup honey (we tested with gallberry honey)
½ cup water
2 tsp. dried crushed green pepper
1 Tbsp. minced onion
2 Tbsp. Worcestershire sauce
¼ tsp. ground black pepper
Dash of garlic powder
Dash of ground red pepper

Bring all ingredients to a boil in a large saucepan over medium-high heat, stirring often. Serve with pork or poultry. **Makes** 3½ cups.

GOOD AND STICKY

Molasses, the cooked-down syrup from sugarcane or sugar beets, adds the characteristic flavor to gingerbread. This sweet syrup, with its acidic taste, also pertly flavors savory sauces and meat glazes like the two sauces that follow.

Citrus-Spiced Barbecue Sauce

Prep: 5 min., Cook: 40 min.

The sweet, citrusy twang of this sauce pairs well with grilled shrimp, poultry, or pork ribs.

1 medium onion, chopped
2 Tbsp. grated orange rind
½ cup molasses
½ cup ketchup
⅓ cup fresh orange juice
2 Tbsp. olive oil
1 Tbsp. white vinegar
1 Tbsp. steak sauce
½ tsp. Worcestershire sauce
½ tsp. prepared mustard
¼ tsp. garlic powder
¼ tsp. salt
¼ tsp. ground red pepper
¼ tsp. hot sauce
⅛ tsp. ground cloves
¼ cup bourbon

Cook first 15 ingredients in a medium saucepan over low heat 30 minutes. Add bourbon, and simmer 10 minutes. **Makes** about 2 cups.

Maple-Molasses Barbecue Sauce

Prep: 10 min., Cook: 10 min.

½ cup finely chopped onion
2 garlic cloves, minced
2 Tbsp. vegetable oil
1 Tbsp. cornstarch
½ cup maple syrup
½ cup water
¼ cup soy sauce
¼ cup molasses
3 Tbsp. cider vinegar
1 tsp. dried crushed red pepper
1 tsp. peeled, minced fresh ginger
¼ cup creamy peanut butter

Sauté onion and garlic in hot oil in a medium saucepan 3 minutes or until tender.
Combine cornstarch and next 7 ingredients; stir well. Add to onion mixture; bring to a boil.
Cook 3 minutes, stirring frequently. Add peanut butter; cook, stirring constantly, 2 minutes or until peanut butter melts. **Makes** 1¾ cups.

CRAZY FOR COLA

Since it came on the market in 1886, Coca-Cola® has been a thirst cure. But this fizzy drink is good for more than quenching thirsts—from flavoring sauces to salads, dinner to dessert. And it's especially good in the next 3 sauces.

Smoky Sweet Barbecue Sauce

Prep: 5 min., Cook: 30 min.

2 cups Worcestershire sauce
1¼ cups ketchup
1 cup cola soft drink
½ cup butter or margarine
1½ Tbsp. sugar
1 Tbsp. salt
2 tsp. freshly ground pepper

Combine all ingredients in a medium saucepan. Bring to a boil; reduce heat, and simmer, stirring constantly, 30 minutes. **Makes** 3¼ cups.

kids love it • quick & easy

Cola Barbecue Sauce
Prep: 10 min., Cook: 8 min.

This recipe was adapted from grillmaster Steven Raichlen's version in his book **Beer-Can Chicken**—*a necessary pairing for Basic Beer-Can Chicken (page 123).*

1 Tbsp. butter
½ small onion, minced
1 Tbsp. minced fresh ginger
1 garlic clove, minced
¾ cup cola soft drink
¾ cup ketchup
½ tsp. grated lemon rind
2 Tbsp. fresh lemon juice
2 Tbsp. Worcestershire sauce

2 Tbsp. steak sauce (we tested with A.1.)
½ tsp. liquid smoke
½ tsp. pepper
Salt to taste

Melt butter in a heavy saucepan over medium heat. Add onion, ginger, and garlic; sauté 3 minutes or until tender.
Stir in cola soft drink; bring mixture to a boil. Stir in ketchup and remaining ingredients; bring to a boil. Reduce heat, and simmer 5 minutes. Serve with poultry. **Makes** about 1½ cups.

Combine all ingredients in a 1-qt. microwave-safe measuring cup, and stir well. Cover with wax paper. Microwave at HIGH 6 minutes or until mixture comes to a boil, stirring after 3 minutes. Use for basting chicken, beef, or pork while cooking. **Makes** 2½ cups.

editor's favorite
Sweet-and-Tangy Barbecue Sauce
Prep: 5 min., Cook: 1 hr.

Vinegar, chili sauce, and red pepper heat things up in this sweet cola-based barbecue sauce.

1 large onion, finely chopped
1 tsp. vegetable oil
¾ cup cola soft drink
¾ cup chili sauce
1 Tbsp. brown sugar
½ tsp. salt
1 Tbsp. dry mustard
1 Tbsp. paprika
⅛ tsp. ground red pepper
2 Tbsp. white vinegar

Cook onion in oil in a large saucepan over low heat, stirring often, 15 minutes or until onion is caramel-colored. Stir in cola and remaining ingredients. Bring to a boil over medium heat. Cover, reduce heat, and simmer, stirring occasionally, 45 minutes. Serve with beef or pork. **Makes** 2 cups.

make ahead • quick & easy
Fiery-Sweet Barbecue Sauce
Prep: 5 min., Cook: 6 min.

Using low-sugar marmalade helps prevent flare-ups on the grill.

1 cup low-sugar orange marmalade
1 cup ketchup
¼ cup cider vinegar
1 Tbsp. soy sauce
¾ tsp. celery seeds
½ tsp. ground red pepper

quick & easy
Big "D" Barbecue Sauce
Prep: 10 min., Cook: 20 min.

This barbecue sauce is so darn good that it will become a permanent condiment in your refrigerator. Make an extra batch, and store in the refrigerator in an airtight container up to three weeks.

2 Tbsp. butter
1 Tbsp. olive oil
1 medium onion, finely chopped
½ green bell pepper, finely chopped
4 garlic cloves, minced
3 medium jalapeño peppers, seeded and minced
1 cup firmly packed brown sugar
1 cup cider vinegar
1 cup chili sauce
1 cup bottled barbecue sauce
1 Tbsp. mustard powder
1 Tbsp. paprika
3 Tbsp. fresh lemon juice
2 Tbsp. Worcestershire sauce
2 Tbsp. hot sauce
2 Tbsp. molasses
¼ tsp. salt

Melt butter with oil in a large Dutch oven over medium heat.
Add onion and next 3 ingredients, and sauté 5 to 6 minutes or until onion is tender.
Stir in brown sugar and remaining ingredients; bring to a boil. Reduce heat to medium-low, and simmer 10 minutes. Pour mixture through a wire-mesh strainer into a bowl, discarding solids. Serve with beef or pork. **Makes** about 3½ cups.

Tangy Sorghum Barbecue Sauce
Prep: 5 min., Cook: 10 min.

For a flavorful glaze, brush this sauce on ribs or pork chops during the last 15 minutes of cooking to prevent it from burning.

1 (8-oz.) can tomato sauce
¾ cup steak sauce
½ to ¾ cup sorghum
¼ cup ketchup
¼ cup lemon juice
2 Tbsp. brown sugar
2 Tbsp. Worcestershire sauce
2 to 4 dashes of hot sauce
Dash of seasoned salt
2 Tbsp. pineapple marmalade (optional)

Cook first 9 ingredients and, if desired, marmalade in a medium saucepan over low heat, stirring occasionally, 10 minutes or until thoroughly heated. Serve with pork or chicken. **Makes** about 3 cups.

Spiced Barbecue Sauce

Prep: 15 min.; Cook: 1 hr., 6 min.

2 Tbsp. vegetable oil
1 medium onion, chopped
4 garlic cloves, halved
1½ cups ketchup
1 cup fresh orange juice
½ cup water
⅓ cup fresh lemon juice
⅓ cup red wine vinegar
¼ cup firmly packed dark brown sugar
¼ cup honey
3 Tbsp. finely chopped crystallized ginger
2 Tbsp. chili powder
1 Tbsp. ground coriander
1 Tbsp. dry mustard
1 Tbsp. Worcestershire sauce
2 Tbsp. liquid smoke
2 Tbsp. dark molasses
1 tsp. salt
¼ tsp. hot sauce

Heat oil in a large saucepan over medium heat; add onion, and cook 5 minutes or until golden, stirring occasionally. Add garlic; cook 1 minute. Stir in ketchup and remaining ingredients; bring to a boil. Reduce heat, and simmer, uncovered, 1 hour or until sauce is thickened, stirring often. Pour mixture through a wire-mesh strainer into a container, discarding onion, garlic, and ginger. Cool to room temperature. Serve with pork or chicken. **Makes** 3¾ cups.

make ahead • quick & easy
Peppery Barbecue Sauce

Prep: 10 min.

2 cups firmly packed brown sugar
2 Tbsp. pepper
1 to 1½ tsp. salt
4 garlic cloves, minced
4 cups ketchup
1 cup white vinegar
2 Tbsp. vegetable oil
2 Tbsp. prepared mustard
2 Tbsp. Worcestershire sauce
2 Tbsp. hot sauce

Stir together all ingredients. Store in refrigerator up to 2 weeks. Serve with beef or pork. **Makes** 6 cups.

quick & easy
Peach of the Old South Barbecue Sauce for Ribs

Prep: 4 min., Cook: 20 min.

Bourbon lends a distinctive flavor to this peach-sweetened barbecue sauce.

2 cups tomato puree
½ cup fresh lemon juice
½ cup sweetened bourbon
½ cup peach preserves
½ cup Dijon mustard
¼ cup firmly packed light brown sugar
2 Tbsp. hot sauce
1 tsp. salt

Combine all ingredients in a saucepan; stir well. Bring to a boil; cover, reduce heat, and simmer 20 minutes, stirring occasionally. Use as a basting sauce for ribs. **Makes** 4 cups.

quick & easy
Apple Barbecue Sauce

Prep: 4 min., Cook: 25 min.

Apple jelly teams with vinegar and hot sauce to conjure up tangy-sweet flavors especially tasty on smoked pork.

½ cup apple jelly
1 (8-oz.) can tomato sauce
¼ cup white vinegar
2 Tbsp. light brown sugar
2 Tbsp. water
1 tsp. hot sauce

Bring all ingredients to a boil in a saucepan, stirring until smooth. Reduce heat, and simmer, stirring occasionally, 20 to 25 minutes. **Makes** 1⅓ cups.

Ranch Barbecue Sauce
Prep: 5 min., Cook: 20 min.

You can vary the flavor this recipe takes on by the brand of bottled sauce you select.

1 (18-oz.) bottle barbecue sauce (we tested with Stubb's Original)
1 (1-oz.) envelope Ranch dressing mix
¼ cup honey
½ tsp. dry mustard

Stir together all ingredients in a saucepan over medium-high heat; bring to a boil. Reduce heat, and simmer, stirring occasionally, 20 minutes. Serve with poultry. **Makes** about 1¼ cups.

Chipotle Barbecue Sauce
Prep: 5 min.

Fiery peppers crank up the heat in this simple sauce.

2 (18-oz.) bottles smoke-flavor barbecue sauce
6 Tbsp. fresh lime juice (about 2 limes)
2 Tbsp. minced garlic
3 canned chipotle peppers in adobo sauce, undrained and chopped
1 Tbsp. adobo sauce from can

Combine all ingredients, stirring well. Serve with beef or pork. **Makes** 3½ cups.

VINEGAR CONTROVERSY

Vinegar sauces rule in North Carolina. The following two vinegar-based sauces lend a taste of Lexington-style and Eastern-style pig pickin'.

Cider Vinegar Barbecue Sauce
Prep: 10 min., Cook: 7 min.

This sauce is often referred to as Lexington Style Dip, but there are many variations. Most folks can't resist adding their own touch by adjusting the sugar or spice. Bob Garner, author of **North Carolina Barbecue: Flavored by Time,** *likes to combine the best of eastern and western Carolina-style barbecue in this sweet vinegar-based sauce.*

1½ cups cider vinegar
⅓ cup firmly packed brown sugar
¼ cup ketchup
1 Tbsp. hot sauce (we tested with Texas Pete)
1 tsp. browning-and-seasoning sauce (we tested with Kitchen Bouquet)
½ tsp. salt
½ tsp. onion powder
½ tsp. pepper
½ tsp. Worcestershire sauce

Stir together all ingredients in a saucepan; cook over medium heat, stirring constantly, 7 minutes or until sugar dissolves. Serve with North Carolina Smoked Pork Shoulder (page 107). **Makes** 2 cups.

Zesty Barbecue Sauce
Prep: 8 min., Cook: 5 min.

½ cup lemon juice
⅓ cup cider vinegar
¼ cup water
¼ cup tomato juice
4 tsp. sugar
1 tsp. dry mustard
1 tsp. hot sauce
½ tsp. salt
½ tsp. onion powder
½ tsp. paprika
½ tsp. ground red pepper
½ tsp. black pepper
⅛ tsp. garlic powder
⅛ tsp. dried oregano

Combine all ingredients in a medium saucepan. Bring mixture to a boil.
Transfer mixture to a serving container; cover and chill. Serve with meat or poultry. **Makes** 1¼ cups.

kids love it • quick & easy
Honey-Mustard Barbecue Sauce
Prep: 15 min., Cook: 18 min.

This is a thick, hearty sauce; if you prefer a thinner sauce, add ¼ cup water.

1 bacon slice, diced
1 small onion, diced
1 garlic clove, minced
1 cup cider vinegar
¾ cup prepared mustard
¼ cup firmly packed brown sugar
¼ cup honey
1 tsp. black pepper
1 tsp. Worcestershire sauce
¼ tsp. ground red pepper

Cook bacon in a medium saucepan until crisp; remove bacon, and drain on paper towels, reserving drippings in saucepan.
Sauté onion and garlic in hot drippings about 3 minutes or until tender. Stir in bacon, vinegar, and remaining ingredients; bring to a boil. Reduce heat, and simmer, stirring occasionally, 10 minutes. Serve with meat or poultry. **Makes** 1½ cups.

quick & easy
Spicy-Sweet Mustard Sauce
Prep: 10 min, Cook: 20 min.

Smoked pork or grilled bratwursts welcome a gracious helping of this mustardy concoction.

½ cup butter or margarine
2 beef bouillon cubes
3 egg yolks, lightly beaten
½ cup sugar
½ cup prepared mustard
¼ cup cider vinegar
1 tsp. salt

Combine butter and bouillon cubes in top of a double boiler. Place over simmering water, and cook, whisking constantly, until butter melts and bouillon cubes dissolve. Gradually whisk in beaten egg yolks. Add sugar and remaining ingredients; cook, whisking often, 20 minutes. Cover and chill. **Makes** 1½ cups.

66 "'Low and slow' is the motto of North Carolina pitmaster Jim 'Trim' Tabb when it comes to barbecue. His succulent pork, Tabb's Barbecue Pork (page 110), is out of this world when drizzled with Honey-Mustard Barbecue Sauce, a South Carolina specialty." 99

—Scott Jones, *Southern Living* Staff

White Barbecue Sauce

Prep: 5 min.

1½ cups mayonnaise
¼ cup water
¼ cup white wine vinegar
1 Tbsp. coarsely ground pepper
1 Tbsp. Creole mustard
1 tsp. salt
1 tsp. sugar
2 garlic cloves, minced
2 tsp. prepared horseradish

Whisk together all ingredients until blended. Serve with chicken. **Makes** 2 cups.

ORIGIN OF WHITE SAUCE

The color spectrum of barbecue sauce is rich and diverse—one reason why sampling different styles from all over the South is so much fun and so delicious. Ask the average person the color of his or her favorite sauce, and you'll probably get an answer such as brick red, mahogany, or caramel.

Pose the same question to a resident of North Alabama, though, and you're sure to get only one answer: white.

"It's the only sauce we know here, because it's what everyone grows up on," says world barbecue champion Chris Lilly of Big Bob Gibson Bar-B-Q in Decatur, Alabama. Bob Gibson is credited with concocting white sauce back in 1925.

Today, this tangy, mayonnaise-based condiment, traditionally used to dress chicken, is as synonymous with the state of Alabama as legendary football coach Paul "Bear" Bryant. "We marinate with it, use it to baste, plus we use it as an all-purpose table sauce," explains Chris.

—Scott Jones, *Southern Living* Staff

SASSY SAUCES

Don't be afraid to sample unique flavors when you journey to the smoker. Try these playful flavors for your next barbecue.

Asian Barbecue Sauce

Prep: 3 min., Cook: 5 min.

1 cup ketchup
2 Tbsp. brown sugar
2 Tbsp. red wine vinegar
1 tsp. dry hot mustard
1 large garlic clove, minced
2 tsp. chili puree with garlic

Combine first 5 ingredients in a small saucepan. Bring to a boil; remove from heat. Stir in chili puree. Use as a basting sauce for chicken, beef, or pork. **Makes** 1⅓ cups.

Tomatillo Barbecue Sauce

Prep: 15 min., Cook: 2 hrs.

2½ lb. green tomatoes, coarsely chopped
1½ lb. tomatillos, husked and coarsely chopped
2 garlic cloves, pressed
½ to 1 cup sugar
1 cup white vinegar
1 large sweet onion, coarsely chopped (about 1½ cups)
1 Tbsp. dry mustard
1 tsp. salt
½ tsp. dried crushed red pepper

Cook all ingredients in a large stockpot over medium-low heat 2 hours or until green tomatoes and tomatillos are tender. Cool.
Process mixture, in batches, in a food processor or blender until smooth, stopping to scrape down sides. Serve over grilled chicken, fish, or shrimp. **Makes** 3 cups.

Tomatillo Sauce

Prep: 10 min., Cook: 20 min., Other: 8 hrs.
(pictured on page 191)

1¼ lb. small tomatillos (about 30)
1 medium onion, chopped
1 Tbsp. olive oil
4 tsp. minced garlic
1 cup water
1 jalapeño pepper, minced
½ cup chopped fresh cilantro
1 Tbsp. fresh lime juice
1 tsp. salt

Remove husks from tomatillos; wash thoroughly.
Sauté onion in hot olive oil in a large saucepan over medium-high heat 5 minutes or until softened. Add garlic, and sauté 1 minute. Stir in tomatillos, 1 cup water, and jalapeño; bring to a boil. Reduce heat to medium; cover and simmer, stirring occasionally, 10 to 12 minutes or until tomatillos are softened. Remove from heat; cool slightly.
Process tomatillo mixture, cilantro, lime juice, and salt in a food processor or blender until smooth. Cover; chill at least 8 hours. Serve with chicken, fish, or shrimp. **Makes** about 3½ cups.

kids love it • quick & easy
Blueberry-Balsamic Barbecue Sauce

Prep: 5 min., Cook: 15 min.

Try this sweet and tangy sauce the next time you grill chicken, pork, or tuna. If fresh blueberries aren't available, use 2 cups thawed frozen blueberries.

2 cups fresh blueberries
¼ cup balsamic vinegar
3 Tbsp. sugar
3 Tbsp. ketchup
½ tsp. garlic powder
¼ tsp. salt

Place all ingredients in a saucepan. Bring to a boil; reduce heat, and simmer 15 minutes or until slightly thick. Remove from heat; cool. Place blueberry mixture in a blender; process until smooth. **Makes** about 1½ cups.

Blueberry Barbecue Sauce

Prep: 15 min., Cook: 15 min.

The combination of fresh blueberries with mustard and butter makes this sauce delectable on chicken or pork.

2 Tbsp. minced onion
1½ tsp. chopped fresh jalapeño pepper
1½ tsp. olive oil
1 cup fresh blueberries
2 Tbsp. rice vinegar
2 Tbsp. ketchup
1½ Tbsp. brown sugar
1½ Tbsp. Dijon mustard
½ tsp. hot sauce
2 Tbsp. unsalted butter
⅛ tsp. salt
⅛ tsp. freshly ground pepper

Cook onion and jalapeño pepper in hot oil in a medium saucepan over medium-high heat, stirring constantly, until tender. Add blueberries and next 5 ingredients; bring to a boil. Reduce heat, and simmer, uncovered, 15 minutes, stirring often.
Pour blueberry mixture into container of an electric blender; process until smooth, stopping once to scrape down sides. Pour blueberry mixture through a wire-mesh strainer into a small saucepan, pressing against strainer with back of a spoon to press out any remaining liquid.
Add butter, salt, and pepper to blueberry mixture; cook over medium heat until butter melts, stirring occasionally. **Makes** ⅔ cup.

Raspberry Barbecue Sauce

Prep: 5 min., Cook: 7 min.

1 (10-oz.) jar seedless raspberry preserves
⅓ cup bottled barbecue sauce (we tested with KC Masterpiece)
2 Tbsp. raspberry vinegar
2 Tbsp. Dijon mustard
1½ tsp. hot sauce

Bring first 4 ingredients to a boil in a small saucepan. Reduce heat to medium, and cook 2 minutes or until slightly thickened. Stir in hot sauce. Serve with pork or chicken. **Makes** 1 cup.

Fragrant Ginger-Hot Pepper Sauce
Prep: 5 min., Cook: 5 min.

A little of this mighty Asian seasoning blend goes a long way. Serve with smoked pork or chicken.

1 Tbsp. vegetable oil
¼ cup minced peeled fresh ginger
2 tsp. dried crushed red pepper
2 large garlic cloves, minced
¼ cup chopped fresh cilantro
¼ cup minced green onions
2½ Tbsp. water
½ tsp. salt

Heat vegetable oil in a small skillet over medium heat. Add minced fresh ginger, red pepper, and garlic; sauté 2 minutes. Remove from heat; spoon into a small bowl, and stir in remaining ingredients. **Makes** ½ cup.

Mango-Pineapple Hot Sauce
Prep: 10 min., Cook: 30 min., Other: 1 hr.

This potent blend offers a sweet-hot finish for smoked fish and pork. Or to make a quick appetizer for a last-minute barbecue, pour some of the sauce over a block of cream cheese and serve with assorted crackers. Always handle habaneros with kitchen gloves. If you prefer a milder finish, use only one habanero.

1 cup mango nectar
1 cup pineapple juice
5 Tbsp. cider vinegar
4 garlic cloves, minced
1 to 2 habanero peppers, seeded and chopped
1¼ tsp. salt
1 tsp. ground turmeric

Stir together all ingredients in a 1-qt. saucepan over medium-high heat; bring to a boil, stirring often. Cover, reduce heat to low, and simmer 30 minutes. Remove pan from heat, and let stand at room temperature 1 hour or until completely cool. **Makes** 1⅔ cups.

Smoky Hot Sauce
Prep: 10 min., Cook: 35 min., Other: 8 hrs.

1 large onion, chopped
1 Tbsp. olive oil
4 tsp. minced garlic
5 medium tomatoes, coarsely chopped (about 1½ lb.)
¾ cup water
1 chicken bouillon cube
1 canned chipotle pepper in adobo sauce
2 Tbsp. adobo sauce from can
1 Tbsp. balsamic vinegar
1 tsp. hot sauce
¼ tsp. salt

Sauté onion in hot oil in a large saucepan over medium-high heat 5 minutes or until softened. Add garlic; sauté 1 minute. Stir in tomatoes and remaining ingredients. Bring to a boil. Reduce heat; simmer, stirring occasionally, 25 minutes. Remove from heat; cool slightly.
Remove chipotle pepper, if desired. Process tomato mixture in a food processor or blender until smooth. **Cover** and chill at least 8 hours. Serve with chicken or fish. **Makes** about 3 cups.

Herbed Lemon Barbecue Sauce
Prep: 5 min.

¾ cup lemon juice
2 garlic cloves, peeled
1 Tbsp. onion powder
1½ tsp. salt
1½ tsp. paprika
1½ cups vegetable oil
1 Tbsp. dried basil
1 tsp. dried thyme, crushed

Process first 5 ingredients in a blender 1 minute. With blender on high, add oil in a slow, steady stream; process 1 minute. Add basil and thyme; process on low 30 seconds. Serve with fish or chicken. **Makes** 2 cups.

Smoky Hot Sauce,
at left

Tomatillo Sauce,
page 189

A rub is a blend of seasonings—usually dried herbs and spices—applied to meat, seafood, or poultry before cooking.

■ A rub is often left on the food for a while before cooking to allow the flavors to penetrate.

■ When a small amount of liquid—such as olive oil or crushed garlic with its juice—is added to a rub, it becomes a wet rub paste. A wet rub is easy to apply to meat because it clings well to the food.

■ For maximum flavor, you can apply a dry rub or wet rub to food up to 24 hours before cooking.

■ Dry rubs can be stored in an airtight container in a cool, dry place up to 6 months.

■ Wet rubs can be stored in an airtight container in the refrigerator up to 1 week.

Garlic-Pepper Brisket Rub
Prep: 5 min.

¼ cup kosher salt
¼ cup sugar
¼ cup black pepper
¾ cup paprika
2 Tbsp. garlic powder
2 Tbsp. garlic salt
2 Tbsp. onion powder
2 Tbsp. chili powder
2 tsp. ground red pepper

Combine all ingredients. Store in an airtight container up to 6 months. **Makes** 2 cups.

All-Purpose Barbecue Rub
Prep: 5 min.

¼ cup coarse salt
¼ cup dark brown sugar
¼ cup sweet paprika
2 Tbsp. pepper

Combine all ingredients. Store in an airtight jar, away from heat, up to 6 months. **Makes** about ¾ cup.

Sweet 'n' Spicy Barbecue Rub
Prep: 10 min.

1¼ cups firmly packed dark brown sugar
⅓ cup kosher salt
¼ cup granulated garlic
¼ cup paprika
1 Tbsp. chili powder
1 Tbsp. ground red pepper
1 Tbsp. ground cumin
1 Tbsp. lemon pepper
1 Tbsp. onion powder
2 tsp. dry mustard
2 tsp. ground black pepper
1 tsp. ground cinnamon

Combine all ingredients. Store in an airtight container up to 6 months. **Makes** about 2½ cups.

make ahead
Southwestern Spice Blend
Prep: 5 min.

1 Tbsp. salt
2 tsp. garlic powder
2 tsp. chili powder
2 tsp. ground cumin
2 tsp. pepper
½ tsp. unsweetened cocoa

Combine all ingredients. Store in airtight container up to 6 months. Use as a meat or poultry rub or to flavor chilis and soups. **Makes** ¼ cup.

Chipotle Rub
Prep: 5 min.

2 to 3 canned chipotle peppers in adobo sauce
¼ cup firmly packed brown sugar
1 Tbsp. chili powder
1 tsp. salt

Chop chipotle peppers; stir together peppers, brown sugar, chili powder, and salt to form a paste. Store in refrigerator up to a week. **Makes** ⅓ cup.

A marinade is a seasoned liquid added to uncooked food for flavor and sometimes tenderizing. Most contain an acid—such as wine, citrus juice, or vinegar—that helps tenderize meat. The more acid a recipe contains, the more tenderizing ability it has.

■ Marinate food in such nonmetal containers as glass dishes, plastic bowls, or heavy-duty plastic bags that won't react with acidic components in the marinade.

■ Allow about ½ cup marinade for every pound of meat, poultry, or seafood.

■ Always marinate food, covered, in the refrigerator, turning occasionally.

■ To simply add flavor, marinate most foods 30 minutes to 2 hours.

■ To tenderize meat, marinating 8 hours is ideal, but you can marinate large cuts of meat up to 24 hours with good results. Meat that marinates longer than that can become mushy.

■ Never reuse a marinade in which raw meat, fish, or poultry has been soaked until you first bring it to a boil. This kills any bacteria that may have been transferred from the raw food.

Beer Marinade

Prep: 5 min.

Red beer is actually a medium dark beer or ale. The name comes from the reddish tint it gets from aging in redwood barrels.

1 (12-oz.) can red beer
¼ cup ketchup
2 tsp. dry mustard
¼ tsp. salt
¼ tsp. pepper
1 garlic clove, crushed

Combine all ingredients; stir well. Use to marinate chicken or pork. **Makes** 1¾ cups.

Horseradish Marinade

Prep: 5 min.

¼ cup dry red wine
2 Tbsp. minced fresh thyme
2 Tbsp. Worcestershire sauce
2 Tbsp. red wine vinegar
2 Tbsp. prepared horseradish
2 Tbsp. tomato paste
1½ tsp. freshly ground pepper
4 garlic cloves, minced

Combine all ingredients; stir well. Use to marinate beef. **Makes** ¾ cup.

Browned Garlic and Burgundy Marinade

Prep: 10 min., Cook: 5 min.

1 Tbsp. olive oil
3 garlic cloves, thinly sliced
¾ cup dry red wine
3 Tbsp. soy sauce
1 tsp. dried tarragon

Heat oil in a small nonstick skillet over medium-high heat until hot. Add garlic; sauté 3 minutes or until brown. Remove from heat; stir in wine, soy sauce, and tarragon. Use to marinate beef. **Makes** 1 cup.

Red Wine-Mustard Marinade

Prep: 5 min.

½ cup dry red wine
¼ cup finely chopped shallot
3 Tbsp. green peppercorn mustard with white wine
1 Tbsp. freshly ground pepper
1 Tbsp. balsamic vinegar
1½ tsp. chopped fresh rosemary
1 large garlic clove, minced

Combine all ingredients; stir well. Use to marinate beef, pork, or lamb. **Makes** 1 cup.

Green Tomato Pickles

Green Tomato Pickles

Prep: 15 min.; Cook: 30 min.; Other: 6 hrs., 10 min.

5 lb. green tomatoes, chopped
1 large onion, chopped
2 Tbsp. pickling spices
1½ cups firmly packed brown sugar
2 cups cider vinegar (5% acidity)
2 tsp. mustard seeds
2 tsp. whole allspice
2 tsp. celery seeds
1½ tsp. whole cloves
3 cups water

Sprinkle tomato and onion with pickling spices; let stand 4 to 6 hours. Drain and pat dry with paper towels; set aside.

Combine brown sugar and vinegar in a Dutch oven; cook over medium heat, stirring constantly, until sugar dissolves.

Place mustard seeds and next 3 ingredients on 6-inch square of cheesecloth; tie with string. Add spice bag, tomato, onion, and 3 cups water to vinegar mixture. Bring to a boil, stirring constantly; reduce heat, and simmer, stirring occasionally, 25 minutes or until tomato and onion are tender. Remove and discard spice bag.

Pour hot mixture into hot, sterilized jars, filling to ½ inch from top. Remove air bubbles; wipe jar rims. Cover at once with metal lids, and screw on bands.

Process jars in boiling-water bath 10 minutes. **Makes** 7 pt.

Pickled Green Tomatoes

Prep: 30 min., Cook: 5 min., Other: 10 min.

8 cups white vinegar (5% acidity)
4 cups sugar
¼ cup mustard seeds
1 Tbsp. celery seeds
1 tsp. ground turmeric
4 lb. green tomatoes, cut into ¼-inch-thick slices
4 medium onions, sliced
1 medium-size red bell pepper, chopped

Bring first 5 ingredients to a boil in a large saucepan, stirring often. Boil, stirring often, until sugar melts. Remove from heat.

Pack tomato and onion into hot, sterilized jars; top evenly with bell pepper. Cover vegetables with hot syrup, filling to ½ inch from top. Remove air bubbles; wipe jar rims. Cover at once with metal lids, and screw on bands.

Process jars in a boiling-water bath 10 minutes. **Makes** 12 pt.

Refrigerator Squash Pickles

Prep: 15 min., Cook: 5 min., Other: 3 hrs.

⅔ cup salt
3 qt. water
8 cups thinly sliced yellow squash (2½ lb.)
2½ cups sugar
2 cups white vinegar (5% acidity)
2 tsp. mustard seeds
2 sweet onions, thinly sliced
2 green bell peppers, thinly sliced
1 (4-oz.) jar sliced pimiento, drained

Dissolve salt in 3 qt. water in a large bowl; add squash. Submerge squash in water using a plate to hold slices down; cover and let stand 3 hours. Drain.

Bring sugar, vinegar, and mustard seeds to a boil in a large nonaluminum Dutch oven or stockpot, stirring until sugar dissolves. Add squash, onion, bell pepper, and pimiento; return to a boil. Remove from heat, and cool. Store in airtight containers in the refrigerator up to 2 weeks. **Makes** 2 qt.

Pickled Asparagus

Prep: 15 min., Cook: 6 min., Other: 8 hrs.

4 cups white vinegar (5% acidity)
3 cups water
½ cup sugar
¼ cup canning-and-pickling salt
1 Tbsp. dried crushed red pepper
1 Tbsp. pickling spices
3 lb. fresh asparagus (about 3 bunches)
6 fresh dill sprigs
3 garlic cloves

Cook first 6 ingredients in a medium saucepan over medium-high heat about 4 to 6 minutes or until sugar is dissolved. Remove saucepan from stove, and cool mixture completely.
Snap off tough ends of asparagus (Step 1).
Pack 1 bunch asparagus, 2 dill sprigs, and 1 garlic clove into 1 (1-qt.) canning jar; repeat process with 2 remaining jars, asparagus, dill sprigs, and garlic cloves (Step 2).
Pour vinegar mixture evenly into jars (Step 3); seal jars. Chill at least 8 hours; store in refrigerator up to 1 week.
Makes 3 qt.

Pickled Onion and Cucumber

Prep: 25 min., Other: 1 day

5 lb. sweet onions, thinly sliced and separated into rings
8 medium cucumbers, thinly sliced
1 gal. white vinegar (5% acidity)
2 tsp. pepper
1 tsp. salt

Stir together all ingredients in a large bowl; cover and chill 24 hours. Store in the refrigerator up to 2 weeks.
Makes 8 qt.

Pickled Onion Rings

Prep: 20 min., Cook: 10 min., Other: 8 hrs.

4 large white onions, sliced and separated into rings (about 1½ lb.)
6 Tbsp. chopped fresh dill
5 cups white vinegar (5% acidity)
¾ cup water
1 cup sugar
2 Tbsp. canning-and-pickling salt

Combine onions and dill in a large plastic bowl (do not use glass).
Combine vinegar and remaining 3 ingredients in a medium saucepan; bring to a boil over medium-high heat. Remove from heat. Pour hot vinegar mixture over onion rings and dill in bowl; cover and chill at least 8 hours. Store in an airtight container in the refrigerator up to 1 month. Serve with a slotted spoon. **Makes** 3 qt.

FRESH IS BEST

Always start with the freshest and ripest produce available. It's best to begin pickling within 24 hours after fruits and vegetables are picked. This reduces the chance that they will be bruised or scraped, which decreases the quality of the finished pickled product.

Pickled Onion
and Cucumber

Freezer Cucumber Pickles

Prep: 30 min., Other: 2 days

3½ cups thinly sliced cucumber

2 small onions, sliced and separated into rings

1 Tbsp. salt

1 cup sugar

½ cup white vinegar (5% acidity)

3 Tbsp. water

Combine first 3 ingredients in a large bowl; set aside.

Cook sugar, vinegar, and 3 Tbsp. water in a small saucepan over medium heat, stirring until sugar dissolves. Pour over cucumber mixture.

Cover and chill 48 hours.

Spoon into half-pt. jars or freezer containers; seal, label, and freeze pickles up to 6 months. Thaw in the refrigerator before serving; use thawed pickles within a week. **Makes** about 3 pt.

Cucumber Pickle Spears

Prep: 15 min.; Cook: 5 min.; Other: 5 days, 2 hrs.

4 large pickling cucumbers (about 1 lb.), each cut
   lengthwise into 6 spears
2 tsp. salt
3 large fresh dill sprigs
1 garlic clove, halved
1 cup white vinegar (5% acidity)
1 cup water
¼ cup sugar

Place cucumber spears in a large bowl. Sprinkle with 2 tsp. salt; toss gently to coat. Cover and chill 2 hours.

Drain cucumber spears in a colander. Rinse under cold water; drain well. Pack cucumber spears into a wide-mouth 1-qt. jar. Add dill and garlic to jar; set aside.

Combine vinegar, water, and sugar in a small saucepan; bring to a boil, stirring until sugar dissolves. Pour hot liquid over cucumber spears. Cover jar with metal lid, and screw on band. Cool completely. Cover and marinate in refrigerator 5 days before serving. Store in refrigerator up to 1 month.
Makes 24 spears.

Peppery Texas
Freezer Pickles

Peppery Texas Freezer Pickles
Prep: 15 min.; Other: 2 days, 8 hrs.

2 lb. pickling cucumbers, sliced
1 cup chopped fresh cilantro
6 small dried red chile peppers
4 garlic cloves, thinly sliced
1 large sweet onion, sliced
3 cups white vinegar (5% acidity)
1 cup water
⅓ cup sugar
2 Tbsp. canning-and-pickling salt
1 Tbsp. pickling spices

Place first 5 ingredients in a large plastic bowl (do not use glass).
Combine vinegar, 1 cup water, and remaining 3 ingredients in a 4-cup glass measuring cup. Microwave at HIGH 3 minutes; remove from microwave, and stir until sugar dissolves. Pour hot mixture evenly over cucumber mixture. Cover and chill 48 hours.
Spoon evenly into qt. canning jars or freezer containers, leaving ½ inch of room at the top; seal, label, and freeze pickles 8 hours or up to 6 months. Thaw in refrigerator before serving; use thawed pickles within 1 week. **Makes** 3 qt.

Bread-and-Butter Pickles
Prep: 10 min., Cook: 8 min.

1 cup sugar
½ cup white vinegar (5% acidity)
1 tsp. salt
½ tsp. celery seeds
½ tsp. mustard seeds
½ tsp. ground turmeric
3 medium pickling cucumbers, cut into ¼-inch slices (about 3 cups)
3 small onions, thinly sliced (about 2 cups)

Combine first 6 ingredients in a large microwaveable bowl, stirring well. Add cucumber and onion; stir well.
Microwave at HIGH 8 minutes, stirring every 2 minutes. Pack mixture evenly into hot, sterilized jars, filling to ½ inch from top. Cover with metal lids, and screw on bands. Cool completely. Store in the refrigerator up to 1 month. **Makes** 2 pt.

Pickled Black-Eyed Peas
Prep: 15 min., Other: 2 hrs.

2 (16-oz.) cans black-eyed peas, rinsed and drained
⅔ cup vegetable oil
⅓ cup white wine vinegar
1 small onion, diced
1 garlic clove, minced
½ tsp. salt
⅛ tsp. pepper

Stir together all ingredients; cover and chill mixture at least 2 hours. Serve with tortilla chips. **Makes** 5 cups.

Marinated Black-Eyed Peas: Substitute olive oil for vegetable oil and ½ red onion for onion; increase pepper to ½ tsp. Add 1 (16-oz.) can whole kernel corn, drained; 1 jalapeño pepper, minced; and ½ red bell pepper, chopped.

Pickled Sugar Snap Peas
Prep: 20 min., Cook: 5 min., Other: 20 min.

2 (3½-inch) cinnamon sticks
1 to 2 tsp. whole cloves
2½ cups white vinegar (5% acidity)
2½ cups water
½ cup sugar
1 Tbsp. pickling spices
¼ to ½ tsp. ground red pepper
2 lb. fresh sugar snap peas
4 to 6 garlic cloves, thinly sliced

Place cinnamon and cloves in a 4-inch square of cheesecloth; tie with a string.
Bring vinegar and next 4 ingredients to a boil in a large saucepan, stirring often; add spice bag. Cool; remove spice bag.
Pack peas and garlic evenly in hot, sterilized jars. Pour cooled vinegar mixture evenly over pea mixture, filling to ½ inch from top. Remove air bubbles; wipe jar rims. Cover at once with metal lids; screw on bands.
Process jars in a boiling-water bath 20 minutes. **Makes** 2 qt.

Note: To store in refrigerator up to 1 month, omit boiling-water bath.

Dilled Green Beans

Prep: 20 min., Cook: 5 min., Other: 10 min.

2 lb. green beans
7 hot red peppers*
7 garlic cloves, quartered
3½ tsp. mustard seeds
3½ tsp. dill seeds
5 cups white vinegar (5% acidity)
5 cups water
½ cup pickling salt

Pack beans into hot jars, trimming to fit ½ inch from top. Add 1 pepper, 1 garlic clove (quartered), ½ tsp. mustard seeds, and ½ tsp. dill seeds to each jar.
Bring vinegar, 5 cups water, and pickling salt to a boil; pour into each jar, filling to ½ inch from top. Remove air bubbles; wipe jar rims. Cover at once with metal lids, and screw on bands.
Process jars in a boiling-water bath 10 minutes. **Makes** 7 pt.

*Substitute 1¾ tsp. dried crushed red pepper for hot red peppers, if desired. Add ¼ tsp. per jar.

Refrigerator Okra Dills

Prep: 5 min., Cook: 5 min., Other: 3 days

1 lb. small fresh okra
3 small dried red chile peppers
2 garlic cloves, minced
2 Tbsp. fresh celery leaves
1 tsp. dill seeds
1⅓ cups water
⅔ cup white vinegar (5% acidity)
2½ Tbsp. salt

Combine first 5 ingredients in a large bowl.
Bring 1⅓ cups water, white vinegar, and salt to a boil in a small nonaluminum saucepan, stirring until salt dissolves; pour over okra mixture, and cool.
Cover and chill, turning occasionally, 3 days. Serve immediately, or store in an airtight container in the refrigerator up to 2 weeks. **Makes** about 3 pt.

Spicy Pickled Okra

Prep: 10 min., Cook: 4 min.

2½ cups white vinegar (5% acidity)
2 cups water
3 Tbsp. sugar
2 Tbsp. kosher salt
1 tsp. white peppercorns
1 tsp. coriander seeds
1 tsp. fennel seeds
1 tsp. cumin seeds
4 fresh dill sprigs
2 green or red jalapeño peppers, halved lengthwise
1½ lb. small okra pods

Combine first 8 ingredients in a large saucepan; bring to a boil. Cook 1 minute or until sugar and salt dissolve, stirring frequently. Remove from heat; stir in fresh dill sprigs, jalapeños, and okra pods. Cool completely; pour mixture into an airtight container. Cover and chill. **Makes** about 5 cups.

Pickled Shrimp

Prep: 20 min., Other: 12 hrs.

With its mild flavor, shrimp blends well with pickling flavors so popular as a barbecue accompaniment.

5 lb. unpeeled, cooked jumbo shrimp
1 (4-oz.) jar capers, drained
2 medium-size white onions, sliced
1 large red bell pepper, sliced
2 tsp. celery seeds
3 lemons, thinly sliced
2 (0.7-oz.) envelopes Italian dressing mix
½ cup vegetable oil
½ cup cider vinegar
1 Tbsp. prepared horseradish

Peel shrimp, and, if desired, devein.
Layer a 13- x 9-inch baking dish with one-third each of shrimp, capers, onion slices, bell pepper slices, celery seeds, and lemon slices. Repeat layers twice.
Whisk together dressing mix and remaining 3 ingredients. Pour evenly over shrimp. Cover and chill at least 12 hours. **Makes** 8 servings.

Spicy Pickled Okra

quick & easy
Walnut-Cranberry Relish
Prep: 5 min., Cook: 5 min.

1 (16-oz.) can whole-berry cranberry sauce
⅓ cup strawberry preserves
1½ Tbsp. sugar
¼ tsp. ground cinnamon
½ cup coarsely chopped walnuts, toasted
1 Tbsp. balsamic vinegar or red wine (we tested with Pinot Noir)

Combine first 4 ingredients in a medium saucepan. Cook over medium heat, stirring often, just until thoroughly heated. Remove from heat; stir in walnuts and vinegar. Cover and chill until ready to serve. Serve with smoked turkey or ham. **Makes** 2¼ cups.

Hot Relish
Prep: 1 hr., Cook: 45 min., Other: 10 min.

6 large red tomatoes
6 large green tomatoes
3 large onions
1 large red bell pepper
2 cups sugar
3 cups white vinegar (5% acidity)
⅓ cup black peppercorns, cracked
2 to 3 jalapeño peppers, finely chopped
2 Tbsp. salt
1 Tbsp. ground black pepper

Chop first 4 ingredients coarsely. Pulse in a food processor 2 to 3 times or until chopped; drain.
Combine tomato mixture, sugar, and remaining ingredients in a large saucepan; bring to a boil over medium-low heat, stirring constantly. Reduce heat, and simmer, stirring often, 45 minutes.
Pack mixture into hot, sterilized jars, filling to ½ inch from top. Remove air bubbles; wipe jar rims. Cover at once with metal lids, and screw on bands.
Process in boiling-water bath 10 minutes. **Makes** 10 (12-oz.) jars.

Grandma's Pepper Relish
Prep: 35 min., Cook: 10 min.

¾ cup sugar
½ cup cider vinegar
½ cup malt vinegar
1 tsp. mustard seeds
1 tsp. celery seeds
¾ tsp. salt
⅛ tsp. turmeric
3 medium-size red bell peppers, seeded and diced
3 medium-size green bell peppers, seeded and diced
2 medium-size Vidalia onions, diced

Combine first 7 ingredients in a large saucepan, and bring to a boil over medium-high heat.
Stir in peppers and onions; reduce heat, and simmer 5 minutes. Remove from heat, and cool. Store in refrigerator. **Makes** about 4½ cups.

Sweet White Corn and Tomato Relish
Prep: 15 min., Cook: 1 min., Other: 3 hrs.

4 ears fresh sweet white corn (we tested with Silver Queen)
2 large tomatoes, peeled and chopped
3 green onions, sliced
2 Tbsp. lemon juice
1 Tbsp. olive oil
½ tsp. salt
½ tsp. pepper
¼ tsp. garlic salt
⅛ tsp. hot sauce

Cook corn in boiling water to cover 1 minute in a large saucepan; drain and cool. Cut kernels from cobs.
Stir together corn, tomato, and remaining ingredients; cover and chill 3 hours. Store in refrigerator. **Makes** 3 cups.

204 SAUCES, MARINADES, AND MORE

Sweet Pepper-and-Onion Relish with Pine Nuts

Prep: 10 min., Cook: 25 min.

1 tsp. olive oil
8 cups vertically sliced Vidalia or other sweet onion (about 1¾ lb.)
1½ cups red bell pepper strips
¾ tsp. dried thyme
2 Tbsp. pine nuts, toasted
1½ Tbsp. rice vinegar
1 Tbsp. honey
¼ tsp. salt
⅛ tsp. coarsely ground pepper

Heat oil in a large nonstick skillet coated with cooking spray over medium heat. Add onion, bell pepper, and thyme; cook 25 minutes or until golden brown, stirring frequently. Remove from heat. Add pine nuts and remaining ingredients, and stir well. Store in refrigerator. Serve at room temperature. **Makes** 2 cups.

Sweet Pepper-and-Onion Relish with Pine Nuts

Chowchow

Prep: 1 hr., 30 min.; Cook: 8 min.; Other: 8 hrs., 15 min.

5 green bell peppers
5 red bell peppers
2 large green tomatoes
2 large onions
½ small cabbage
¼ cup pickling salt
3 cups sugar
2 cups white vinegar (5% acidity)
1 cup water
1 Tbsp. mustard seeds
1½ tsp. celery seeds
¾ tsp. turmeric

Chop first 5 ingredients.
Stir together chopped vegetables and salt in a large Dutch oven. Cover and chill 8 hours. Rinse and drain; return mixture to Dutch oven. Stir in sugar and remaining ingredients. Bring to a boil; reduce heat, and simmer 3 minutes.
Pack hot mixture into hot, sterilized jars, filling to ½ inch from top. Remove air bubbles; wipe jar rims. Cover at once with metal lids, and screw on bands.
Process jars in boiling-water bath 15 minutes. **Makes** 5 pt.

Sweet Pickle Relish

Prep: 30 min.; Cook: 15 min.; Other: 2 hrs., 10 min.

4 cups chopped cucumber
2 cups chopped onion
1 green bell pepper, chopped
1 red bell pepper, chopped
¼ cup pickling salt
1¾ cups sugar
1 cup cider vinegar or white vinegar (5% acidity)
1½ tsp. celery seeds
1½ tsp. mustard seeds

Combine first 4 ingredients in a large bowl; sprinkle evenly with pickling salt, and cover vegetables with cold water. Let stand 2 hours. Drain.
Combine sugar, vinegar, and spices in a Dutch oven; bring to a boil, and add vegetables. Return to a boil; reduce heat, and simmer 10 minutes.
Pack hot mixture into hot, sterilized jars, filling to ½ inch from top. Remove air bubbles; wipe jar rims. Cover at once with metal lids, and screw on bands.
Process in boiling water bath 10 minutes. **Makes** 4 (½-pt.) jars.

Pear Chutney
Prep: 30 min.; Cook: 2 hrs., 5 min.; Other: 10 min.

4½ lb. firm ripe pears, peeled and chopped
1 small green bell pepper, minced
1 cup raisins
4 cups sugar
1 cup crystallized ginger, chopped
3 cups white vinegar (5% acidity)
1 cup water
1½ tsp. salt
½ tsp. ground cinnamon
¼ tsp. ground cloves
¼ tsp. ground nutmeg
¼ tsp. ground allspice
1 (3-oz.) package liquid pectin

Bring all ingredients except pectin to a boil in a large Dutch oven. Reduce heat, and simmer, stirring occasionally, 2 hours or until pear is tender. Stir in pectin; return mixture to a boil, and boil, stirring constantly, 1 minute. Remove from heat, and skim off foam with a metal spoon.
Pour hot chutney into hot, sterilized jars, filling each to ¼ inch from top; wipe jar rims. Cover at once with metal lids, and screw on bands.
Process jars in boiling-water bath 10 minutes. **Makes** 11 (6-oz.) jars.

Note: If chutney is not processed in a water bath, you may store jars in refrigerator up to 1 week.

Tomato Chutney
Prep: 15 min., Cook: 2 hrs.

2 (14½-oz.) cans diced tomatoes, undrained
1 cup firmly packed light brown sugar
½ cup granulated sugar
2 small green bell peppers, diced
1 medium onion, diced
2 Tbsp. ketchup
1 tsp. pepper
⅛ to ¼ tsp. hot sauce

Bring all ingredients to a boil in a medium saucepan, stirring occasionally; reduce heat, and simmer, stirring occasionally, 1½ to 2 hours or until thickened. Store in refrigerator. **Makes** about 5 cups.

Cranberry-Ginger Chutney
Prep: 10 min., Cook: 20 min., Other: 8 hrs.

1 (12-oz.) package fresh cranberries
1½ cups sugar
1 cup fresh orange juice
2 celery ribs, chopped
1 cup golden raisins
1 medium apple, chopped
1 Tbsp. grated orange rind
1 tsp. minced fresh ginger
1 cup chopped walnuts, toasted

Bring cranberries, sugar, and orange juice to a boil in a large saucepan. Reduce heat, and simmer 15 minutes. Remove from heat.
Stir in celery and next 4 ingredients. Chill mixture 8 hours. Stir in walnuts. Store in refrigerator. **Makes** 6 cups.

quick & easy
Tomato-Garlic Chutney
Prep: 13 min., Cook: 8 min.

1 Tbsp. vegetable oil
1 tsp. mustard seeds, crushed
8 garlic cloves, minced
2 cups chopped seeded plum tomato
1½ tsp. curry powder
½ tsp. salt

Combine first 3 ingredients, and cook over low heat 1 minute.
Stir in chopped plum tomato, curry powder, and salt; cook tomato mixture 8 minutes or until creamy, stirring occasionally. Store in refrigerator. **Makes** 1¼ cups.

Fresh Mango Salsa
Prep: 18 min., Other: 3 hrs.

A cool summer accompaniment awaits grilled fish or pork with this fruity salsa with a kick.

2 ripe mangoes, peeled and finely chopped*
½ red bell pepper, finely chopped
½ red onion, finely chopped
2½ Tbsp. chopped fresh cilantro
2 to 3 Tbsp. chopped fresh mint
1 jalapeño pepper, seeded and minced
2 Tbsp. fresh lime juice
½ tsp. salt
¼ tsp. pepper

Stir together all ingredients. Cover and chill 3 hours. Store in refrigerator. **Makes** 2 cups.

*Substitute 1 (26-oz.) jar refrigerated mango slices, drained and finely chopped, for fresh mangoes.

Cranberry-Jalapeño Salsa
Prep: 10 min.

You'll never serve smoked turkey, pork, or ham plain again when you try this chile-inspired cranberry sauce. It's especially tasty around the holidays.

1 (12-oz.) package fresh cranberries
1 medium-size navel orange, unpeeled and coarsely
    chopped
3 Tbsp. crystallized ginger
2 jalapeño peppers, seeded and coarsely chopped
¼ cup fresh mint leaves
1 cup sugar
Garnishes: fresh mint sprigs, orange wedges

Pulse fresh cranberries in a food processor until minced. Transfer minced cranberries to a small bowl. **Pulse** orange and next 4 ingredients in a food processor 3 to 5 times or until mixture is finely chopped. Stir into cranberries; cover and chill, if desired. Store in refrigerator. Garnish, if desired. **Makes** 2 cups.

Salsa Verde
Prep: 5 min., Cook: 20 min.

A dollop of this tomatillo salsa nicely complements smoked pork, chicken, or fish.

6 fresh tomatillos (about 8 oz.)
1 jalapeño pepper
¼ tsp. salt
1 garlic clove, sliced
¼ cup water
¼ cup minced fresh cilantro

Discard husks and stems from tomatillos. Place tomatillos and jalapeño in a saucepan; cover with water, and bring to a boil. Cook 15 minutes or until tender, and drain.
Combine tomatillos, jalapeño, salt, and garlic in a blender or food processor; process until smooth.
Place a nonstick skillet coated with cooking spray over medium-high heat until hot. Pour tomatillo mixture into pan (mixture will boil vigorously), and cook 2 minutes. Add ¼ cup water; cook 1 minute or until thoroughly heated. Stir in cilantro. Store in refrigerator. **Makes** ½ cup.

Peachy Green Tomato Salsa
Prep: 20 min., Other: 1 hr.

Serve with grilled or fried chicken, catfish, or pork.

2 green tomatoes, chopped
1 large peach, chopped
3 green onions, sliced
¼ cup olive oil
⅛ cup white wine vinegar
1 Tbsp. minced fresh cilantro
1 Tbsp. lemon juice
½ Tbsp. liquid from hot peppers in vinegar
½ Tbsp. honey
½ tsp. salt

Stir together all ingredients. Cover and chill 1 hour. Store in refrigerator. **Makes** 3 cups.

kids love it
Green Tomato-Blueberry Jam
Prep: 35 min., Cook: 5 min., Other: 10 min.

5 cups fresh blueberries, stemmed*
4 large green tomatoes, coarsely chopped (about 4 lb.)
1½ cups water
5 cups sugar
3 (1¾-oz.) packages powdered pectin (we tested with Sure-Jell Fruit Pectin)
¼ cup lemon juice
2 tsp. ground cinnamon
½ tsp. ground nutmeg

Pulse blueberries and chopped tomato in batches in a blender or food processor 3 or 4 times or until mixture is almost smooth.

Cook blueberry mixture, 1½ cups water, and sugar in a Dutch oven over medium heat, stirring constantly, until sugar dissolves.

Stir in fruit pectin and remaining ingredients. Bring to a boil; cook, stirring constantly, 5 minutes or until mixture thickens.

Pour hot mixture into hot, sterilized jars, filling to ¼ inch from top. Remove air bubbles; wipe jar rims. Cover at once with metal lids, and screw on bands.

Process jars in boiling-water bath 10 minutes. **Makes** 5 pt.

*Substitute 5 cups frozen blueberries, thawed, if desired.

Peach-Rosemary Jam
Prep: 25 min., Cook: 10 min., Other: 10 min.

4 cups peeled and chopped fresh peaches or nectarines
1 tsp. grated lime rind
¼ cup fresh lime juice
2 fresh rosemary sprigs
1 (1.75-oz.) package powdered fruit pectin
5 cups sugar

Bring first 5 ingredients to a full rolling boil in a Dutch oven. Boil 1 minute, stirring constantly. Add sugar to peach mixture, and bring to a full rolling boil; boil 1 minute, stirring constantly. Remove from heat. Remove and discard rosemary sprigs; skim off any foam.

Pour hot mixture immediately into hot, sterilized jars, filling to ¼ inch from top. Remove air bubbles; wipe jar rims. Cover at once with metal lids, and screw on bands.

Process in boiling-water bath 10 minutes. **Makes** 7 (½-pt.) jars.

quick & easy
Freezer Garlic Pepper Jelly
Prep: 4 min., Cook: 10 min.

2 (16-oz.) jars apple jelly
2 Tbsp. dried parsley flakes
1 Tbsp. pressed garlic
½ tsp. dried crushed red pepper
4 tsp. white vinegar

Melt apple jelly in a medium saucepan over low heat, stirring often. Stir in parsley and remaining ingredients. Pour into jars or freezer containers. Cool. Cover and freeze up to 6 months. (Jelly will not freeze solid.) Use as a basting sauce for chicken or pork, or serve over cream cheese or Brie. **Makes** 3 cups.

Peach-Rosemary Jam

Spicy Blueberry-Citrus
Marmalade

Spicy Blueberry-Citrus Marmalade

Prep: 15 min., Cook: 40 min., Other: 10 min.

1 orange
1 lemon
1 lime
2 cups water
½ tsp. dried crushed red pepper
2 cups fresh or frozen blueberries, thawed
2 cups sugar

Cut rinds from citrus fruit into thin strips. Set aside. Squeeze juice and pulp from orange, lemon, and lime into a bowl. Set aside.

Bring rind strips, 2 cups water, and red pepper to a boil in a saucepan. Cover, reduce heat, and simmer 25 minutes or until rinds are very tender.

Add blueberries, sugar, and citrus pulp and juice to saucepan. Bring to a full rolling boil; boil, uncovered, stirring often, 15 minutes or until a gel forms. Remove from heat; skim off any foam.

Pour hot mixture immediately into hot, sterilized jars, filling to ¼ inch from top. Remove air bubbles; wipe jar rims. Cover at once with metal lids, and screw on bands.

Process in boiling water-bath 10 minutes. **Makes** 5 (½-pt.) jars.

Green Tomato Marmalade

Prep: 20 min.; Cook: 3 hrs., 50 min.; Other: 10 min.

1 cup water
2 oranges, thinly sliced
1 lemon, thinly sliced
6 large green tomatoes, chopped (about 4 lb.)
4 cups sugar
½ tsp. salt

Cook first 3 ingredients in a Dutch oven over medium heat 17 to 20 minutes or until fruit is tender. Add tomato and remaining ingredients, stirring until sugar dissolves.

Bring to a boil, stirring constantly; reduce heat, and simmer, stirring occasionally, 3½ hours or until mixture thickens.

Pour hot mixture into hot, sterilized jars, filling to ¼ inch from top. Remove air bubbles; wipe jar rims. Cover at once with metal lids, and screw on bands.

Process jars in boiling-water bath 10 minutes. **Makes** 3 pt.

For dessert after the barbecue, grill pound cake slices and serve warm with one of the following two sweet butter spreads.

kids love it • quick & easy
Blackberry Butter
Prep: 5 min.

2 to 3 Tbsp. seedless blackberry jam
½ cup softened butter

Stir blackberry jam into butter. Cover and chill until ready to serve. **Makes** about ½ cup.

quick & easy
Pecan-Honey Butter
Prep: 5 min.

½ cup butter, softened
⅓ cup finely chopped pecans, toasted
2 Tbsp. wildflower honey
⅛ to ¼ tsp. ground cinnamon

Stir together all ingredients until blended. Cover and chill until ready to serve. **Makes** about ¾ cup.

quick & easy
Garlic-Basil Butter
Prep: 5 min.

If you're looking for an alternative to plain ol' butter to serve on Texas toast or grilled corn on the cob, try this herbed version.

½ cup butter, softened
1 Tbsp. finely chopped fresh basil
1 garlic clove, minced

Combine all ingredients, stirring well. Cover and chill until ready to serve. **Makes** ½ cup.

quick & easy
Jalapeño-Chili Butter
Prep: 5 min.

Throw corn on the cob to grill alongside the barbecue, and smear it with this feisty butter blend while hot from the grill.

½ cup butter, softened
1 jalapeño pepper, seeded and minced
1 tsp. chili powder

Combine all ingredients, stirring well. Cover and chill until ready to serve. **Makes** ½ cup.

editor's favorite
Roasted Garlic Beurre Blanc
Prep: 10 min,. Cook: 1 hr.

Drizzle this garlicky butter blend over grilled seafood or veggies.

6 garlic cloves
Olive oil
Salt and black pepper to taste
½ cup fresh lemon juice (about 2 lemons)
½ cup dry white wine
1 cup whipping cream
¼ cup cold butter, cut into pieces
1 tsp. kosher salt
½ tsp. ground red pepper

Place garlic in center of an aluminum foil sheet. Drizzle garlic lightly with oil; sprinkle with salt and black pepper to taste.
Bake garlic at 350° for 20 to 25 minutes or until golden.
Squeeze out pulp from each garlic clove into a medium saucepan. Add lemon juice and white wine to garlic. Cook, uncovered, over medium-high heat about 20 minutes or until reduced by three-fourths. Stir in whipping cream; reduce heat and simmer, uncovered, 10 to 15 minutes or until reduced by half. Remove from heat; gradually whisk in butter, a few pieces at a time, until sauce is slightly thickened and smooth. Stir in 1 tsp. salt and ground red pepper. **Makes** 2 cups.

Sweet-Hot Honey Mustard
Prep: 5 min., Cook: 12 min.

This mustard is a delicious complement to smoked ham or turkey. Spread it on a grilled chicken sandwich or over the crust of a quiche before adding the filling. Straight from the jar, it makes a bold and spicy dip for egg rolls.

2 cups sugar
1½ cups dry mustard
2 cups white vinegar
3 large eggs, lightly beaten
½ cup honey

Whisk together sugar and mustard in a heavy 3-qt. saucepan; gradually whisk in vinegar and eggs until blended.
Cook mustard mixture over medium heat, whisking constantly, 10 to 12 minutes or until smooth and thickened. Remove from heat, and whisk in honey. Cool and store in airtight containers in the refrigerator for up to 2 weeks. **Makes** 4 cups.

Sweet-Hot Ketchup
Prep: 5 min.

1 cup ketchup
1 tsp. grated lime rind
3 Tbsp. fresh lime juice
2 Tbsp. honey
1 tsp. chipotle chile pepper seasoning

Stir together all ingredients. Cover and chill until ready to serve. **Makes** 1⅓ cups.

editor's favorite
Roasted Red Pepper Rémoulade
Prep: 10 min.

¼ cup egg substitute
½ cup vegetable oil
½ (12-oz.) jar roasted red bell peppers, drained
¼ cup onions, minced
1 Tbsp. Creole mustard
1 tsp. dry mustard
1 tsp. lemon juice
1 garlic clove, minced
½ tsp. sugar
½ tsp. salt
½ tsp. ground cumin
¼ tsp. ground red pepper

Place egg substitute in bowl of a food processor. With processor running, pour oil through food chute in a slow, steady stream; process until thickened, stopping to scrape down sides. Pour mixture into a small bowl.
Process roasted red bell peppers and remaining 9 ingredients in food processor, pulsing until smooth. Fold roasted pepper mixture into egg mixture. Cover and chill until ready to serve. **Makes** 1 cup.

Lime-Red Pepper Mayonnaise
Prep: 5 min.

½ cup mayonnaise
½ tsp. grated lime rind
¼ tsp. ground red pepper
2 Tbsp. fresh lime juice

Stir together all ingredients; cover and chill until ready to serve. **Makes** ½ cup.

Lemon-Rosemary Mayonnaise
Prep: 5 min.

If you prefer a milder flavor, substitute fresh parsley for rosemary.

2 cups mayonnaise
2 Tbsp. chopped fresh rosemary
1½ tsp. grated lemon rind
1 garlic clove, pressed

Stir together all ingredients. Cover and chill until ready to serve. **Makes** about 2 cups.

Fresh Herb Mayonnaise
Prep: 5 min.

2 cups mayonnaise
2 Tbsp. chopped fresh parsley
2 Tbsp. chopped fresh chives
1 Tbsp. chopped fresh basil
1 Tbsp. chopped fresh dill
1 Tbsp. chopped fresh oregano

Stir together all ingredients.
Cover and chill until ready to serve. **Makes** about 2¼ cups.

MAYONNAISE APLENTY

These mayonnaises can be used in a variety of ways: Use in place of tartar sauce when grilling or smoking fresh seafood, spoon over grilled tuna, or spread on a smoked turkey sandwich.

Uptown Collards,
page 246

On the Side

Round out a barbecue feast
with a crisp salad, saucy slaw,
sweet baked beans, or soulful
greens. Whatever the choice,
these lively sides are
sure to satisfy.

Lettuce-Wedge Salad
Prep: 30 min., Cook: 15 min.

Shredded fresh basil and crumbled bacon sprinkled atop a homemade dressing update a lettuce-wedge salad that offers a nice and simple start to a barbecue menu.

4 to 6 bacon slices
1 medium onion, sliced
1 cup buttermilk
½ cup sour cream
1 (1-oz.) envelope Ranch dressing mix
¼ cup chopped fresh basil
2 garlic cloves
1 large head iceberg lettuce, cut into 4 wedges
Shredded fresh basil (optional)

Cook bacon in a large skillet until crisp; remove bacon, and drain on paper towels, reserving 1 tsp. drippings in skillet. Crumble bacon, and set aside.
Sauté onion in hot drippings in skillet over medium heat 10 minutes or until tender and lightly browned. Remove from heat; cool.
Process buttermilk and next 4 ingredients in a blender or food processor until smooth, stopping to scrape down sides. Stir in onion.
Top each lettuce wedge with dressing; sprinkle with bacon, and, if desired, top with shredded basil. **Makes** 4 servings.

quick & easy
Red Leaf Lettuce Salad with Sweet-and-Sour Dressing
Prep: 5 min.

This sweet-and-sour dressed salad mimics the flavors in many barbecue sauces.

1 bunch Red Leaf lettuce, torn
1 cup frozen sweet peas, thawed
1 cup (4 oz.) shredded mozzarella cheese
½ cup toasted slivered almonds
6 bacon slices, cooked and crumbled
Sweet-and-Sour Dressing

Combine lettuce, peas, cheese, almonds, and bacon. Toss with Sweet-and-Sour Dressing just before serving. **Makes** 4 servings.

Sweet-and-Sour Dressing
Prep: 5 min.

⅓ cup sugar
2½ Tbsp. white vinegar
1 Tbsp. diced onion
¼ tsp. salt
¼ tsp. garlic salt
⅛ tsp. pepper
½ cup vegetable oil

Pulse first 6 ingredients in a blender 2 to 3 times or until smooth. With blender running, pour oil through food chute in a slow, steady stream; process until smooth. **Makes** about 1 cup.

Chopped Cilantro Salad
Prep: 25 min.

6 fresh tomatillos, husks removed
⅔ cup loosely packed fresh cilantro leaves
6 Tbsp. fresh lime juice (about 3 limes)
2 garlic cloves, halved
2 tsp. chopped jalapeño pepper (about 1 small)
¾ cup vegetable oil
1 cup finely chopped green onions
1 tsp. salt
½ tsp. pepper
5 cups loosely packed, coarsely chopped romaine lettuce
4 cups loosely packed, coarsely chopped cabbage
2 medium tomatoes, seeded and chopped (about 1½ cups)
1½ cups chopped, peeled jícama
1½ cups fresh corn kernels (about 3 ears)
½ cup crumbled feta cheese
2 ripe avocados, chopped
Tortilla chips (optional)

Cut tomatillos into quarters. Process tomatillos, cilantro, and next 3 ingredients in a blender 20 seconds or until pureed; pour into a medium bowl. Whisk together cilantro puree and oil; add green onions, salt, and pepper, stirring well.
Stir together romaine lettuce and next 5 ingredients in a large bowl. Gently toss avocado and lettuce mixture with cilantro mixture. Serve with tortilla chips, if desired. **Makes** 8 servings.

Chipotle Caesar Salad
Prep: 20 min.

Add a chipotle pepper or two to a bottled Caesar dressing for a quicker take on this salad.

1 large jícama
2 heads romaine lettuce, torn
1 large red bell pepper, thinly sliced
Chipotle Caesar Dressing

Cut jícama into thin slices. Cut each slice into a star using a 1½-inch star-shaped cookie cutter (about 15 stars).

Toss together lettuce, bell pepper, and desired amount of dressing in a large bowl. Top with jícama stars. **Makes** 8 servings.

Chipotle Caesar Dressing
Prep: 10 min.

2 garlic cloves
1 to 2 canned chipotle peppers
½ tsp. salt
⅓ cup fresh lemon juice
⅓ cup egg substitute
⅓ cup shredded Parmesan cheese
½ cup olive oil

Pulse first 3 ingredients in a food processor 3 to 4 times or until garlic is minced. Add lemon juice, egg substitute, and Parmesan cheese. With food processor running, pour oil through food chute in a slow, steady stream; process until smooth. Cover and chill until ready to serve. **Makes** 1¼ cups.

Grilled Romaine Salad with Buttermilk-Chive Dressing
Prep: 10 min., Cook: 5 min.

Nestle romaine halves on the grill next to the barbecue for a warm and wilted salad to start the meal.

4 bunches romaine hearts
1 red onion
1 to 2 Tbsp. olive oil
Buttermilk-Chive Dressing
Kosher salt to taste
Freshly ground pepper to taste
½ cup freshly shaved or shredded Parmesan cheese

Cut romaine hearts in half lengthwise, keeping leaves intact. Cut red onion crosswise into ½-inch slices, keeping rings intact; brush romaine and onions with olive oil, and set aside.

Coat food grate evenly with vegetable cooking spray, or brush lightly with vegetable oil. Place food on grate; grill over medium heat (300° to 350°).

Place romaine halves, cut sides down, on food grate. Grill, uncovered, 3 to 5 minutes or until just wilted. If desired, rotate halves once to get crisscross grill marks. Brush warm romaine halves with Buttermilk-Chive Dressing, coating lightly.

Place 2 romaine halves on each of 4 salad plates. Sprinkle with salt and pepper to taste. Top each evenly with onion slices and freshly shaved Parmesan cheese. Serve immediately with remaining Buttermilk-Chive Dressing. **Makes** 4 servings.

Buttermilk-Chive Dressing
Prep: 5 min.

¾ cup buttermilk
½ cup mayonnaise
2 Tbsp. chopped fresh chives
1 Tbsp. minced green onions
1 garlic clove, minced
½ tsp. salt
¼ tsp. freshly ground pepper

Whisk together all ingredients. Cover; chill until ready to use. **Makes** 1¼ cups.

Mixed Salad Greens with Warm Goat Cheese
Prep: 15 min., Cook: 5 min.

Pecan-encrusted slices of creamy goat cheese crown a fresh mix of five salad greens. Buy bags of washed, torn salad greens to save preparation time and effort.

2 heads Boston lettuce, torn
2 heads Bibb lettuce, torn
2 heads romaine lettuce, torn
3 bunches arugula, torn
2 bunches watercress, torn
3 cups seedless red grapes
1 (1-lb.) log goat cheese
1⅔ cups chicken broth, divided
1 to 1½ cups ground pecans
½ cup chopped fresh parsley
⅓ cup red wine vinegar
3 Tbsp. fresh lemon juice
3 Tbsp. walnut oil
2 Tbsp. safflower oil
1 Tbsp. Dijon mustard
2 green onions, chopped
1 garlic clove, minced
1 Tbsp. sugar
¼ tsp. salt
¼ tsp. freshly ground pepper

Combine first 6 ingredients in a large bowl, tossing gently; cover and chill thoroughly.

Cut goat cheese into ¼-inch rounds. Dip each round in 1 cup broth; roll in pecans and then in parsley. Place on a lightly greased baking sheet. Bake, uncovered, at 325° for 5 minutes or until toasted.

Combine remaining ⅔ cup broth, vinegar, and remaining 9 ingredients in container of an electric blender; process 1 minute. Drizzle over salad greens, and toss gently; place cheese on top of salad. Serve immediately. **Makes** 8 servings.

Garden Salad with Buttermilk Dressing
Prep: 8 min., Other: 2 hrs.

¾ cup mayonnaise or salad dressing
½ cup buttermilk
1 Tbsp. chopped fresh parsley
1 Tbsp. finely chopped onion
1 garlic clove, minced
¼ tsp. salt
Dash of pepper
4 cups mixed salad greens

Combine first 7 ingredients; stir with a wire whisk until blended. Cover and chill at least 2 hours. Serve with greens. **Makes** 4 servings.

Tossed Spinach Salad
Prep: 20 min.

1 (10-oz.) package fresh spinach*
1 medium-size red onion, thinly sliced
2 large hard-cooked eggs, chopped
1 cup garlic-seasoned croutons
2 Tbsp. grated Parmesan cheese
Zesty Lemon Dressing

Toss first 5 ingredients in a large bowl; serve with Dressing. **Makes** 6 servings.

*Substitute 1 (10-oz.) package salad greens for spinach, if desired.

Zesty Lemon Dressing
Prep: 10 min.

¼ cup lemon olive oil (we tested with Stutz Limonato California Extra Virgin Lemon and Olive Oil)
3 Tbsp. lemon juice
1 Tbsp. red wine vinegar
1 tsp. Dijon mustard
½ tsp. salt
¼ tsp. freshly ground pepper
6 oz. Canadian bacon, cut into thin strips

Whisk together first 6 ingredients. Add Canadian bacon just before serving. **Makes** ½ cup.

Black Bean and Black-Eyed Pea Salad
Prep: 20 min., Other: 30 min.

1 tsp. grated lime rind
½ cup fresh lime juice (about 4 limes)
¼ cup olive oil
1 tsp. brown sugar
1 tsp. chili powder
½ tsp. ground cumin
½ to 1 tsp. salt
1 (15-oz.) can black beans, rinsed and drained
1 (15.5-oz.) can black-eyed peas, rinsed and drained
1½ cups frozen whole kernel corn, thawed
½ small green bell pepper, chopped
⅓ cup chopped fresh cilantro
Romaine lettuce
2 large avocados, sliced
Garnishes: lime wedges, fresh cilantro sprigs

Whisk together first 7 ingredients in a large bowl. Add black beans and next 4 ingredients, tossing to coat. Cover and chill at least 30 minutes.
Serve over lettuce; arrange avocado slices around salad. Garnish, if desired. **Makes** 6 servings.

Pea Salad
Prep: 10 min.

1 (16-oz.) can small sweet peas, drained
1 (16-oz.) can medium-size sweet peas, drained
6 green onions, sliced
2 large hard-cooked eggs, chopped
¾ cup diced sharp Cheddar cheese
½ cup mayonnaise
1 tsp. sugar
1 tsp. fresh dill, minced
1 tsp. lemon juice
¼ tsp. salt
¼ tsp. pepper

Stir together all ingredients in a large bowl. **Makes** 4 to 6 servings.

Fresh Mozzarella-
Tomato-Basil Salad

Fresh Mozzarella-Tomato-Basil Salad

Prep: 10 min., Other: 4 hrs.

For an extra sprinkling of color, use multicolored peppercorns and grind them over the salad just before serving.

½ lb. fresh mozzarella cheese
2 large red tomatoes, sliced
1 large yellow tomato, sliced
½ tsp. salt
3 Tbsp. extra-virgin olive oil
Freshly ground pepper
½ cup shredded or chopped fresh basil

Remove cheese from brine, and cut into 12 slices; sprinkle tomato slices evenly with salt. Alternate tomato and cheese slices on a platter; drizzle with olive oil. Cover and chill 4 hours. Just before serving, sprinkle with freshly ground pepper and shredded basil. **Makes** 6 servings.

Note: Fresh mozzarella is a soft white cheese available at gourmet grocery stores or cheese shops. It's usually packed in brine, a strong solution of water and salt used for pickling or preserving foods.

Italian Tomato Salad

Prep: 20 min., Other: 8 hrs.

6 plum tomatoes, chopped*
1 small red onion, thinly sliced (optional)
1 Tbsp. minced fresh basil
1 Tbsp. minced fresh oregano
1 garlic clove, minced
¼ tsp. salt
⅛ tsp. pepper
3 Tbsp. olive oil
3 Tbsp. red wine vinegar
¼ cup crumbled Gorgonzola cheese
Garnish: croutons

Combine chopped tomato and, if desired, onion in a large bowl.
Combine basil and next 6 ingredients in a small bowl; add to tomato mixture, tossing to coat. Sprinkle with cheese. Chill 8 hours. Garnish, if desired. **Makes** 4½ cups.

*Substitute 3 large tomatoes, if desired.

Asparagus, Roasted Beet, and Goat Cheese Salad

Prep: 15 min., Cook: 47 min.

18 small fresh beets (about 6 lb.)
1 cup olive oil
⅓ cup red wine vinegar
½ tsp. salt, divided
½ tsp. freshly ground pepper, divided
60 small fresh asparagus
1 (11-oz.) log goat cheese
1 Tbsp. chopped fresh chives
Cracked pepper (optional)
Chopped fresh chives (optional)
Gourmet mixed salad greens (optional)

Arrange beets in a single layer on a lightly greased baking sheet; bake at 425° for 40 to 45 minutes or until tender, stirring every 15 minutes. Cool beets completely.
Whisk together oil, vinegar, ¼ tsp. salt, and ¼ tsp. ground pepper in a small bowl.
Peel beets, and cut into wedges. Toss together beets, ½ cup vinaigrette, remaining ¼ tsp. salt, and remaining ¼ tsp. ground pepper; set aside.
Snap off tough ends of asparagus, discarding ends; cook asparagus in boiling water to cover 1 to 2 minutes or until crisp-tender. Plunge into ice water to stop the cooking process, and drain. Combine asparagus and ½ cup vinaigrette; set aside.
Cut cheese into 6 equal slices. Place 1 cheese slice in a 3-inch round cutter or ring mold; sprinkle with ½ tsp. chives. Press chives into cheese; remove cutter. Repeat procedure with remaining cheese and 2½ tsp. chives.
Arrange asparagus over cheese. Surround with beets, and drizzle with remaining vinaigrette. Sprinkle with cracked pepper and chives, if desired; serve with salad greens, if desired. **Makes** 6 servings.

Cucumber Salad with Roasted Red Bell Pepper Dressing

Prep: 5 min.

8 cups gourmet mixed salad greens
2 cucumbers, diced
1 small red onion, sliced
Roasted Red Bell Pepper Dressing

Combine salad greens, diced cucumbers, and onion; serve with Roasted Red Bell Pepper Dressing. **Makes** 6 to 8 servings.

Roasted Red Bell Pepper Dressing

Prep: 5 min.

1 (7-oz.) jar roasted red bell peppers, drained
2 large garlic cloves, chopped
1 cup fat-free yogurt
1 tsp. salt

Pulse ingredients in a blender 5 to 6 times or until smooth. **Makes** about 2 cups.

Avocado Salad

Prep: 10 min., Other: 1 hr.

2 large ripe avocados, coarsely chopped
4 large radishes, chopped
2 celery ribs, chopped
2 green onions, chopped
2 Tbsp. fresh lemon juice
2 Tbsp. olive oil
½ tsp. salt
¼ to ½ tsp. freshly ground pepper

Combine all ingredients. Cover and chill 1 hour. **Makes** 2½ cups.

Fried Okra Salad

Prep: 25 min., Cook: 4 min. per batch, Other: 20 min.

Crispy fried small whole pods of okra perch atop greens and tomato slices for a distinctly Southern take on salad.

1 lb. small fresh okra
2 cups buttermilk
1 lb. bacon, chopped
1 cup cornmeal
1 cup all-purpose flour
1¼ tsp. salt, divided
¾ tsp. pepper, divided
Canola oil
½ small onion, coarsely chopped
¼ cup canola oil
3 Tbsp. red wine vinegar
3 Tbsp. honey
1½ Tbsp. Dijon mustard
1 tsp. paprika
1 lb. Bibb lettuce
6 tomatoes, sliced
Garnish: fresh basil sprigs

Stir together okra and buttermilk in a large bowl; let stand 20 minutes. Drain okra.

Cook chopped bacon in a large skillet over medium heat until crisp; drain on paper towels. Reserve ¼ cup bacon drippings.

Combine cornmeal, flour, 1 tsp. salt, and ½ tsp. pepper in a large zip-top freezer bag; add okra a few at a time, sealing and shaking to coat each batch.

Pour oil to a depth of ½ inch into a large heavy skillet. Fry okra in batches in hot oil 2 minutes on each side or until golden. Drain well on paper towels.

Process reserved ¼ cup drippings, remaining ¼ tsp. salt, remaining ¼ tsp. pepper, onion, and next 5 ingredients in a blender or food processor until smooth, stopping once to scrape down sides. Pour into a 1-cup glass measuring cup.

Microwave dressing mixture at HIGH 30 to 45 seconds or until thoroughly heated.

Line a large serving platter with lettuce; arrange tomato and okra on top. Sprinkle with bacon, and drizzle with warm dressing. Garnish, if desired. Serve immediately. **Makes** 6 main-dish or 10 side-dish servings.

Kentucky Bibb Salad with Fried Green Tomatoes
Prep: 20 min., Cook: 8 min. per batch

½ cup cornmeal
1 tsp. dried mint
1 tsp. ground cumin
½ tsp. salt
½ cup buttermilk
3 large green tomatoes, cut into ¼-inch-thick slices
Vegetable or peanut oil
2 large heads Bibb lettuce, rinsed and torn
½ cup toasted walnuts
Rose Vinaigrette
Garnishes: gourmet edible petite rose petals; chopped green, red, and yellow bell peppers; chopped red onion

Whisk together first 5 ingredients in a bowl until smooth; dip tomato slices evenly in batter.
Pour oil to a depth of 2 inches into a large heavy skillet. Fry tomato slices, in batches, in hot oil over medium-high heat 4 minutes on each side or until slices are golden.
Arrange lettuce evenly on 6 plates; top each with 2 tomato slices. Sprinkle evenly with walnuts; drizzle with Rose Vinaigrette. Garnish, if desired. **Makes** 6 servings.

Note: For extra-crispy fried tomatoes, dip in batter twice.

Rose Vinaigrette
Prep: 10 min.

3 large shallots, finely chopped
¼ tsp. salt
1 Tbsp. honey
⅓ cup red wine vinegar
2 tsp. rose water (optional)
⅓ cup vegetable oil
3 Tbsp. walnut oil*

Stir together first 4 ingredients and, if desired, rose water; whisk in oils. **Makes** ¾ cup.

*Substitute 3 Tbsp. vegetable oil for walnut oil, if desired.

Bacon-Mandarin Salad

Bacon-Mandarin Salad
Prep: 15 min., Cook: 18 min.

Wash the lettuces the night before. Wrap in a damp paper towel, and chill in zip-top plastic bags; cook the bacon, and toast the almonds, too. Assemble and dress right before serving.

½ cup olive oil
¼ cup red wine vinegar
¼ cup sugar
1 Tbsp. chopped fresh basil
⅛ tsp. hot sauce
2 (15-oz.) cans mandarin oranges, drained and chilled*
1 bunch Red Leaf lettuce, torn
1 head romaine lettuce, torn
1 lb. bacon, cooked and crumbled
1 (4-oz.) package sliced almonds, toasted

Whisk together first 5 ingredients in a large bowl, blending well. Add oranges and lettuces, tossing gently to coat. Sprinkle with crumbled bacon and sliced almonds. Serve immediately. **Makes** 12 servings.

*Substitute fresh orange segments for canned mandarin oranges, if desired.

Orange-Walnut Salad
Prep: 20 min., Cook: 6 min.

2 heads Bibb lettuce, torn into bite-size pieces
1 (10-oz.) package fresh spinach, torn
2 oranges, peeled, seeded, and sectioned
½ medium onion, sliced and separated into rings
½ cup coarsely chopped walnuts
2 tsp. butter or margarine, melted
Sweet-and-Sour Dressing

Place first 4 ingredients in a large salad bowl. Sauté walnuts in butter in a small skillet over medium heat until toasted; add to salad. Toss with Sweet-and-Sour Dressing. **Makes** 6 servings.

Sweet-and-Sour Dressing
Prep: 2 min.

1 cup vegetable oil
½ cup white vinegar
½ cup sugar
1 tsp. salt
1 tsp. dry mustard
1 tsp. paprika
1 tsp. grated onion
1 tsp. celery seeds

Process first 7 ingredients in a blender until smooth. Stir in celery seeds. Cover and chill until ready to serve. Stir again just before serving. **Makes** 1¾ cups.

Cantaloupe-Spinach Salad with Pistachio-Lime Vinaigrette
Prep: 15 min.

1 large cantaloupe
6 cups torn fresh spinach leaves
½ cup pistachios, coarsely chopped
Pistachio-Lime Vinaigrette

Peel, seed, and cut cantaloupe into thin wedges; cut wedges vertically into ½-inch slices.
Place spinach on individual serving plates; arrange cantaloupe on top, and sprinkle with pistachios. Serve with Pistachio-Lime Vinaigrette. **Makes** 6 to 8 servings.

Pistachio-Lime Vinaigrette
Prep: 5 min.

⅓ cup fresh lime juice
⅓ cup honey
¼ cup chopped red onion
1 tsp. dried crushed red pepper
½ tsp. salt
¼ cup chopped fresh cilantro
¾ cup vegetable oil
1 cup pistachios

Process first 6 ingredients in a blender until smooth. With blender running, add oil in a slow, steady stream. Turn blender off; add pistachios, and pulse until pistachios are finely chopped. Store in refrigerator. **Makes** about 2 cups.

Strawberry Salad with Cinnamon Vinaigrette
Prep: 20 min.

This salad's dressing offers a wonderful balance of tastes. It's so delicious, we gave it our highest rating.

1 (11-oz.) can mandarin oranges, drained
1 pt. fresh strawberries, stemmed and quartered
1 small red onion, thinly sliced
½ cup coarsely chopped pecans, toasted
1 ripe avocado, sliced
1 (10-oz.) package romaine lettuce
Cinnamon Vinaigrette

Combine first 6 ingredients in a large bowl. Drizzle with half of Cinnamon Vinaigrette, tossing to coat. Serve remaining vinaigrette with salad. **Makes** 6 to 8 servings.

Cinnamon Vinaigrette
Prep: 5 min., Other: 2 hrs.

⅓ cup olive oil
⅓ cup raspberry vinegar
1 Tbsp. sugar
½ tsp. salt
½ tsp. ground cinnamon
¼ tsp. pepper
½ tsp. hot sauce

Combine all ingredients in a jar; cover tightly, and shake vigorously. Chill at least 2 hours. Shake well before serving. **Makes** ⅔ cup.

quick & easy
Cranberry-Gorgonzola Green Salad
Prep: 20 min.

⅓ cup vegetable oil
¼ cup seasoned rice vinegar
¾ tsp. Dijon mustard
1 garlic clove, pressed
1 small head Bibb lettuce, torn
1 bunch Green Leaf lettuce, torn
1 Granny Smith or pippin apple, diced
⅓ cup coarsely chopped walnuts, toasted
⅓ cup dried cranberries
⅓ cup crumbled Gorgonzola cheese

Combine first 4 ingredients; stir with a wire whisk until blended. Set aside.
Just before serving, combine Bibb lettuce and remaining 5 ingredients in a large bowl. Pour dressing over salad; toss gently. **Makes** 8 servings.

Cranberry-Strawberry-Jícama Salad

Prep: 30 min.

The raw jícama in this salad adds flavor and crunch. Sometimes referred to as the Mexican potato, jícama has a sweet, nutty taste and can be eaten raw or cooked.

½ cup olive oil
½ cup orange juice
¼ cup cranberry-orange relish (we tested with Ocean Spray Cran-Fruit Crushed Fruit For Chicken)
1 small shallot, peeled and chopped
2 Tbsp. balsamic vinegar
¼ tsp. ground red pepper
¼ tsp. salt
¼ tsp. freshly ground black pepper
1 large jícama, peeled
2 (5-oz.) packages gourmet mixed salad greens
2 cups sliced fresh strawberries
½ cup sweetened dried cranberries, finely chopped
2 large navel oranges, peeled and sectioned (optional)
Garnish: shaved Pecorino Romano or Parmesan cheese

Process first 8 ingredients in a blender until smooth, stopping to scrape down sides.
Cut jícama into cubes (or, if desired, cut into ¼-inch-thick slices; cut with a 1½-inch star-shaped cutter).
Place jícama, salad greens, strawberries, cranberries, and, if desired, orange sections in a large bowl. Drizzle with vinaigrette, and gently toss to coat. Garnish, if desired. **Makes** 8 to 10 servings.

Watermelon-Prosciutto Salad

Prep: 20 min., Cook: 5 min.

¼ lb. prosciutto, cut into thin strips
1 Tbsp. chopped fresh basil
3 Tbsp. white balsamic vinegar
2 tsp. honey
⅛ tsp. paprika
⅓ cup olive oil
3 cups seeded and cubed watermelon
2 bunches watercress
½ tsp. freshly ground pepper
Garnish: watermelon wedges

Brown prosciutto in a small nonstick skillet over medium heat 5 minutes. Remove prosciutto, and set aside.
Whisk together basil and next 3 ingredients; gradually whisk in oil until blended.
Arrange watermelon cubes over watercress. Sprinkle with prosciutto and pepper, and drizzle with vinaigrette. Garnish, if desired. Serve immediately. **Makes** 4 servings.

quick & easy
Fruit Salad with Honey-Pecan Dressing

Prep: 5 min.

2½ cups fresh orange sections
2½ cups fresh grapefruit sections
1 ripe avocado, sliced
3⅓ cups sliced strawberries
10 cups Bibb lettuce leaves
Honey-Pecan Dressing

Arrange fresh orange and grapefruit sections, sliced avocado, and sliced strawberries over Bibb lettuce leaves; drizzle with Honey-Pecan Dressing. **Makes** 6 to 8 servings.

Honey-Pecan Dressing

Prep: 5 min.

3 Tbsp. sugar
1 Tbsp. chopped sweet onion
½ tsp. dry mustard
¼ tsp. salt
½ cup honey
¼ cup red wine vinegar
1 cup vegetable oil
1 cup chopped pecans, toasted

Pulse first 6 ingredients in a blender 2 to 3 times until blended. With blender running, pour oil through food chute in a slow, steady stream; process until smooth. Stir in pecans. **Makes** 2½ cups.

Summer Fruit Salad with Blueberry Vinaigrette
Prep: 10 min., Other: 1 hr.

2 cups fresh or frozen blueberries
1 cup fresh strawberries, halved
2 nectarines, sliced
8 cups mixed salad greens
Blueberry Vinaigrette
½ cup slivered almonds, toasted (optional)

Combine first 4 ingredients in a large bowl. Cover and chill 1 hour.
Drizzle ⅓ cup Blueberry Vinaigrette over blueberry mixture, tossing to coat.
Sprinkle with slivered almonds, if desired. **Makes** 4 servings.

Blueberry Vinaigrette
Prep: 5 min.

¼ cup Blueberry Chutney
¼ cup minced onion
⅓ cup balsamic vinegar
1 tsp. salt
½ tsp. pepper
⅔ cup vegetable oil

Whisk together first 5 ingredients. Gradually whisk in oil until blended. Refrigerate leftover vinaigrette up to 2 weeks. **Makes** 1½ cups.

Blueberry Chutney
Prep: 15 min., Cook: 40 min.

1 large Granny Smith apple, peeled and diced
½ cup sugar
½ cup orange juice
1 Tbsp. grated orange rind
1 tsp. ground ginger
¼ to ½ tsp. dried crushed red pepper
¼ tsp. ground black pepper
4 cups fresh or frozen blueberries
3 Tbsp. balsamic vinegar

Bring first 7 ingredients to a boil in a medium saucepan. Reduce heat to low; simmer, stirring occasionally, 15 minutes or until apple is tender. Stir in blueberries and vinegar; bring to a boil.
Reduce heat to medium; cook, stirring occasionally, 40 minutes or until thickened. **Makes** 3 cups.

Fruity Spring Mix Salad
Prep: 15 min.

You can make the salad dressing and sugared almonds several days ahead and store in airtight containers.

1 head Bibb lettuce, torn
10 oz. gourmet mixed salad greens*
2 cups fresh chopped pineapple (1-inch cubes)
2 kiwifruit, peeled and sliced
1 (11-oz.) can mandarin oranges, drained and chilled
16 seedless green or red grapes, cut in half lengthwise
Sweet-Hot Vinaigrette
Sugared Almonds

Toss first 6 ingredients together in a large glass bowl. Drizzle evenly with Sweet-Hot Vinaigrette, and sprinkle with Sugared Almonds. **Makes** 6 to 8 servings.

*Substitute 10 cups of your favorite salad greens, loosely packed and torn, if desired.

Sweet-Hot Vinaigrette
Prep: 5 min., Other: 30 min.

¼ cup vegetable oil
¼ cup balsamic vinegar
2 Tbsp. sugar
¼ tsp. salt
¼ tsp. pepper
¼ tsp. hot sauce

Whisk together all ingredients. Cover; chill 30 minutes. **Makes** ½ cup.

Sugared Almonds
Prep: 2 min., Cook: 10 min., Other: 20 min.

1 cup slivered almonds
½ cup sugar

Stir together all ingredients in a heavy saucepan over medium heat, and cook, stirring constantly, 10 minutes or until golden. Spread mixture in an even layer on lightly greased wax paper, and cool 20 minutes. Break into pieces, and store in an airtight container. **Makes** 1 cup.

SLAW SECRET

Look for prepackaged broccoli slaw mix in the produce department of your grocery store. The fine shreds of broccoli stalks, which resemble shredded cabbage, need no cooking and are ready to toss into slaws, leaving you more time to tend the barbecue. These four recipes, using the nutritious slaw mix, offer lots of variety.

make ahead • quick & easy

Cilantro Slaw

Prep: 10 min.

¼ cup finely chopped fresh cilantro
¼ cup Dijon mustard
3 Tbsp. mayonnaise
1 Tbsp. white wine vinegar
1 (12-oz.) package broccoli slaw mix

Whisk together first 4 ingredients in a large bowl; add broccoli slaw, tossing to coat. **Makes** 4 cups.

make ahead • quick & easy

Broccoli Slaw

Prep: 20 min.

This is a terrific dish to take to a barbecue after a busy day because you can make it the night before.

1 (12-oz.) package broccoli slaw mix
1 cup seedless red grapes, halved
1 Granny Smith apple, diced
1 cup Vidalia onion dressing or poppy seed dressing
2 oranges, peeled and sectioned
Toasted chopped pecans (optional)

Stir together first 5 ingredients in a large bowl. Top with chopped pecans, if desired. **Makes** 8 servings.

quick & easy

Blue Cheese-Bacon Slaw

Prep: 15 min.

1 (16-oz.) bottle Ranch dressing
1 cup crumbled blue cheese
2 (12-oz.) packages broccoli slaw mix
1 small onion, chopped
6 bacon slices, cooked and crumbled

Stir together Ranch dressing and blue cheese in a large bowl. Rinse slaw mix with cold water; drain well. Combine slaw mix, onion, and bacon; toss. Top with dressing just before serving. **Makes** 8 servings.

make ahead

Broccoli-Squash Slaw

Prep: 20 min., Other: 2 hrs.

¼ cup mayonnaise
¼ cup honey
2 Tbsp. fresh lemon juice
1 tsp. salt
½ tsp. black pepper
⅛ to ¼ tsp. ground red pepper
1 (12-oz.) package broccoli slaw mix
2 medium-size yellow squash, cut in half lengthwise and thinly sliced
1 red bell pepper, chopped
½ cup chopped pecans, toasted

Whisk together first 6 ingredients in a small bowl. Combine broccoli slaw, squash, and bell pepper in a large bowl. Add half of mayonnaise mixture (about ¼ cup), tossing to coat. Cover and chill both slaw mixture and remaining mayonnaise mixture at least 2 hours or up to 24 hours.

Drain slaw mixture, just before serving, discarding excess liquid; return to bowl. Add reserved half of mayonnaise mixture and pecans, tossing to coat. **Makes** 4 servings.

'Cue: What type of coleslaw goes best with barbecue?
A: There are two basic types of coleslaw: vinegar based and creamy. Vinegar-based coleslaws mirror the tangy flavors of barbecue sauce for those adventuresome palates that can't get enough. Creamy coleslaws tame the heat of hot sauces—literally if dairy products are in the slaw, and figuratively if the slaws are mayonnaise based. So pick a slaw that complements your preferences.

make ahead
Sweet-and-Tart
Red Cabbage Coleslaw
Prep: 20 min., Other: 1 hr.

Pineapple juice and sugar sweeten this German-style coleslaw.

⅓ cup pineapple juice
¼ cup sugar
¼ cup olive oil
¼ cup lemon or lime juice
¼ cup rice wine vinegar
½ tsp. salt
½ tsp. pepper
⅛ tsp. hot sauce
1 large red cabbage, finely shredded
1 small Granny Smith apple, chopped
1 large carrot, shredded
1 small sweet onion, minced
5 to 6 bacon slices, cooked and crumbled

Whisk together first 8 ingredients in a large bowl until sugar dissolves.
Add cabbage and next 3 ingredients, tossing to coat. Cover and chill at least 1 hour. Sprinkle with bacon before serving. **Makes** 8 cups.

make ahead
Spectacular Overnight Slaw
Prep: 8 min., Cook: 4 min., Other: 8 hrs.

This slaw is true to its name! Chilling the slaw overnight allows the flavors to blend, resulting in a taste sensation.

1 medium cabbage, finely shredded
1 medium-size red onion, thinly sliced
½ cup chopped green bell pepper
½ cup chopped red bell pepper
½ cup sliced pimiento-stuffed olives
½ cup sugar
½ cup vegetable oil
½ cup white wine vinegar
1 tsp. salt
1 tsp. celery seeds
1 tsp. mustard seeds
2 tsp. Dijon mustard

Combine first 5 ingredients in a large bowl; stir well. Combine sugar and remaining 6 ingredients in a small saucepan; bring to a boil. Boil 1 minute. Pour over cabbage mixture; toss well. Cover and chill 8 hours. Toss well. **Makes** 12 servings.

make ahead
Tangy Marinated Coleslaw
Prep: 5 min., Other: 8 hrs.

4 cups coarsely shredded green cabbage
1 medium cucumber, thinly sliced
1 cup coarsely shredded carrot
½ cup diced red onion
½ cup diced green bell pepper
¼ cup cider vinegar
1 Tbsp. sugar
1 Tbsp. Dijon mustard
1 Tbsp. vegetable oil
2 tsp. prepared horseradish
½ tsp. pepper
¼ tsp. salt

Combine first 5 ingredients in a large bowl; toss well. **Combine** vinegar and remaining 6 ingredients in a jar. Cover tightly, and shake vigorously. Pour over vegetables; toss gently. Cover and chill 8 hours. Serve chilled or at room temperature. **Makes** 6 cups.

Chinese Cabbage Slaw
Prep: 15 min., Cook: 5 min.

1 head bok choy, shredded
1 bunch green onions, diced
2 Tbsp. butter or margarine
¼ cup sliced almonds
¼ cup sesame seeds
½ cup vegetable oil
¼ cup sesame oil
6 Tbsp. rice wine vinegar
¼ cup sugar
1 tsp. salt
1 tsp. pepper

Place bok choy and green onions in a large bowl.
Melt butter in a skillet. Add almonds and sesame seeds; sauté mixture over medium-high heat 5 minutes or until lightly browned. Drain and cool slightly. Add to bok choy mixture.
Stir together oils and remaining 4 ingredients. Toss with bok choy mixture. Serve immediately. **Makes** 4 servings.

Buttermilk-Dressing Coleslaw
Prep: 15 min., Other: 2 hrs.

½ cup sugar
½ cup mayonnaise
¼ cup milk
¼ cup buttermilk
2½ Tbsp. lemon juice
1½ Tbsp. white vinegar
½ tsp. salt
⅛ tsp. pepper
2 (10-oz.) packages finely shredded cabbage
1 carrot, shredded

Whisk together first 8 ingredients in a large bowl until blended. Add cabbage and carrot, and toss to coat. Cover and chill at least 2 hours. **Makes** 8 to 10 servings.

Memphis-Style Coleslaw
Prep: 8 min., Other: 4 hrs.

2 cups mayonnaise
¼ cup sugar
¼ cup Dijon mustard
¼ cup cider vinegar
1½ to 2 Tbsp. celery seeds
1 tsp. salt
⅛ tsp. pepper
1 medium cabbage, shredded
2 carrots, grated
1 green bell pepper, diced
2 Tbsp. grated onion

Stir together first 7 ingredients in a large bowl; add cabbage and remaining ingredients, tossing gently. Cover and chill 3 to 4 hours; serve with a slotted spoon. **Makes** 12 servings.

Barbecue Slaw
Prep: 5 min., Other: 3 hrs.

Move over, ordinary coleslaw—this easy barbecue-flavored variation is sure to become a favorite in your family.

⅓ cup sugar
⅓ cup ketchup
⅓ cup white vinegar
11 cups shredded cabbage (about 1 medium cabbage)

Combine first 3 ingredients in a small saucepan; bring to a boil, stirring until sugar dissolves. Pour hot vinegar mixture over cabbage; toss well. Cover and chill at least 3 hours. **Makes** 8 servings.

Bacon Potato Salad

Bacon Potato Salad
Prep: 15 min., Cook: 18 min., Other: 1 hr.

6 to 8 medium potatoes (about 3 lb.), peeled and cut
    into 1-inch cubes
½ lb. bacon, cooked and crumbled
6 green onions, chopped
2 celery ribs, finely chopped
2 Tbsp. diced pimiento, drained
¾ tsp. salt
¼ tsp. pepper
½ cup mayonnaise
½ cup sour cream
Garnishes: paprika, celery sticks

Cook potatoes in boiling water to cover in a Dutch oven over medium heat 15 to 18 minutes or until tender. Drain and cool slightly.
Place potatoes in a large bowl. Add bacon, chopped green onions, and next 4 ingredients.
Stir together mayonnaise and sour cream until blended. Pour over potato mixture, tossing gently to coat. Cover and chill at least 1 hour. Garnish, if desired. **Makes** 6 servings.

Southern-Style Potato Salad
Prep: 15 min., Cook: 40 min.

4 lb. potatoes (about 4 large)
3 large hard-cooked eggs, peeled and grated
1 cup mayonnaise
½ cup sour cream
¼ cup celery, finely chopped
2 Tbsp. onion, finely chopped
2 Tbsp. sweet pickle relish
1 Tbsp. mustard
1 tsp. salt
½ tsp. freshly ground pepper
½ lb. bacon, cooked and crumbled

Cook potatoes in boiling water to cover 40 minutes or until tender; drain and cool. Peel potatoes, and cut into 1-inch cubes.
Stir together potatoes and egg in a large bowl.
Stir together mayonnaise and next 7 ingredients; gently stir into potato mixture. Cover and chill. Sprinkle with bacon just before serving. **Makes** 8 servings.

Lemon-Basil Potato Salad
Prep: 20 min., Cook: 25 min.

2½ lb. small Yukon gold potatoes, cut into eighths*
¼ cup lemon juice
4 garlic cloves, minced
¾ cup chopped fresh basil
1 Tbsp. Dijon mustard
1 tsp. salt
½ tsp. freshly ground pepper
⅔ cup olive oil
½ medium-size red onion, chopped
1 (10-oz.) package leaf spinach, cut into thin strips
10 thick bacon slices, cooked and crumbled

Arrange potato evenly on a lightly greased 15- x 10-inch jelly-roll pan; coat potato with cooking spray.
Bake at 475°, stirring occasionally, 20 to 25 minutes or until tender and golden.
Whisk together lemon juice and next 5 ingredients; whisk in oil in a slow, steady stream. Gently toss potato and onion with ½ cup vinaigrette.
Arrange spinach evenly in 6 bowls, and drizzle with remaining vinaigrette. Top with potato mixture; sprinkle with bacon. **Makes** 6 servings.

*Substitute 2½ lb. small new potatoes, if desired.

Sweet Potato Salad with Rosemary-Honey Vinaigrette
Prep: 10 min., Cook: 35 min.

4½ cups peeled, cubed sweet potato
2 Tbsp. olive oil, divided
¼ cup honey
3 Tbsp. white wine vinegar
2 Tbsp. chopped fresh rosemary
2 garlic cloves, minced
½ tsp. salt
½ tsp. freshly ground pepper

Line a 15- x 10-inch jelly-roll pan with aluminum foil. Coat foil with vegetable cooking spray.
Toss together sweet potato and 1 Tbsp. oil in pan.
Bake at 450° for 35 minutes or until tender.
Whisk together remaining 1 Tbsp. oil, honey, and next 5 ingredients in a large bowl. Add sweet potato; toss well. Cool. **Makes** 6 servings.

Not every barbecue region considers beans an essential side dish. However, in such states as Texas, Alabama, and Missouri, a plate of 'cue without beans in some shape or form—whether great Northern, black, pinto, or pork and beans—just wouldn't be proper.

Beans are prepared in a variety of styles and flavored with a wide assortment of seasonings. Whichever you choose, you'll love these recipes that showcase the best of the bean.

Red Beans and Rice

Prep: 12 min., Cook: 30 min.

2 tsp. olive oil
6 oz. smoked turkey sausage
1¼ cups chopped onion
1 tsp. minced garlic
1½ cups uncooked long-grain rice
½ tsp. dried thyme
½ tsp. ground red pepper
3 bay leaves
2 (15-oz.) cans kidney beans, drained
2 (14-oz.) cans beef broth
1½ cups seeded, chopped tomato
3 Tbsp. sliced green onions

Coat a Dutch oven with cooking spray; add oil. Place over medium-high heat until hot. Add sausage, onion, and garlic; sauté 5 minutes or until onion is tender. Add rice and next 3 ingredients; sauté 30 seconds. Stir in beans and beef broth. Bring to a boil; cover, reduce heat, and simmer 20 minutes or until liquid is absorbed and rice is tender. Remove and discard bay leaves.

To serve, spoon into 4 individual bowls, and top evenly with tomato and green onions. **Makes** 4 servings.

Spicy Pinto Beans

Prep: 10 min.; Cook: 2 hrs., 30 min.; Other: 1 hr.

1 cup dried pinto beans
4¼ cups cold water
1 tsp. olive oil
1 cup chopped onion
2 medium garlic cloves, crushed
½ cup diced ham
3 jalapeño peppers, seeded and chopped
2 Tbsp. red wine vinegar
2 tsp. brown sugar
½ tsp. salt
¼ tsp. pepper

Sort and wash beans; place beans in a large saucepan. Cover with water to a depth of 2 inches above beans. Bring to a boil; cover, remove from heat, and let stand 1 hour. Drain beans, and return to saucepan; add 4¼ cups water. Bring to a boil; cover, reduce heat, and simmer, partially covered, 2 hours or until tender.

Heat oil in a large nonstick skillet over medium-high heat until hot. Add onion, and sauté 5 minutes. Add garlic, ham, and chopped pepper; sauté 5 more minutes. Add onion mixture to beans in saucepan. Add vinegar and remaining ingredients; stir well. Bring to a boil; cover, reduce heat, and simmer 20 minutes. **Makes** 4 servings.

Baked Beans

Prep: 10 min., Cook: 45 min.

4 bacon slices
1 (28-oz.) can pork and beans, drained
1 small onion, diced
¼ cup firmly packed brown sugar
¼ cup sorghum
¼ cup ketchup
1 tsp. Worcestershire sauce
½ tsp. dry mustard

Cook bacon in a large skillet over medium-high heat 3 to 4 minutes. Stir together pork and beans and next 6 ingredients in a lightly greased 1-qt. baking dish. Top mixture with bacon.

Bake, uncovered, at 350° for 45 minutes. **Makes** 4 to 6 servings.

Mexican Pinto Beans

Prep: 15 min., Cook: 2 hrs., Other: 1 hr.

1 cup dried pinto beans
3 cups chicken broth
3 bacon slices, diced
1 small onion, chopped
1 small green bell pepper, chopped
2 tsp. ground cumin
2 tsp. chili powder
¾ tsp. salt
½ tsp. pepper

Sort and wash pinto beans; place in a large saucepan. Cover with water 2 inches above beans, and bring to a boil. Boil beans 1 minute. Cover, remove from heat, and let soak 1 hour. Drain.

Bring beans, broth, and remaining ingredients to a boil. Cover, reduce heat, and simmer 2 hours or until beans are tender and mixture is desired consistency. **Makes** 4 cups.

Slow-Cooker Barbecue Beans

Prep: 5 min., Cook: 1 hr.

This recipe is perfect for using leftover barbecue. Although it calls for pork, feel free to use chopped or shredded chicken, turkey, or brisket. If time is a concern, pick up meat from your favorite barbecue joint (just make sure you get it without sauce to prevent the beans from being too soupy).

½ lb. chopped or shredded barbecue pork
1 (32-oz.) can pork and beans, undrained
1 (14½-oz.) can diced tomatoes with green pepper, celery, and onion, drained
¼ cup spicy brown mustard
3 Tbsp. brown sugar
2 Tbsp. Worcestershire sauce
1 Tbsp. molasses (optional)

Stir together first 6 ingredients, and, if desired, molasses in a 6-qt. slow cooker. Cover; cook on HIGH 1 hour. (You can keep this recipe warm on LOW for up to 2 hours before serving.) **Makes** 8 servings.

TRY BEANS THE TEXAS WAY

Barbecue lovers in the middle and eastern South like baked beans (usually varieties that are the size of your pinkie fingernail or a bit smaller) seasoned with molasses and shades of ketchup, mustard, and spices. Texans, however, tend to see beans as a backdrop for sliced raw onions and jalapeños served alongside brisket. Most Lone Star barbecue plates sporting beans offer pinto beans made from dried pintos slowly cooked with water, salt, pepper, and sometimes cumin or other Southwestern spices. The recipe below highlights how Texans take their beans. Enjoy!

Tex-Mex Pinto Beans

Prep: 20 min., Cook: 3 hrs., Other: 8 hrs.

To turn these baked beans into a hearty main dish, stir in cooked ground beef before serving.

1 lb. dried pinto beans
10 cups water
2 tsp. vegetable oil
1 medium onion, diced
4 garlic cloves, crushed
1 (14.5-oz.) can stewed tomatoes, undrained and chopped
¼ cup Worcestershire sauce
2 Tbsp. mild picante sauce
1 tsp. chopped fresh cilantro
1 tsp. salt
1 tsp. ground cumin
¼ tsp. chili powder
1 cup (4 oz.) shredded sharp Cheddar cheese

Sort and wash beans; place in a large Dutch oven. Cover with water 2 inches above beans; let soak at least 8 hours. Drain. Add 10 cups water and vegetable oil to beans; bring to a boil. Reduce heat, and simmer, uncovered, 1½ hours.

Add onion and next 8 ingredients; bring to a boil. Reduce heat; simmer, uncovered, 1½ hours or until beans are tender and mixture is desired consistency. **To serve,** ladle beans into individual serving bowls. Top evenly with cheese. **Makes** 7 servings.

Spicy Baked Beans

Prep: 15 min., Cook: 55 min.

1 lb. ground pork sausage
1 onion, chopped
2 (28-oz.) cans bold-and-spicy baked beans
1 (15-oz.) can black beans, drained
1 (15-oz.) can light or dark kidney beans, drained
3 cups bottled barbecue sauce
½ cup firmly packed dark brown sugar
¼ cup yellow mustard
1 tsp. black pepper
½ tsp. ground red pepper
1 tsp. garlic powder (optional)

Cook pork sausage in an ovenproof Dutch oven over medium-high heat, stirring until sausage crumbles and is no longer pink. Drain, reserving 2 tsp. drippings in Dutch oven. Return sausage to Dutch oven, and stir in onion, next 8 ingredients, and, if desired, garlic powder.

Bake, uncovered, at 350° for 45 minutes or until thickened and bubbly. **Makes** 12 servings.

Baked Beans and Peppers

Prep: 25 min.; Cook: 3 hrs., 5 min.

10 bacon slices
4 (28-oz.) cans baked beans
5 green bell peppers, cut into 1-inch pieces
3 large onions, chopped
2 cups ketchup
½ cup firmly packed brown sugar
2 Tbsp. prepared mustard
1 Tbsp. white vinegar

Cook bacon in a large skillet until crisp; reserve 2 Tbsp. drippings. Crumble bacon.
Stir together bacon, bacon drippings, beans, and next 5 ingredients in a roasting pan.
Bake, covered, at 350° for 3 hours. Stir in vinegar.
Makes 15 servings.

Three-Bean Barbecue Bake

Prep: 15 min., Cook: 55 min.

2 tsp. vegetable oil
1½ cups chopped onion
1 cup chopped green bell pepper
1 cup chopped red bell pepper
2 garlic cloves, minced
¾ cup ketchup
½ cup firmly packed brown sugar
¼ cup molasses
1 Tbsp. cider vinegar
1 tsp. dry mustard
1 (15.8-oz.) can great Northern beans, drained
1 (16-oz.) can kidney beans, drained
1 (16-oz.) can lima beans, drained

Heat oil in a large nonstick skillet over medium-high heat. Add onion, peppers, and garlic; sauté 5 minutes or until tender. Stir in ketchup and next 4 ingredients; bring to a boil. Stir in beans.
Pour mixture into an 11- x 7-inch baking dish coated with cooking spray. Bake, uncovered, at 325° for 55 minutes or until bubbly. **Makes** 4 servings.

Note: If you want a more traditional baked bean dish, top the bean mixture with 5 bacon slices before baking. Bake as directed above.

Spicy Molasses Baked Beans

Prep: 10 min., Cook: 1 hr.

1 cup chopped onion
1 jalapeño pepper, seeded and minced
2 (15.8-oz.) cans great Northern beans, drained
1 (16-oz.) can pinto beans, drained
½ cup ketchup
½ cup water
3 Tbsp. dark brown sugar
3 Tbsp. molasses
2 Tbsp. yellow mustard
1 tsp. chili powder
½ tsp. liquid smoke

Coat a small nonstick skillet with cooking spray, and place over medium-high heat until hot. Add onion and jalapeño pepper; sauté 2 minutes or until tender. Combine onion mixture, beans, and remaining ingredients in a large bowl; stir well.
Spoon bean mixture into a lightly greased 2-qt. casserole. Bake, uncovered, at 350° for 1 hour or until thick and bubbly. **Makes** 10 servings.

quick & easy
Stovetop "Baked Beans"

Prep: 15 min., Cook: 20 min.

1 Tbsp. butter or margarine
1¼ cups chopped onion
¾ cup chopped green bell pepper
2 garlic cloves, minced
1 cup ketchup
¼ cup firmly packed brown sugar
¼ cup maple syrup
2 Tbsp. Worcestershire sauce
2 tsp. liquid smoke
2 tsp. prepared mustard
1 (16-oz.) can red beans, drained
1 (15.8-oz.) can great Northern beans, drained

Melt butter in a medium saucepan over medium-high heat. Add onion, bell pepper, and garlic; sauté 4 minutes.
Stir in ketchup and remaining ingredients; bring to a boil. Reduce heat; simmer 15 minutes, stirring occasionally. **Makes** 8 servings.

Root Beer Baked Beans

Prep: 5 min.; Cook: 1 hr., 7 min.

You don't actually taste the root beer in this recipe—it's just used for sweetening instead of the traditional brown sugar.

3 bacon slices
1 small onion, diced
2 (16-oz.) cans pork and beans
½ cup root beer (not diet)
¼ cup hickory-smoked barbecue sauce
½ tsp. dry mustard
⅛ tsp. hot sauce

Cook bacon in a skillet over medium heat until crisp; remove and drain on paper towels, reserving 2 Tbsp. drippings in skillet. Crumble bacon.

Sauté diced onion in hot bacon drippings in skillet over high heat 5 minutes or until tender. Stir together onion, crumbled bacon, pork and beans, and remaining ingredients in a lightly greased 1-qt. baking dish.

Bake, uncovered, at 400° for 55 minutes or until sauce is thickened. **Makes** 4 servings.

In the South it's not uncommon to find deviled eggs at a barbecue—sometimes as an appetizer while the 'cue cooks, sometimes as a side dish to rival the baked beans or potato salad in popularity.

make ahead • quick & easy

Spicy-Sweet Deviled Eggs

Prep: 15 min.

12 large hard-cooked eggs, peeled
½ cup mayonnaise
3 Tbsp. mango chutney
⅛ tsp. ground red pepper
Kosher salt to taste
Garnish: sliced fresh chives

Cut eggs in half lengthwise; carefully remove yolks.
Mash yolks in a small bowl; stir in mayonnaise, chutney, and red pepper until blended.
Spoon yolk mixture evenly into egg white halves. Sprinkle evenly with salt to taste. Garnish, if desired. Chill until ready to serve. **Makes** 2 dozen.

make ahead

Barbecue Deviled Eggs

Prep: 20 min., Cook: 6 min., Other: 15 min.

Finely chopped pork is the secret to the filling in Barbecue Deviled Eggs. The recipe serves a crowd of 12, but the eggs will be gone before you know it.

12 large eggs
¼ cup mayonnaise
⅓ cup finely chopped smoked pork
1 Tbsp. Dijon mustard
¼ tsp. salt
½ tsp. pepper
⅛ tsp. hot sauce
Garnish: paprika

Place eggs in a single layer in a large saucepan; add water to a depth of 3 inches. Bring to a boil; cover, remove from heat, and let stand 15 minutes.
Drain and fill pan with cold water and ice. Tap each egg firmly on the counter until cracks form all over shell. Peel under cold running water.
Cut eggs in half lengthwise; carefully remove yolks.
Mash yolks in a medium bowl with mayonnaise. Stir in pork and next 4 ingredients; blend well.
Spoon yolk mixture evenly into egg white halves. Garnish, if desired. **Makes** 2 dozen.

Barbecue Deviled Eggs

Creole Deviled Eggs
Prep: 20 min.

Hot sauce and red pepper deliver a powerful punch to these stuffed eggs.

16 large hard-cooked eggs, peeled
½ cup mayonnaise
1 Tbsp. lemon juice
5 drops of hot sauce
¼ tsp. salt
½ tsp. ground red pepper
2 Tbsp. finely chopped fresh chives
2 Tbsp. finely chopped fresh parsley
2 Tbsp. finely chopped red bell pepper
Garnishes: red bell pepper strips, chopped fresh chives, fresh parsley sprigs
Additional ground red pepper

Cut eggs in half lengthwise; carefully remove yolks. **Process** yolks, mayonnaise, and next 4 ingredients in a food processor until smooth, stopping once to scrape down sides. Add chives, parsley, and chopped red bell pepper; pulse just until blended.
Spoon yolk mixture evenly into egg white halves. Garnish, if desired; sprinkle with additional ground red pepper. Chill thoroughly before serving. **Makes** 32 deviled eggs.

HOW TO COOK THE PERFECT EGG

■ Place the desired number of eggs in a single layer in a saucepan. Add enough water to measure at least 1 inch above eggs. Cover and quickly bring to a boil.
■ Remove from heat. Let stand, covered, in hot water 15 minutes for large eggs. (Adjust time up or down by about 3 minutes for each size larger or smaller.)
■ Pour off water. Immediately run cold water over eggs or place them in ice water until completely cooled.
■ To remove shell, gently tap each egg all over and roll between hands to loosen egg shell; then hold egg under cold running water as you peel off shell.

Deviled Eggs with Capers
Prep: 15 min.

6 large hard-cooked eggs, peeled
2 Tbsp. mayonnaise
1 Tbsp. butter, softened
2 tsp. capers
1 tsp. chopped fresh chives
⅛ tsp. dry mustard
Salt and pepper to taste
Paprika (optional)
Fresh parsley sprigs (optional)

Cut eggs in half lengthwise; carefully remove yolks. **Mash** yolks in a small bowl; stir in mayonnaise and next 4 ingredients. Stir in salt and pepper to taste. Spoon or pipe egg yolk mixture evenly into egg white halves.
Cover and chill until ready to serve. Sprinkle with paprika and top with parsley sprigs, if desired. **Makes** 1 dozen.

Pecan-Stuffed Deviled Eggs
Prep: 15 min.

Top these eggs with fresh parsley sprigs and sliced pimientos or chopped pecans for a festive presentation. You might be tempted to use chopped onion, but we found that grating the onion gives the filling a better texture.

6 large hard-cooked eggs, peeled
¼ cup mayonnaise
1 tsp. grated onion
1 tsp. white vinegar
½ tsp. chopped fresh parsley
½ tsp. dry mustard
⅛ tsp. salt
⅓ cup coarsely chopped pecans

Cut eggs in half lengthwise; carefully remove yolks. **Mash** yolks in a small bowl. Stir in mayonnaise and next 5 ingredients, and blend well. Stir in pecans.
Spoon or pipe yolk mixture evenly into egg white halves. **Makes** 1 dozen.

Mexican Deviled Eggs

Mexican Deviled Eggs
Prep: 10 min.

Although these eggs are not too spicy, you can prepare a milder version by reducing the amount of minced jalapeños.

6 large hard-cooked eggs, peeled
¼ cup mayonnaise
2 Tbsp. pickled jalapeño slices, minced
1 Tbsp. prepared mustard
¼ tsp. ground cumin
⅛ tsp. salt
Garnishes: chili powder, fresh parsley sprigs

Cut eggs in half lengthwise; carefully remove yolks.
Mash egg yolks in a small bowl. Stir in mayonnaise and next 4 ingredients, and blend well.
Spoon or pipe yolk mixture evenly into egg white halves. Garnish, if desired. **Makes** 1 dozen.

Tex-Mex Deviled Eggs
Prep: 10 min.

6 large hard-cooked eggs, peeled
1 Tbsp. diced green onions
1 Tbsp. chopped fresh cilantro
1 small serrano chile pepper or jalapeño pepper, seeded and finely chopped
¼ cup mayonnaise
1 tsp. prepared mustard
½ tsp. salt
¼ cup (1 oz.) shredded Cheddar cheese
Chili powder

Cut eggs in half lengthwise; carefully remove yolks.
Mash yolks in a small bowl, and stir in green onions and next 5 ingredients.
Spoon evenly into egg white halves; sprinkle with cheese and chili powder. Cover and chill. **Makes** 1 dozen.

Roasted Asparagus

VEGETABLES TAKE THE 'CUE

Southern barbecues are typically full of the slaws, salads, and beans we've just seen as side dishes, but don't limit your 'cue to those recipes. Barbecued smoked pork, beef, and chicken—sauced or with no sauce—take to a host of other veggies that offer lots more menu options. These vegetables pair especially well with smoked meats and poultry.

Snap off and discard tough ends of asparagus.
Arrange asparagus evenly on a lightly greased 15- x 10-inch jelly-roll pan. Drizzle with olive oil, and sprinkle with salt and pepper; toss to coat.
Bake asparagus at 400° for 15 minutes or just until tender.
Melt butter in a large skillet over medium heat. Cook, stirring occasionally, 4 minutes or until butter is lightly browned. Remove from heat; stir in soy sauce and balsamic vinegar. Drizzle over asparagus, tossing to coat. Serve immediately. **Makes** 12 servings.

editor's favorite • quick & easy
Roasted Asparagus
Prep: 10 min., Cook: 7 min.

2 lb. medium-size fresh asparagus, trimmed
½ cup pine nuts, toasted
1 plum tomato, seeded and chopped

Spray asparagus lightly with cooking spray, and arrange asparagus in an aluminum foil-lined pan.
Bake at 425° for 7 minutes.
Sprinkle asparagus with pine nuts and tomatoes.
Makes 8 servings.

quick & easy
Balsamic-Browned Butter Asparagus
Prep: 10 min., Cook: 15 min.

The secret to browning butter without burning it is to use smell as a test for doneness—it should have a nutty aroma.

4 lb. fresh asparagus
2 Tbsp. extra-virgin olive oil
½ tsp. kosher salt
¼ tsp. cracked pepper
¼ cup butter
4 tsp. lite soy sauce
2 tsp. balsamic vinegar

quick & easy
Gingered Green Beans
Prep: 10 min., Cook: 10 min.

Look for fresh ginger (also called gingeroot) in the specialty produce section of your grocery store. Peel it with a vegetable peeler, and mince with a sharp knife.

3 cups water
1 extra-large ham-flavored bouillon cube
1 lb. fresh green beans, trimmed
2 Tbsp. butter or margarine
1 small sweet onion, diced
2 garlic cloves, minced
2 Tbsp. peeled and minced fresh ginger
½ tsp. salt
½ tsp. seasoned pepper
¼ cup finely chopped pecans, toasted
Garnish: toasted pecan halves

Bring 3 cups water to a boil in a large saucepan over medium-high heat. Stir in bouillon cube until dissolved. Add green beans, and cook 4 to 6 minutes or until crisp-tender; drain.
Melt butter in a large nonstick skillet over medium-high heat. Add onion, garlic, and ginger; sauté 2 minutes. Add beans, salt, and pepper; sauté 1 minute or until thoroughly heated. Transfer to a serving dish; sprinkle with pecans. Garnish, if desired. **Makes** 6 servings.

Broccoli with
Orange Sauce

Garlic-Tarragon Green Beans
Prep: 20 min., Cook: 15 min.

2 qt. water
2 Tbsp. salt
2 lb. thin fresh green beans
2 garlic cloves, minced
½ tsp. dried tarragon
2 Tbsp. olive oil
½ tsp. salt
½ tsp. pepper

Bring 2 qt. water and 2 Tbsp. salt to a boil in a Dutch oven; add beans. Cook 6 minutes or until crisp-tender; drain. Plunge into ice water to stop the cooking process; drain.

Sauté garlic and tarragon in hot oil in Dutch oven over medium heat 2 to 3 minutes or until garlic is tender. (Do not brown garlic.) Add beans, salt, and pepper, and cook, stirring constantly, 2 minutes or until thoroughly heated. **Makes** 10 to 12 servings.

Broccoli with Orange Sauce
Prep: 20 min., Cook: 11 min.

2 oranges
1½ lb. fresh broccoli, cut into florets
1 tsp. butter or margarine
1 small onion, chopped
2 tsp. finely chopped crystallized ginger
1 (8-oz.) container low-fat lemon yogurt

Grate 1 orange to equal 1 tsp. grated rind; set aside. Peel and section oranges, removing seeds; set aside.

Place broccoli florets in a steamer basket over boiling water, and cook 3 to 4 minutes or until crisp-tender.

Melt butter in a nonstick skillet over medium-high heat; add onion and ginger, and sauté until tender. Remove from heat.

Toss together broccoli florets, onion mixture, 1 tsp. orange rind, and orange sections in a large bowl. Stir in yogurt. Serve immediately. **Makes** 6 servings.

Butterbeans, Bacon, and Tomatoes
Prep: 20 min., Cook: 1 hr.

3 bacon slices, chopped
1 medium onion, finely chopped
1 small green bell pepper, chopped
3 garlic cloves, minced
1 bay leaf
3 medium tomatoes, chopped
4 cups chicken broth
4 cups fresh or frozen butterbeans, thawed
2 Tbsp. minced fresh parsley
1 tsp. salt
1 tsp. pepper
1 tsp. Worcestershire sauce
½ tsp. hot sauce

Cook bacon in a Dutch oven until crisp. Stir in onion and next 3 ingredients; sauté until vegetables are tender. Stir in tomato, and cook 3 minutes.

Stir in broth and butterbeans; bring to a boil. Cover; reduce heat. Simmer, stirring occasionally, 30 minutes.

Simmer, uncovered, 20 minutes; stir often. Add parsley and remaining ingredients. Cook, stirring often, 5 minutes. Remove bay leaf; discard. **Makes** 6 servings.

Tangy Beets

Prep: 5 min., Cook: 8 min.

For a festive look, spoon beets over a bed of gourmet mixed salad greens.

½ cup sugar
2 Tbsp. all-purpose flour
½ cup white vinegar
¼ cup water
⅛ tsp. salt
2 Tbsp. butter or margarine
2 (15-oz.) cans sliced beets, drained

Combine sugar and flour in a heavy saucepan; whisk in vinegar and ¼ cup water. Bring to a boil over medium heat, and boil, whisking constantly, 1 minute or until thickened. Remove from heat; stir in salt and butter.

Stir beets into sugar mixture, and cook over low heat 5 minutes or until thoroughly heated, stirring often.

Serve immediately; or cool, spoon beet mixture into an airtight container, and chill up to 8 hours. **Makes** 8 servings.

Brown Sugar-Glazed Carrots

Prep: 5 min., Cook: 35 min.

1 lb. medium carrots
¾ tsp. salt, divided
2 Tbsp. butter or margarine
½ cup minced onion
1½ Tbsp. dark brown sugar
⅔ cup apple juice
¼ tsp. pepper

Cut carrots diagonally into ¼-inch-thick slices. Cook in boiling water to cover with ½ tsp. salt 5 minutes or until crisp-tender. Drain and rinse with cold water. Pat dry with paper towels.

Melt butter in a large skillet over low heat; add onion, and cook, stirring constantly, 10 minutes. Add brown sugar; cook, stirring constantly, 5 minutes. Add juice; cook, stirring occasionally, 10 minutes. Stir in carrot, remaining ¼ tsp. salt, and pepper. **Makes** 4 to 6 servings.

Carrots with Horseradish Glaze

Prep: 5 min., Cook: 20 min.

1 (1-lb.) package baby carrots
1¼ tsp. salt, divided
3 Tbsp. butter
⅓ cup honey
2 Tbsp. prepared horseradish

Cook carrots and 1 tsp. salt in boiling water to cover in a large saucepan 15 minutes or until tender; drain.

Melt 3 Tbsp. butter in saucepan over medium-high heat; stir in honey, horseradish, and remaining ¼ tsp. salt. Add carrots, and cook, stirring gently, 5 minutes. **Makes** 4 servings.

Glazed Carrots with Bacon and Onion

Prep: 5 min., Cook: 30 min.

1 (1-lb.) package baby carrots
3 bacon slices
1 small onion, chopped
3 Tbsp. brown sugar
¼ tsp. pepper

Cook carrots in boiling water to cover in a large saucepan 15 minutes or until carrots are tender; drain.

Cook bacon in a skillet until crisp; remove bacon, and drain on paper towels, reserving 1 Tbsp. drippings in skillet. Crumble bacon; set aside.

Sauté onion in reserved drippings over medium-high heat 3 minutes or until tender. Stir in brown sugar, pepper, and carrots. Cook, stirring often, 5 minutes or until carrots are glazed and thoroughly heated.

Transfer carrots to a serving dish, and sprinkle with crumbled bacon. **Makes** 4 servings.

Uptown Collards

Prep: 30 min., Cook: 1 hr.

7 lb. fresh collard greens
1 medium onion, quartered
1 cup water
1 cup dry white wine
1 Tbsp. sugar
1 Tbsp. bacon drippings
1 red bell pepper, diced

Remove and discard stems from greens. Wash leaves thoroughly, and cut into 1-inch-wide strips; set aside. **Pulse** onion in a food processor 3 or 4 times or until minced.

Bring onion and next 4 ingredients to a boil in a Dutch oven. Add greens and bell pepper; cook, covered, over medium heat 45 minutes to 1 hour or until greens are tender. **Makes** 8 to 10 servings.

Garlicky Collard Greens

Prep: 10 min., Cook: 55 min.

½ cup diced prosciutto
3 Tbsp. butter
½ cup diced onion
2 Tbsp. minced garlic
2 lb. fresh collard greens
3 cups chicken broth

Heat a large Dutch oven over medium-high heat. Add prosciutto; sauté 2 minutes. Add butter, onion, and garlic; sauté until onion is tender. Add greens and broth. Bring to a boil; reduce heat, and simmer 30 to 45 minutes or until greens are tender. **Makes** 10 cups.

Sweet Skillet Turnips

Prep: 20 min., Cook: 25 min.

1 Tbsp. butter or margarine
1 small onion, finely chopped
1 lb. turnips, peeled and shredded
½ cup chicken broth
1 Tbsp. sugar
½ tsp. salt
¼ tsp. pepper

Melt butter in a large skillet over medium heat; add onion, and sauté 3 to 5 minutes or until tender.
Stir in turnip and remaining ingredients. Cook, stirring often, 20 minutes or until turnip is tender. (Turnips will turn a light brown-caramel color as they cook.) **Makes** 2 to 3 servings.

Scalloped Turnip Casserole

Prep: 15 min., Cook: 55 min.

2 lb. turnips, peeled and chopped
¼ cup butter or margarine, divided
1 small onion, finely chopped
½ cup milk
1½ cups (6 oz.) grated white Cheddar cheese, divided
½ tsp. salt
½ tsp. pepper
⅓ cup Italian-seasoned breadcrumbs

Combine turnip and water to cover in a large saucepan. Bring to a boil; cook 20 minutes or until tender. Drain well; transfer to a large bowl, and mash with a potato masher.
Melt 1 Tbsp. butter in a skillet over medium heat; add onion, and sauté 3 minutes or until tender.
Add onion, milk, 1 cup Cheddar cheese, salt, pepper, and remaining 3 Tbsp. butter to mashed turnips, stirring to combine. Spoon into a lightly greased 11- x 7-inch baking dish. Sprinkle evenly with breadcrumbs and remaining ½ cup Cheddar cheese.
Bake, uncovered, at 350° for 30 minutes or until lightly browned. **Makes** 4 servings.

Spinach Soufflé

Prep: 15 min., Cook: 40 min., Other: 5 min.

1 (10-oz.) package frozen chopped spinach, thawed
2 Tbsp. butter
1 medium onion, chopped (about ¾ cup)
2 garlic cloves, minced
3 large eggs
2 Tbsp. all-purpose flour
½ tsp. salt
¼ tsp. nutmeg
¼ tsp. pepper
1 cup milk
1 cup freshly grated Parmesan or Romano cheese

Drain spinach well, pressing between paper towels to remove all excess liquid.
Melt butter in a large skillet over medium heat; add onion and garlic, and sauté 5 minutes or until garlic is lightly browned and onion is tender. Remove from heat, and stir in spinach until well blended; cool.
Whisk together eggs and next 4 ingredients in a large bowl. Whisk in milk and freshly grated Parmesan cheese; stir in spinach mixture, and pour into a lightly greased 8-inch square baking dish.
Bake at 350° for 33 to 35 minutes or until set. Let stand 5 minutes before serving. **Makes** 4 to 6 servings.

Buttermilk Batter-Fried Onion Rings

Prep: 20 min., Cook: 10 min.

These rings are best served the moment they come out of the fryer.

2 large onions
1 cup all-purpose flour
2 cups buttermilk
1 Tbsp. sugar
1 tsp. baking powder
½ tsp. salt
Peanut oil

Cut onions into ½-inch slices, and separate into rings. Set aside.

Whisk together flour and next 4 ingredients until smooth.

Pour oil to a depth of 2 inches into a Dutch oven; heat to 375°.

Dip onion rings in batter, coating well. Fry, a few rings at a time, until golden.

Drain on paper towels. Serve immediately. **Makes** 4 servings.

■ Cut onions into ½-inch slices. Separate into rings.

■ Whisk together flour and first 4 ingredients until smooth. Dip onion rings in batter, coating well.

■ Fry rings, a few at a time, until golden. Drain on paper towels.

Sweet Onion Pudding

Prep: 1 hr., Cook: 30 min.

2 cups whipping cream
1 (3-oz.) package shredded Parmesan cheese
6 large eggs, lightly beaten
3 Tbsp. all-purpose flour
2 Tbsp. sugar
2 tsp. baking powder
1 tsp. salt
½ cup butter or margarine
6 medium-size sweet onions, thinly sliced

Stir together first 3 ingredients in a large bowl. Combine flour and next 3 ingredients in a small bowl; gradually stir into egg mixture. Set aside.

Melt butter in a large skillet over medium heat; add onion, and cook, stirring often, 30 to 40 minutes or until onion is caramel colored. Remove onion from heat.

Stir onion into egg mixture; spoon into a lightly greased 13- x 9-inch baking dish.

Bake, uncovered, at 350° for 30 minutes or until set. **Makes** 8 servings.

Buttermilk Fried Corn

Prep: 15 min., Cook: 15 min., Other: 30 min.

2 cups fresh corn kernels (4 ears)
1½ cups buttermilk
⅔ cup all-purpose flour
⅔ cup cornmeal
1 tsp. salt
½ tsp. pepper
Corn oil

Combine corn kernels and buttermilk in a large bowl; let stand 30 minutes. Drain.

Combine flour and next 3 ingredients in a large zip-top freezer bag. Add corn to flour mixture, a small amount at a time, and shake bag to coat corn.

Pour oil to depth of 1 inch in a Dutch oven; heat to 375°. Fry corn, a small amount at a time, in hot oil 2 minutes or until golden. Drain on paper towels. Serve as a side dish or sprinkle on salads, soups, or casseroles. **Makes** 2 cups.

Sweet Corn Pudding

Prep: 10 min.; Cook: 1 hr., 5 min.; Other: 10 min.

1 cup soft breadcrumbs

6 Tbsp. self-rising white cornmeal mix

1½ Tbsp. sugar

½ tsp. salt

3 large eggs

1¼ cups milk

½ cup half-and-half

2 Tbsp. butter, melted

1 (20-oz.) package frozen cream style corn, thawed

Garnish: chopped green onions

Combine first 4 ingredients in a large bowl.

Whisk eggs in a large bowl until pale and foamy; whisk in milk, half-and-half, and butter. Whisk egg mixture into breadcrumb mixture; stir in corn. Pour into a lightly greased 9-inch square baking dish.

Bake at 325° for 1 hour to 1 hour and 5 minutes or until set. Let stand 10 minutes before serving. Garnish, if desired. **Makes** 6 servings.

Lemon-Scented Sugar Snap Peas
Prep: 15 min., Cook: 10 min.

2 lb. fresh sugar snap peas
2 Tbsp. butter or margarine
2 garlic cloves, minced
2 tsp. grated lemon rind
1 Tbsp. fresh lemon juice
¾ tsp. salt
½ tsp. freshly ground pepper

Cook peas in boiling salted water to cover 5 minutes or until crisp-tender in a large saucepan. Drain and plunge into ice water to stop the cooking process; drain.

Melt butter in a medium skillet over medium-high heat; add peas, and sauté 3 minutes. Add garlic and remaining ingredients. Sauté 2 minutes or until thoroughly heated. **Makes** 4 to 6 servings.

Orange-Ginger Peas
Prep: 5 min., Cook: 7 min.

This dish is equally good without ginger; if you don't have ginger or don't like it, leave it out.

1 (16-oz.) package frozen sweet peas
1 cup water
1 Tbsp. grated orange rind
2 Tbsp. honey
¼ to ½ tsp. salt
¼ tsp. ground red pepper
1 (1-inch) piece fresh ginger, peeled (optional)

Combine first 6 ingredients and, if desired, ginger in a large saucepan over medium-high heat. Bring to a boil; reduce heat, and simmer 3 minutes. Remove and discard ginger. Serve with a slotted spoon. **Makes** 8 servings.

Green Peas with Crispy Bacon
Prep: 20 min., Cook: 18 min.

The addition of mint and orange brightens this often under-rated legume, while the bacon lends a smoky flavor. When in season, use fresh sweet green peas.

2 hickory-smoked bacon slices
1 shallot, sliced
½ tsp. grated orange rind
½ cup fresh orange juice
½ tsp. pepper
¼ tsp. salt
1 (16-oz.) bag frozen sweet peas, thawed*
1 tsp. butter or margarine
1 Tbsp. chopped fresh mint
Garnishes: fresh mint sprig, orange rind curl

Cook bacon in a medium skillet until crisp; remove and drain on paper towels, reserving 1 tsp. drippings in skillet. Crumble bacon, and set aside.

Sauté shallot in hot bacon drippings over medium-high heat 2 minutes or until tender. Stir in orange rind, orange juice, pepper, and salt. Cook, stirring occasionally, 5 minutes or until reduced by half. Add peas, and cook 5 more minutes; stir in butter and mint.

Transfer peas to a serving dish, and sprinkle with crumbled bacon. Garnish, if desired. **Makes** 6 servings.

*Substitute 3 cups shelled fresh sweet peas for frozen, if desired. Cook peas in boiling water 5 minutes, and proceed with recipe.

Green Peas with Crispy Bacon

Peppery Peas
O' Plenty

Rosemary-Roasted Cherry Tomatoes
Prep: 5 min., Cook: 15 min.

Fragrant rosemary boosts the flavor of these juicy tomatoes. If you can't find cherry tomatoes, then dependable year-round tomatoes, such as plum, are terrific substitutes.

2 pt. cherry tomatoes
1 tsp. olive oil
1½ tsp. chopped fresh rosemary
2 garlic cloves, minced
¼ tsp. salt
¼ tsp. pepper

Combine all ingredients in a zip-top freezer bag. Gently shake until tomatoes are well coated. Transfer to an aluminum foil-lined jelly-roll pan coated with cooking spray.
Bake, uncovered, at 425°, stirring occasionally, 15 minutes or until tomatoes begin to burst. **Makes** 4 servings.

Peppery Peas O' Plenty
Prep: 15 min., Cook: 40 min.

4 hickory-smoked bacon slices (we tested with Bryan Sweet Hickory)
1 large onion, chopped
1 cup frozen black-eyed peas
1 cup frozen purple hull peas
1 cup frozen crowder peas
1 cup frozen butter peas
1 cup frozen field peas with snaps
1 (32-oz.) container chicken broth
1 Tbsp. Asian garlic-chili sauce (we tested with A Taste of Thai)
¾ to 1 tsp. salt
1 Tbsp. freshly ground pepper

Cook bacon in Dutch oven until crisp; remove bacon, and drain on paper towels, reserving drippings in pan. Crumble bacon.
Sauté onion in hot drippings in Dutch oven over medium-high heat 8 minutes or until translucent. Add black-eyed peas and next 8 ingredients, and cook 20 to 25 minutes, uncovered. Top with crumbled bacon. **Makes** 4 to 6 servings.

Grilled Summer Squash and Tomatoes
Prep: 5 min., Cook: 10 min., Other: 30 min.

¼ cup olive oil
2 Tbsp. balsamic vinegar
1 tsp. salt
½ tsp. pepper
4 garlic cloves, minced
4 medium-size green tomatoes, cut into ¼-inch-thick slices
1 lb. yellow squash, cut diagonally into ½-inch-thick slices

Combine first 5 ingredients in a shallow dish or zip-top freezer bag; add tomato and squash. Cover or seal; chill 30 minutes.
Remove vegetables from marinade, reserving marinade.
Grill vegetables, covered with grill lid, over medium-high heat (350° to 400°) 10 minutes, turning occasionally. Toss with reserved marinade. **Makes** 6 servings.

Two-Cheese Squash Casserole

Prep: 30 min., Cook: 1 hr.

4 lb. yellow squash, sliced
4 Tbsp. butter or margarine, divided
1 large sweet onion, finely chopped
2 garlic cloves, minced
2½ cups soft breadcrumbs, divided
1¼ cups shredded Parmesan cheese, divided
1 cup (4 oz.) shredded Cheddar cheese
½ cup chopped fresh chives
½ cup minced fresh parsley
1 (8-oz.) container sour cream
1 tsp. salt
1 tsp. freshly ground pepper
2 large eggs, lightly beaten
¼ tsp. garlic salt

Cook squash in boiling water to cover in a large skillet 8 to 10 minutes or just until tender. Drain well; gently press between paper towels.

Melt 2 Tbsp. butter in a large skillet over medium-high heat; add onion and garlic, and sauté 5 to 6 minutes or until tender. Remove skillet from heat; stir in squash, 1 cup breadcrumbs, ¾ cup Parmesan cheese, and next 7 ingredients. Spoon into a lightly greased 13- x 9-inch baking dish.

Melt remaining 2 Tbsp. butter. Stir together melted butter, remaining 1½ cups soft breadcrumbs, remaining ½ cup Parmesan cheese, and garlic salt. Sprinkle mixture evenly over top of casserole.

Bake, uncovered, at 350° for 35 to 40 minutes or until set. **Makes** 8 to 10 servings.

Crunchy Squash Casserole
Prep: 40 min., Cook: 1 hr., Other: 10 min.

The sauce takes a few extra minutes to make, but the rich results are worth the effort. Make this casserole up to a day ahead, or freeze it earlier in the week.

2 Tbsp. butter or margarine
3 lb. yellow squash, thinly sliced
1 small onion, chopped
1¼ tsp. salt
½ tsp. pepper
2 (8-oz.) cans sliced or chopped water chestnuts, drained
Swiss Cheese Cream Sauce
2 (2-oz.) jars diced pimientos, drained (optional)
Buttery Parmesan Topping

Melt butter in a large skillet over medium heat; add squash and next 3 ingredients, and sauté 10 minutes or until vegetables are tender.

Stir in water chestnuts, Swiss Cheese Cream Sauce, and, if desired, diced pimientos. Spoon squash mixture into a lightly greased 13- x 9-inch baking dish.

Bake, uncovered, at 350° for 15 minutes. Sprinkle evenly with Buttery Parmesan Topping; bake 30 more minutes or until set and golden. Let stand 10 minutes before serving. **Makes** 10 to 12 servings.

Swiss Cheese Cream Sauce
Prep: 25 min., Cook: 15 min.

6 Tbsp. butter or margarine, melted
6 Tbsp. all-purpose flour
3 cups milk
½ tsp. salt
1 cup (4 oz.) shredded Swiss cheese
2 large eggs

Melt butter in a heavy saucepan over medium heat; whisk in all-purpose flour until smooth. Gradually whisk in milk and salt.

Bring mixture to a boil over medium-high heat, whisking constantly. Boil, whisking constantly, 1 minute. Remove from heat, and stir in cheese until melted and blended.

Beat eggs with a fork until thick and pale. Gradually stir about one-fourth hot milk mixture into eggs; add egg mixture to remaining hot milk mixture, stirring constantly. **Makes** 4 cups.

Buttery Parmesan Topping
Prep: 10 min.

8 white bread slices, cut into ¼-inch cubes
½ cup grated Parmesan cheese
½ cup butter or margarine, melted
2 Tbsp. dried parsley flakes

Pulse bread cubes in a food processor until mixture resembles fine crumbs. Transfer breadcrumbs to a large mixing bowl. Stir in Parmesan cheese, butter, and parsley. **Makes** 3 cups.

Roasted Baby Vegetables
Prep: 25 min., Cook: 40 min.

1 lb. fresh baby beets with tops
¼ cup olive oil, divided
2 Tbsp. chopped fresh rosemary
1 tsp. coarse-grain sea salt, divided
¼ tsp. pepper, divided
1 lb. baby carrots with tops
8 shallots
2 medium-size baking potatoes, quartered
4 small turnips, peeled and quartered

Cut tops from beets, leaving 1-inch stems. Peel beets, and cut in half lengthwise. Place on a 12-inch square of aluminum foil. Drizzle with 1 Tbsp. olive oil; sprinkle with rosemary, ¼ tsp. salt, and ⅛ tsp. pepper. Fold up foil sides, forming a bowl. Place bowl in 1 end of a large roasting pan; set aside.

Cut tops from carrots, leaving 2-inch stems. Scrape carrots, if desired, and set aside.

Cut an X in top of 4 unpeeled shallots; cut remaining shallots in half lengthwise.

Toss together carrots, whole and cut shallots, potato, turnip, remaining 3 Tbsp. oil, remaining ¾ tsp. salt, and remaining ⅛ tsp. pepper. Place in remaining end of roasting pan.

Bake, uncovered, at 500° for 30 to 40 minutes or until tender. Use roasted whole shallots to garnish meats. **Makes** 4 servings.

Note: If you can't find baby vegetables, cut large carrots and beets into quarters or eighths. For even roasting, vegetables should be about the same size.

Fried Okra

Fried Okra
Prep: 12 min., Cook: 4 min. per batch, Other: 45 min.

1 lb. fresh okra
2 cups buttermilk
1 cup self-rising cornmeal
1 cup self-rising flour
1 tsp. salt
¼ tsp. ground red pepper
Vegetable oil
¼ cup bacon drippings

Cut off and discard tip and stem ends from okra; cut okra into ½-inch-thick slices. Stir into buttermilk; cover and chill 45 minutes.
Combine cornmeal and next 3 ingredients in a medium bowl.
Remove okra from buttermilk with a slotted spoon, and discard buttermilk. Dredge okra, in batches, in cornmeal mixture.
Pour oil to depth of 2 inches into a Dutch oven or cast-iron skillet; add bacon drippings, and heat to 375°. Fry okra, in batches, 4 minutes or until golden; drain on paper towels. **Makes** 4 servings.

Fried Okra Pods: Trim stem end, but do not trim tips or slice okra. Proceed as directed.

Garden Succotash
Prep: 25 min., Cook: 40 min.

¾ cup fresh lima or butterbeans
1¼ cups fresh corn kernels (2 small ears)
1 cup chopped shiitake mushrooms
1 red bell pepper, seeded and diced
1 green bell pepper, seeded and diced
¾ tsp. salt
¼ tsp. pepper
2 Tbsp. olive oil
½ tsp. chopped garlic
¼ cup dry white wine
¾ cup whipping cream
2 Tbsp. butter
1 medium tomato, peeled, seeded, and chopped
1 Tbsp. chopped fresh parsley
1 Tbsp. chopped fresh chives

Place beans in boiling water to cover in a small saucepan; simmer 3 minutes or until crisp-tender. Drain; rinse with cold water, and drain.
Sauté corn kernels, chopped mushrooms, bell peppers, salt, and pepper in hot oil in a medium skillet over medium-high heat for 5 minutes or until corn is crisp-tender. Add chopped garlic, and sauté 30 seconds. Stir in white wine, and cook 1 minute.
Add whipping cream and beans; reduce heat to medium low, and simmer, covered, 25 to 30 minutes or until beans are tender. Remove from heat, and stir in butter. Add chopped tomato, parsley, and chives, and stir just until combined. **Makes** 6 servings.

Roasted Smashed Sweet Potatoes
Prep: 20 min., Cook: 40 min.

3 lb. sweet potatoes, peeled and cut into 1½-inch chunks
3 Tbsp. olive oil
¾ tsp. salt
½ tsp. freshly ground pepper
¼ cup butter or margarine, cut into pieces
⅔ cup half-and-half, heated
¼ cup firmly packed light brown sugar

Place sweet potato chunks in a large greased roasting pan; drizzle with olive oil. Sprinkle with salt and pepper; toss well. Spread sweet potato chunks in a single layer. Roast, uncovered, at 400° for 30 to 40 minutes or until sweet potatoes are very tender and roasted in appearance, stirring occasionally.
Transfer roasted sweet potatoes to a large bowl while still warm; add butter and mash with a potato masher. Add half-and-half and brown sugar; mash until fluffy. Serve warm. **Makes** 8 servings.

Make Ahead: Transfer roasted sweet potatoes to a Dutch oven or large saucepan; add butter and mash. Cover; chill overnight. Before serving, let mixture stand at room temperature about 30 minutes. Add half-and-half and brown sugar; cook over low heat until thoroughly heated, mashing until fluffy.

Cheesy Mashed Potatoes
Prep: 15 min., Cook: 35 min.

2 lb. Yukon gold potatoes, peeled and cubed
2 (4-oz.) packages spiced Gournay cheese product (buttery garlic-and-herb spreadable cheese)
⅔ cup half-and-half
¼ cup butter or margarine
¼ tsp. salt
¼ tsp. pepper

Bring potato and water to cover to a boil in a large saucepan; reduce heat, and cook 15 to 20 minutes or until tender. Drain and return to saucepan. Cook over medium heat 30 seconds. Remove from heat.
Add cheese and next 4 ingredients; beat at medium speed with an electric mixer until smooth. Spoon into a 2½-qt. baking dish. Bake, uncovered, at 350° for 15 minutes. **Makes** 4 to 6 servings.

Simple Mashed Potatoes
Prep: 15 min., Cook: 35 min.

4 lb. Yukon gold potatoes, peeled and quartered
1¾ tsp. salt, divided
¾ cup milk
½ cup butter, softened
½ tsp. pepper

Bring potatoes, 1 tsp. salt, and water to cover to a boil in a Dutch oven; cover, reduce heat, and simmer 30 minutes or until tender. Drain.
Mash potatoes with remaining ¾ tsp. salt, milk, butter, and pepper until smooth. **Makes** 8 servings.

kids love it
Out-of-This-World Scalloped Potatoes
Prep: 20 min.; Cook: 2 hrs., 40 min.

¼ cup butter or margarine
¼ cup all-purpose flour
3 cups milk
1 (10-oz.) block Cheddar cheese, shredded
½ cup thinly sliced green onions
1 tsp. salt
¼ tsp. pepper
4 lb. potatoes, thinly sliced
1½ cups soft breadcrumbs
¼ cup butter or margarine, melted
¼ cup grated Parmesan cheese

Melt ¼ cup butter in a large saucepan over medium heat. Whisk in flour, and cook, whisking constantly, 2 to 3 minutes or until flour is lightly browned. Whisk milk into butter mixture; bring to a boil. Reduce heat, and simmer 6 minutes or until thickened. Stir in Cheddar cheese and next 3 ingredients, stirring until cheese melts.
Spread ¼ cup cheese sauce evenly in a greased 13- x 9-inch baking dish. Layer half of potatoes over sauce; top with half of remaining sauce. Repeat with remaining potatoes and remaining cheese sauce.
Bake, covered, at 325° 1½ to 2 hours.
Stir together breadcrumbs, melted butter, and Parmesan cheese in a medium bowl; spread evenly over potatoes. Bake, uncovered, 20 to 30 more minutes or until potatoes are tender. **Makes** 8 to 10 servings.

Barbecue Scalloped Potatoes
Prep: 15 min.; Cook: 1 hr., 25 min.

3 large baking potatoes (about 2½ lb.)
1½ tsp. salt, divided
1 (10¾-oz.) can cream of mushroom soup, undiluted
1 (5-oz.) can evaporated milk
¼ cup spicy barbecue sauce
¼ tsp. onion salt
2 cups (8 oz.) shredded sharp Cheddar cheese
⅛ tsp. paprika

Cook potatoes with 1 tsp. salt in boiling water to cover 30 to 40 minutes or just until tender in a large saucepan. Cool slightly; peel and slice. Set aside.
Stir together remaining ½ tsp. salt, soup, and next 3 ingredients until blended.
Layer half each of potato slices, sauce mixture, and cheese in a lightly greased 2-qt. round baking dish. Repeat layers; sprinkle top evenly with paprika.
Bake, uncovered, at 350° for 45 minutes or until golden. **Makes** 6 servings.

Smoky Mashed Potato Bake
Prep: 20 min., Cook: 1 hr.

3 garlic cloves, minced
1 tsp. olive oil
3½ lb. new potatoes, cut into 1-inch pieces
¾ cup (3 oz.) shredded smoked Gouda cheese, divided
1 cup half-and-half
2 to 3 chipotle peppers in adobo sauce, minced
½ cup light butter
½ (8-oz.) package cream cheese, softened
¼ tsp. salt

Sauté garlic in hot oil in a skillet coated with cooking spray over medium-high heat 2 to 3 minutes or until tender. Set aside.
Cook potato in a Dutch oven in boiling water to cover 30 minutes or until tender; drain.
Mash potato in a large bowl. Stir in garlic, ¼ cup Gouda cheese, half-and-half, and next 4 ingredients until blended. Spoon mixture into a 13- x 9-inch baking dish coated with cooking spray. Sprinkle with remaining ½ cup Gouda cheese.
Bake, uncovered, at 350° for 30 minutes or until cheese is melted. **Makes** 10 servings.

Potato-and-Gruyère Casserole
Prep: 20 min.; Cook: 1 hr., 45 min.

Gruyère cheese is known for its rich, nutty flavor. You can substitute Swiss or Cheddar cheese.

12 medium Yukon gold potatoes (about 4 lb.)
2 tsp. salt, divided
2 Tbsp. butter or margarine
1 large sweet onion, chopped
½ tsp. pepper
2 cups (8 oz.) shredded Gruyère cheese*
Cream Sauce

Peel and thinly slice potatoes.
Bring potatoes, 1 tsp. salt, and water to cover to a boil in a Dutch oven; cook 8 to 10 minutes. Remove from heat; drain and set aside.
Melt butter in a large skillet over medium-high heat; add chopped onion, and sauté 12 to 15 minutes or until golden brown.
Layer half of potatoes in a lightly greased 13- x 9-inch baking dish or 2 (8-inch) square baking dishes; sprinkle with ½ tsp. salt and ¼ tsp. pepper. Top with half each of onions, Gruyère cheese, and Cream Sauce. Repeat layers once, ending with Cream Sauce.
Bake at 350° for 1 hour and 15 minutes or until golden brown. **Makes** 10 to 12 servings.

*Substitute 1 (8-oz.) block Swiss cheese, shredded, or 1 (8-oz.) block sharp white Cheddar cheese, shredded, if desired.

Cream Sauce
Prep: 5 min., Cook: 25 min.

¼ cup butter or margarine
⅓ cup all-purpose flour
2½ cups milk
1 cup dry white wine
¼ tsp. salt

Melt butter in a heavy saucepan over low heat; whisk in flour until smooth. Cook, whisking constantly, 1 minute. Gradually whisk in milk and wine; cook over medium heat, whisking constantly, 18 to 20 minutes or until mixture is thickened and bubbly. Stir in salt. **Makes** 3½ cups.

Hot Corned Beef-Potato Hash

Prep: 10 min., Cook: 15 min.

8 oz. thinly sliced lean corned beef
1 lb. small red potatoes (about 8 potatoes), thinly sliced
1 cup thinly sliced leek (about 1 medium leek)
1 (10-oz.) bag angel hair slaw
1 Tbsp. vegetable oil
6 Tbsp. red wine vinegar
2 tsp. spicy brown mustard
1 tsp. sugar
½ tsp. salt
½ tsp. garlic powder
½ tsp. pepper

Cut corned beef slices crosswise into thin strips; set aside.
Place potatoes in a large saucepan. Cover with water; bring to a boil. Cook 5 minutes. Add leek; cook 2 more minutes. Drain well. Combine potato mixture and slaw in a large bowl; toss well. Set aside.
Heat oil in a large nonstick skillet over medium heat. Add corned beef; sauté 2 minutes. Add vinegar and next 5 ingredients; cook 1 minute, stirring frequently. Pour vinaigrette over potato mixture; toss until well blended and wilted. Serve immediately. **Makes** 4 servings.

Old-Fashioned Beef Hash

Prep: 5 min., Cook: 15 min.

1 cup cubed cooked lean beef
1 cup peeled, cubed red potato
½ cup chopped onion
1 Tbsp. chopped fresh parsley
¼ tsp. salt
¼ tsp. pepper
1 Tbsp. vegetable oil
⅓ cup milk

Combine first 6 ingredients. Cook mixture in hot oil in a large skillet over medium-high heat 10 minutes or until mixture is browned and potatoes are tender, stirring occasionally. Stir in milk; cover, reduce heat, and simmer 5 minutes. **Makes** 2 servings.

Beef Hash

Prep: 10 min., Cook: 30 min.

1 cup hot water
1 beef bouillon cube
3 medium potatoes, peeled and cubed (1½ lb.)
1 medium onion, chopped
1 garlic clove, minced
2 Tbsp. vegetable oil
2 cups chopped cooked eye of round roast
½ tsp. salt
1 tsp. pepper
2 Tbsp. chopped fresh parsley (optional)

Stir together 1 cup hot water and beef bouillon cube until cube dissolves.
Sauté potato, onion, and garlic in hot oil in a large skillet over medium-high heat 10 minutes. Add beef; cover, reduce heat, and cook, stirring occasionally, 15 minutes or until potato is tender.
Stir in bouillon mixture, ½ tsp. salt, 1 tsp. pepper, and, if desired, parsley; cover and simmer 5 minutes. **Makes** 4 servings.

Potato-Smoked Sausage Hash

Prep: 10 min., Cook: 20 min.

1 (16-oz.) package smoked sausage, sliced
1 medium onion, chopped
1 medium-size green bell pepper, chopped
½ (32-oz.) package frozen Southern-style hash browns
½ tsp. salt
½ tsp. pepper

Brown smoked sausage slices in a large nonstick skillet about 5 minutes on each side; remove sausage slices from pan, reserving drippings in skillet.
Sauté onion and green pepper in reserved drippings 3 minutes or until crisp-tender. Add hash browns, and cook, stirring occasionally, 5 minutes or until brown. Stir in sausage, salt, and pepper; cook 2 minutes or until thoroughly heated. **Makes** 4 servings.

Jim Gibson's Barbecue Hash

Prep: 15 min., Cook: 1 hr.

"When you're making hash, it's a great time to have company," advises Jim Gibson of Beaufort, South Carolina. Multiply this recipe by 5 to feed about 50 people, and increase the cooking time to about 3 hours. Leftovers make great sloppy joes.*

2 medium onions, chopped
1 Tbsp. vegetable oil
1 lb. ground beef
1 lb. ground pork
6 Tbsp. Worcestershire sauce
1 (28-oz.) can crushed tomatoes
¼ cup prepared mustard
¼ cup white vinegar
¾ tsp. salt
½ tsp. pepper
Hot cooked rice

Sauté onions in hot oil in a Dutch oven over medium heat until tender. Add ground beef and pork, and cook, stirring until meat crumbles and is no longer pink; drain. Stir in Worcestershire sauce.
Stir in next 3 ingredients, and bring to a boil; cook over low heat, stirring often, 45 minutes. Add salt and pepper. Serve with hot cooked rice. **Makes** 10 servings.

Savory Sweet Potato Hash

Prep: 15 min., Cook: 20 min.

4 bacon slices, diced
1 Tbsp. olive oil
½ medium onion, diced
3 medium-size sweet potatoes, chopped
1 large Granny Smith apple, peeled and chopped
½ cup chicken broth
¼ tsp. dried thyme
¼ tsp. ground allspice
½ cup chopped toasted pecans
1 Tbsp. chopped fresh parsley

Sauté bacon in hot oil in a large nonstick skillet over medium-high heat 3 minutes or until brown. Add onion, and sauté 2 minutes. Stir in sweet potatoes, and sauté 5 minutes. Stir in apple and next 3 ingredients, and cook, stirring often, 8 to 10 minutes or until potatoes and apple are tender.
Spoon mixture into a serving dish, and sprinkle evenly with pecans and parsley. **Makes** 4 to 6 servings.

Savory Sweet Potato Hash

TALE OF TWO STEWS

Burgoo and Brunswick stew, distinguished by their regional differences, vie for serving rights alongside barbecue. Burgoo (ber-GOO), native to Kentucky, is a thick stew flavored with chicken, vegetables, and mutton (lamb aged more than two years). Both Brunswick County, Virginia, and St. Simons Island, Georgia, claim to be the home of hearty Brunswick stew. Seasoned with barbecue pork, chicken, and sometimes ground beef, Georgia's stew is more tomatoey than Virginia's. Brunswick stew also shows up on barbecue menus in North Carolina and other spots in the Southeast. Wherever you are and whichever stew you prefer, our versions will satisfy your hankering.

Kentucky Burgoo
Prep: 25 min., Cook: 2 hrs.

1 lb. lean boneless chuck roast
1½ tsp. vegetable oil
8 cups no-salt-added beef broth
1 lb. skinned and boned chicken thighs
4 cups peeled, cubed baking potato (about 1½ lb.)
2½ cups chopped carrot
1 cup chopped celery
1 cup chopped onion
1½ tsp. curry powder
1 tsp. dried thyme
½ tsp. salt
1 (14.5-oz.) can diced tomatoes, undrained
1 garlic clove, minced
2 cups frozen whole kernel corn, thawed
1 (10-oz.) package frozen lima beans, thawed

Trim fat from roast, and cut roast into 1-inch cubes. Heat vegetable oil in a large Dutch oven; add roast cubes, and brown well on all sides. Add broth; bring to a boil. Cover, reduce heat, and simmer 1 hour.
Trim any fat from chicken thighs, and cut the chicken into 1-inch cubes. Add chicken cubes and next 9 ingredients; simmer, uncovered, 30 minutes or until the vegetables are tender.
Add corn and lima beans to stew; cook 15 more minutes or until the beans are tender. **Makes** 10 servings.

Classic Kentucky Burgoo
Prep: 25 min., Cook: 4 hrs., Other: 8 hrs.

Kentucky burgoo is a stew of Southern origin. It usually includes at least two types of meat and a garden's worth of fresh vegetables. This recipe serves a crowd, and you can easily freeze any leftovers.

1 (4- to 5-lb.) hen
2 lb. beef or veal stew meat
1½ to 2 lb. beef or veal bones
1 celery rib with leaves, cut into 1-inch pieces
1 carrot, scraped and cut into 1-inch pieces
1 small onion, quartered
1 (6-oz.) can tomato paste
3 qt. water
1 red bell pepper
1 to 1½ Tbsp. salt
1½ to 2 tsp. black pepper
½ tsp. ground red pepper
2 Tbsp. lemon juice
1 Tbsp. Worcestershire sauce
6 onions, finely chopped
8 to 10 tomatoes, peeled and chopped
1 turnip, peeled and finely chopped
2 green bell peppers, finely chopped
2 cups fresh butterbeans
2 cups thinly sliced celery
2 cups finely chopped cabbage
2 cups sliced fresh okra
2 cups fresh corn kernels (4 ears)

Combine first 14 ingredients in a large Dutch oven. Bring to a boil; cover, reduce heat, and simmer 1 hour. Cool. Strain meat mixture, reserving meat and liquid; discard vegetables. Remove skin, gristle, and meat from bone; finely chop meat. Return meat to liquid; cover and chill 8 hours.
Discard fat layer on mixture; add onion and remaining ingredients. Bring mixture to a boil; reduce heat, and simmer, uncovered, 3 hours or to desired consistency, stirring mixture often to prevent sticking.
Makes 30 cups.

Note: Classic Kentucky Burgoo freezes well. To serve, thaw and cook until stew is thoroughly heated.

Brunswick Stew
Prep: 40 min.; Cook: 2 hrs., 40 min.

1 (4½-lb.) pork roast
1 (4½-lb.) hen
3 (16-oz.) cans whole tomatoes, undrained and chopped
1 (8-oz.) can tomato sauce
3 large onions, chopped
2 small green bell peppers, chopped
¾ cup white vinegar
¼ cup sugar
¼ cup all-purpose flour
1 cup water
1 tsp. salt
½ tsp. pepper
½ tsp. ground turmeric
2 Tbsp. hot sauce
1 (16-oz.) package frozen white shoepeg corn

Place pork roast, fat side up, on a rack of a roasting pan. Insert meat thermometer, being careful not to touch bone or fat. Bake at 325° for 2 hours or until thermometer registers 160°. Cool. Trim and discard fat; cut pork into 2-inch pieces.

Meanwhile, place hen in a Dutch oven, and cover with water. Bring to a boil; cover, reduce heat, and simmer 2 hours or until tender. Remove hen from broth, and cool. (Reserve broth for another use.) Bone hen, and cut meat into 2-inch pieces.

Coarsely grind pork and chicken in food processor or with meat grinder. Combine ground meat, tomatoes, and next 5 ingredients in a large Dutch oven.

Combine flour and water in a bowl, stirring until smooth; stir into meat mixture. Stir in salt and next 3 ingredients. Cook over medium heat 30 minutes, stirring occasionally. Add water, if needed, to reach desired consistency. Stir in corn, and cook 10 more minutes. **Makes** 22 cups.

Note: This stew freezes well in individual-size containers.

Chicken Brunswick Stew
Prep: 30 min; Cook: 4 hrs., 55 min.

2 (2½-lb.) whole chickens
2 qt. water
1 Tbsp. salt
1½ cups ketchup, divided
2 Tbsp. light brown sugar
1½ tsp. dry mustard
1½ tsp. grated fresh ginger
½ lemon, sliced
1 garlic clove, minced
1 Tbsp. butter or margarine
¼ cup white vinegar
3 Tbsp. vegetable oil
1 Tbsp. Worcestershire sauce
¾ tsp. hot sauce
½ tsp. pepper
2 (28-oz.) cans crushed tomatoes
2 (15.25-oz.) cans whole kernel corn, undrained
2 (14¾-oz.) cans cream-style corn
1 large onion, chopped
¼ cup firmly packed light brown sugar
1 Tbsp. salt
1 Tbsp. pepper

Bring first 3 ingredients to a boil in a large heavy stockpot; cover, reduce heat, and simmer 45 minutes or until chicken is tender. Drain chicken, reserving 1 qt. broth in pot; skin, bone, and shred chicken, and return to pot.

Cook ½ cup ketchup and next 11 ingredients in a small saucepan over medium heat, stirring occasionally, 10 minutes.

Stir ketchup mixture, remaining 1 cup ketchup, tomatoes, and next 6 ingredients into chicken and broth; simmer, stirring often, 4 hours or until thickened. **Makes** 3½ qt.

Pecan-Chocolate Chip
Cookies, page 270

Sweet Tooth

The only things possibly more
irresistible than succulent barbecue
are crunchy cookies, juicy cobblers,
and fruit-speckled ice creams.
These and more delightful desserts
are sure to cure your most insatiable
sugar craving.

Melt-in-Your-Mouth Iced Sugar Cookies

Prep: 45 min., Cook: 9 min. per batch

1 cup butter, softened
1½ cups sugar
1 large egg
3 cups all-purpose flour
½ tsp. baking soda
½ tsp. salt
1 tsp. cream of tartar
2 tsp. vanilla extract
Royal Icing
Assorted colors food coloring paste
Decorator sprinkles

Beat butter in a large bowl at medium speed with an electric mixer 2 minutes or until creamy. Gradually add sugar, beating well. Add egg, and beat well. Combine flour and next 3 ingredients. Add to butter mixture, beating at low speed just until blended. Stir in vanilla.

Roll dough to ¼-inch thickness on a lightly floured surface. Cut with 3-inch cookie cutters. Place 1-inch apart on ungreased baking sheets. Bake at 350° for 9 minutes. Cool completely on wire racks.

Spoon about ⅔ cup white Royal Icing into a decorating bag fitted with decorating tip #3 (small round tip). Pipe white icing to outline cookies and detail as desired.

Divide remaining Royal Icing into a separate bowl for each color of icing desired; color as desired with food coloring paste. Slowly stir just enough water into each bowl of icing to make "flow-in icing" that is still thick but flows into a smooth surface after stirring. (Add water a little at a time; if flow-in icing is too watery, it may not dry properly and may run under outline into another color area.)

Fill decorating bags (using no tips) about half full of flow-in icing. Snip off small tip of each cone. Pipe desired colors of icing to cover areas between the Royal Icing outline; spread icing into corners and hard-to-reach areas using wooden picks, as necessary.

Add flow-in icing 1 color at a time, allowing icing to dry before changing colors. Avoid using excess icing to prevent spilling over into another color area. If air bubbles form in icing, use a sterilized straight pin to remove them.

Decorate with decorator sprinkles while icing is still wet. **Makes** 3½ dozen.

Royal Icing

Prep: 10 min., Cook: 9 min.

This icing dries very quickly, so keep it covered with a damp cloth at all times while in the bowl to help keep it moist.

3 egg whites
1 (16-oz.) package powdered sugar, sifted and divided
½ tsp. cream of tartar

Combine egg whites, 1 cup powdered sugar, and cream of tartar in top of a double boiler. Place over simmering water. Cook, stirring constantly with a wire whisk, 9 minutes or until mixture reaches 160°. Remove from heat. Transfer to a large mixing bowl, and add remaining powdered sugar.

Beat at high speed with an electric mixer 5 to 8 minutes or until stiff peaks form. **Makes** 2 cups.

Gingersnaps

Prep: 10 min., Cook: 8 min. per batch

¾ cup shortening
1 cup sugar
1 large egg
¼ cup molasses
2 cups all-purpose flour
2 tsp. baking soda
¼ tsp. salt
1 Tbsp. ground ginger
1 tsp. ground cinnamon
Additional sugar

Beat shortening in a large bowl at medium speed with an electric mixer; gradually add 1 cup sugar, beating well. Add egg and molasses; mix thoroughly.

Combine flour and next 4 ingredients; add flour mixture one-fourth at a time to creamed mixture, mixing after each addition.

Shape dough into ¾-inch balls, and roll in sugar. Place on ungreased baking sheets, and bake at 350° for 8 minutes. (Tops will crack.) Remove to wire racks to cool. **Makes** 8 dozen.

Note: To make larger gingersnaps, shape cookie dough into 1-inch balls, and bake 10 minutes; the yield will be 4 dozen.

Molasses Sugar Cookies
Prep: 25 min., Cook: 10 min. per batch, Other: 40 min.

If you can't find whole wheat pastry flour, increase the all-purpose flour to 1¾ cups and use ¼ cup whole wheat flour.

½ cup applesauce
1¼ cups sugar, divided
6 Tbsp. butter, softened
¼ cup dark molasses
1 large egg
1 cup all-purpose flour
1 cup whole wheat pastry flour
2 tsp. baking soda
1 tsp. ground cinnamon
½ tsp. salt
½ tsp. ground ginger
½ tsp. ground cloves

Spoon applesauce onto several layers of heavy-duty paper towels; spread to ½-inch thickness. Cover with additional paper towels; let stand 5 minutes. Scrape into a bowl using a rubber spatula.

Combine applesauce, 1 cup sugar, and butter; beat at medium speed with an electric mixer until well blended (about 3 minutes). Add molasses and egg; beat well.

Combine flours and remaining 5 ingredients, stirring well with a whisk. Gradually add flour mixture to sugar mixture, beating until blended. Cover and freeze dough 30 minutes or until firm.

With moist hands, shape dough into 32 (1-inch) balls. Roll balls in remaining ¼ cup sugar. Place 3 inches apart on baking sheets coated with cooking spray. Bake at 375° for 8 to 10 minutes. Cool on pans 5 minutes. Remove from pans; cool completely on wire racks. **Makes** 32 cookies.

Old-Fashioned Peanut Butter Cookies

Prep: 25 min., Cook: 8 min. per batch, Other: 3 hrs.

1 cup butter or margarine, softened
1 cup creamy peanut butter
1 cup granulated sugar
1 cup firmly packed brown sugar
2 large eggs
2½ cups all-purpose flour
2 tsp. baking soda
¼ tsp. salt
1 tsp. vanilla extract
Additional granulated sugar

Beat butter and peanut butter at medium speed with an electric mixer until creamy; gradually add sugars, beating well. Add eggs, beating well.

Combine flour, soda, and salt in a medium bowl; add to butter mixture, beating well. Stir in vanilla. Cover and chill 3 hours.

Shape into 1¼-inch balls; place 3 inches apart on ungreased baking sheets. Dip a fork in additional sugar; flatten cookies in a crisscross design. Bake at 375° for 7 to 8 minutes. Remove to wire racks to cool.

Makes 6 dozen.

Peanut Butter Turtle Cookies

Prep: 25 min., Cook: 24 min., Other: 2 min.

½ cup unsalted butter, softened
½ cup granulated sugar
½ cup firmly packed light brown sugar
⅔ cup creamy peanut butter
1 large egg
2 cups all-purpose baking mix
⅔ cup almond toffee bits
⅔ cup coarsely chopped peanuts
⅔ cup milk chocolate morsels
10 oz. vanilla caramels
2 to 3 Tbsp. whipping cream
½ tsp. vanilla extract
⅔ cup milk chocolate morsels, melted

Beat first 4 ingredients at medium speed with an electric mixer until creamy. Add egg, beating until blended. Add baking mix, beating at low speed just until blended. Stir in toffee bits, chopped peanuts, and ⅔ cup chocolate morsels.

Drop dough by rounded tablespoonfuls onto ungreased baking sheets; flatten dough with hand.

Bake at 350° for 10 to 12 minutes or until golden brown. Cool cookies on baking sheets 1 minute; remove cookies to wire racks.

Microwave caramels and 2 Tbsp. cream in a glass bowl at HIGH 1 minute; stir. Continue to microwave at 30-second intervals, stirring until caramels melt and mixture is smooth; add remaining cream, if necessary. Stir in vanilla. Spoon mixture evenly onto tops of cookies; drizzle evenly with chocolate. **Makes** 3 dozen.

Brown Sugar-Oatmeal Cookies

Prep: 10 min., Cook: 14 min. per batch, Other: 2 min.

1 cup butter or margarine, softened
2 cups firmly packed brown sugar
2 large eggs
½ tsp. baking soda
¼ cup hot water
2 cups all-purpose flour
1 tsp. baking powder
½ tsp. salt
4 cups uncooked regular oats
1 cup sweetened flaked coconut
1 cup chopped pecans

Beat butter at medium speed with an electric mixer until creamy; gradually add brown sugar, beating well. Add eggs; beat well.

Combine soda and water, stirring well. Combine flour, baking powder, salt, and soda mixture; gradually add to butter mixture, beating well. Stir in oats and remaining ingredients.

Drop dough by heaping teaspoonfuls onto greased baking sheets. Bake at 350° for 14 minutes or until lightly browned. Cool 2 minutes on sheets; remove to wire racks to cool completely. **Makes** about 6 dozen.

Clear-the-Cupboard Cookies

Prep: 20 min., Cook: 10 min. per batch

1 cup shortening
1 cup granulated sugar
1 cup firmly packed light brown sugar
2 large eggs
2 cups all-purpose flour
1 tsp. baking soda
1 tsp. baking powder
1 tsp. salt
1 cup uncooked regular oats
1 cup sweetened flaked coconut
1 cup crisp rice cereal
1 tsp. vanilla extract
1 cup chopped pecans, toasted (optional)

Beat shortening at medium speed with an electric mixer until fluffy; add sugars, beating well. Add eggs, beating until blended.

Combine flour and next 4 ingredients; gradually add to sugar mixture, beating after each addition. Stir in coconut, cereal, vanilla, and, if desired, pecans.

Drop by tablespoonfuls onto baking sheets.

Bake at 350° for 10 minutes or until lightly golden. Remove to wire racks to cool. **Makes** 4½ dozen.

COOKIES AND 'CUE—A GREAT PAIR

Cookies are terrific post-barbecue treats—they can be made ahead and make plenty to feed a crowd. They also make crisp partners for another summertime favorite: homemade ice cream!

Oatmeal-Raisin Cookies

Prep: 11 min., Cook: 8 min. per batch

1 cup butter or margarine, softened
1 cup granulated sugar
1 cup firmly packed brown sugar
2 large eggs
1 Tbsp. vanilla extract
2 cups all-purpose flour
1 tsp. baking soda
½ tsp. baking powder
½ tsp. salt
1½ cups quick-cooking oats, uncooked
1 cup raisins
1½ cups chopped pecans

Beat butter at medium speed with an electric mixer until creamy; gradually add sugars, beating well. Add eggs and vanilla; beat well.

Combine flour and next 3 ingredients; gradually add to butter mixture, beating well. Stir in oats, raisins, and pecans.

Drop dough by heaping teaspoonfuls onto greased baking sheets.

Bake at 375° for 8 minutes or until lightly browned. Cool slightly on baking sheets; remove to wire racks to cool completely. **Makes** 7 dozen.

Nutty Oatmeal-Chocolate Chunk Cookies

Prep: 10 min., Cook: 8 min. per batch

2½ cups uncooked regular oats
1 cup butter or margarine, softened
1 cup granulated sugar
1 cup firmly packed brown sugar
2 large eggs
1 Tbsp. vanilla extract
2 cups all-purpose flour
1 tsp. baking powder
1 tsp. baking soda
½ tsp. salt
3 (1.55-oz.) milk chocolate candy bars, chopped
1½ cups chopped pecans

Process oats in a blender or food processor until ground.

Beat butter and sugars at medium speed with an electric mixer until fluffy. Add eggs and vanilla; beat until blended.

Combine ground oats, flour, and next 3 ingredients. Add to butter mixture, beating until blended. Stir in chocolate and pecans.

Drop dough by tablespoonfuls onto ungreased baking sheets.

Bake at 375° for 7 to 8 minutes or until golden brown; remove to wire racks to cool. **Makes** 6 dozen.

Orange-Macadamia Nut Cookies

Prep: 15 min., Cook: 10 min. per batch, Other: 2 hrs.

Macadamia nuts and white chocolate pair up for a taste sensation in this delicious drop cookie.

¾ cup butter or margarine, softened
½ cup granulated sugar
½ cup firmly packed brown sugar
1 large egg
1 Tbsp. grated orange rind
¾ tsp. vanilla extract
¼ tsp. orange extract
1⅓ cups all-purpose flour
½ cup quick-cooking oats, uncooked
¾ tsp. baking powder
½ tsp. baking soda
1 (3.5-oz.) jar lightly salted macadamia nuts, coarsely chopped
1 cup white chocolate morsels or chunks

Beat butter at medium speed with an electric mixer 2 minutes or until creamy. Gradually add sugars, beating well. Add egg, orange rind, and flavorings.

Combine flour and next 3 ingredients in a medium bowl. Add to butter mixture, beating at low speed just until blended. Stir in nuts and white chocolate morsels. Cover and chill 2 hours.

Drop dough by rounded tablespoonfuls onto ungreased baking sheets.

Bake at 350° for 9 to 10 minutes or just until edges are golden. Cool 1 minute on baking sheets; remove to wire racks, and cool completely. **Makes** about 3 dozen.

White Chocolate-Macadamia Nut Cookies

Prep: 10 min., Cook: 10 min. per batch

½ cup butter or margarine, softened
½ cup shortening
¾ cup firmly packed brown sugar
½ cup granulated sugar
1 large egg
1½ tsp. vanilla extract
2 cups all-purpose flour
1 tsp. baking soda
½ tsp. salt
1 (6-oz.) package white chocolate baking bars, cut into chunks
1 (7-oz.) jar macadamia nuts, chopped

Beat butter and shortening at medium speed with an electric mixer until creamy; gradually add sugars, beating well. Add egg and vanilla; beat well.
Combine flour, soda, and salt; gradually add to butter mixture, beating well. Stir in white chocolate and nuts.
Drop dough by rounded teaspoonfuls 2 inches apart onto lightly greased baking sheets. Bake at 350° for 8 to 10 minutes or until lightly browned. Cool slightly on baking sheets; remove to wire racks to cool completely. **Makes** 5 dozen.

Cranberry-White Chocolate Cookies

Prep: 15 min., Cook: 12 min. per batch

2½ cups all-purpose flour
1 tsp. baking powder
¼ tsp. salt
⅛ tsp. baking soda
½ cup butter, softened
1⅓ cups sugar
2 large eggs
1½ cups white chocolate morsels
1 (6-oz.) package sweetened dried cranberries (we tested with Craisins)

Combine flour and next 3 ingredients; set aside. Beat butter at medium speed with an electric mixer until creamy; gradually add sugar, beating well. Add eggs, 1 at a time, beating until blended after each addition.

Add flour mixture to butter mixture gradually, beating at low speed until blended. Stir in white chocolate morsels and cranberries.
Drop cookie dough by heaping tablespoonfuls onto lightly greased baking sheets.
Bake at 350° for 10 to 12 minutes or until lightly browned on bottom. Remove to wire racks to cool completely. **Makes** about 3 dozen.

Heavenly Chocolate Chunk Cookies

Prep: 15 min., Cook: 14 min.

Megamorsels give a big chocolate taste to every bite of these deluxe chocolate chip cookies.

2 cups plus 2 Tbsp. all-purpose flour
½ tsp. baking soda
½ tsp. salt
¾ cup butter or margarine
2 Tbsp. instant coffee granules
1 cup firmly packed brown sugar
½ cup granulated sugar
1 large egg
1 egg yolk
1 (11.5-oz.) package semisweet chocolate megamorsels
1 cup walnut halves, toasted

Combine first 3 ingredients in a medium bowl; stir well.
Combine butter and coffee granules in a small saucepan or skillet. Cook over medium-low heat until butter melts and coffee granules dissolve, stirring occasionally. Remove from heat, and cool to room temperature (don't let butter resolidify).
Combine butter mixture, sugars, egg, and egg yolk in a large bowl. Beat at medium speed with an electric mixer until blended. Gradually add flour mixture, beating at low speed just until blended. Stir in megamorsels and walnuts.
Drop dough by heaping tablespoonfuls 2 inches apart onto ungreased baking sheets. Bake at 325° for 12 to 14 minutes. Cool slightly on baking sheets. Remove to wire racks to cool completely. **Makes** 20 cookies.

Chocolate-Chocolate Chip Cookies
Prep: 10 min., Cook: 10 min. per batch

½ cup butter
4 (1-oz.) unsweetened chocolate baking squares,
    chopped
3 cups (18 oz.) semisweet chocolate morsels, divided
1½ cups all-purpose flour
½ tsp. baking powder
½ tsp. salt
4 large eggs
1½ cups sugar
2 tsp. vanilla extract
2 cups chopped pecans, toasted

Combine butter, unsweetened chocolate, and 1½ cups chocolate morsels in a large heavy saucepan. Cook over low heat, stirring constantly, until butter and chocolate melt; cool. Combine flour, baking powder, and salt in a small bowl; set aside.

Beat eggs, sugar, and vanilla in a medium mixing bowl at medium speed with an electric mixer. Gradually add flour mixture to egg mixture, beating well. Add chocolate mixture; beat well. Stir in remaining 1½ cups chocolate morsels and pecans.

Drop dough by 2 tablespoonfuls 1 inch apart onto parchment paper- or wax paper-lined baking sheets. Bake at 350° for 10 minutes. Cool slightly on baking sheets; remove to wire racks to cool completely. **Makes** about 2½ dozen.

Ultimate Chocolate Chip Cookies
Prep: 30 min., Cook: 14 min. per batch

¾ cup butter, softened
¾ cup granulated sugar
¾ cup firmly packed dark brown sugar
2 large eggs
1½ tsp. vanilla extract
2¼ cups plus 2 Tbsp. all-purpose flour
1 tsp. baking soda
¾ tsp. salt
2 cups (12-oz. package) semisweet chocolate morsels

Beat butter and sugars at medium speed with an electric mixer until creamy. Add eggs and vanilla, beating until blended.

Combine flour, soda, and salt in a small bowl; gradually add to butter mixture, beating well. Stir in morsels.

Drop by tablespoonfuls onto lightly greased baking sheets. Bake at 350° for 8 to 14 minutes or until desired degree of doneness. Remove to wire racks to cool completely. **Makes** about 5 dozen.

Peanut Butter-Chocolate Chip Cookies: Decrease salt to ½ tsp. Add 1 cup creamy peanut butter with butter and sugars. Increase flour to 2½ cups plus 2 Tbsp. Proceed as directed. (Dough will look a little moist.)

Oatmeal-Raisin-Chocolate Chip Cookies: Reduce flour to 2 cups. Add 1 cup uncooked quick-cooking oats to dry ingredients and 1 cup raisins with morsels. Proceed as directed.

Pecan-Chocolate Chip Cookies: Add 1½ cups chopped, toasted pecans with morsels. Proceed as directed.

Toffee-Chocolate Chip Cookies: Reduce morsels to 1 cup. Add ½ cup slivered toasted almonds and 1 cup toffee bits (we tested with Hershey's Heath Bits O'Brickle Toffee Bits). Proceed as directed.

Dark Chocolate Chip Cookies: Substitute 2 cups (12-oz. package) dark chocolate morsels (we tested with Hershey's Special Dark Chips) for semisweet chocolate morsels. Proceed as directed.

Chunky Cherry-Double Chip Cookies: Microwave 1 Tbsp. water and ½ cup dried cherries in a glass bowl at HIGH 30 seconds, stirring once. Let stand 10 minutes. Substitute 2 cups (11.5-oz. package) semisweet chocolate chunks for morsels. Add 1 cup white chocolate morsels, ⅓ cup slivered toasted almonds, and cherries with chocolate chunks. Proceed as directed.

Coconut-Macadamia Chunk Cookies: Substitute 2 cups (11.5-oz. package) semisweet chocolate chunks for morsels. Add 1 cup white chocolate morsels, ½ cup sweetened flaked coconut, and ½ cup macadamia nuts with chocolate chunks. Proceed as directed.

Pecan-Chocolate
Chip Cookies

Millionaire Shortbread

Prep: 15 min., Cook: 55 min., Other: 45 min.

1½ cups butter, softened and divided
2 cups all-purpose flour
¾ cup white rice flour*
½ cup granulated sugar
1 (14-oz.) can sweetened condensed milk
¼ cup light corn syrup
1 cup firmly packed light brown sugar
1½ cups semisweet chocolate morsels

Pulse 1 cup butter, flours, and granulated sugar in a food processor 10 to 15 times or until crumbly. Press mixture evenly into a 15- x 10-inch jelly-roll pan coated with cooking spray for baking.
Bake at 350° for 18 to 20 minutes or until light golden brown.
Stir together remaining ½ cup butter, condensed milk, and corn syrup in a 2-qt. heavy saucepan over low heat 4 minutes or until butter is melted and mixture is blended. Add brown sugar, and cook, stirring constantly, 25 to 30 minutes or until caramel colored and thickened. Pour evenly over baked cookie in pan, and spread into an even layer. Chill 30 minutes or until caramel is set.
Microwave morsels in a small glass bowl at HIGH 1 minute or until almost melted. Stir until smooth. Spread over caramel layer in pan. (The chocolate layer will be thin.) Chill 15 minutes or until chocolate is firm. Cut into 2-inch squares; if desired, cut each square into 2 triangles. **Makes** about 3 dozen squares or 6 dozen triangles.

*Substitute ¾ cup all-purpose flour, if desired.

Butter-Mint Shortbread

Prep: 10 min., Cook: 25 min., Other: 10 min.

1 cup butter, softened
¾ cup powdered sugar
½ tsp. mint extract
½ tsp. vanilla extract
2 cups all-purpose flour
Additional powdered sugar

Beat butter and ¾ cup powdered sugar at medium speed with an electric mixer until light and fluffy.

Add extracts, beating until blended. Gradually add flour, beating at low speed until blended. Press dough into an ungreased 15- x 10-inch jelly-roll pan.
Bake at 325° for 25 minutes or until golden. Cool in pan on a wire rack 10 minutes. Cut into squares; sprinkle with additional powdered sugar. Remove from pan; cool on wire rack. **Makes** 3 dozen.

Peanut Butter Shortbread

Prep: 10 min., Cook: 12 min. per batch

⅔ cup creamy peanut butter
½ Basic Butter Cookie Dough recipe
36 milk chocolate kisses

Knead peanut butter into Basic Butter Cookie Dough until smooth and well blended.
Shape dough into 1-inch balls, and place on lightly greased baking sheets. Make an indentation in center of each ball with thumb or spoon handle.
Bake at 350° for 12 minutes or until lightly browned. Immediately press chocolate kiss in center of each cookie. Remove to wire racks to cool. **Makes** 3 dozen.

Basic Butter Cookie Dough

Prep: 20 min.

1 cup butter or margarine, softened
½ cup firmly packed brown sugar
½ cup granulated sugar
1 large egg
3½ cups all-purpose flour
2 tsp. baking powder
½ tsp. salt
2 Tbsp. milk
2 tsp. vanilla extract

Beat butter in a large mixing bowl at medium speed with an electric mixer until creamy. Gradually add sugars, beating well. Add egg, beating well.
Combine flour, baking powder, and salt; add to butter mixture alternately with milk, beginning and ending with flour mixture. Beat at low speed after each addition until mixture is blended. Stir in vanilla.
Divide dough into 2 equal portions; wrap each portion in plastic wrap. Chill. **Makes** 2¼ pounds.

Note: Cookie dough may be frozen up to 1 month.

Peanut-Toffee Shortbread

Prep: 30 min., Cook: 20 min., Other: 5 min.

1 cup butter, softened
⅔ cup firmly packed light brown sugar
⅓ cup cornstarch
2 cups all-purpose flour
¼ tsp. salt
2 tsp. vanilla extract
2 cups coarsely chopped honey-roasted peanuts, divided
2 cups (12-oz. package) semisweet chocolate morsels

Beat butter at medium speed with an electric mixer until creamy. Combine brown sugar and cornstarch; gradually add to butter, beating well. Gradually add flour and salt to butter mixture, beating at low speed just until blended. Add vanilla and 1 cup peanuts, beating at low speed just until blended.
Turn dough out onto a lightly greased baking sheet; pat or roll dough into an 11- x 14-inch rectangle; leave at least a 1-inch border on all sides of baking sheet.
Bake at 350° for 20 minutes or until golden brown. Remove baking sheet to a wire rack; sprinkle shortbread evenly with chocolate morsels. Let stand 5 minutes; gently spread melted morsels over shortbread. Sprinkle with remaining 1 cup peanuts; cool completely. Cut or break into 2- to 3-inch irregular-shaped pieces. **Makes** about 2½ to 3 dozen pieces.

Marble-Topped Hazelnut Shortbread

Prep: 15 min., Cook: 41 min., Other: 40 min.

½ cup chopped hazelnuts or macadamia nuts
2 cups cake flour
¾ cup powdered sugar
¼ tsp. salt
1 cup butter, softened
4 (1-oz.) semisweet chocolate baking squares
1 (2-oz.) vanilla bark coating square

Bake hazelnuts in a shallow pan at 350°, stirring occasionally, 5 to 10 minutes or until toasted; set aside.
Reduce temperature to 325°.
Combine flour, sugar, and salt in a large mixing bowl; add butter, and beat at low speed with an electric mixer until blended. Press dough into an aluminum foil-lined 10-inch round cakepan.
Bake at 325° for 25 to 30 minutes or until lightly browned.
Microwave chocolate in a small microwave-safe bowl at HIGH, stirring twice, 1 minute or until melted. Spread over shortbread.
Place vanilla bark coating square in a small zip-top freezer bag; seal. Submerge in hot water until bark coating melts. Snip a tiny hole in 1 corner of bag, and drizzle lines ¾ inch apart over chocolate.
Swirl melted coating and chocolate with a wooden pick. Sprinkle with hazelnuts.
Cool in pan on a wire rack 40 minutes. Cut into wedges. **Makes** 16 servings.

Peanut-Toffee Shortbread

Banana-Split Brownies

Prep: 10 min., Cook: 45 min.

1 (17.6-oz) package chocolate double-fudge
    brownie mix (we tested with Duncan Hines Chocolate
    Lover's Double Fudge Brownie Mix)
½ cup dried cherries
¼ cup water
1 medium banana, sliced
1 tsp. vanilla extract
½ cup sliced almonds (optional), toasted
Toppings: ice cream, hot fudge, and caramel sauces;
    toasted flaked coconut; grated milk chocolate;
    chopped pecans; candy-coated chocolate pieces;
    whipped cream; maraschino cherries with stems

Prepare brownie mix according to package direc-
tions, following cakelike instructions.
Microwave cherries and ¼ cup water on HIGH 1½
minutes. Drain and cool.
Stir cherries, banana, vanilla, and, if desired, almonds
into batter.
Pour into a lightly greased 8-inch square baking pan.
Bake at 350° for 40 to 45 minutes. Cool and cut
brownies into squares. Serve with desired toppings.
Makes 1 dozen.

Banana-Split Brownies

Mississippi Mud Brownies

Prep: 5 min., Cook: 25 min., Other: 50 min.

1 (20.5-oz.) package low-fat fudge brownie mix
⅔ cup water
1 tsp. vanilla extract
½ cup reduced-fat semisweet chocolate morsels
2 cups miniature marshmallows
1 (16-oz.) container reduced-fat ready-to-spread
    chocolate-flavored frosting

Combine brownie mix, ⅔ cup water, and vanilla; stir
well. Fold in chocolate morsels.
Spread batter in a lightly greased 13- x 9-inch pan.
Bake at 350° for 23 minutes.
Sprinkle marshmallows over hot brownies; return
pan to oven, and bake 2 more minutes. Cool completely (about 20 minutes) in pan on a wire rack.
Spread frosting over brownies; let stand at least
30 minutes. Cut into 24 squares. **Makes** 2 dozen.

Double-Chocolate Brownies

Prep: 10 min., Cook: 35 min.

1 cup butter or margarine, softened
2 cups sugar
4 large eggs
1 cup unsweetened cocoa
1 tsp. vanilla extract
1 cup all-purpose flour
1 cup chopped pecans
⅔ cup white chocolate or semisweet chocolate morsels

Beat butter at medium speed with an electric mixer
until creamy; gradually add sugar, beating well. Add
eggs, 1 at a time, beating just until blended.
Add cocoa and vanilla; beat at low speed 1 minute or
until blended. Gradually add flour, beating well.
Stir in pecans and chocolate morsels. Pour batter into
a greased 13- x 9-inch baking pan.
Bake at 350° for 30 to 35 minutes or until done. Cool
and cut into squares. **Makes** 2 dozen.

Pecan Squares
Prep: 20 min., Cook: 50 min.

2 cups all-purpose flour

⅔ cup powdered sugar

¾ cup butter, softened

½ cup firmly packed brown sugar

½ cup honey

⅔ cup butter

3 Tbsp. whipping cream

3½ cups coarsely chopped pecans

Sift together 2 cups flour and ⅔ cup powdered sugar. Cut in ¾ cup softened butter using a pastry blender or fork just until mixture resembles coarse meal.

Pat mixture on bottom and 1½ inches up sides of a lightly greased 13- x 9-inch baking dish.

Bake at 350° for 20 minutes or until edges are lightly browned. Cool.

Bring brown sugar, honey, ⅔ cup butter, and whipping cream to a boil in a saucepan over medium-high heat. Stir in pecans, and pour hot filling into prepared crust.

Bake at 350° for 25 to 30 minutes or until golden and bubbly. Cool completely before cutting into 2-inch squares. **Makes** about 28 squares.

Citrus Bars

Citrus Bars

Prep: 15 min., Cook: 52 min.

1 cup butter, softened
2¼ cups all-purpose flour, divided
½ cup powdered sugar
1¾ cups granulated sugar
⅓ cup fresh lemon juice
1 tsp. finely grated orange rind
⅓ cup fresh orange juice
4 large eggs, beaten
1 tsp. baking powder
¼ tsp. salt
1 Tbsp. powdered sugar
Garnish: orange and lemon rind strips

Beat butter at medium speed with an electric mixer until creamy; add 2 cups flour and ½ cup powdered sugar. Beat until mixture forms a smooth dough. Press mixture into a lightly greased 13- x 9-inch baking pan.
Bake at 350° for 20 to 22 minutes or until lightly browned.
Whisk together remaining ¼ cup flour, granulated sugar, and next 6 ingredients; pour over baked crust.
Bake at 350° for 28 to 30 minutes or until set. Cool in pan or on wire rack. Sprinkle evenly with 1 Tbsp. powdered sugar, and cut into bars. Garnish, if desired. **Makes** 2 dozen.

Lemon Bars Deluxe

Prep: 15 min., Cook: 50 min.

2¼ cups all-purpose flour, divided
½ cup sifted powdered sugar
1 cup butter or margarine
½ tsp. baking powder
4 large eggs, lightly beaten
2 cups granulated sugar
⅓ cup lemon juice
Additional powdered sugar

Combine 2 cups flour and ½ cup powdered sugar; cut in butter with pastry blender until mixture is crumbly. Firmly press mixture in a greased 13- x 9-inch pan. Bake at 350° for 20 to 25 minutes or until lightly browned.

Combine remaining ¼ cup flour and baking powder in a small bowl; stir well. Combine eggs, 2 cups sugar, and lemon juice in a large bowl; stir in flour mixture. Pour over prepared crust. Bake at 350° for 25 minutes or until set and lightly browned. Cool completely in pan on a wire rack. Sprinkle with additional powdered sugar; cut into bars. **Makes** 2½ dozen.

Apple Squares

Prep: 20 min., Cook: 50 min.

2½ cups all-purpose flour
½ tsp. baking powder
½ tsp. salt
¾ cup shortening
1 large egg, lightly beaten
¼ cup cold water
1 Tbsp. white vinegar
¾ cup granulated sugar
3 Tbsp. all-purpose flour
½ tsp. salt
½ tsp. ground cinnamon
¼ tsp. ground nutmeg
8 large cooking apples, peeled and chopped
1 cup sifted powdered sugar
1 to 2 Tbsp. warm water or milk
½ tsp. vanilla extract or fresh lemon juice

Combine 2½ cups flour, baking powder, and ½ tsp. salt in a medium bowl; cut in shortening with pastry blender until mixture is crumbly. Stir in egg. Sprinkle cold water and vinegar, 1 Tbsp. at a time, evenly over surface; stir with a fork until dry ingredients are moistened. Shape into a ball; chill.
Roll half of pastry to ⅛-inch thickness on a lightly floured surface. Place in a greased 15- x 10-inch jelly-roll pan; trim off excess pastry along edges. Combine ¾ cup sugar and next 4 ingredients in a large bowl; stir well. Add chopped apple, and toss to coat. Spoon apple mixture into prepared pastry shell.
Roll remaining pastry to ⅛-inch thickness on a lightly floured surface. Transfer to top of apple mixture. Fold edges under; crimp. Cut slits in top of pastry to allow steam to escape. Bake at 375° for 45 to 50 minutes or until lightly browned. Cool completely in pan on a wire rack. Combine powdered sugar and remaining ingredients in a small bowl; stir well. Drizzle on top of pastry. Cut into squares. **Makes** 15 servings.

Caramel-Pecan
Cheesecake Bars

Chocolate-Caramel
Sheet Cake

Caramel-Pecan Cheesecake Bars

Prep: 15 min., Cook: 48 min., Other: 8 hrs.

2 cups graham cracker crumbs
½ cup butter, melted
4 (8-oz.) packages cream cheese, softened
¾ cup sugar
¼ cup all-purpose flour
3 large eggs
1 Tbsp. vanilla extract
Quick Caramel-Pecan Frosting (page 279)

Stir together graham cracker crumbs and butter; press into bottom of a lightly greased 13- x 9-inch baking pan.

Bake at 350° for 8 minutes. Remove from oven, and cool on a wire rack.

Beat cream cheese at medium speed with an electric mixer until smooth. Combine sugar and flour; gradually add to cream cheese, beating just until blended.

Add eggs, 1 at a time, beating until blended after each addition. Stir in vanilla. Pour mixture over prepared crust, spreading evenly to edges of pan.

Bake at 350° for 40 minutes or until set. Remove from oven, and cool on a wire rack.

Pour warm Quick Caramel-Pecan Frosting over cheesecake, spreading evenly to edges of pan. Cover and chill 8 hours. Cut into bars. **Makes** 2 dozen.

Chocolate-Caramel Sheet Cake

Prep: 15 min., Cook: 25 min.

1 cup butter
1 cup water
¼ cup unsweetened cocoa
½ cup buttermilk
2 large eggs
1 tsp. baking soda
1 tsp. vanilla extract
2 cups sugar
2 cups all-purpose flour
½ tsp. salt
Quick Caramel Frosting
1½ cups coarsely chopped pecans, toasted

Cook first 3 ingredients in a small saucepan over low heat, stirring constantly, until butter melts and mixture is smooth; remove from heat.

Beat buttermilk and next 3 ingredients at medium speed with an electric mixer until smooth; add cocoa mixture, beating until blended.

Combine sugar, flour, and salt; gradually add to buttermilk mixture, beating just until blended. (Batter will be thin.) Pour batter into a greased and floured 15- x 10-inch jelly-roll pan.

Bake at 350° for 20 to 25 minutes or until a wooden pick inserted in center comes out clean. Cool cake completely in pan on a wire rack.

Pour warm Quick Caramel Frosting over cake, spreading evenly to edges of pan. Sprinkle evenly with pecans. **Makes** 15 servings.

Quick Caramel Frosting

Prep: 5 min., Cook: 10 min.

2 (14-oz.) cans sweetened condensed milk
½ cup firmly packed light brown sugar
½ cup butter
1 tsp. vanilla extract

Place all ingredients in a heavy 3-qt. saucepan; bring to a boil, stirring constantly, over medium-low heat. Cook, stirring constantly, 3 to 5 minutes or until mixture reaches a pudding-like thickness. Remove from heat. **Makes** 2½ cups.

Quick Caramel-Pecan Frosting: Prepare Quick Caramel Frosting as directed; remove from heat, and stir in 1½ cups chopped toasted pecans.

Chocolate-Peanut Butter Cake

Prep: 20 min., Cook: 35 min.

Fat-free and reduced-fat ingredients make this rich cake a guilt-free indulgence.

¼ cup reduced-fat creamy peanut butter
⅓ cup fat-free cream cheese, softened
3 Tbsp. butter, softened
1½ cups sugar
½ cup frozen egg substitute, thawed
2 cups sifted cake flour
¼ cup plus 2 Tbsp. unsweetened cocoa
1 tsp. baking soda
¼ tsp. salt
1 cup fat-free buttermilk
1 tsp. vanilla extract
Chocolate Frosting
2 Tbsp. finely chopped unsalted peanuts

Beat first 3 ingredients at medium speed with an electric mixer until creamy; gradually add sugar, beating well. Add egg substitute, beating well.

Combine flour and next 3 ingredients in a medium bowl; stir well with a wire whisk. Add to peanut butter mixture alternately with buttermilk, beginning and ending with flour mixture. Mix batter just until blended after each addition. Stir in vanilla.

Pour batter into a 13- x 9-inch pan coated with cooking spray. Bake at 350° for 30 to 35 minutes or until a wooden pick inserted in center comes out clean. Cool completely on a wire rack. Spread Chocolate Frosting over cooled cake, and sprinkle with chopped peanuts. **Makes** 15 servings.

Chocolate Frosting

Prep: 10 min.

¼ cup plus 2 Tbsp. fat-free evaporated milk
2 Tbsp. reduced-fat creamy peanut butter
3 cups sifted powdered sugar
¼ cup unsweetened cocoa
¼ tsp. salt
1 tsp. vanilla extract

Combine evaporated milk and peanut butter in a small saucepan; cook over low heat until peanut butter melts and mixture is smooth. Combine milk mixture with powdered sugar and remaining ingredients, stirring until frosting cools. **Makes** 1⅓ cups.

Cream Cheese Coffee Cake
Prep: 15 min., Cook: 40 min.

½ cup butter, softened
1 (8-oz.) package cream cheese, softened
1½ cups sugar
2 large eggs
2 cups all-purpose flour
2 tsp. baking powder
½ tsp. baking soda
½ tsp. salt
½ cup milk
1 tsp. vanilla extract
Brown Sugar-Pecan Topping

Beat butter and cream cheese at medium speed with an electric mixer until creamy; gradually add sugar, beating well. Add eggs, 1 at a time, beating after each addition.
Combine flour, baking powder, baking soda, and salt; add to butter mixture alternately with milk, beginning and ending with flour mixture. Mix at low speed just until blended after each addition. Stir in vanilla.
Pour batter into a greased 13- x 9-inch pan. Sprinkle with topping. Bake at 350° for 40 minutes or until a wooden pick inserted in center comes out clean. Cool in pan on a wire rack. **Makes** 12 servings.

Brown Sugar-Pecan Topping
Prep: 5 min.

½ cup all-purpose flour
½ cup firmly packed brown sugar
½ cup chopped pecans
¼ cup butter, melted

Combine all ingredients. **Makes** 1½ cups.

Blueberry 'n' Cheese Coffee Cake
Prep: 25 min., Cook: 55 min.

This easy coffee cake showcases fresh juicy blueberries, chunks of cream cheese, and a lemon-sugar topping.

½ cup butter or margarine, softened
1¼ cups sugar
2 large eggs
2 cups all-purpose flour
1 tsp. baking powder
1 tsp. salt
¾ cup milk
¼ cup water
2 cups fresh blueberries
1 (8-oz.) package cream cheese, softened and cubed
½ cup all-purpose flour
½ cup sugar
2 Tbsp. grated lemon rind
2 Tbsp. butter or margarine, softened

Beat ½ cup butter at medium speed with an electric mixer until creamy; gradually add 1¼ cups sugar, beating well. Add eggs, 1 at a time, beating until blended after each addition.
Combine 2 cups flour, baking powder, and salt; stir well. Combine milk and water; stir well. Add flour mixture to butter mixture alternately with milk mixture, beginning and ending with flour mixture. Mix at low speed after each addition until mixture is blended.
Gently stir in blueberries and cream cheese. Pour batter into a greased 9-inch square pan.
Combine ½ cup flour and remaining 3 ingredients; stir well with a fork. Sprinkle mixture over batter.
Bake at 375° for 50 to 55 minutes or until golden. Serve warm, or cool completely on a wire rack. **Makes** 16 servings.

> "Whether laden with fruit or sprinkled with streusel, coffee cake is typically fluffy and light, yet rich but not too sweet. Most coffee cakes can be made a day ahead and are equally as good at room temperature." —Julie Gunter, *Southern Living* Books

Chocolate Truffle Cake

Prep: 30 min.; Cook: 42 min.; Other: 1 hr., 5 min.

8 (1-oz.) semisweet chocolate baking squares

2½ cups milk

1 cup butter, softened

3 large eggs

2 tsp. vanilla extract

2⅔ cups all-purpose flour

2 cups sugar

1¼ tsp. baking soda

½ tsp. salt

Chocolate Truffle Filling, divided

10 (1-oz.) semisweet chocolate baking squares, coarsely
   chopped

½ cup plus 2 Tbsp. whipping cream

1 to 2 (1-oz.) semisweet chocolate baking squares, finely
   grated

Stir together first 3 ingredients in a large heavy saucepan over low heat, and cook, stirring constantly, 8 to 10 minutes or until chocolate melts and mixture is smooth. Remove from heat, and cool slightly (about 10 minutes).

Whisk together eggs and vanilla in a large bowl. Gradually whisk in melted chocolate mixture until blended and smooth.

Combine flour and next 3 ingredients; whisk into chocolate mixture until blended and smooth.

Pour batter into 3 greased and floured 9-inch round cakepans.

Bake at 325° for 25 to 30 minutes or until a wooden pick inserted in center comes out clean. Cool cake layers in pans on wire racks 10 minutes. Remove from pans, and cool completely on wire racks.

Spread ½ cup plus 2 Tbsp. Chocolate Truffle Filling evenly on top of 1 cake layer. Top with 1 cake layer; spread ½ cup plus 2 Tbsp. Chocolate Truffle Filling evenly on top, reserving remaining ½ cup Chocolate Truffle Filling. Top with remaining cake layer.

Microwave coarsely chopped semisweet chocolate and whipping cream in a 2-qt. microwave-safe bowl at HIGH 1½ to 2 minutes, stirring after 1 minute and then every 30 seconds until chocolate melts and mixture is smooth and slightly thickened. Cool slightly (about 15 minutes).

Spread warm semisweet chocolate mixture over top and sides of cake. Chill cake 30 minutes or until chocolate glaze is firm. Pipe border using a rosette tip around bottom of cake with remaining ½ cup Chocolate Truffle Filling. Sprinkle finely grated semisweet chocolate evenly over top of cake. **Makes** 12 servings.

Chocolate Truffle Filling

Prep: 10 min.

4 (1-oz.) semisweet chocolate baking squares

6 Tbsp. butter

¼ to ½ cup whipping cream

2½ cups powdered sugar, sifted

Microwave semisweet chocolate baking squares and 6 Tbsp. butter in a large microwave-safe bowl at HIGH 1½ to 2 minutes or until melted and smooth, stirring every 30 seconds. Stir in ¼ cup whipping cream. Stir in 2½ cups powdered sugar, adding remaining ¼ cup whipping cream, 1 Tbsp. at a time, if necessary, until mixture is smooth and creamy. Cool completely. **Makes** 1¾ cups.

FOR GREAT CAKES

■ All-purpose flour is presifted, so there's no need to sift it unless the recipe specifies. Always sift cake flour before measuring.

■ You can substitute all-purpose flour for cake flour by using 2 Tbsp. less per cup.

■ There's no good substitute for real eggs and butter when making a cake.

■ Be sure to use the correct pan size, measuring across the top. An incorrect pan size can cause a cake to be flat and shrunken or to rise to a peak and fall.

■ Use wax paper to lightly grease sides and bottoms of pans with shortening.

■ Always preheat the oven 10 minutes before baking.

■ When oven is preheated, place pans on center rack of oven; don't let pans touch.

■ Before frosting a cake, cool layers completely and gently brush away loose crumbs.

Chocolate-Praline Cake
Prep: 30 min., Cook: 18 min., Other: 10 min.

Chocolate and pralines are perfect partners in this delightfully Southern cake. It's sure to be a winner at your next barbecue.

1 cup boiling water
1 cup butter or margarine, cut into pieces
¼ cup unsweetened cocoa
½ cup buttermilk
2 large eggs
1 tsp. baking soda
1 tsp. vanilla extract
2 cups sugar
2 cups all-purpose flour
½ tsp. salt
Chocolate Frosting
Praline Topping
Garnish: pecan halves

Pour boiling water over butter and cocoa, stirring until butter melts and mixture is smooth.

Beat buttermilk, 2 eggs, baking soda, and vanilla at medium speed with an electric mixer until smooth. Add butter mixture to buttermilk mixture, beating until blended.

Combine sugar, flour, and salt; gradually add to buttermilk mixture, beating until blended.

Coat 3 (9-inch) round cakepans with cooking spray, and line pans with wax paper. Pour cake batter evenly into pans.

Bake at 350° for 16 to 18 minutes or until a wooden cake pick comes out clean and cake pulls away from sides of pan. Cool in pans on wire racks 10 minutes. Remove from pans, and cool completely on wire racks.

Spread about ½ cup Chocolate Frosting between cake layers, and spread remaining frosting on sides of cake.

Prepare Praline Topping; pour topping slowly over center of cake, gently spreading to edges, allowing some topping to run over sides. Freeze, if desired; thaw at room temperature 4 to 6 hours. Garnish, if desired. **Makes** 12 servings.

Chocolate Frosting
Prep: 5 min., Other: 15 min.

2 cups (12-oz. package) semisweet chocolate morsels
⅓ cup whipping cream
¼ cup butter or margarine, cut into pieces

Microwave chocolate morsels and whipping cream in a glass bowl at HIGH 1 minute or until morsels are melted. Whisk until smooth.

Gradually add butter, whisking until smooth. Cool, whisking often, 10 to 15 minutes or until spreading consistency. **Makes** about 2 cups.

Praline Topping
Prep: 10 min., Cook: 3 min.

Do not prepare this frosting ahead, as it will harden very quickly.

¼ cup butter or margarine
1 cup firmly packed brown sugar
⅓ cup whipping cream
1 cup powdered sugar
1 tsp. vanilla extract
1 cup chopped pecans, toasted

Bring first 3 ingredients to a boil in a 2-qt. saucepan over medium heat, stirring often, and boil 1 minute. Remove from heat, and whisk in powdered sugar and vanilla extract until smooth.

Stir in toasted pecans, stirring gently 2 minutes or until mixture begins to cool and thicken slightly. Pour over cake immediately. **Makes** about 1¾ cups.

Carrot Cake Supreme

Prep: 25 min., Cook: 30 min., Other: 15 min.

Buttermilk Glaze adds extra moistness to this cake and makes it incredibly rich. Cover and chill the cake, and serve it the second day; it'll slice neater.

2 cups all-purpose flour
2 tsp. baking soda
½ tsp. salt
2 tsp. ground cinnamon
3 large eggs
2 cups sugar
¾ cup vegetable oil
¾ cup buttermilk
2 tsp. vanilla extract
2 cups grated carrot
1 (8-oz.) can crushed pineapple, drained
1 (3.5-oz.) can sweetened flaked coconut
1 cup chopped pecans
Buttermilk Glaze (page 285)
Deluxe Cream Cheese Frosting (page 285)

Grease 3 (9-inch) round cakepans; line with wax paper. Lightly grease and flour wax paper. Set aside.

Stir together first 4 ingredients. Beat eggs and next 4 ingredients at medium speed with an electric mixer until smooth.

Add flour mixture to egg mixture, beating at low speed until blended. Fold in carrot and next 3 ingredients. Pour batter into prepared pans.

Bake at 350° for 25 to 30 minutes or until a wooden pick inserted in center comes out clean.

Drizzle warm Buttermilk Glaze evenly over warm cake layers; cool in pans on wire racks 15 minutes. Remove from pans, inverting layers. Peel off wax paper; invert again, glaze side up. Cool completely on wire racks.

Spread Deluxe Cream Cheese Frosting between layers and on top and sides of cake. Chill cake several hours before slicing. Store in refrigerator. **Makes** 16 servings.

Buttermilk Glaze
Prep: 3 min., Cook: 5 min.

1 cup sugar
1½ tsp. baking soda
½ cup buttermilk
½ cup butter or margarine
1 Tbsp. light corn syrup
1 tsp. vanilla extract

Bring first 5 ingredients to a boil in a Dutch oven over medium heat. Boil 4 minutes, stirring constantly until glaze is golden. Remove from heat, and stir in vanilla. Cool slightly. **Makes** 1½ cups.

Deluxe Cream Cheese Frosting
Prep: 7 min.

1 (8-oz.) package cream cheese, softened
1 (3-oz.) package cream cheese, softened
¾ cup butter, softened
1 (16-oz.) package powdered sugar, sifted
1½ tsp. vanilla extract

Beat first 3 ingredients at medium speed with an electric mixer until smooth. Gradually add powdered sugar, beating at low speed until light and fluffy. Stir in vanilla. **Makes** 3½ cups.

Pig Pickin' Cake
Prep: 15 min.; Cook: 30 min.; Other: 4 hrs., 10 min.

This cake is simple, quick, and good—but what about its name? It's called a Pig Pickin' Cake because its citrus lift is the perfect ending to a barbecue, or pig pickin'.

1 (18.25-oz.) package yellow cake mix
⅓ cup water
⅓ cup vegetable oil
3 large eggs
1 (11-oz.) can mandarin oranges, drained
1 (15-oz.) can crushed pineapple, undrained
1 (3.4-oz.) package vanilla instant pudding mix
1 (12-oz.) container frozen whipped topping, thawed
½ cup chopped pecans
Garnish: chopped pecans

Beat first 4 ingredients in a large bowl at medium speed with an electric mixer until blended. Stir in oranges. Pour batter into 3 greased and floured 8-inch round cakepans. (Layers will be thin.)
Bake at 350° for 25 to 30 minutes or until a wooden pick inserted in center comes out clean. Cool layers in pans on wire racks 10 minutes; remove layers from pans, and cool completely on wire racks.
Stir together crushed pineapple and next 3 ingredients. Spread pineapple mixture evenly between layers and on top of cake. Chill cake 3 to 4 hours. Garnish, if desired. **Makes** 12 servings.

Pig Pickin' Cake

Blue Ribbon Angel Food Cake

Prep: 20 min., Cook: 35 min., Other: 1 hr.

1½ cups sifted cake flour
12 egg whites
1¼ tsp. cream of tartar
¼ tsp. salt
1 tsp. vanilla extract
¼ tsp. almond extract
1⅓ cups sugar

Sift flour 4 times, and set aside.

Beat egg whites and next 4 ingredients at high speed with an electric mixer until soft peaks form (about 5 minutes). Gradually add sugar, ⅓ cup at a time, beating until blended after each addition. Fold in flour. Pour batter into an ungreased 10-inch tube pan.

Bake at 375° for 35 minutes. Invert pan on a wire rack, and let stand 1 hour or until cake is completely cool. Run a knife around cake to loosen edges. **Makes** 16 servings.

Brown Sugar Angel Food Cake

Prep: 15 min., Cook: 50 min.

2 cups firmly packed brown sugar, divided
1¼ cups sifted cake flour
12 egg whites
1½ tsp. cream of tartar
1 tsp. salt
2 tsp. vanilla extract
Powdered sugar

Sift 1 cup brown sugar and cake flour together into a small bowl; set aside. Beat egg whites in a large mixing bowl at medium speed until foamy. Add cream of tartar and salt; beat until soft peaks form. Add remaining 1 cup brown sugar, 2 Tbsp. at a time, beating until stiff peaks form and brown sugar dissolves. Sift flour mixture over egg whites, ¼ cup at a time, folding in after each addition. Fold in vanilla.

Spoon batter into an ungreased 10-inch tube pan. Break air pockets by cutting through batter with a knife. Bake at 350° for 50 minutes or until cake springs back when lightly touched. Remove cake from oven. Invert pan; cool completely. Loosen cake from pan, using a narrow metal spatula; remove cake. Sprinkle with powdered sugar. **Makes** 12 servings.

Lemon Buttermilk Cake with Lemon Curd Sauce

Prep: 20 min.; Cook: 1 hr., 15 min.; Other: 10 min.

1 cup butter, softened
2⅓ cups sugar, divided
3 large eggs
3 cups all-purpose flour
½ tsp. baking soda
½ tsp. salt
1 cup buttermilk
1½ Tbsp. grated lemon rind
½ cup plus 3 Tbsp. fresh lemon juice, divided
3 Tbsp. fine, dry breadcrumbs
Lemon Curd Sauce

Beat butter at medium speed with an electric mixer until creamy; gradually add 2 cups sugar, beating well. Add eggs, 1 at a time, beating after each addition.

Combine flour, baking soda, and salt; add to butter mixture alternately with buttermilk, beginning and ending with flour mixture. Mix at low speed after each addition until blended. Stir in rind and 3 Tbsp. juice. Pour into a buttered 12-cup Bundt pan coated with breadcrumbs. Bake at 350° for 1 hour to 1 hour and 15 minutes or until a wooden pick inserted in center comes out clean. Cool in pan on a wire rack 10 minutes; remove from pan. Place on wire rack.

Combine remaining ⅓ cup sugar and remaining ½ cup lemon juice in a saucepan; cook over medium-low heat until sugar dissolves, stirring often. Prick cake at 1-inch intervals with a long wooden skewer or cake tester. Spoon juice mixture over top of warm cake; cool completely on wire rack. Serve with Lemon Curd Sauce. **Makes** 16 servings.

Lemon Curd Sauce

Prep: 5 min., Cook: 15 min.

2 cups sugar
6 large eggs, lightly beaten
¼ cup grated lemon rind
¾ cup fresh lemon juice
¾ cup butter, softened

Combine first 4 ingredients in top of a double boiler; bring water to a boil. Reduce heat to medium; cook, stirring constantly, until mixture coats a spoon. Cool slightly. Add butter, 1 Tbsp. at a time, whisking until blended. Serve immediately or chill. **Makes** 4 cups.

Lemon Tea Bread

Prep: 15 min., Cook: 1 hr., Other: 10 min.

½ cup butter, softened

1 cup granulated sugar

2 large eggs

1½ cups all-purpose flour

1 tsp. baking powder

½ tsp. salt

½ cup milk

2 Tbsp. grated lemon rind, divided

1 cup powdered sugar

2 Tbsp. fresh lemon juice

1 Tbsp. granulated sugar

Beat softened butter at medium speed with an electric mixer until creamy. Gradually add 1 cup granulated sugar, beating until light and fluffy. Add eggs, 1 at a time, beating just until blended after each addition.

Stir together flour, baking powder, and salt; add to butter mixture alternately with milk, beating at low speed just until blended, beginning and ending with flour mixture.

Stir in 1 Tbsp. lemon rind. Spoon batter into greased and floured 8- x 4-inch loafpan.

Bake at 350° for 1 hour or until a wooden pick inserted in center comes out clean. Cool in pan 10 minutes. Remove bread from pan, and cool completely on a wire rack.

Stir together powdered sugar and lemon juice until smooth; spoon evenly over top of bread, letting excess drip down sides.

Stir together remaining 1 Tbsp. lemon rind and 1 Tbsp. granulated sugar; sprinkle on top of bread.

Makes 1 (8-inch) loaf.

Blueberry Cheesecake

Prep: 20 min.; Cook: 1 hr., 15 min.; Other: 9 hrs.

Believe it or not, this decadent cheesecake is made from reduced-fat and fat-free products.

1 cup graham cracker crumbs
3 Tbsp. butter, melted
1 Tbsp. sugar
2 (8-oz.) packages ⅓-less-fat cream cheese
1 (8-oz.) package fat-free cream cheese
1 cup sugar
3 Tbsp. all-purpose flour
½ tsp. salt
2 large eggs
2 egg whites
1 (8-oz.) container light sour cream
1 tsp. vanilla extract
1 Tbsp. grated lemon rind
1½ cups fresh or frozen blueberries
1 cup fat-free frozen whipped topping, thawed
¼ cup light sour cream

Combine graham cracker crumbs, melted butter, and 1 Tbsp. sugar in a small bowl.

Press mixture on bottom and 1½ inches up sides of a 9-inch springform pan coated with cooking spray. **Bake** at 350° for 5 minutes. Remove from oven.

Beat cream cheeses at medium speed with an electric mixer until smooth.

Combine 1 cup sugar, flour, and salt. Add to cream cheese, beating until blended. Add eggs, 1 at a time, beating well after each addition. Add egg whites, beating until blended.

Add 8-oz. container sour cream, vanilla, and lemon rind, beating just until blended. Gently stir in blueberries. Pour mixture into prepared pan.

Bake at 300° for 1 hour and 10 minutes or until center of cheesecake is firm. Turn off oven, and let cheesecake stand in oven, with oven door partially open, 30 minutes.

Remove cheesecake from oven; cool in pan on a wire rack 30 minutes.

Cover cheesecake; chill 8 hours. Release sides of pan.

Stir together whipped topping and ¼ cup sour cream. Spread over cheesecake. **Makes** 12 servings.

Blackberry Cobbler

Prep: 25 min., Cook: 1 hr., Other: 10 min.

8 cups fresh blackberries
2¼ cups sugar
⅓ cup all-purpose flour
1 tsp. lemon juice
Pastry, divided
¼ cup butter or margarine, cut up
Additional sugar (optional)
Vanilla ice cream
Blackberry Syrup

Stir together first 4 ingredients; let mixture stand 10 minutes or until sugar dissolves.
Roll half of Pastry to ¼-inch thickness; cut into 1½-inch-wide strips. Place on a greased baking sheet.
Bake at 425° for 10 minutes or until lightly browned. Remove to a wire rack to cool. Break strips into pieces.
Spoon half of blackberry mixture into a lightly greased 13- x 9-inch baking dish; top with pastry pieces. Spoon remaining blackberry mixture over pastry; dot with butter.
Roll remaining Pastry to ¼-inch thickness; cut into 1-inch strips, and arrange in a lattice design over filling. Sprinkle with sugar, if desired. Place cobbler on a baking sheet.
Bake at 350° for 50 minutes or until golden. Serve with vanilla ice cream and Blackberry Syrup. **Makes** 8 servings.

Pastry

Prep: 5 min.

2½ cups all-purpose flour
1¾ tsp. baking powder
¾ tsp. salt
½ cup shortening
⅔ cup milk

Combine first 3 ingredients in a medium bowl; cut in shortening with a pastry blender until crumbly. Add milk, stirring with a fork until dry ingredients are moistened and mixture forms a soft ball.
Turn dough out onto a floured surface; knead 6 to 8 times. **Makes** pastry for 1 (13- x 9-inch) cobbler.

Blackberry Syrup

Prep: 10 min., Cook: 5 min.

3 cups fresh blackberries
1¼ cups sugar
¼ cup light corn syrup
1 tsp. cornstarch

Process blackberries in a blender until smooth, stopping to scrape down sides. Pour through a fine wire-mesh strainer into a medium saucepan, discarding solids. Stir in remaining ingredients; bring to a boil over medium heat, stirring occasionally.
Boil, stirring occasionally, 1 minute. Remove from heat; cool. Serve with cobbler, pound cake, fruit, pancakes, or ice cream. **Makes** 1⅔ cups.

Nectarine Cobbler with Blueberry Muffin Crust

Prep: 30 min., Cook: 30 min.

4 lb. nectarines, peeled and sliced
¾ cup sugar
2 Tbsp. all-purpose flour
¼ cup butter
2 cups all-purpose flour
¼ cup sugar
1 Tbsp. baking powder
½ tsp. salt
1 cup milk
¼ cup vegetable oil
1 large egg, lightly beaten
1 cup fresh or frozen blueberries
Vanilla ice cream

Toss together first 3 ingredients in a large bowl.
Melt butter in a large skillet over medium-high heat. Add nectarine mixture to skillet; bring to a boil, and cook, stirring often, 5 minutes. Spoon hot nectarine mixture into a lightly greased 13- x 9-inch baking dish.
Combine 2 cups flour and next 3 ingredients in a large mixing bowl; make a well in center of mixture. Stir together milk, oil, and egg; add to dry ingredients, and stir just until moistened. Gently fold in blueberries. Spoon blueberry mixture evenly over hot nectarine mixture.
Bake at 400° for 25 minutes or until crust is golden brown. Serve with ice cream. **Makes** 8 servings.

Too-Easy Cherry Cobbler

Prep: 15 min., Cook: 45 min.

This recipe calls for trimming crusts from bread slices. Shave off some prep time by using store-bought crustless white bread for the topping.

2 (20-oz.) cans cherry pie filling
1 (15-oz.) can pitted dark sweet cherries in heavy syrup, drained
¼ cup all-purpose flour, divided
½ tsp. almond extract
5 white bread slices
1¼ cups sugar
½ cup butter or margarine, melted
1 large egg
1½ tsp. grated lemon rind

Stir together pie filling, cherries, and 2 Tbsp. flour. Stir in almond extract. Place in a lightly greased 8-inch square baking dish.

Trim crusts from bread slices; cut each slice into 5 strips. Arrange bread strips over fruit mixture.
Stir together remaining 2 Tbsp. flour, sugar, and next 3 ingredients; drizzle over bread strips.
Bake at 350° for 35 to 45 minutes or until golden and bubbly. **Makes** 4 to 6 servings.

Too-Easy Peach Cobbler: Substitute 2 (16-oz.) packages frozen sliced peaches, thawed and drained, for cherry pie filling and canned cherries. Omit almond extract and grated lemon rind. Proceed as directed.

Too-Easy Berry Cobbler: Substitute 1 (21-oz.) can blueberry pie filling and 2 (10-oz.) packages frozen whole strawberries, thawed, for cherry pie filling and canned cherries. Omit almond extract; add 1 tsp. vanilla extract and 1 tsp. lemon juice. Proceed as directed.

Crumb-Topped Apple Pie
Prep: 20 min., Cook: 42 min.

If you could pick one grand apple pie to bake, this streusel-topped version is the one to try. The thin apple slices are covered with a mound of brown sugar, oats, and pecans. After just one bite, we gave the pie our highest rating.

2 cups all-purpose flour
⅔ cup firmly packed brown sugar
½ cup uncooked regular oats
½ tsp. salt
⅓ cup chopped pecans
¾ cup butter or margarine, melted
4 cups peeled, thinly sliced cooking apple (about 3 apples)
⅓ cup granulated sugar
1½ tsp. cornstarch
⅛ tsp. salt
¼ cup water
½ tsp. vanilla extract

Combine first 5 ingredients in a medium bowl; add butter, and stir until blended. Measure 1 cup firmly packed mixture; set aside for pie topping. Press remaining mixture in bottom and up sides of a well-greased 9-inch pieplate. Arrange apple slices in pieplate; set aside.

Combine ⅓ cup granulated sugar, cornstarch, and ⅛ tsp. salt in a small saucepan; stir in water. Bring to a boil over medium heat; stir in vanilla. Pour hot mixture over apples; crumble reserved topping over pie.

Bake at 350° for 42 minutes, covering with aluminum foil during last 15 minutes to prevent overbrowning, if necessary. Serve with ice cream, if desired. **Makes** 8 servings.

Quick Tip: *Vanilla ice cream makes even the best pie even better. Top a slice of one of these fruit pies with a generous scoop of ice cream while the pie is still warm—it'll be swimming in vanilla goodness!*

Blueberry Pie
Prep: 15 min., Cook: 35 min.

5 cups fresh blueberries*
1 Tbsp. lemon juice
Double-Crust Pastry
1 cup sugar
⅓ cup all-purpose flour
⅛ tsp. salt
½ tsp. ground cinnamon
2 Tbsp. butter or margarine
1 large egg, lightly beaten
1 tsp. sugar

Sprinkle berries with lemon juice; set aside.
Roll half of pastry to ⅛-inch thickness on a floured surface. Place in a 9-inch pieplate.
Combine 1 cup sugar and next 3 ingredients; add to berries, stirring well. Pour into pastry shell, and dot with butter.
Roll remaining pastry to ⅛-inch thickness. Place over filling; seal and crimp edges. Cut slits in top of crust to allow steam to escape. Brush top of pastry with beaten egg, and sprinkle with 1 tsp. sugar.
Bake at 400° for 35 minutes or until golden. Cover edges with aluminum foil to prevent overbrowning, if necessary. Serve warm with vanilla ice cream, if desired. **Makes** 8 servings.

*Substitute 2 (14-oz.) packages frozen blueberries, thawed and drained, if desired. Just be sure to increase the flour to ½ cup.

Double-Crust Pastry
Prep: 5 min.

2 cups all-purpose flour
1 tsp. salt
⅔ cup plus 2 Tbsp. shortening
4 to 5 Tbsp. ice water

Combine flour and salt; cut in shortening with a pastry blender until mixture is crumbly. Sprinkle ice water, 1 Tbsp. at a time, evenly over surface of mixture; stir with a fork until dry ingredients are moistened. Shape into a ball; chill until ready to use. Roll and fit pastry into pieplate as pie recipe directs. **Makes** 8 servings.

Mango Cream Pie

Prep: 10 min., Cook: 17 min., Other: 8 hrs.

½ (15-oz.) package refrigerated piecrusts

2½ cups mango nectar

1 cup whipping cream

3 egg yolks

¾ cup sugar

⅓ cup cornstarch

⅛ tsp. salt

2 Tbsp. butter or margarine

1½ tsp. vanilla extract

Garnishes: whipped cream, fresh mango slices, fresh
mint leaves

Fit piecrust into a 9-inch pieplate according to package directions; fold edges under, and crimp. Bake at 425° for 7 minutes or until lightly browned; cool.

Combine nectar and next 5 ingredients in a medium saucepan. Bring to a boil over medium heat, whisking constantly; boil, whisking constantly, 1 minute or until mixture thickens. Remove from heat.

Stir in butter and vanilla. Cover tightly with plastic wrap, and cool to room temperature. Spoon mixture into prepared piecrust; cover and chill 8 hours. Garnish, if desired. **Makes** 6 to 8 servings.

Coconut Cream Pie

Prep: 10 min., Cook: 10 min., Other: 1 hr.

A silky cream pie offers the perfect complement to spicy barbecue.

½ (15-oz.) package refrigerated piecrusts
½ cup sugar
¼ cup cornstarch
2 cups half-and-half
4 egg yolks
3 Tbsp. butter
1 cup sweetened flaked coconut
2½ tsp. vanilla extract, divided
2 cups whipping cream
⅓ cup sugar
Garnish: toasted coconut

Fit piecrust into a 9-inch pieplate according to package directions; fold edges under, and crimp. Prick bottom and sides of piecrust with a fork.

Bake piecrust according to package directions for a one-crust pie.

Combine ½ cup sugar and cornstarch in a heavy saucepan. Whisk together half-and-half and egg yolks. Gradually whisk egg mixture into sugar mixture; bring to a boil over medium heat, whisking constantly. Boil 1 minute; remove from heat.

Stir in butter, 1 cup coconut, and 1 tsp. vanilla. Cover with plastic wrap, placing plastic wrap directly on filling in pan; let stand 30 minutes. Spoon custard mixture into prepared crust; cover and chill 30 minutes or until set.

Beat whipping cream at high speed with an electric mixer until foamy; gradually add ⅓ cup sugar and remaining 1½ tsp. vanilla. Beat until soft peaks form.

Spread or pipe whipped cream over pie filling. Store pie in refrigerator. Garnish, if desired. **Makes** 6 to 8 servings.

Banana Cream Pie

Prep: 11 min.; Cook: 8 min.; Other: 1 hr., 30 min.

For a kid-friendly version, omit the crème de cacao. Increase the milk by ¼ cup, and toss the bananas in 1 Tbsp. lemon juice.

1 cup chocolate graham cracker crumbs (about
   10 crackers)
¼ cup butter or margarine, melted
1 (3.4-oz.) package banana cream instant pudding mix
1 cup milk
¼ cup plus 1 Tbsp. crème de cacao or other chocolate-
   flavored liqueur, divided
1¾ cups frozen whipped topping, thawed and divided
1¼ cups peeled, sliced banana

Combine cracker crumbs and butter, stirring well. Press into bottom and up sides of a 9-inch pieplate.
Bake at 350° for 8 minutes. Remove from oven, and cool on a wire rack.
Combine pudding mix, milk, and ¼ cup liqueur in a medium bowl; stir with a wire whisk until smooth. Gently fold 1 cup whipped topping into mixture.
Toss banana slices with remaining 1 Tbsp. liqueur, and arrange over prepared crust. Spoon pudding mixture over banana slices. Cover and chill 1½ hours or until set. Pipe or spoon remaining ¾ cup whipped topping around edge of pie just before serving.
Makes 8 servings.

make ahead
Boston Cream Pie

Prep: 20 min.; Cook: 20 min.; Other: 1 hr., 10 min.

Traditionally called a pie, this is really a two-layer cake filled with thick custard and topped with a slick layer of chocolate.

½ cup butter or margarine, softened
1 cup sugar
3 large eggs
2 cups sifted cake flour
2 tsp. baking powder
¼ tsp. salt
½ cup milk
2 tsp. vanilla extract
½ tsp. butter extract (optional)
Cream Filling
Chocolate Glaze

Beat butter at medium speed with an electric mixer until creamy; gradually add sugar, beating 5 to 7 minutes. Add eggs, 1 at a time, beating after each addition.
Combine flour, baking powder, and salt; add to butter mixture alternately with milk, beginning and ending with flour mixture. Mix at low speed after each addition until blended. Stir in vanilla extract and, if desired, butter extract.
Pour batter into 2 greased and floured 9-inch round cakepans. Bake at 350° for 18 to 20 minutes or until a wooden pick inserted in center comes out clean. Cool in pans on wire racks 10 minutes; remove from pans, and cool completely on wire racks.
Spread Cream Filling between cake layers. Spread Chocolate Glaze over top of cake, letting excess drip down sides. Chill at least 1 hour. Store in refrigerator.
Makes 12 servings.

Cream Filling
Prep: 8 min.

½ cup sugar
3 Tbsp. cornstarch
¼ tsp. salt
2 cups milk
4 egg yolks, lightly beaten
1 tsp. vanilla extract

Combine first 3 ingredients in a heavy saucepan. Add milk and egg yolks; stir with a wire whisk until blended.
Cook over medium heat, stirring constantly, until mixture comes to a boil. Boil 1 minute or until thickened, stirring constantly; remove from heat. Stir in vanilla. Cool. **Makes** 2¼ cups.

Chocolate Glaze
Prep: 5 min., Cook: 5 min.

2 Tbsp. butter or margarine
1 (1-oz.) unsweetened chocolate baking square
1 cup sifted powdered sugar
2 Tbsp. boiling water

Combine butter and chocolate in a small heavy saucepan. Cook over low heat until chocolate melts. Cool 3 to 4 minutes. Add sugar and water; beat until smooth, using a wooden spoon. **Makes** ¾ cup.

Lemon Meringue Pie

Prep: 25 min., Cook: 50 min., Other: 10 min.

Sealing meringue to the outer edge of crust over a hot filling ensures that the meringue topping cooks completely without shrinking.

1 (15-oz.) package refrigerated piecrusts
Lemon Meringue Pie Filling
6 egg whites
½ tsp. vanilla extract
6 Tbsp. sugar

Unfold and stack piecrusts on a lightly floured surface. Roll into 1 (12-inch) circle. Fit piecrust into a 9-inch pieplate (about 1 inch deep); fold edges under, and crimp. Prick bottom and sides of piecrust with a fork. Freeze piecrust 10 minutes.

Line piecrust with parchment paper; fill with pie weights or dried beans.

Bake at 425° for 10 minutes. Remove weights and parchment paper; bake 12 to 15 more minutes or until crust is lightly browned. (Shield edges with aluminum foil if they brown too quickly.)

Prepare Lemon Meringue Pie Filling; pour into piecrust. Cover with plastic wrap, placing directly on filling. (Proceed immediately with next step to ensure that the meringue is spread over the pie filling while it's still warm.)

Beat egg whites and vanilla at high speed with an electric mixer until foamy.

Add sugar, 1 Tbsp. at a time, and beat 2 to 4 minutes or until stiff peaks form and sugar dissolves.

Remove plastic wrap from pie, and spread meringue evenly over warm Lemon Meringue Pie Filling, sealing edges.

Bake at 325° for 25 minutes or until golden brown. Cool pie completely on a wire rack. Store leftovers in the refrigerator. **Makes** 8 to 10 servings.

Lemon Meringue Pie Filling

Prep: 10 min., Cook: 10 min.

1 cup sugar
¼ cup cornstarch
⅛ tsp. salt
4 large egg yolks
2 cups milk
⅓ cup fresh lemon juice
3 Tbsp. butter or margarine
1 tsp. grated lemon rind
½ tsp. vanilla extract

Whisk together first 3 ingredients in a heavy non-aluminum medium saucepan.

Whisk together egg yolks, milk, and lemon juice in a bowl; whisk into sugar mixture in pan over medium heat.

Bring to a boil, and boil, whisking constantly, 1 minute.

Remove pan from heat; stir in butter, lemon rind, and vanilla extract until smooth. **Makes** enough for 1 (9-inch) pie.

Mocha Fudge Pie
Prep: 20 min., Cook: 22 min.

⅓ cup hot water

4 tsp. instant coffee granules, divided

½ (19.85-oz.) box light fudge brownie mix (about 2 cups)

2 tsp. vanilla extract, divided

2 egg whites

¾ cup milk

3 Tbsp. Kahlúa or other coffee liqueur, divided

1 (3.9-oz.) package chocolate instant pudding mix

3 cups frozen whipped topping, thawed and divided

Garnish: chocolate curls

Combine hot water and 2 tsp. coffee granules in a medium bowl; stir well. Add ½ box brownie mix, 1 tsp. vanilla, and egg whites; stir until well blended. Pour mixture into a 9-inch pieplate coated with cooking spray. Bake at 325° for 22 minutes. Cool completely.

Combine milk, 2 Tbsp. Kahlúa, 1 tsp. coffee granules, remaining 1 tsp. vanilla, and pudding mix in a medium bowl; beat at medium speed with an electric mixer 1 minute. Gently fold in 1½ cups whipped topping. Spread pudding mixture evenly over crust.

Combine remaining 1 tsp. coffee granules and remaining 1 Tbsp. Kahlúa in a bowl; stir well. Gently fold in remaining 1½ cups whipped topping. Spread whipped topping mixture over pudding mixture. Garnish, if desired. Serve immediately, or store loosely covered in refrigerator. **Makes** 8 servings.

Note: Store remaining brownie mix in a zip-top freezer bag in refrigerator; use mix to make another pie or a small pan of brownies. To make brownies, combine about 2 cups mix, ¼ cup water, and 1 lightly beaten egg white in a bowl. Stir just until combined. Spread in a lightly greased 8-inch square pan. Bake at 350° for 23 to 25 minutes.

Fudge Pie

Prep: 25 min., Cook: 30 min.

Strong brewed coffee brings out the rich, fudgy flavor of this easy chocolate pie—it's a "must try." If you usually use instant coffee granules, use 2 tsp. granules per 1 cup water to make the strong coffee.

2 cups (12-oz. package) semisweet chocolate morsels
¼ cup butter or margarine, softened
¾ cup firmly packed brown sugar
3 large eggs
2 tsp. strong brewed coffee
1 tsp. vanilla extract
1½ cups chopped pecans, divided
¼ cup all-purpose flour
1 unbaked 9-inch pastry shell
1 cup whipping cream, whipped

Microwave chocolate in a 1-qt. glass bowl at HIGH 1½ minutes or until melted, stirring twice.
Beat butter at medium speed with an electric mixer until creamy; gradually add sugar, beating well. Add eggs, 1 at a time, beating after each addition. Stir in melted chocolate, coffee, and vanilla. Gradually add 1 cup pecans and flour, stirring well.
Spoon chocolate mixture into pastry shell; sprinkle with remaining ½ cup pecans. Bake at 375° for 30 minutes or until a knife inserted in center comes out almost clean. Cool completely on a wire rack. Serve with whipped cream. **Makes** 8 to 10 servings.

Chocolate Sauce

Prep: 5 min., Cook: 3 min.

If you have chocolate fever, this sauce makes a satisfying topping for any chocolate or nut pie or for simply drizzling over ice cream.

1 cup (4 oz.) semisweet chocolate morsels
¼ cup whipping cream
2 Tbsp. butter

Stir together all ingredients in a small saucepan over low heat, and cook, stirring constantly, until chocolate and butter melt and sauce is warm. **Makes** 1 cup.

Bourbon-Chocolate-Pecan Pie

Prep: 10 min., Cook: 1 hr.

½ (15-oz.) package refrigerated piecrusts
4 large eggs
1 cup light corn syrup
6 Tbsp. butter or margarine, melted
½ cup granulated sugar
¼ cup firmly packed light brown sugar
3 Tbsp. bourbon
1 Tbsp. all-purpose flour
1 Tbsp. vanilla extract
1 cup coarsely chopped pecans
1 cup (6-oz. package) semisweet chocolate morsels

Fit piecrust into a 9-inch pieplate according to package directions; fold edges under, and crimp.
Whisk together eggs and next 7 ingredients in a large bowl until mixture is smooth; stir in chopped pecans and morsels. Pour into piecrust.
Bake on lowest oven rack at 350° for 1 hour or until set. **Makes** 8 servings.

Coconut-Macadamia Nut Pie

Prep: 10 min.; Cook: 1 hr., 8 min.; Other: 15 min.

½ (15-oz.) package refrigerated piecrusts
1 cup sugar
3 large eggs
1 cup light corn syrup
¼ cup whipping cream
1 Tbsp. butter or margarine, melted
1 tsp. vanilla extract
¾ cup coarsely chopped macadamia nuts
1 cup sweetened flaked coconut
Garnishes: whipped cream, chopped macadamia nuts, toasted sweetened flaked coconut

Fit piecrust into a 9-inch pieplate according to package directions; fold edges under, and crimp. Freeze 15 minutes. Bake at 425° for 6 to 8 minutes or until golden; cool on a wire rack.
Whisk together sugar and next 5 ingredients in a medium bowl; stir in nuts and coconut. Pour into prepared piecrust.
Bake at 350° for 55 minutes to 1 hour. Cool on a wire rack. Garnish, if desired. **Makes** 8 servings.

Spiked Strawberry-Lime Ice-Cream Pie
Prep: 30 min.; Cook: 10 min.; Other: 3 hrs., 30 min.

This pie softens quickly due to the alcohol content, which lowers the freezing temperature of the ice cream.

4 cups pretzel twists
½ cup butter, melted
2 Tbsp. granulated sugar
1 (½-gal.) container premium strawberry ice cream (we tested with Blue Bell Ice Cream)
1 (16-oz.) container fresh strawberries, stemmed
½ cup powdered sugar
1 (6-oz.) can frozen limeade concentrate, partially thawed
½ cup tequila
¼ cup orange liqueur (we tested with Triple Sec)
Garnishes: lime rind curls, fresh whole strawberries, pretzels

Process first 3 ingredients in a food processor until pretzels are finely crushed. Firmly press mixture into a lightly greased 10-inch springform pan.

Bake at 350° for 10 minutes. Cool completely in pan on a wire rack.

Let strawberry ice cream stand at room temperature 20 minutes or until slightly softened.

Process strawberries and powdered sugar in food processor until pureed, stopping to scrape down sides.

Place ice cream in a large bowl; cut into large (3-inch) pieces. Fold strawberry mixture, limeade concentrate, tequila, and orange liqueur into ice cream until well blended. Spoon mixture into prepared crust in springform pan. Freeze 3 hours or until firm. Let stand 10 minutes at room temperature before serving. Garnish, if desired. **Makes** 10 to 12 servings.

Strawberry-Lime Ice-Cream Pie: Omit tequila and orange liqueur, and add 1 (6-oz.) can frozen orange juice concentrate, partially thawed. Proceed with recipe as directed. Let stand 15 minutes at room temperature before serving. Garnish, if desired.

Strawberry Smoothie Ice-Cream Pie
Prep: 50 min.; Cook: 10 min.; Other: 5 hrs., 5 min.

1 (7-oz.) package waffle cones, broken into pieces
6 Tbsp. butter, melted
1 Tbsp. granulated sugar
2 (1-qt.) containers premium vanilla ice cream, divided (we tested with Häagen-Dazs)
1 (16-oz.) container fresh strawberries, stemmed
¼ cup powdered sugar, divided
1 pt. fresh blueberries
2 ripe bananas
Garnishes: waffle cone pieces, fresh whole strawberries, fresh blueberries

Process first 3 ingredients in a food processor until finely crushed. Firmly press mixture onto bottom of a lightly greased 10-inch springform pan.

Bake at 350° for 10 minutes. Cool completely in pan on a wire rack.

Let vanilla ice cream stand at room temperature 20 minutes or until slightly softened.

Process strawberries and 2 Tbsp. powdered sugar in a food processor until pureed, stopping to scrape down sides. Remove strawberry mixture; set aside.

Process blueberries and 1 Tbsp. powdered sugar in food processor until pureed, stopping to scrape down side; set aside.

Mash bananas with a fork in a large bowl; stir in remaining 1 Tbsp. powdered sugar. Set aside.

Place 1 qt. ice cream in a large bowl; cut into large (3-inch) pieces. Fold strawberry mixture into ice cream until blended. Freeze until slightly firm.

Divide remaining 1 qt. ice cream in half, placing halves in separate bowls. Stir blueberry mixture into half and mashed banana mixture into remaining half. Place bowls in freezer.

Spread half of strawberry mixture evenly into prepared crust in springform pan. Place pan and remaining strawberry mixture in freezer. Freeze 30 minutes or until strawberry layer in pan is slightly firm. Spread banana mixture evenly over strawberry layer in pan; return pan to freezer, and freeze 30 minutes or until banana layer is slightly firm. Repeat procedure with blueberry mixture. Spread remaining strawberry mixture over blueberry layer in pan, and freeze 3 hours or until all layers are firm. Let pie stand at room temperature 15 minutes before serving. Garnish, if desired. **Makes** 10 to 12 servings.

Strawberry Smoothie Ice-Cream Pie

Layered Fruit Congealed Salad
Prep: 30 min.; Cook: 50 min.; Other: 4 hrs., 15 min.

Don't cover bowls or glasses during each chill time (except at the very end). This shortens the required time in the refrigerator as you move through the steps.

1 small navel orange
2 cups water
2½ cups sugar, divided
2 (3-oz.) packages peach-flavored gelatin
4 cups boiling water, divided
½ cup half-and-half
¼ cup cold water
2 tsp. unflavored gelatin
½ (8-oz.) package cream cheese
¼ tsp. vanilla extract
2 (3-oz.) packages raspberry-flavored gelatin
2 cups fresh raspberries

Cut orange into thin (⅛-inch-thick) slices, discarding ends.

Stir together 2 cups water and 2 cups sugar in a large saucepan over medium-high heat. Bring to a boil, and stir until sugar dissolves. Gently stir in orange slices, and bring to a simmer; reduce heat to low, and simmer, occasionally pressing orange slices into liquid, 40 minutes. Remove orange slices using a slotted spoon, and place in a single layer on wax paper; cool completely. Discard liquid in pan.

Place 1 orange slice in bottom of each of 6 (1½- to 2-cup) water glasses, discarding or reserving remaining orange slices for another use. (Orange slices will not lie flat against bottoms of glasses.) Set aside.

Remove and discard 2 Tbsp. peach-flavored gelatin from 1 package. Stir together remaining peach-flavored gelatin and 2 cups boiling water in a bowl 1 to 2 minutes or until gelatin dissolves. Pour about ⅓ cup peach-flavored gelatin mixture over orange slice in each glass. Chill 1 hour or until firm.

Stir together half-and-half and ¼ cup cold water in a medium saucepan. Sprinkle with 2 tsp. unflavored gelatin, and stir.

Place pan over medium heat; stir in remaining ½ cup sugar, and cook, stirring often, 3 to 5 minutes or until sugar and gelatin dissolve. (Do not boil.) Remove pan from heat.

Microwave cream cheese at MEDIUM (50% power) 45 seconds or until very soft; stir until smooth. Whisk cream cheese into half-and-half mixture until smooth; whisk in vanilla extract, and chill 30 minutes or until slightly cool. Spoon about 3 Tbsp. cream cheese mixture in an even layer over firm peach layer in each glass; chill.

Remove and discard 2 Tbsp. raspberry-flavored gelatin from 1 package. Stir together remaining raspberry-flavored gelatin and remaining 2 cups boiling water l to 2 minutes or until gelatin dissolves.

Chill 45 minutes or until consistency of unbeaten egg white.

Stir in fresh raspberries, and spoon about ½ cup raspberry mixture in an even layer over cream cheese mixture in each glass. Cover and chill at least 2 hours or up to 24 hours before serving. **Makes** 6 servings.

FOR THE LOVE OF LAYERS

■ Use clear glass or acrylic bowls or other see-through containers to show off layers.
■ Think outside the round bowl. Go for a fun and unexpected shape, such as a square, rectangle, or scallop-edged bowl; a trifle bowl is also a good option. With so much from which to choose, don't forget glassware for some unique individual serving possibilities.

Strawberry-Sugar Biscuit Trifle

Prep: 35 min., Cook: 50 min., Other: 4 hrs.

When prepping for this recipe, make the custard first; then bake the biscuits, and prepare the fruit.

Sugar Biscuits
6 Tbsp. orange liqueur or orange juice, divided
2½ lb. fresh strawberries, halved
Trifle Custard
1½ cups whipping cream
¼ cup plus 2 Tbsp. powdered sugar
Garnishes: strawberries, mint leaves

Cut Sugar Biscuits in half; brush cut sides evenly with 5 Tbsp. orange liqueur.

Line bottom of a 4-qt. bowl or trifle bowl with 8 Sugar Biscuit halves.

Arrange strawberry halves around lower edge of bowl.

Spoon one-third of Trifle Custard evenly over Sugar Biscuit halves; top with one-third of remaining strawberry halves. Repeat layers as shown in photo below.

Drizzle remaining 1 Tbsp. orange liqueur evenly over top. Cover and chill 3 to 4 hours.

Beat whipping cream until foamy; gradually add powdered sugar, beating until soft peaks form.

Spread whipped cream over trifle, and serve immediately. Garnish, if desired. **Makes** 10 to 12 servings.

Sugar Biscuits
Prep: 10 min., Cook: 20 min.

1 (12-count) package frozen buttermilk biscuits
2 Tbsp. whipping cream
1 Tbsp. sugar
¼ tsp. ground cinnamon

Brush tops of frozen biscuits with whipping cream; sprinkle evenly with sugar and ground cinnamon. Place biscuits on a lightly greased baking sheet.

Bake at 350° for 20 minutes. Cool. **Makes** 1 dozen.

Trifle Custard
Prep: 5 min., Cook: 8 min., Other: 2 hrs.

1 cup sugar
⅓ cup cornstarch
6 egg yolks
2 cups milk
1¾ cups half-and-half
1 tsp. vanilla extract

Whisk together all ingredients in a heavy saucepan. Bring to a boil over medium heat; whisk constantly. Boil, whisking constantly, 1 minute or until thickened. Remove from heat. Place pan in ice water; whisk occasionally until cool. Chill 2 hours. **Makes** 4 cups.

Peaches 'n' Cream Trifle
Prep: 35 min.; Other: 8 hrs., 20 min.

3 Tbsp. sugar
7 fresh ripe peaches, peeled and sliced (4 cups)
1¾ cups whipping cream
¼ cup sifted powdered sugar
Crème Anglaise
6 cups pound cake, cut into 1-inch cubes
½ cup amaretto liqueur
¼ cup sliced almonds, toasted

Sprinkle sugar over peaches; toss and let stand 20 minutes or until juicy.

Combine whipping cream and powdered sugar in a chilled mixing bowl. Beat at medium speed with an electric mixer until soft peaks form. Fold half of whipped cream into Crème Anglaise.

Place half of cake cubes in a 3-qt. trifle bowl. Sprinkle ¼ cup liqueur over cubes. Top with half each of Crème Anglaise mixture and peaches. Repeat layers.

Spread remaining Crème Anglaise mixture on top of trifle. Cover and chill 8 hours. Sprinkle with almonds before serving. **Makes** 14 servings.

Crème Anglaise
Prep: 4 min., Cook: 14 min., Other: 10 min.

2 cups milk, or 1 cup milk and 1 cup half-and-half
½ cup sugar
5 egg yolks
1 tsp. vanilla extract

Bring milk to a simmer over medium heat. Beat sugar and egg yolks at high speed with an electric mixer until pale and mixture forms a ribbon.

Gradually add hot milk to egg yolk mixture, whisking until blended; return to saucepan. Cook over low heat, stirring constantly, until custard thickens and coats a spoon. Remove from heat; pour through a wire-mesh strainer into a bowl, and cool 10 minutes. Stir in vanilla. Cover and chill. **Makes** 2 cups.

THE CLASSIC TRIFLE

Full of fruit, cream, and tender cake or biscuit layers, trifles end a spicy barbecue meal on a cool and creamy note.

Jumbleberry Trifle

Jumbleberry Trifle
Prep: 45 min., Other: 50 min.

1 (10-oz.) package frozen unsweetened raspberries, thawed
1 (18-oz.) jar seedless blackberry jam or preserves, divided
1 (10.75-oz.) frozen pound cake, thawed
2 Tbsp. cream sherry
1½ cups whipping cream
1 (10-oz.) jar lemon curd
Garnishes: whipped cream, fresh raspberries and blackberries, fresh mint sprigs, lemon rind strips

Stir together raspberries and 1 cup jam. Press mixture through a wire-mesh strainer into a bowl; discard seeds. Cover sauce, and chill 20 minutes.

Cut pound cake into ¼-inch-thick slices. Spread remaining jam on 1 side of half of slices; top with remaining slices. Cut sandwiches into ½-inch cubes; drizzle with sherry, and set aside.

Beat whipping cream and lemon curd at low speed with an electric mixer until blended. Gradually increase mixer speed, beating until medium peaks form. Cover and chill 30 minutes.

Spoon 1 Tbsp. berry sauce into 8 large wine glasses; top with about ¼ cup each of cake cubes and lemon curd mixture. Repeat layers once, ending with berry sauce. Serve immediately, or chill until ready to serve. Garnish, if desired. **Makes** 8 servings.

Very Berry Sundaes

Warm Cookie Sundaes
Prep: 5 min., Cook: 30 min., Other: 5 min.

We liked the cookie cups soft, but for a more crisp cookie increase the bake time.

6 packaged refrigerated ready-to-bake peanut butter
  cookie dough rounds with mini peanut butter cups
  (we tested with Pillsbury Ready to Bake Peanut
  Butter Cup Cookies)
Vanilla ice cream
Toppings: hot fudge sauce, whipped cream, chopped
  peanuts

Place each cookie dough round into a lightly greased 8-oz. ramekin or individual soufflé dish.
Bake at 350° for 25 to 30 minutes or until cookies are lightly browned. Cool 5 minutes. Scoop vanilla ice cream into each ramekin; top sundaes with desired toppings. Serve immediately. **Makes** 6 servings.

Note: For testing purposes only, we used half of an 18-oz. package of Pillsbury Ready to Bake Peanut Butter Cup Cookies.

Very Berry Sundaes
Prep: 10 min., Other: 2 hrs.

We used blueberries, blackberries, and raspberries for mixed fresh berries.

2¼ cups fresh strawberries, halved
2¼ cups mixed fresh berries
3 Tbsp. sugar
2 Tbsp. orange liqueur
2 tsp. grated orange rind
½ tsp. chopped mint
3 cups fruit sorbet
Garnishes: orange zest, fresh mint sprigs

Combine strawberries and next 5 ingredients, tossing lightly to combine. Cover and chill up to 2 hours.
Scoop ½ cup sorbet into each of 6 serving dishes.
Spoon ⅔ cup berries over sorbet in each dish. Garnish, if desired. Serve immediately. **Makes** 6 servings.

S'mores Sundaes
Prep: 10 min., Other: 1 hr.

2 cups low-fat chocolate chunk ice cream, slightly
  softened (we tested with Healthy Choice Chocolate
  Chocolate Chunk Premium Low Fat Ice Cream)
20 graham cracker sticks, crushed (we tested with Honey
  Maid Grahams Honey Sticks)
¼ cup marshmallow crème
4 tsp. semisweet chocolate mini-morsels
8 whole graham cracker sticks

Stir together softened ice cream and crushed graham crackers in a small bowl. Freeze 1 hour or until firm.
Spoon ice-cream mixture into 4 bowls; top evenly with marshmallow crème and chocolate mini-morsels. Serve each with 2 graham cracker sticks. **Makes** 4 servings.

Chocolate Pudding
Prep: 15 min., Cook: 10 min.

4 cups whipping cream
6 Tbsp. cornstarch
1 cup sugar
1 cup (6-oz. package) semisweet chocolate morsels
1 tsp. vanilla extract

Stir together 6 Tbsp. whipping cream and cornstarch, stirring until a paste forms.
Bring remaining whipping cream to a simmer in a 2-qt. saucepan over medium heat. Stir in cornstarch mixture, sugar, chocolate morsels, and vanilla; cook, stirring constantly, until chocolate melts.
Cook mixture, stirring often, 8 minutes or until thick and creamy. Serve warm or cool. **Makes** 5 cups.

Bittersweet Chocolate Pudding
Prep: 10 min., Cook: 14 min.

3½ cups milk, divided
1 cup Dutch process or unsweetened cocoa
3 Tbsp. cornstarch
¼ tsp. salt
1 cup sugar
1 egg, lightly beaten
1 large egg yolk, lightly beaten
2 (1-oz.) bittersweet chocolate baking squares, coarsely
   chopped
1 Tbsp. vanilla extract

Combine 1 cup milk, cocoa, cornstarch, and salt in a large bowl; stir well with a whisk. Set aside.
Cook remaining 2½ cups milk in a large, heavy saucepan over medium-high heat to 180° or until tiny bubbles form around edge (do not boil). Remove from heat; stir in sugar with a whisk until sugar dissolves. Add cocoa mixture to pan, stirring until blended. Bring to a boil over medium heat; cook 2 minutes, stirring constantly.
Combine egg and egg yolk in a medium bowl, stirring well with a whisk. Gradually add milk mixture to egg mixture, stirring constantly. Return mixture to pan. Cook over medium heat until thick (about 2 minutes); stir constantly. Remove from heat. Stir in chocolate and vanilla; stir until chocolate melts. Serve warm or chilled. **Makes** 8 servings.

kids love it
Best-Ever Banana Pudding
Prep: 25 min., Cook: 25 min.

⅔ cup sugar
¼ cup all-purpose flour
Dash of salt
1 (14-oz.) can sweetened condensed milk
2½ cups milk
4 large eggs, separated
2 tsp. vanilla extract
1 (12-oz.) package vanilla wafers
6 large bananas
⅓ cup sugar
½ tsp. banana extract or vanilla extract

Combine first 3 ingredients in a heavy saucepan. Whisk together milks and egg yolks; stir into dry ingredients.
Cook over medium heat, whisking constantly, until smooth and thickened. Remove from heat; stir in vanilla.
Arrange one-third of wafers in bottom of a 3-qt. baking dish. Slice 2 bananas; layer over wafers. Pour one-third of pudding mixture over bananas. Repeat layers of sliced bananas and pudding twice; arrange remaining wafers around edge of dish.
Beat egg whites at high speed with an electric mixer until foamy.
Add ⅓ cup sugar, 1 Tbsp. at a time, beating until soft peaks form and sugar dissolves. Fold in banana extract; spread over pudding, sealing to edge.
Bake at 325° for 25 minutes or until golden brown.
Makes 8 to 10 servings.

❝While all things barbecue tend to fall squarely along regional and state lines, desserts are all over the map.**❞**

—Scott Jones, *Southern Living* Staff

**Peanut Butter-
Banana Pudding**

Peanut Butter-Banana Pudding
Prep: 10 min., Other: 2 hrs.

1 (3.4-oz.) package French vanilla instant pudding mix
2 cups milk
⅓ cup creamy peanut butter
1 (8-oz.) carton sour cream
42 vanilla wafers
6 small bananas, divided
1 (8-oz.) container frozen whipped topping, thawed

Prepare pudding mix according to package directions, using a whisk and 2 cups milk. (Do not use an electric mixer.) Add peanut butter and sour cream, stirring well with a wire whisk.
Line a 2½-qt. casserole with 14 vanilla wafers. Peel and slice 4 bananas. Top wafers with one-third each of pudding mixture, banana slices, and whipped topping. Repeat layers twice using remaining wafers, pudding mixture, banana slices, and whipped topping.
Cover and chill at least 2 hours. To garnish, peel and slice remaining 2 bananas; arrange slices around outer edges of dish. **Makes** 8 to 10 servings.

Cinnamon-Raisin Bread Pudding
Prep: 15 min.; Cook: 1 hr., 30 min.

4 cups milk
5 large eggs
10 to 12 white bread slices, torn into pieces
3 cups vanilla wafer crumbs (about 55 wafers)
¾ cup sugar
½ tsp. ground cinnamon
1¼ cups raisins

Whisk together milk and eggs in a large bowl. Add bread and remaining ingredients, stirring until blended.
Pour mixture into an aluminum foil-lined 11- x 7-inch baking dish; cover with foil, and place in a larger pan. Add water to larger pan to a depth of 1 to 1½ inches.
Bake at 350° for 1 hour. Uncover and bake 20 to 30 more minutes. Serve with caramel sauce or softened ice cream, if desired. **Makes** 10 servings.

Bread Pudding with Whiskey Sauce
Prep: 10 min., Cook: 1 hr., Other: 10 min.

1 (1-lb.) loaf dry French bread*
4 cups milk
4 large eggs, beaten
2 cups sugar
2 Tbsp. vanilla extract
1 cup raisins
2 apples, peeled, cored, and cubed
1 (8-oz.) can crushed pineapple, drained
¼ cup butter, melted
Whiskey Sauce

Tear bread into small pieces; place in a large bowl. Add milk to bowl; let mixture stand 10 minutes. Stir mixture well with a wooden spoon. Add eggs, sugar, and vanilla; stir well. Stir in raisins, apple, and pineapple.
Pour butter in a 13- x 9-inch pan; tilt pan to coat evenly. Spoon pudding mixture into pan.
Bake, uncovered, at 350° for 55 minutes to 1 hour. Remove from oven, and cool slightly. Serve warm with Whiskey Sauce. **Makes** 16 servings.

*To dry out fresh bread, tear bread into small pieces; bake at 200° for 1 hour, turning once.

Whiskey Sauce
Prep: 5 min., Cook: 6 min., Other: 2 min.

½ cup melted butter
1 cup sugar
⅓ cup bourbon, divided
1 large egg, beaten

Combine butter and sugar in a heavy saucepan; cook over medium heat until sugar dissolves. Add half of bourbon, and simmer 3 minutes, stirring well.
Reduce heat to medium-low, and add egg; stir well. Remove from heat, and let stand 2 minutes. Stir in remaining bourbon. **Makes** about 2 cups.

make ahead

make ahead

Layered Almond-Cream Cheese Bread Pudding with Amaretto Cream Sauce

Prep: 30 min., Cook: 1 hr., Other: 30 min.

1 (16-oz.) loaf white bread, sliced and divided
1 (8-oz.) package cream cheese, softened
9 large eggs, divided
¼ cup sugar
3 tsp. vanilla extract, divided
1¼ cups almond filling (we tested with Solo Almond Filling)
1 cup butter, melted and divided
2½ cups half-and-half
Dash of salt
2 Tbsp. almond filling
2 Tbsp. sugar
1 egg yolk
¼ cup slivered almonds
Amaretto Cream Sauce (page 309)

Coat a 13- x 9-inch pan with cooking spray. Arrange 4½ bread slices in bottom of prepared pan, cutting slices as necessary to fit pan.

Beat cream cheese, 1 egg, ¼ cup sugar, and 1 tsp. vanilla with an electric mixer until smooth. Spread half of cream cheese mixture over bread in pan.

Whisk together 1¼ cups almond filling and ½ cup melted butter. Spread half of almond mixture over cream cheese mixture. Repeat layers once, using 4½ bread slices, remaining cream cheese mixture, and remaining almond mixture.

Cut remaining bread slices into 1-inch cubes; sprinkle evenly over almond mixture.

Whisk together remaining 8 eggs, remaining 2 tsp. vanilla, half-and-half, and salt in a large bowl; pour over bread cubes. Cover and chill 30 minutes or until most of egg mixture is absorbed.

Whisk together remaining ½ cup melted butter, 2 Tbsp. almond filling, 2 Tbsp. sugar, and egg yolk until blended. Drizzle evenly over bread pudding; sprinkle with almonds. Bake at 325° for 1 hour or until set. Serve warm or chilled with Amaretto Cream Sauce.
Makes 12 servings.

Amaretto Cream Sauce
Prep: 5 min., Cook: 10 min.

½ cup amaretto liqueur
2 Tbsp. cornstarch
1½ cups whipping cream
½ cup sugar

Combine liqueur and cornstarch, stirring until smooth.
Cook cream in a heavy saucepan over medium heat, stirring often, just until bubbles appear; gradually stir in liqueur mixture. Bring to a boil over medium heat, and boil, stirring constantly, 30 seconds. Remove from heat; stir in sugar, and cool completely. **Makes** about 2½ cups.

Chocolate-Cherry Bread Pudding
Prep: 15 min., Cook: 1 hr., Other: 15 min.

Juicy cherries and triple chocolate flavor combine for a five-star dessert.

1 (6-oz.) jar maraschino cherries
3 large eggs, lightly beaten
3 cups chocolate milk
¾ cup sugar
3 Tbsp. butter or margarine, melted
1 Tbsp. unsweetened cocoa
6 cups cubed French bread
1 cup (6-oz. package) semisweet chocolate morsels
Garnishes: sweetened whipped cream, additional maraschino cherries

Drain cherries, reserving 1 Tbsp. cherry juice. Coarsely chop cherries.
Combine eggs, 1 Tbsp. reserved cherry juice, milk, and next 3 ingredients in a large bowl, stirring well. Add bread cubes, and let stand 15 minutes, stirring occasionally. Stir in cherries and chocolate morsels.
Spoon mixture into a lightly greased 9-inch square pan. Bake, uncovered, at 350° for 50 minutes to 1 hour or until set. Garnish, if desired. Serve bread pudding warm or at room temperature. **Makes** 8 to 10 servings.

Summer Pudding
Prep: 15 min., Cook: 15 min., Other: 2 hrs.

2 cups fresh raspberries
1 cup fresh blackberries
1 cup quartered fresh strawberries
½ cup sugar
1 Tbsp. grated lemon rind
2 Tbsp. fresh lemon juice
½ tsp. vanilla extract
⅛ tsp. salt
2 Tbsp. raspberry or blackberry liqueur (optional)
1 fresh lemon verbena sprig (optional)
½ tsp. crushed green peppercorns (optional)
2 cups day-old white bread slices, cut into ½-inch cubes (we tested with Sara Lee Honey White Bakery Bread)
Garnishes: fresh blackberries, fresh blueberries, fresh strawberries

Combine first 8 ingredients and, if desired, liqueur, lemon verbena, and peppercorns in a large nonaluminum bowl. Cover and let stand at room temperature at least 1½ hours.
Spread bread cubes evenly on a baking sheet; bake at 350° for 10 to 15 minutes or until toasted. Cool.
Stir bread into berry mixture, and let stand for 30 minutes. Remove lemon verbena, and discard.
Spoon pudding mixture into 4 (8-oz.) individual serving dishes. Garnish, if desired. **Makes** 4 servings.

Summer Pudding

Blueberry Bread Pudding

make ahead
Blueberry Bread Pudding
Prep: 15 min.; Cook: 1 hr.; Other: 8 hrs., 5 min.

Make this easy, decadent recipe the day before, and chill; then bake and serve hot.

1 (16-oz.) French bread loaf, cubed
1 (8-oz.) package cream cheese, cut into pieces
3 cups fresh blueberries, divided
6 large eggs
4 cups milk
½ cup sugar
¼ cup butter or margarine, melted
¼ cup maple syrup
1 (10-oz.) jar blueberry preserves
Garnishes: fresh mint leaves, edible pansies

Arrange half of bread cubes in a lightly greased 13- x 9-inch pan. Sprinkle evenly with cream cheese and 1 cup blueberries; top with remaining bread cubes.

Whisk together eggs, 4 cups milk, sugar, butter, and maple syrup; pour over bread mixture, pressing bread cubes to absorb egg mixture. Cover and chill 8 hours.

Bake, covered, at 350° for 30 minutes. Uncover and bake 30 more minutes or until lightly browned and set. Let stand 5 minutes before serving.

Stir together remaining 2 cups blueberries and blueberry preserves in a saucepan over low heat until warm. Serve blueberry mixture over bread pudding. Garnish, if desired. **Makes** 10 to 12 servings.

editor's favorite • make ahead
Creamy Rice Pudding
Prep: 5 min., Cook: 43 min.

There's no need to save this dish for dessert—you can try it for breakfast, too. Speed up the recipe by cooking it over medium heat rather than low, but remember to stir constantly.

1 qt. milk
1 cup regular rice, uncooked
½ tsp. salt
1½ tsp. vanilla extract
4 egg yolks, beaten
½ cup sugar
½ cup half-and-half
1 tsp. ground cinnamon
1 cup raisins

Combine first 4 ingredients in a medium saucepan. Cover and cook over low heat about 40 minutes or until rice is tender, stirring occasionally.

Combine egg yolks and next 3 ingredients in a small bowl. Gradually stir about one-fourth of hot mixture into yolk mixture; add yolk mixture to remaining hot mixture. Cook over low heat, stirring constantly, until mixture reaches 160° and is thickened and bubbly (about 3 minutes). Stir in raisins. Serve warm or chilled. **Makes** 10 servings.

Bourbon Balls
Prep: 45 min., Other: 9 hrs.

1 (16-oz.) package powdered sugar
⅓ cup bourbon (we tested with Woodford Reserve
    Distiller's Select Bourbon)
¼ cup butter, softened
50 pecan halves (about 1¼ cups)
2 cups (12-oz. package) semisweet chocolate morsels
1 Tbsp. shortening

Stir together first 3 ingredients until blended. Cover and chill 8 hours.

Shape mixture into 1-inch balls. Gently press pecan halves into 2 sides of each ball. Chill 8 hours.

Melt chocolate and shortening in a saucepan over medium heat. Remove from heat. Dip bourbon balls in chocolate, and place on wax paper.

Chill 1 hour or until hardened. **Makes** 25 balls.

Fast Fudge
Prep: 18 min., Cook: 8 min.

2 cups sugar
⅔ cup evaporated milk
½ cup butter
12 large marshmallows
Pinch of salt
1 cup (6-oz. package) semisweet chocolate morsels
1 cup chopped pecans
1 tsp. vanilla extract

Combine first 5 ingredients in a large heavy saucepan. Cook over medium heat, stirring constantly, until mixture comes to a boil; boil 5 minutes, stirring constantly. Remove from heat.

Add chocolate morsels to marshmallow mixture, stirring until chocolate melts. Add pecans and vanilla, stirring well. Spread evenly in a buttered 8- or 9-inch square pan. Cool and cut into squares in pan. **Makes** 3 dozen squares (2 lb.).

Buttermilk Fudge
Prep: 10 min., Cook: 18 min., Other: 15 min.

2 cups sugar
1 cup buttermilk
½ cup butter
2 Tbsp. light corn syrup
1 tsp. baking soda
¾ cup chopped pecans, toasted (optional)
1 tsp. vanilla extract

Butter sides of a heavy 4-qt. saucepan; add sugar and next 4 ingredients. Cook over medium heat, stirring constantly, 18 minutes or until candy thermometer registers 236°. Remove from heat, and cool, undisturbed, until temperature drops to 180° (about 15 minutes).

Add pecans, if desired, and vanilla; beat with a wooden spoon until mixture thickens and just begins to lose its gloss (about 5 minutes). Quickly pour into a buttered 9- x 5-inch loafpan. Cool completely; cut into squares. **Makes** 3 dozen squares (1¼ lb.).

Buckeyes
Prep: 25 min.

1¼ cups butter, softened
1 (18-oz.) jar creamy peanut butter
7 cups sifted powdered sugar (about 1½ lb.)
3 cups (18 oz.) semisweet chocolate morsels
1½ Tbsp. shortening

Process butter and peanut butter in food processor until thoroughly blended. Add 3 cups powdered sugar, and process until smooth. Gradually add remaining powdered sugar in 2 batches, processing after each addition until mixture pulls away from sides and is no longer crumbly. Shape mixture into 1-inch balls. Cover and chill thoroughly.

Combine chocolate morsels and shortening in top of a double boiler; bring water to a boil. Reduce heat to low; cook until chocolate melts, stirring occasionally. Remove pan from heat, leaving chocolate mixture over hot water. Use a wooden pick to dip each ball in chocolate, coating three-fourths of ball; place on wax paper. Carefully smooth wooden pick holes. Let candies stand until chocolate hardens. Store in an airtight container in refrigerator. **Makes** 8 dozen.

Peanutty Ice-Cream Sandwiches

Prep: 20 min.; Cook: 16 min.; Other: 1 hr., 30 min.

⅔ cup butter or margarine
2 cups quick-cooking oats, uncooked
¾ cup firmly packed dark brown sugar
½ cup finely chopped dry-roasted peanuts
1 large egg, lightly beaten
¼ cup all-purpose flour
¼ tsp. baking powder
¼ tsp. salt
1 tsp. vanilla extract
½ cup chunky peanut butter
3 cups vanilla ice cream, softened
1 cup coarsely chopped dry-roasted peanuts

Melt butter in a Dutch oven over medium heat. Remove from heat; stir in oats and next 7 ingredients.
Drop oat mixture by tablespoonfuls 3 inches apart onto a parchment paper-lined baking sheet. Spread each dollop of cookie batter to form a 3-inch circle.
Bake at 350° for 9 to 11 minutes or until edges are golden. Remove from pan; cool completely on a wire rack.
Swirl peanut butter into softened ice cream. Freeze 30 minutes. Scoop ice cream evenly on flat sides of half of cookies; top with remaining cookies, flat sides down. Roll sides of sandwiches in coarsely chopped peanuts. Place in plastic or wax paper sandwich bags, and freeze at least 1 hour. **Makes** 9 servings.

Note: Do not substitute a greased baking sheet for parchment paper. The cookies will slide and tear.

Easy Chocolate-Mint Ice-Cream Sandwich

Peanutty Ice-Cream Sandwiches

Easy Chocolate-Mint Ice-Cream Sandwiches

Prep: 15 min.; Other: 1 hr., 30 min.

This recipe uses packaged chewy cookies, but check your local bakery for freshly baked ones if you prefer.

2 pt. vanilla ice cream, softened
15 mint-and-cream-filled chocolate sandwich cookies, chopped (we tested with Oreo Double Delight Mint 'n Creme)
1 (8.5-oz.) package large chewy chocolate cookies (we tested with Archway Original Dutch Cocoa)

Stir together softened ice cream and sandwich cookie pieces. Freeze 30 minutes. Spread ice cream evenly on 1 side of 5 large chewy cookies; top with remaining large chewy cookies. Place in plastic or wax paper sandwich bags, and freeze at least 1 hour. **Makes** 5 servings.

Butter Pecan Ice-Cream Sandwiches: Omit mint-and-cream-filled sandwich cookies. Substitute 2 pt. butter pecan ice cream for vanilla ice cream and 1 (8.75-oz.) package large chewy sugar cookies for chewy chocolate cookies. Proceed as directed.

Mocha-Almond-Fudge Ice-Cream Sandwiches: Omit mint-and-cream-filled chocolate sandwich cookies. Substitute 2 pt. mocha-flavored ice cream with chocolate-covered almonds for vanilla ice cream (we tested with Starbucks Coffee Almond Fudge Ice Cream). Proceed as directed.

Oatmeal-Rum-Raisin Ice-Cream Sandwiches: Omit mint-and-cream-filled sandwich cookies. Substitute 1 (8.75-oz.) package large, chewy oatmeal cookies for chewy chocolate cookies. Pour ¼ cup dark rum over ½ cup golden raisins; let stand 2 hours. Drain and discard rum; stir rum-soaked raisins into softened ice cream. Proceed as directed.

Mocha Ice Cream

Prep: 15 min., Cook: 14 min., Other: 3 hrs.

1 (8-oz.) package semisweet chocolate baking squares, coarsely chopped
¼ cup strong brewed coffee
2 cups whipping cream
1 cup half-and-half
¾ cup sugar, divided
3 Tbsp. instant coffee granules
4 egg yolks

Microwave chocolate in a 1-qt. microwave-safe bowl at HIGH 1½ minutes or until melted, stirring twice; stir in brewed coffee. Set chocolate mixture aside.
Bring whipping cream, half-and-half, ½ cup sugar, and coffee granules to a boil in a heavy saucepan over medium-high heat, stirring until sugar and coffee dissolve.
Beat yolks and remaining ¼ cup sugar at high speed with an electric mixer until thick and pale. With mixer at low speed, gradually pour hot cream mixture into yolk mixture; return to saucepan.
Cook over medium heat, stirring constantly, 6 to 8 minutes or until mixture thickens and coats a spoon. Remove from heat; stir in chocolate mixture. Cover and chill 2 hours.
Pour chilled mixture into freezer container of a 5-qt. hand-turned or electric freezer. Freeze according to manufacturer's instructions.
Pack freezer with additional ice and rock salt, and let stand 1 hour. Serve ice cream with cookies, if desired.
Makes 5 cups.

**No-Cook Fig-Mint
Ice Cream**

No-Cook Vanilla Ice Cream
Prep: 5 min.; Other: 2 hrs., 15 min.

1 (14-oz.) can sweetened condensed milk
1 (5-oz.) can evaporated milk
2 Tbsp. sugar
2 tsp. vanilla
2 cups whole milk

Whisk all ingredients in a 2-qt. pitcher or large bowl until blended. Cover and chill 30 minutes.

Pour milk mixture into freezer container of a 1-qt. electric ice-cream maker, and freeze according to manufacturer's instructions.

Remove container with ice cream from ice-cream maker, and place in freezer 15 minutes. Transfer to an airtight container; freeze until firm, about 1 to 1½ hours. **Makes** 1 qt.

Note: For testing purposes only, we used a Rival 4-qt. Durable Plastic Bucket Ice Cream Maker and a Cuisinart Automatic Frozen Yogurt-Ice Cream & Sorbet Maker.

No-Cook Fig-Mint Ice Cream: Prepare No-Cook Vanilla Ice Cream as directed. Remove container with prepared ice cream from ice-cream maker, and place in freezer. Freeze 15 minutes. Stir together 2 cups chopped peeled fresh figs, ¼ cup fresh lemon juice, 2 Tbsp. sugar, and 2 tsp. chopped fresh mint. Stir mixture into prepared ice-cream mixture. Place in an airtight container; freeze until firm. **Makes** 1½ qt.

Note: We used Black Mission Figs; any seasonal fresh figs, including green figs, should work in this recipe.

ICE CREAM AND BBQ: A NATURAL PAIR

Ice cream and barbecue go hand in hand in the South—there's no better way to cool down from a long day of smoking or barbecuing. Get the whole family involved by making homemade ice cream while the barbecue cooks.

Old-Fashioned Vanilla Ice Cream
Prep: 40 min., Cook: 30 min., Other: 5 hrs.

Homemade vanilla ice cream is hard to beat to cool down a hot summer day and a spicy barbecue meal.

6 egg yolks, lightly beaten
2⅓ cups sugar
4 cups milk
5 cups half-and-half
¼ tsp. salt
2 Tbsp. vanilla extract

Combine first 3 ingredients in a large saucepan. Cook over low heat, stirring constantly, 25 to 30 minutes or until mixture thickens and coats a spoon; cover and chill at least 4 hours.

Stir in half-and-half, salt, and vanilla; pour into freezer container of a 4- or 5-qt. hand-turned or electric freezer. Freeze according to manufacturer's instructions.

Pack freezer with additional ice and rock salt, and let stand 1 hour. Serve ice cream immediately; or spoon into an airtight container, and freeze until firm. **Makes** 3½ qt.

Coffee Ice Cream
Prep: 15 min., Other: 1 hr.

⅔ cup hot water
1 Tbsp. instant coffee granules
2 (14-oz.) cans sweetened condensed milk
1 qt. half-and-half
1½ Tbsp. vanilla extract

Combine hot water and instant coffee granules in a small bowl, stirring until granules dissolve. Cool slightly.

Combine coffee, sweetened condensed milk, and remaining ingredients in a bowl, mixing well.

Pour ice-cream mixture into freezer container of a 1-gal. hand-turned or electric freezer. Freeze according to manufacturer's instructions.

Pack freezer with additional ice and rock salt; let stand at least 1 hour before serving, if desired. **Makes** about 2 qt.

Chocolate Ice Cream
Prep: 10 min., Other: 1 hr.

2 (14-oz.) cans sweetened condensed milk
1 qt. half-and-half
1½ Tbsp. vanilla extract
1 cup chocolate syrup

Combine all ingredients in a large bowl, mixing well.
Pour ice-cream mixture into freezer container of a 1-gal. hand-turned or electric freezer. Freeze according to manufacturer's instructions.
Pack freezer with additional ice and rock salt; let stand at least 1 hour before serving, if desired. **Makes** about 2 qt.

Chocolate Chip Ice Cream: Substitute 1 cup (6-oz. package) semisweet chocolate mini-morsels for 1 cup chocolate syrup. Proceed as directed.

Cookies and Cream Ice Cream: Substitute 15 cream-filled chocolate sandwich cookies, crumbled, for 1 cup chocolate syrup. Proceed as directed.

Caramel-Pecan Crunch Ice Cream
Prep: 15 min., Cook: 14 min., Other: 1 hr.

Ice cream has never been so good. Buttery pecans and ribbons of caramel are just waiting for you—and a big bowl and a spoon!

2 Tbsp. butter or margarine, melted
1 cup chopped pecans
½ cup sugar
8 cups half-and-half
1 cup firmly packed brown sugar
2 (12-oz.) jars caramel topping
1 Tbsp. vanilla extract

Combine first 3 ingredients in an 8-inch cast-iron skillet, and cook over medium heat, stirring constantly, 12 to 14 minutes or until sugar is golden. Pour mixture onto greased wax paper. Cool completely; break into small pieces. Set aside.

Combine half-and-half and remaining 3 ingredients; stir until brown sugar and caramel topping dissolve. Pour mixture into freezer container of a 6-qt. hand-turned or electric freezer.
Add reserved pecan crunch pieces. Freeze according to manufacturer's instructions.
Pack freezer with additional ice and rock salt, and let stand 1 hour before serving. **Makes** 1½ gal.

Butter Pecan Ice Cream
Prep: 10 min., Cook: 13 min., Other: 1 hr.

This recipe is so good you may want to double or triple it, and invite over your friends. If you do, make the ice cream in a 1-gal. freezer.

¾ cup firmly packed brown sugar
½ cup water
⅛ tsp. salt
2 large eggs, lightly beaten
2 Tbsp. butter
1 cup milk
1 tsp. vanilla extract
1 cup whipping cream
½ cup finely chopped pecans, toasted

Combine first 3 ingredients in top of a double boiler; bring water in bottom of double boiler to a boil. Reduce heat to low; cook, stirring constantly, 3 to 4 minutes or until sugar dissolves. Gradually stir a small amount of hot mixture into eggs; add to remaining hot mixture, stirring constantly. Cook over medium heat, stirring constantly, until thermometer registers 160° and mixture thickens (about 4 to 5 minutes). Remove from heat; stir in butter, and cool. Stir in milk and remaining ingredients.
Pour mixture into freezer container of a 2-qt. hand-turned or electric freezer. Freeze according to manufacturer's instructions.
Pack freezer with additional ice and rock salt, and let stand 1 hour before serving. **Makes** 1 qt.

Peanut Butter Ice Cream
Prep: 15 min., Cook: 25 min., Other: 1 hr.

1 (12-oz.) jar chunky peanut butter
1½ qt. half-and-half
6 large eggs
1 (14-oz.) can sweetened condensed milk
1 cup milk
1 Tbsp. vanilla extract
2 cups sugar
2 Tbsp. all-purpose flour

Cook peanut butter, 2 cups half-and-half, and eggs in a Dutch oven over low heat, whisking constantly, 7 minutes or until a thermometer registers 160°. Whisk in remaining 4 cups half-and-half, condensed milk, milk, and vanilla.

Combine sugar and flour; whisk into hot mixture until sugar dissolves.

Pour into freezer container of a 5-qt. hand-turned or electric freezer. Freeze according to manufacturer's instructions.

Pack freezer with additional ice and rock salt, and let stand 1 hour before serving. **Makes** 1 gal.

Toasted Coconut Ice Cream
Prep: 10 min., Cook: 30 min., Other: 4 hrs.

2 cups sweetened flaked coconut
4 cups milk
1 cup sugar
6 egg yolks
2 cups half-and-half
1 (16-oz.) can cream of coconut
2 tsp. vanilla extract
Garnish: toasted coconut

Bake 2 cups coconut in a shallow pan at 350°, stirring occasionally, 10 minutes or until toasted.

Whisk together milk, sugar, and egg yolks in a heavy saucepan. Cook over medium heat, whisking constantly, 20 minutes or until mixture thickens and coats a spoon. (Do not boil.) Remove from heat; whisk in coconut, half-and-half, cream of coconut, and vanilla. Cover and chill 3 hours.

Pour into freezer container of a 1-gal. hand-turned or electric freezer. Freeze according to manufacturer's instructions.

Pack freezer with additional ice and rock salt; let stand 1 hour before serving. Garnish, if desired. **Makes** 4 qt.

Low-Fat Strawberry Cheesecake Ice Cream
Prep: 18 min., Other: 1 hr.

Experience decadence guilt-free with this low-fat indulgence. There really is room for dessert after all that barbecue!

3 cups strawberries, halved
1 (6-oz.) block fat-free cream cheese (about ⅔ cup), softened
2 (12-oz.) cans evaporated fat-free milk
1 (14-oz.) can fat-free sweetened condensed skim milk
1 tsp. vanilla extract
1 cup frozen reduced-calorie whipped topping, thawed

Place strawberries in a food processor; process until finely chopped, scraping sides of bowl once. Set aside.

Place cream cheese in a large bowl; mash with a fork until smooth. Add milks and vanilla; stir with a whisk until smooth. Stir in strawberries. Gently fold in whipped topping.

Pour into freezer container of a 1-gal. hand-turned or electric freezer; freeze according to manufacturer's instructions. Spoon ice cream into a freezer-safe container; cover and freeze 1 hour or until firm. **Makes** 2½ qt.

Strawberry Ice Cream
Prep: 45 min., Cook: 16 min.

Summer's fresh strawberries make a big difference in this ice cream.

2 cups sugar, divided
¼ cup all-purpose flour
Dash of salt
3 cups milk
4 large eggs, lightly beaten
3 cups sieved or pureed fresh strawberries
3 cups whipping cream
1 Tbsp. vanilla extract
2 tsp. almond extract

Combine 1½ cups sugar, flour, and salt; set mixture aside.

Heat milk in top of a double boiler until hot; add a small amount of milk to sugar mixture, stirring to make a smooth paste. Stir sugar mixture into remaining milk; cook over medium heat, stirring constantly, until slightly thickened. Cover and cook 10 minutes, stirring often.

Stir about one-fourth of hot mixture into beaten eggs; add to remaining hot mixture. Cook 1 minute, stirring constantly. Cool.

Combine strawberries, remaining ½ cup sugar, whipping cream, and flavorings; stir into custard.

Pour into freezer container of a 1-gal. hand-turned or electric freezer. Freeze according to manufacturer's instructions. Mixture does not require standing time before serving. **Makes** 4 qt.

Lemon-Buttermilk Ice Cream
Prep: 15 min., Other: 1 hr.

Three different kinds of milk provide a rich, creamy consistency. This ice cream is at its peak served as soon as it's firm. Let stand at room temperature 30 minutes so that it's soft enough to scoop.

1½ cups sugar
1 cup fresh lemon juice (about 10 lemons)
2 cups half-and-half
2 cups whole milk
2 cups fat-free buttermilk

Combine sugar and juice in a large bowl, stirring with a whisk until sugar dissolves. Add half-and-half, whole milk, and buttermilk.

Pour into freezer container of a 1-gal. hand-turned or electric freezer; freeze according to manufacturer's instructions. Spoon ice cream into a freezer-safe container. Cover and freeze 1 hour or until firm. **Makes** 9 cups.

Fresh Lime Ice Cream
Prep: 10 min., Other: 1 hr.

2½ cups sugar
6 cups half-and-half
1 Tbsp. grated lime rind
¾ cup fresh lime juice (about 6 limes)
⅛ tsp. salt

Combine all ingredients; pour into freezer container of a 4- or 5-qt. hand-turned or electric freezer. Freeze according to manufacturer's instructions.

Pack freezer with additional ice and rock salt, and let stand 1 hour before serving. **Makes** 2½ qt.

Orange Ice Cream: Substitute orange rind and fresh lemon juice for lime rind and juice. Proceed as directed.

**Lemon-Buttermilk
Ice Cream**

Lemon Ice Cream

Prep: 8 min., Other: 6 hrs.

This is one of our staffs' longtime favorite recipes, and it's so easy to make. You don't even need an ice-cream freezer.

2 cups sugar
2 cups milk
2 cups half-and-half
2 tsp. grated lemon rind
1 cup fresh lemon juice
6 drops of yellow liquid food coloring
Garnish: fresh mint sprigs

Stir together first 6 ingredients in a large bowl. Pour mixture into a 13- x 9-inch pan; cover and freeze at least 2 hours.

Process half of mixture in a food processor or blender until smooth. Remove mixture from processor, and set aside.

Repeat procedure with remaining mixture. Return all of mixture to pan.

Cover and freeze at least 4 hours or until firm. Garnish, if desired. **Makes** 1½ qt.

South Seas Ice Cream with Sweet-Heat Salsa and Cinnamon Crisps

Prep: 30 min., Cook: 10 min., Other: 8 hrs.

½ gal. vanilla ice cream, slightly softened
1 (15-oz.) can cream of coconut
¾ cup sweetened flaked coconut, lightly toasted
¾ cup chopped macadamia nuts
1 small lime
1½ cups chopped fresh mango
1½ cups chopped fresh pineapple
1 kiwifruit, peeled and diced
½ cup peeled, seeded, and chopped cucumber
2 Tbsp. Asian sweet chili sauce (we tested with Yeo's Chili Sauce Sweet)
¼ tsp. freshly ground pepper
2 Tbsp. fresh mint leaves, chopped
¼ cup sugar
2 tsp. ground cinnamon
4 (8-inch) flour tortillas
4 Tbsp. butter, melted

Stir together first 4 ingredients in a large bowl; freeze 8 hours or until firm.

Grate lime rind in a large bowl; squeeze juice from lime, and combine with grated rind. Stir in chopped mango and next 6 ingredients. Cover salsa, and chill 2 hours.

Combine sugar and cinnamon in a small bowl.

Brush 1 side of tortillas with melted butter; cut each into 8 wedges or decorative shapes using a cookie cutter. Arrange in a single layer on an aluminum foil-lined baking sheet, and sprinkle evenly with sugar mixture.

Bake at 400° for 7 to 10 minutes or until lightly browned. Cool.

Spoon ice-cream mixture into 8 bowls; top evenly with salsa mixture, and serve with cinnamon crisps. Serve immediately. **Makes** 8 servings.

Great Barbecue Menus

Party Planner

Southerners fire up the smoker or grill year-round for casual gatherings.
So invite some friends over and get grillin'!

Friday Night Barbecue

Serves 8

Baked Vidalia Onion Dip, page 74
* BBQ Grilled Salmon, page 135
* Fried Okra, page 255
Southern-Style Potato Salad, page 233
Brown Sugar-Oatmeal Cookies, page 267

Super Bowl Sunday

Serves 8

Pecan-Crusted Artichoke and
Cheese Spread, page 75

Mini Mexican Quiches, page 90
Jerk Smoked Chicken, page 122
* Black Bean and Black-Eyed Pea Salad, page 219
Double-Chocolate Brownies, page 274
Cola and beer bar

Southwest Fiesta

Serves 6

Guacamole, page 70
Margaritas from Scratch, page 59
Beef Fajitas with Pico de Gallo, page 103
South Seas Ice Cream with
Sweet-Heat Salsa and Cinnamon Crisps, page 321

4th of July

Serves 6

Sweet-and-Sour Baby Back Ribs, page 113
Grilled Corn with Creamy Chipotle Sauce, page 137
Lemon-Basil Potato Salad, page 233
Homemade Lemonade, page 46
Peanutty Ice-Cream Sandwiches, page 312

Daylong Smokeout

Serves 8

Smoky Pecans, page 80
Texas-Smoked Beer-Marinated Brisket, page 96
Jim Gibson's Barbecue Hash, page 259
Tex-Mex Pinto Beans, page 235
Texas toast
* Simple Southern Iced Tea, page 50
Coconut Cream Pie, page 293

Birthday Bash

Serves 6

Chipotle Pulled-Pork
Barbecue Sandwiches, page 161

Baked Beans, page 234
Bacon Potato Salad, page 233
Chocolate-Praline Cake, page 282

Couples' Wedding Shower

Serves 12

Sun-Dried Tomato Cheesecake, page 82

* Peach-Glazed Barbecue
Pork Chops and Peaches, page 116

* Kentucky Bibb Salad with
Fried Green Tomatoes, page 223

* Lemon Meringue Pie, page 295

Winter Warm-Up

Serves 6

Kentucky Burgoo, page 260
Yeast rolls
Too-Easy Cherry Cobbler, page 290

* Indicates recipes to double

Family Gatherings

Whip up a meal that'll leave family and loved ones speechless—or divvy up the meal with a potluck-style dinner.

Simple Weeknight Fixin's
Serves 4
Barbecue Chopped Steaks, page 105
Broccoli with Orange Sauce, page 244
Tossed green salad
Ranch dressing
Chocolate Pudding, page 305

Summertime by the Pool
Serves 6
* Mojitos, page 65
Hickory-Smoked Barbecue Shrimp, page 132
Grilled Balsamic-Glazed Peaches, page 142
Cucumber Salad with
Roasted Red Bell Pepper Dressing, page 222
Strawberry Smoothie Ice-Cream Pie, page 298

Sunday Potluck
Serves 6
Guinness-Braised Beef Brisket, page 173
Barbecue Scalloped Potatoes, page 257
Butterbeans, Bacon, and Tomatoes, page 244
Tangy Marinated Coleslaw, page 230
Strawberry-Sugar Biscuit Trifle, page 302

Family Reunion
Serves 8 to 10
Barbecue Pork Shoulder, page 109
Two-Cheese Squash Casserole, page 253
Chipotle Caesar Salad, page 217
Pig Pickin' Cake, page 285

Holiday Happenings

Enjoy barbecue even on the most special days of the year with these simple holiday menus.

Easter Delight
Serves 6 to 8
Barbecue Deviled Eggs, page 239
Best BBQ Chicken Ever, page 129
Sweet Corn Pudding, page 250
Fruity Spring Mix Salad, page 228
Citrus Bars, page 277

Giving Thanks for Turkey
Serves 4 to 6
Hickory-Smoked Bourbon Turkey, page 130
Brown Sugar-Glazed Carrots, page 245
Spinach Soufflé, page 247
Cranberry Tea, page 52
Pecan Squares, page 275

A Barbecue Christmas
Serves 12
Pecan Cheese Ball, page 69
* Sage-Smoked Maple Quail, page 117
Potato-and-Gruyère Casserole, page 257
Balsamic-Browned Butter
Asparagus, page 243
Bread Pudding with
Whiskey Sauce, page 307

Smokin' New Year's Day
Serves 8 to 10
Pork Chops with Tangy Barbecue
Sauce, page 111
Uptown Collards, page 246
* Peppery Peas O'Plenty, page 252
Cornbread
Buttermilk Fudge, page 311
* Bourbon-Barrel Coffee, page 68

* Indicates recipes to double

Food Safety

Whether you're barbecuing outdoors or cooking indoors, follow these simple guidelines to ensure that food is safe for family and friends.

Gathering and Storing Groceries

■ **Put** meat and poultry at the bottom of your grocery list, and select right before you check out.

■ **Place** packages of raw meat or poultry into plastic bags to collect leaking juices and prevent cross-contamination.

■ **Immediately** refrigerate meat and poultry once you get home.

■ **Freeze** poultry or ground beef right away if you don't plan to use it within one or two days. Freeze any other meats within three or four days of purchase.

Thawing

■ **Thaw** meat and poultry thoroughly before grilling. This allows even cooking for all cuts.

■ **Never** defrost food at room temperature. The safest method for thawing meat or poultry is in the refrigerator. You may also thaw unopened, airtight packages weighing 3 lb. or less by submerging in cold **water;** change the water every 30 minutes.

■ If you're in a hurry, defrost food in the **microwave.** This is only recommended if the food is to be grilled immediately upon thawing.

Marinating

■ **Marinating** is an excellent way to tenderize meats (acid breaks down connective tissues in the meat) and impart full flavors of herbs and spice. Depending on the type and size of meat, marinating can take from 30 minutes up to a couple of days.

■ **Delicate** fish and seafood are generally marinated an hour or less. The larger and tougher the cut of meat or poultry, the longer marinating time it will take.

■ **Always** marinate food in the refrigerator; never marinate on the counter.

■ If some of the marinade will later be used as a sauce for cooked food, **reserve** some marinade for this use before marinating or basting raw food.

■ If leftover marinade is to later be used on cooked meat, always bring the leftover marinade to a **full boil** to destroy any harmful bacteria that may be present.

Thermometers—Two Are Better Than One

■ Smoking and barbecuing often cause food to quickly brown on the exterior—but this does not mean it's done on the inside. Whether you're smoking or barbecuing, to test for doneness, always **use two** thermometers—one to test the temperature of the air inside the smoker or grill and the other to test the food temperature.

■ **Safe** air temperatures inside the grill for smoking and barbecuing are between 225° and 300°. Many smoking recipes call for keeping the air temperature between 225° and 250°.

■ **Always** insert a meat thermometer into the thickest portion of the food, without touching the bone, to test when the food is at a safe temperature. Use the chart below to determine the correct level of doneness.

Is It Done?

Whole poultry (dark meat)	180°F
Poultry breasts	170°F
Ground beef	160°F
Beef, Veal, and Lamb (steaks, roasts, and chops)	145°F
Pork	160°F
Fish	Flakes with a fork

Leftovers

■ When the barbecue festivities are over and your guests have full tummies and smiles on their faces, remember to refrigerate any leftovers within two hours of removing foods from the smoker (and within one hour if you're outdoors and the outdoor temperature is above 90°). Then you can safely enjoy the fruits of your labor the next day!

Metric Equivalents

The recipes that appear in this cookbook use the standard U.S. method for measuring liquid and dry or solid ingredients (teaspoons, tablespoons, and cups). The information in the following charts is provided to help cooks outside the United States successfully use these recipes. All equivalents are approximate.

Metric Equivalents for Different Types of Ingredients

A standard cup measure of a dry or solid ingredient will vary in weight depending on the type of ingredient. A standard cup of liquid is the same volume for any type of liquid. Use the following chart when converting standard cup measures to grams (weight) or milliliters (volume).

Standard Cup	Fine Powder (ex. flour)	Grain (ex. rice)	Granular (ex. sugar)	Liquid Solids (ex. butter)	Liquid (ex. milk)
1	140 g	150 g	190 g	200 g	240 ml
¾	105 g	113 g	143 g	150 g	180 ml
⅔	93 g	100 g	125 g	133 g	160 ml
½	70 g	75 g	95 g	100 g	120 ml
⅓	47 g	50 g	63 g	67 g	80 ml
¼	35 g	38 g	48 g	50 g	60 ml
⅛	18 g	19 g	24 g	25 g	30 ml

Useful Equivalents for Dry Ingredients by Weight

(To convert ounces to grams, multiply the number of ounces by 30.)

1 oz	=	1/16 lb	=	30 g
4 oz	=	¼ lb	=	120 g
8 oz	=	½ lb	=	240 g
12 oz	=	¾ lb	=	360 g
16 oz	=	1 lb	=	480 g

Useful Equivalents for Length

(To convert inches to centimeters, multiply the number of inches by 2.5.)

1 in			=	2.5 cm		
6 in	=	½ ft	=	15 cm		
12 in	=	1 ft	=	30 cm		
36 in	=	3 ft	= 1 yd	=	90 cm		
40 in			=	100 cm	=	1 m

Useful Equivalents for Liquid Ingredients by Volume

¼ tsp				=	1 ml
½ tsp				=	2 ml
1 tsp				=	5 ml
3 tsp	= 1 Tbsp		= ½ fl oz	=	15 ml
	2 Tbsp	= ⅛ cup	= 1 fl oz	=	30 ml
	4 Tbsp	= ¼ cup	= 2 fl oz	=	60 ml
	5⅓ Tbsp	= ⅓ cup	= 3 fl oz	=	80 ml
	8 Tbsp	= ½ cup	= 4 fl oz	=	120 ml
	10⅔ Tbsp	= ⅔ cup	= 5 fl oz	=	160 ml
	12 Tbsp	= ¾ cup	= 6 fl oz	=	180 ml
	16 Tbsp	= 1 cup	= 8 fl oz	=	240 ml
	1 pt	= 2 cups	= 16 fl oz	=	480 ml
	1 qt	= 4 cups	= 32 fl oz	=	960 ml
			33 fl oz	=	1000 ml	= 1 L

Useful Equivalents for Cooking/Oven Temperatures

	Fahrenheit	Celsius	Gas Mark
Freeze water	32° F	0° C	
Room temperature	68° F	20° C	
Boil water	212° F	100° C	
Bake	325° F	160° C	3
	350° F	180° C	4
	375° F	190° C	5
	400° F	200° C	6
	425° F	220° C	7
	450° F	230° C	8
Broil			Grill

Index

Almonds, Sugared, 228
Appetizers. *See also* Salsas, Spreads.
Biscuits with Olive-Parsley Spread, Cream Cheese-and-Olive, 79
Bruschetta, Roasted Red Pepper, 89
Cheese
Ball, Easy Chut-Nut, 68
Ball, Party Cheese, 69
Ball, Pecan Cheese, 69
Cheesecakes, Pesto-Chicken, 88
Cheesecake Squares, Savory Kalamata, 81
Cheesecake, Sun-Dried Tomato, 82
Cheesecake, Three-Layer, 82
Goat Cheese Wrapped in Phyllo, 90
Southwestern Cheese Appetizer, 86
Sticks, Parmesan-Bacon, 78
Straws, Parmesan Cheese, 79
Wafers, Spicy Cheese-Walnut, 80
Crab Fritters, 92
Crisps, Garlic-Pepper Parmesan, 78
Dips
Artichoke Dip, Florentine, 72
Blue Cheese-Bacon Dip, 73
Chipotle-Black Bean Dip, Creamy, 72
Guacamole, 70
Guacamole with Garlic and Parsley, Roasted Poblano, 70
Hummus, White Bean, 72
Nacho Dip, Layered, 72
Roasted Corn and Avocado Dip, 70
Tomato-Basil Dip, 70
Vidalia Onion Dip, Baked, 74
Firecrackers, Texas, 91
Hot Browns, Baby, 87
Meatballs, Spicy Party, 87
Mushrooms, Crab-Stuffed, 93
Nuts, Mexico, 81
Olives, Marinated Spanish, 84
Olives Scaciati, 84
Pecans, Smoky, 80
Pecans, Spicy, 81
Pesto, 88
Pita Chips, Garlic, 79
Quiches, Mini Mexican, 90
Quiches, Mini Spinach, 90
Sandwiches, Mini Pork, 87
Sauce, Creole, 92
Sausage Balls, 87
Shrimp Cocktail, Cinco de Mayo, 84
Shrimp, Grilled Zucchini-Wrapped, 93
Shrimp with Mustard Sauce, Coconut, 93
Tartlets, Raspberry-Brie, 89
Tarts, Phyllo Potato, 89

Apples
Barbecue Sauce, Apple, 185
Pie, Crumb-Topped Apple, 291
Quencher, Iced Apple, 52
Squares, Apple, 277
Apricot and Green Peppercorn Glaze, Grilled Venison with, 120
Apricot Brisket, Spicy, 155
Artichoke and Cheese Spread, Pecan-Crusted, 75
Artichoke Dip, Florentine, 72
Asparagus
Balsamic-Browned Butter Asparagus, 243
Grilled Asparagus, 138
Grilled Portobello Mushrooms and Asparagus, 141
Pickled Asparagus, 196
Roasted Asparagus, 243
Salad, Asparagus, Roasted Beet, and Goat Cheese, 221
Avocados
Dip, Roasted Corn and Avocado, 70
Guacamole, 70
Guacamole with Garlic and Parsley, Roasted Poblano, 70
Salad, Avocado, 222
Salsa, Avocado-Feta, 77
Salsa, Fresh Avocado, 77

Bacon
Butterbeans, Bacon, and Tomatoes, 244
Carrots with Bacon and Onion, Glazed, 245
Dip, Blue Cheese-Bacon, 73
Green Peas with Crispy Bacon, 251
Pizza, Tex-Mex Chicken-and-Bacon, 169
Salad, Bacon-Mandarin, 224
Salad, Bacon Potato, 233
Shrimp with Bacon and Jalapeños, Grilled, 132
Slaw, Blue Cheese-Bacon, 229
Sticks, Parmesan-Bacon, 78

Bananas
Brownies, Banana-Split, 274
Pie, Banana Cream, 294
Pudding, Best-Ever Banana, 305
Pudding, Peanut Butter-Banana, 307
Smoothies, Banana-Berry, 56
Barbecue
cook-offs and festivals, 26–27
regional styles of, 18–24
where to get, 19, 21, 23, 25
Beans
Baked
Baked Beans, 234
Molasses Baked Beans, Spicy, 237
Peppers, Baked Beans and, 237
Root Beer Baked Beans, 238
Spicy Baked Beans, 236
Stovetop "Baked Beans," 237
Three-Bean Barbecue Bake, 237
Black
Dip, Creamy Chipotle-Black Bean, 72
Salad, Black Bean and Black-Eyed Pea, 219
Salsa, Black Bean, 76
Butterbeans, Bacon, and Tomatoes, 244
Dip, Layered Nacho, 72
Green
Dilled Green Beans, 202
Garlic-Tarragon Green Beans, 244
Gingered Green Beans, 243
Pinto Beans, Mexican, 235
Pinto Beans, Spicy, 234
Pinto Beans, Tex-Mex, 235
Red Beans and Rice, 234
Ribs and Beans, Spicy-Sweet, 176
Slow-Cooker Barbecue Beans, 235
White Bean Hummus, 72
Beef. *See also* Beef, Ground; Grilled/Beef; Smoked/Beef.
Brisket
Apricot Brisket, Spicy, 155
Baked Brisket Au Jus, 153
Baked Brisket, Beer-, 154
Barbecue Beef Brisket, 96
Braised Beef Brisket, Guinness-, 173
Chili Sauce and Beer, Lone Star Brisket in, 152
Chili-Spiced Brisket, 153
Coffee-Baked Brisket, 154
5-Ingredient Brisket, 153
German-Style Beef Brisket, 154
Ketchup 'n' Cola Brisket, 154
Marinated Brisket, Texas-Smoked Beer-, 96
Onion Brisket, Savory, 150

Potatoes, Saucy Brisket and, 152
Red-Sauced Brisket, Traditional, 97
Rub, Brisket, 97
Sandwiches, Knife-and-Fork
    Barbecued Brisket, 173
Sandwiches, Quickest Brisket, 150
Sauce, Brisket Mopping, 97
Sauce, Brisket Red, 97
Smoked Brisket Sandwiches, 99
Smoky Barbecue Brisket, 156
Sweet Potato Mélange, Beef Brisket
    with, 155
Veggies, Brisket with, 153
Burgoo, Classic Kentucky, 260
Corned Beef-Potato Hash, Hot, 258
Hash, Old-Fashioned Beef, 258
Pork Barbecue, Beef and, 174
Prime Rib, Smoked Garlic, 100
Prime Rib, Smoked Herbed, 100
Roasts
    Barbecue, Four-Hour, 150
    Barbecue Roast, 149
    Beefwiches, Barbecue, 149
    Burgoo, Kentucky, 260
    Chuck Roast Barbecue, 172
    Eye of Round, Smoked
        Marinated, 102
    Hash, Beef, 258
    Sandwiches, Barbecue Beef, 173
Spiced Beef Barbecue, 174
Steaks
    Fajitas, Chicken-and-Beef, 128
    Fajitas, Java, 105
    Fajitas with Peppers and Onions,
        Beef-and-Chicken, 105
    Fajitas with Pico de Gallo, Beef, 103
    Strip Steaks, Smoked, 102
Beef, Ground
    Burritos, Barbecue, 157
    Chopped Steaks, Barbecue, 105
    Hash, Jim Gibson's Barbecue, 259
    Meat Loaf, Barbecue, 157
    Meat Loaf Sandwiches, Barbecue, 157
    Pizzas, Individual Barbecue, 159
Beet, and Goat Cheese Salad, Asparagus,
    Roasted, 221
Beets, Tangy, 245
Beverages
    Alcoholic
        Batidas, Citrus, 66
        Bellinis, 62
        Bellinis, Mint, 62
        Cocktail, Pomegranate-
            Champagne, 65
        Coffee, Bourbon-Barrel, 68
        Coffee, Fireside, 68

Daiquiris, Watermelon, 58
Margaritas, Blue, 60
Margaritas from Scratch, 59
Margaritas, Frozen, 59
Margaritas, Strawberry, 60
Margaritas, Watermelon, 60
Martini, Mint Julep, 63
Mimosas, 62
Mojitos, 65
Punch, Bloody Mary, 63
Punch, Champagne, 63
Punch, Citrus-Wine, 62
Sangría, Texas White, 60
Sazerac, 66
Sipper, Creamy Coconut, 66
Sippers, Sunset Vodka-Orange, 65
Slush, Lemon-Rum, 62
Sours, Slushy Whiskey, 66
Sours, Whiskey, 66
Spritzers, Pineapple-Grapefruit, 65
Breeze, Southern, 54
Coolers, Speedy Spring, 52
Coolers, Watermelon-Lemonade, 45
Fizz, Berry Blue, 54
Ice Cubes, Lemonade, 45
Jubilee, Orange, 58
Lemonade, Blackberry, 46
Lemonade, Cranberry, 46
Lemonade, Fizzy Raspberry, 46
Lemonade, Fizzy Strawberry, 46
Lemonade, Homemade, 46
Lemonade, Sweet-Tart, 49
Limeade, Homemade, 46
Limeade, Tangy, 53
Punch, Brunch, 54
Quencher, Iced Apple, 52
Shakes, Peach Melba, 56
Shakes, Tropical, 54
Sippers, Fresh Mint-Citrus, 52
Slush, Peach, 58
Slush, Strawberry-Lemonade, 45
Smoothies
    Banana-Berry Smoothies, 56
    Blackberry Smoothies, 56
    Caffé Latte Smoothies, 58
    Mango Smoothies, 56
Soda, Homemade Orange, 53
Spritzer, Kiwi-Lemonade, 45
Spritzer, Strawberry-Kiwi-
    Lemonade, 45
Teas
    Cranberry Tea, 52
    Ginger Tea, 49
    Iced Hibiscus Tea, 49
    Iced Red Tea, 52
    Iced Tea, Blackberry, 50

Iced Tea, Simple Southern, 50
Mint Tea, Fruity, 49
Passion Tea, 50
Biscuits, Sugar, 302
Biscuits with Olive-Parsley Spread, Cream
    Cheese-and-Olive, 79
Blackberries
    Butter, Blackberry, 211
    Cobbler, Blackberry, 289
    Lemonade, Blackberry, 46
    Smoothies, Blackberry, 56
    Syrup, Blackberry, 289
    Tea, Blackberry Iced, 50
Blueberries
    Bread Pudding, Blueberry, 310
    Cheesecake, Blueberry, 288
    Chutney, Blueberry, 227
    Coffee Cake, Blueberry 'n'
        Cheese, 280
    Jam, Green Tomato-Blueberry, 208
    Marmalade, Spicy Blueberry-
        Citrus, 210
    Pie, Blueberry, 291
    Sauce, Blueberry-Balsamic
        Barbecue, 189
    Sauce, Blueberry Barbecue, 189
    Vinaigrette, Blueberry, 227
Breads
    Lemon Tea Bread, 287
    Pizza Crusts, Quick-and-Easy, 143
    Puddings
        Almond-Cream Cheese Bread
            Pudding with Amaretto Cream
            Sauce, Layered, 308
        Blueberry Bread Pudding, 310
        Chocolate-Cherry Bread
            Pudding, 309
        Cinnamon-Raisin Bread
            Pudding, 307
        Summer Pudding, 309
        Whiskey Sauce, Bread Pudding
            with, 307
Broccoli
    Orange Sauce, Broccoli with, 244
    Slaw, Blue Cheese-Bacon, 229
    Slaw, Broccoli, 229
    Slaw, Broccoli-Squash, 229
    Slaw, Cilantro, 229
Burgoo, Classic Kentucky, 260
Burgoo, Kentucky, 260
Burritos, Barbecue, 157
Butter
    Blackberry Butter, 211
    Cilantro Butter, 141
    Garlic-Basil Butter, 211
    Jalapeño-Chili Butter, 211

Butter *(continued)*

Jalapeño-Lime Butter, Grilled
Corn with, 137
Pecan-Honey Butter, 211
Roasted Garlic Beurre Blanc, 211
Sage Butter, 137

C abbage. *See* **Salads and Salad
Dressings/Slaws.**

Cakes
Angel Food Cake, Blue Ribbon, 286
Angel Food Cake, Brown Sugar, 286
Carrot Cake Supreme, 284
Chocolate-Caramel Sheet Cake, 279
Chocolate-Peanut Butter Cake, 279
Chocolate-Praline Cake, 282
Chocolate Truffle Cake, 281
Coffee Cake, Blueberry 'n' Cheese, 280
Coffee Cake, Cream Cheese, 280
great cakes, 281
Lemon Buttermilk Cake with Lemon
Curd Sauce, 286
Pig Pickin' Cake, 285

Candies
Bourbon Balls, 311
Buckeyes, 311
Fudge, Buttermilk, 311
Fudge, Fast, 311

Caramel
Bars, Caramel-Pecan Cheesecake, 278
Cake, Chocolate-Caramel Sheet, 279
Frosting, Quick Caramel, 279
Frosting, Quick Caramel-Pecan, 279
Ice Cream, Caramel-Pecan
Crunch, 316

Carrots
Cake Supreme, Carrot, 284
Glaze, Carrots with Horseradish, 245
Glazed Carrots, Brown Sugar-, 245
Glazed Carrots with Bacon and
Onion, 245

Casseroles
Potato-and-Gruyère Casserole, 257
Potato Bake, Smoky Mashed, 257
Potatoes, Barbecue Scalloped, 257
Potatoes, Out-of-This-World
Scalloped, 256
Squash Casserole, Crunchy, 254
Squash Casserole, Two-Cheese, 253
Turnip Casserole, Scalloped, 247

Charcoal grills
annual upkeep, 13
lighting coals, 15
safety, 13

Cheese. *See also* **Appetizers/Cheese;
Cheesecakes.**
Casseroles
Casserole, Potato-and-Gruyère, 257
Squash Casserole, Two-Cheese, 253
Turnip Casserole, Scalloped, 247
Coffee Cake, Blueberry 'n' Cheese, 280
Coffee Cake, Cream Cheese, 280
Grits Crust Batter, Cheese, 163
Pinto Beans, Tex-Mex, 235
Pizza, Goat Cheese-and-Grilled
Pepper, 142
Potatoes, Cheesy Mashed, 256
Quesadillas, Barbecue, 163
Salad, Fresh Mozzarella-Tomato-
Basil, 221
Sauce, Swiss Cheese Cream, 254
Slaw, Blue Cheese-Bacon, 229
Spread, Pecan-Crusted Artichoke and
Cheese, 75
Topping, Buttery Parmesan, 254

Cheesecakes
Bars, Caramel-Pecan Cheesecake, 278
Blueberry Cheesecake, 288
Savory
Pesto-Chicken Cheesecakes, 88
Sun-Dried Tomato Cheesecake, 82
Three-Layer Cheesecake, 82

Cherries
Bread Pudding, Chocolate-Cherry, 309
Cobbler, Too-Easy Cherry, 290
Cookies, Chunky Cherry-Double
Chip, 270

Chicken. *See also* **Grilled/Poultry;
Smoked/Poultry.**
Brunswick Stew, 261
Brunswick Stew, Chicken, 261
Burgoo, Classic Kentucky, 260
Burgoo, Kentucky, 260
Cheesecakes, Pesto-Chicken, 88
Cranberry Barbecue Sauce, Chicken
with, 165
Fajitas with Peppers and Onions, Beef-
and-Chicken, 105
Fingers, Barbecue-Battered
Chicken, 166
Firecrackers, Texas, 91
Grilled
Asian Barbecue Chicken, 126
BBQ Chicken Ever, Best, 129
Beer-Can Chicken, Basic, 123
Fajitas, Chicken-and-Beef, 128
Fajitas, Tangy Chicken, 129
Honey-Barbecue Chicken, 126
Marinated Chicken Quarters, 124
Raspberry-Barbecue Chicken, 129

Red Hot Barbecue Chicken, 124
Sweet Barbecue Chicken, 126
White Barbecue Sauce, Chicken
with, 124
Hoisin Barbecue Chicken
Breasts, 165
Oven-Baked Barbecue Chicken, 165
Pizza, Barbecue Chicken, 169
Pizza, Quick 'n' Easy Barbecue
Chicken, 169
Pizza, Tex-Mex Chicken-and-
Bacon, 169
Pulled Chicken with Marinated
Cucumbers, Barbecue, 166
Rub, Garlic Chicken, 125
Salad, Warm Barbecue Chicken, 167
Sandwiches, Carolina Blond
Open-Faced, 167
Seared Chicken with Feisty Hot
Barbecue Dipping Sauce, 164
Shredded Barbecue Chicken, 177
Smoked
Big "D" Smoked Chicken, 125
Jerk Smoked Chicken, 122

Chocolate
Bars and Cookies
Brownies, Banana-Split, 274
Brownies, Double-Chocolate, 274
Brownies, Mississippi Mud, 274
Cherry-Double Chip Cookies,
Chunky, 270
Chocolate Chip Cookies,
Chocolate-, 270
Coconut-Macadamia Chunk
Cookies, 270
Cranberry-White Chocolate
Cookies, 269
Dark Chocolate Chip Cookies, 270
Heavenly Chocolate Chunk
Cookies, 269
Oatmeal-Chocolate Chunk Cookies,
Nutty, 268
Oatmeal-Raisin-Chocolate Chip
Cookies, 270
Peanut Butter-Chocolate Chip
Cookies, 270
Pecan-Chocolate Chip
Cookies, 270
Shortbread, Marble-Topped
Hazelnut, 273
Toffee-Chocolate Chip
Cookies, 270
Ultimate Chocolate Chip
Cookies, 270
White Chocolate-Macadamia Nut
Cookies, 269

Bourbon Balls, 311
Bread Pudding, Chocolate-Cherry, 309
Cakes
    Peanut Butter Cake,
        Chocolate-, 279
    Praline Cake, Chocolate-, 282
    Sheet Cake, Chocolate-
        Caramel, 279
    Truffle Cake, Chocolate, 281
Frostings, Fillings, and Toppings
    Chocolate Frosting, 279, 282
    Chocolate Glaze, 294
    Truffle Filling, Chocolate, 281
Fudge, Fast, 311
Ice Cream, Chocolate, 316
Ice Cream, Chocolate Chip, 316
Ice-Cream Sandwiches, Easy
    Chocolate-Mint, 313
Ice-Cream Sandwiches, Mocha-
    Almond-Fudge, 313
Mocha Ice Cream, 313
Pies
    Bourbon-Chocolate-Pecan Pie, 297
    Fudge Pie, 297
    Mocha Fudge Pie, 296
Pudding, Bittersweet Chocolate, 305
Pudding, Chocolate, 305
Sauce, Chocolate, 297
Sundaes, S'mores, 304
Chutney
Blueberry Chutney, 227
Cranberry-Ginger Chutney, 206
Pear Chutney, 206
Tomato Chutney, 206
Tomato-Garlic Chutney, 206
Coconut
Cookies, Clear-the-Cupboard, 267
Cookies, Coconut-Macadamia
    Chunk, 270
Ice Cream, Toasted Coconut, 317
Pie, Coconut Cream, 293
Pie, Coconut-Macadamia Nut, 297
Shrimp with Mustard Sauce,
    Coconut, 93
Sipper, Creamy Coconut, 66
Coffee. *See also* **Beverages.**
Brisket, Coffee-Baked, 154
Fajitas, Java, 105
Cookies
Bars and Squares
    Apple Squares, 277
    Brownies, Banana-Split, 274
    Brownies, Double-Chocolate, 274
    Brownies, Mississippi Mud, 274
    Caramel-Pecan Cheesecake
        Bars, 278

Citrus Bars, 277
Lemon Bars Deluxe, 277
Pecan Squares, 275
Dough, Basic Butter Cookie, 272
Drop
    Brown Sugar-Oatmeal
        Cookies, 267
    Cherry-Double Chip Cookies,
        Chunky, 270
    Chocolate Chip Cookies,
        Ultimate, 270
    Chocolate-Chocolate Chip
        Cookies, 270
    Chocolate Chunk Cookies,
        Heavenly, 269
    Clear-the-Cupboard Cookies, 267
    Coconut-Macadamia Chunk
        Cookies, 270
    Cranberry-White Chocolate
        Cookies, 269
    Dark Chocolate Chip Cookies, 270
    Oatmeal-Chocolate Chunk Cookies,
        Nutty, 268
    Oatmeal-Raisin-Chocolate Chip
        Cookies, 270
    Oatmeal-Raisin Cookies, 268
    Orange-Macadamia Nut
        Cookies, 268
    Peanut Butter-Chocolate Chip
        Cookies, 270
    Peanut Butter Turtle Cookies, 267
    Pecan-Chocolate Chip
        Cookies, 270
    Toffee-Chocolate Chip
        Cookies, 270
    White Chocolate-Macadamia
        Nut Cookies, 269
Gingersnaps, 264
Peanut Butter Cookies, Old-
    Fashioned, 266
Shortbread, Butter-Mint, 272
Shortbread, Marble-Topped
    Hazelnut, 273
Shortbread, Millionaire, 272
Shortbread, Peanut Butter, 272
Shortbread, Peanut-Toffee, 273
Sugar Cookies, Melt-in-Your-Mouth
    Iced, 264
Sugar Cookies, Molasses, 265
Corn
Fried Corn, Buttermilk, 249
Grilled Corn with Creamy Chipotle
    Sauce, 137
Grilled Corn with Jalapeño-Lime
    Butter, 137
Pudding, Sweet Corn, 250

Roasted Corn and Avocado
    Dip, 70
Salsa, Corn, 76
Salsa, Grilled Corn, 117
White Corn and Tomato Relish,
    Sweet, 204
Cornish Hens, Asian Grilled, 119
Crab
Fritters, Crab, 92
King Crab Legs and Lobster Tails,
    Smoked, 136
Mushrooms, Crab-Stuffed, 93
Cranberries
Chutney, Cranberry-Ginger, 206
Cookies, Cranberry-White
    Chocolate, 269
Lemonade, Cranberry, 46
Relish, Walnut-Cranberry, 204
Salad, Cranberry-Gorgonzola
    Green, 225
Salad, Cranberry-Strawberry-
    Jícama, 226
Salsa, Cranberry-Jalapeño, 207
Sauce, Chicken with Cranberry
    Barbecue, 165
Tea, Cranberry, 52
Cucumbers
Marinated Cucumbers, Barbecue Pulled
    Chicken with, 166
Pickled Onion and Cucumber, 196
Pickles, Bread-and-Butter, 201
Pickles, Freezer Cucumber, 198
Pickle Spears, Cucumber, 199
Pickles, Peppery Texas Freezer, 201
Salad with Roasted Red Bell Pepper
    Dressing, Cucumber, 222

Desserts. *See also* specific types.
Biscuits, Sugar, 302
Boston Cream Pie, 294
Peaches, Grilled Balsamic-Glazed, 142
Sauces
    Amaretto Cream Sauce, 309
    Chocolate Sauce, 297
    Crème Anglaise, 303
    Lemon Curd Sauce, 286
    Whiskey Sauce, 307
Sundaes
    Berry Sundaes, Very, 304
    Cookie Sundaes, Warm, 304
    S'mores Sundaes, 304
Trifle Custard, 302
Trifle, Jumbleberry, 303
Trifle, Peaches 'n' Cream, 303
Trifle, Strawberry-Sugar Biscuit, 302

Direct heat
lighting coals, 15
technique for determining the heat, 14

Eggplant, Sage-Grilled, 137
Eggs
Barbecue Deviled Eggs, 239
Creole Deviled Eggs, 240
Mexican Deviled Eggs, 241
Pecan-Stuffed Deviled Eggs, 240
Spicy-Sweet Deviled Eggs, 239
Tex-Mex Deviled Eggs, 241
with Capers, Deviled Eggs, 240
Entertaining
decorative elements for, 32–33
family reunions, 36–39
flowers for, 34–35
invitations, 36
planning ahead, 36–39
setting up outdoors, 30–32, 38–39
transporting food, 37

Fajitas
Beef-and-Chicken Fajitas with Peppers
and Onions, 105
Beef Fajitas with Pico de Gallo, 103
Chicken-and-Beef Fajitas, 128
Chicken Fajitas, Tangy, 129
Java Fajitas, 105
toppings, 129
Fig-Mint Ice Cream, No-Cook, 315
Fillings
Chocolate Truffle Filling, 281
Cream Filling, 294
Lemon Meringue Pie Filling, 295
Fish. *See also* **Crab, Lobster, Salmon,**
Scallops, Shrimp.
Catfish, Barbecue Baked, 170
Smoked Fish, 134
Trout, Smoked, 134
Tuna, Smoked, 134
Flare-ups, 99
Food safety, 99, 125, 324
Fritters, Crab, 92
Frostings. *See also* **Toppings.**
Caramel Frosting, Quick, 279
Caramel-Pecan Frosting,
Quick, 279
Chocolate Frosting, 279, 282
Cream Cheese Frosting, Deluxe, 285
Fruit. *See also* specific types.
Cake, Pig Pickin', 285
Cobbler, Too-Easy Berry, 290
Pudding, Summer, 309

Salads
Congealed Salad, Layered
Fruit, 300
Honey-Pecan Dressing, Fruit
Salad with, 226
Spring Mix Salad, Fruity, 228
Summer Fruit Salad with Blueberry
Vinaigrette, 227
Salsa, Tropical, 77
Trifle, Jumbleberry, 303

Gadgets for grilling, 11
Game
accompaniments, 121
Duck Breasts, Grilled Wild, 120
Quail, 119
Asian Grilled Quail, 119
Mesquite-Grilled Quail, 119
Sage-Smoked Maple Quail, 117
Venison
Grilled Venison with Apricot
and Green Peppercorn
Glaze, 120
Roast, Grilled Venison, 121
Steaks, Grilled Venison, 120
Tenderloin, Grilled Marinated
Venison, 121
Garlic
Browned Garlic and Burgundy
Marinade, 193
Chicken with Feisty Hot Barbecue
Dipping Sauce, Seared, 164
Chutney, Tomato-Garlic, 206
Green Beans, Dilled, 202
Jelly, Freezer Garlic Pepper, 208
Olives Scaciati, 84
Parmesan Crisps, Garlic-Pepper, 78
Pinto Beans, Tex-Mex, 235
Pita Chips, Garlic, 79
Pork, Smoked Mustard-Sauced, 108
Pork with Texas Caviar, Mesquite-
Smoked, 108
Prime Rib, Smoked Garlic, 100
Prime Rib, Smoked Herbed, 100
Roasted Garlic Beurre Blanc, 211
Rub, Garlic Chicken, 125
Rub, Garlic-Pepper Brisket, 192
Sandwiches, Quickest Brisket, 150
Sauce, Brisket Mopping, 97
Sauce, Spiced Barbecue, 185
Summer Squash and Tomatoes,
Grilled, 252
Gas grills
annual upkeep, 13
safety, 13

Greens
Collard Greens, Garlicky, 247
Collards, Uptown, 246
Grilled. *See also* **Smoked.**
Andouille Grits, Grilled, 145
Beef
Brisket, Barbecue Beef, 96
Chopped Steaks, Barbecue, 105
Fajitas, Java, 105
Fajitas with Pico de Gallo, Beef, 103
Fajitas, Chicken-and-Beef, 128
Fajitas with Peppers and Onions,
Beef-and-Chicken, 105
Fish and Shellfish
Salmon, BBQ Grilled, 135
Shrimp, Grilled Zucchini-
Wrapped, 93
Shrimp with Bacon and Jalapeños,
Grilled, 132
Game
Duck Breasts, Grilled Wild, 120
Quail, Asian Grilled, 119
Quail, Mesquite-Grilled, 119
Venison Roast, Grilled, 121
Venison Steaks, Grilled, 120
Venison Tenderloin, Grilled
Marinated, 121
Venison with Apricot and Green
Peppercorn Glaze, Grilled, 120
Peaches, Grilled Balsamic-Glazed, 142
Pizza, Goat Cheese-and-Grilled
Pepper, 142
Pizzas, Grilled Onion, 144
Pizzas, Grilled Veggie, 145
Pizza with Feta and Spinach, Grilled
Vegetable, 143
Pizza with Smoked Tofu and Roasted
Red Peppers, Grilled, 144
Pork
Baby Back Ribs, Smoky
Chipotle, 112
Baby Back Ribs, Sweet-and-
Sour, 113
Chops and Peaches, Peach-Glazed
Barbecue Pork, 116
Chops with Grilled Corn Salsa,
Barbecue Pork, 117
Chops with Tangy Barbecue Sauce,
Pork, 111
Country-Style Ribs, Barbecued, 114
Spareribs, Maple, 115
Tenderloin, Fiery-Barbecued
Pork, 111
Poultry
Chicken, Asian Barbecue, 126
Chicken, Basic Beer-Can, 123

Chicken Ever, Best BBQ, 129
Chicken Fajitas, Tangy, 129
Chicken, Honey-Barbecue, 126
Chicken Quarters, Marinated, 124
Chicken, Raspberry-Barbecue, 129
Chicken, Red Hot Barbecue, 124
Chicken, Sweet Barbecue, 126
Chicken with White Barbecue
   Sauce, 124
Cornish Hens, Asian Grilled, 119
Vegetables
   Asparagus, Grilled, 138
   Cilantro Butter, Grilled Vegetables
      with, 141
   Corn Salsa, Grilled, 117
   Corn with Creamy Chipotle Sauce,
      Grilled, 137
   Corn with Jalapeño-Lime Butter,
      Grilled, 137
   Eggplant, Sage-Grilled, 137
   Portobello Mushrooms and
      Asparagus, Grilled, 141
   Red Onions, Grilled, 138
   Romaine Salad with Buttermilk-
      Chive Dressing, Grilled, 218
   Summer Squash and Tomatoes,
      Grilled, 252
   Summer Squash, Grilled, 138
   Sweet Potatoes with Orange-
      Chipotle Glaze, Grilled, 141
   Tomatoes, Grilled, 139
   Yellow Squash Halves, Grilled, 138
Grilling
   fish and shellfish, 133
   pizza, 142
   tips, 99
   using a grill, 12
Grits
   Andouille Grits, Grilled, 145
   Crust, Barbecue Pot Pie with Cheese
      Grits, 163
   Crust Batter, Cheese Grits, 163

Hash
   Barbecue Hash, Jim Gibson's, 259
   Beef Hash, 258
   Beef Hash, Old-Fashioned, 258
   Corned Beef-Potato Hash,
      Hot, 258
   Potato-Smoked Sausage Hash, 259
   Sweet Potato Hash, Savory, 259
Honey
   Butter, Pecan-Honey, 211
   Chicken, Honey-Barbecue, 126
   Dressing, Honey-Pecan, 226

Sauce, Honey-Barbecue, 180
Sauce, Honey-Mustard Barbecue, 187
Vinaigrette, Sweet Potato Salad with
   Rosemary-Honey, 233

Ice Creams
   Butter Pecan Ice Cream, 316
   Caramel-Pecan Crunch Ice Cream, 316
   Chocolate Chip Ice Cream, 316
   Chocolate Ice Cream, 316
   Coconut Ice Cream, Toasted, 317
   Coffee Ice Cream, 315
   Cookies and Cream Ice Cream, 316
   Fig-Mint Ice Cream, No-Cook, 315
   Lemon-Buttermilk Ice Cream, 318
   Lemon Ice Cream, 320
   Lime Ice Cream, Fresh, 318
   Mocha Ice Cream, 313
   Orange Ice Cream, 318
   Peanut Butter Ice Cream, 317
   Pie, Spiked Strawberry-Lime Ice-
      Cream, 298
   Pie, Strawberry-Lime Ice-Cream, 298
   Pie, Strawberry Smoothie Ice-
      Cream, 298
   Sandwiches, Butter Pecan Ice-
      Cream, 313
   Sandwiches, Easy Chocolate-Mint
      Ice-Cream, 313
   Sandwiches, Mocha-Almond-Fudge
      Ice-Cream, 313
   Sandwiches, Oatmeal-Rum-Raisin
      Ice-Cream, 313
   Sandwiches, Peanutty Ice-Cream, 312
   South Seas Ice Cream with Sweet-Heat
      Salsa and Cinnamon Crisps, 321
   Strawberry Cheesecake Ice Cream,
      Low-Fat, 317
   Strawberry Ice Cream, 318
   Vanilla Ice Cream, No-Cook, 315
   Vanilla Ice Cream, Old-Fashioned, 315
Indirect heat
   lighting coals, 15
   technique for determining the heat, 14

Jams. *See also* **Jelly, Marmalades.**
   Green Tomato-Blueberry Jam, 208
   Peach-Rosemary Jam, 208
Jelly, Freezer Garlic Pepper, 208
Jícama Salad, Cranberry-Strawberry-, 226

Kiwi-Lemonade Spritzer, 45
Kiwi-Lemonade Spritzer, Strawberry-, 45

Lemon
   Bread, Lemon Tea, 287
   Desserts
      Bars Deluxe, Lemon, 277
      Cake with Lemon Curd Sauce,
         Lemon Buttermilk, 286
      Filling, Lemon Meringue Pie, 295
      Ice Cream, Lemon, 320
      Ice Cream, Lemon-Buttermilk, 318
      Pie, Lemon Meringue, 295
      Sauce, Lemon Curd, 286
   Dressing, Zesty Lemon, 219
   Mayonnaise, Lemon-Rosemary, 213
   Salad, Lemon-Basil Potato, 233
   Sauce, Herbed Lemon Barbecue, 190
   Sugar Snap Peas, Lemon-Scented, 251
Lime
   Butter, Grilled Corn with Jalapeño-
      Lime, 137
   Ice Cream, Fresh Lime, 318
   Ice-Cream Pie, Spiked Strawberry-
      Lime, 298
   Ice-Cream Pie, Strawberry-Lime, 298
   Limeade, Homemade, 46
   Limeade, Tangy, 53
   Mayonnaise, Lime-Red Pepper, 212
   Shrimp with Orange and Lime, Spicy
      Smoked, 133
   Vinaigrette, Pistachio-Lime, 225
Lobster Tails, Smoked King Crab Legs
   and, 136

Mangoes
   Pie, Mango Cream, 292
   Salsa, Fresh Mango, 207
   Sauce, Mango-Pineapple Hot, 190
   Smoothies, Mango, 56
Marinades. *See* **Seasonings/Marinades.**
Marmalades. *See also* **Jams, Jelly.**
   Blueberry-Citrus Marmalade,
      Spicy, 210
   Green Tomato Marmalade, 210
Mayonnaise
   Herb Mayonnaise, Fresh, 213
   Lemon-Rosemary Mayonnaise, 213
   Lime-Red Pepper Mayonnaise, 212
Melons
   Cantaloupe-Spinach Salad with
      Pistachio-Lime Vinaigrette, 225
   Watermelon
      Coolers, Watermelon-
         Lemonade, 45
      Daiquiris, Watermelon, 58
      Margaritas, Watermelon, 60
      Salad, Watermelon-Prosciutto, 226

Microwave

Desserts

Brownies, Banana-Split, 274

Cake, Chocolate Truffle, 281

Cookies, Chunky Cherry-Double Chip, 270

Cookies, Peanut Butter Turtle, 267

Filling, Chocolate Truffle, 281

Frosting, Chocolate, 282

Ice Cream, Mocha, 313

Pie, Fudge, 297

Shortbread, Millionaire, 272

Fizz, Berry Blue, 54

Pickles, Bread-and-Butter, 201

Pickles, Peppery Texas Freezer, 201

Quail, Mesquite-Grilled, 119

Salad, Layered Fruit Congealed, 300

Sauce, Fiery-Sweet Barbecue, 183

Shrimp with Bacon and Jalapeños, Grilled, 132

Mushrooms and Asparagus, Grilled Portobello, 141

Mushrooms, Crab-Stuffed, 93

Mustard

Sauce, Honey-Mustard Barbecue, 187

Sauce, Mustard, 93

Sauce, Spicy-Sweet Mustard, 187

Sweet-Hot Honey Mustard, 212

Nectarine Cobbler with Blueberry Muffin Crust, 289

Okra

Dills, Refrigerator Okra, 202

Fried Okra, 255

Fried Okra Pods, 255

Fried Okra Salad, 222

Pickled Okra, Spicy, 202

Olives

Biscuits with Olive-Parsley Spread, Cream Cheese-and-Olive, 79

Cheesecake Squares, Savory Kalamata, 81

Scaciati, Olives, 84

Spanish Olives, Marinated, 84

Onions

Brisket, Savory Onion, 150

Carrots with Bacon and Onion, Glazed, 245

Fajitas with Peppers and Onions, Beef-and-Chicken, 105

Grilled Onion Pizzas, 144

Pickled Onion and Cucumber, 196

Pickled Onion Rings, 196

Pudding, Sweet Onion, 249

Red Onions, Grilled, 138

Relish with Pine Nuts, Sweet Pepper-and-Onion, 205

Rings, Buttermilk Batter-Fried Onion, 248

Vidalia Onion Dip, Baked, 74

Oranges

Glaze, Grilled Sweet Potatoes with Orange-Chipotle, 141

Peas, Orange-Ginger, 251

Salad, Bacon-Mandarin, 224

Salad, Orange-Walnut, 224

Sauce, Broccoli with Orange, 244

Shrimp with Orange and Lime, Spicy Smoked, 133

Peaches

Barbecue Sauce for Ribs, Peach of the Old South, 185

Cobbler, Too-Easy Peach, 290

Grilled Balsamic-Glazed Peaches, 142

Jam, Peach-Rosemary, 208

Pork Chops and Peaches, Peach-Glazed Barbecue, 116

Salsa, Peachy Green Tomato, 207

Shakes, Peach Melba, 56

Slush, Peach, 58

Trifle, Peaches 'n' Cream, 303

Peanut Butter

Cake, Chocolate-Peanut Butter, 279

Cookies

Chocolate Chip Cookies, Peanut Butter-, 270

Old-Fashioned Peanut Butter Cookies, 266

Shortbread, Peanut Butter, 272

Turtle Cookies, Peanut Butter, 267

Ice Cream, Peanut Butter, 317

Pudding, Peanut Butter-Banana, 307

Pear Chutney, 206

Peas

Black-Eyed Pea Salad, Black Bean and, 219

Black-Eyed Peas, Marinated, 201

Black-Eyed Peas, Pickled, 201

Green Peas with Crispy Bacon, 251

Orange-Ginger Peas, 251

Peppery Peas O' Plenty, 252

Salad, Pea, 219

Sugar Snap Peas, Lemon-Scented, 251

Sugar Snap Peas, Pickled, 201

Pecans

Butter, Pecan-Honey, 211

Cookies, Pecan-Chocolate Chip, 270

Deviled Eggs, Pecan-Stuffed, 240

Dressing, Honey-Pecan, 226

Ice Cream, Butter Pecan, 316

Ice-Cream Sandwiches, Butter Pecan, 313

Mexico Nuts, 81

Pie, Bourbon-Chocolate-Pecan, 297

Smoky Pecans, 80

Spicy Pecans, 81

Squares, Pecan, 275

Topping, Brown Sugar-Pecan, 280

Peppers

Baked Beans and Peppers, 237

Chile

Chipotle Baby Back Ribs, Smoky, 112

Chipotle Barbecue Pork, Saucy, 174

Chipotle Barbecue Sauce, 186

Chipotle-Black Bean Dip, Creamy, 72

Chipotle Glaze, Grilled Sweet Potatoes with Orange-, 141

Chipotle Pulled-Pork Barbecue Sandwiches, 161

Chipotle Rub, 192

Chipotle Sauce, Grilled Corn with Creamy, 137

Poblano Guacamole with Garlic and Parsley, Roasted, 70

Spread, Chile-Cheese, 76

Chowchow, 205

Deviled Eggs, Tex-Mex, 241

Firecrackers, Texas, 91

Green Bell Pepper Sauce, 171

Grilled Pepper Pizza, Goat Cheese-and-, 142

Hot Pepper Sauce, Fragrant Ginger-, 190

Jalapeño

Butter, Grilled Corn with Jalapeño-Lime, 137

Butter, Jalapeño-Chili, 211

Pinto Beans, Spicy, 234

Salsa, Cranberry-Jalapeño, 207

Sauce, Sweet Jalapeño Barbecue, 125

Red

Relish with Pine Nuts, Sweet Pepper-and-Onion, 205

Roasted Red Bell Pepper Dressing, 222

Roasted Red Pepper Bruschetta, 89

Roasted Red Pepper Rémoulade, 212

Relish, Grandma's Pepper, 204

Stuffed Peppers, Barbecue Shrimp and Cornbread-, 171

Pesto, 88

Pickles. *See also* **Relishes.**
  Bread-and-Butter Pickles, 201
  Cucumber Pickles, Freezer, 198
  Cucumber Pickle Spears, 199
  Freezer Pickles, Peppery Texas, 201
  Green Tomato Pickles, 195
  Okra Dills, Refrigerator, 202
  Squash Pickles, Refrigerator, 195
Pies and Pastries
  Apple Pie, Crumb-Topped, 291
  Banana Cream Pie, 294
  Blueberry Pie, 291
  Boston Cream Pie, 294
  Bourbon-Chocolate-Pecan Pie, 297
  Cobblers
    Berry Cobbler, Too-Easy, 290
    Blackberry Cobbler, 289
    Cherry Cobbler, Too-Easy, 290
    Nectarine Cobbler with Blueberry
      Muffin Crust, 289
    Peach Cobbler, Too-Easy, 290
  Coconut Cream Pie, 293
  Coconut-Macadamia Nut Pie, 297
  Fudge Pie, 297
  Ice-Cream Pie, Spiked Strawberry-
    Lime, 298
  Ice-Cream Pie, Strawberry-
    Lime, 298
  Ice-Cream Pie, Strawberry
    Smoothie, 298
  Lemon Meringue Pie, 295
  Mango Cream Pie, 292
  Mocha Fudge Pie, 296
  Pastries
    Double-Crust Pastry, 291
    Firecrackers, Texas, 91
    Pastry, 289
    Phyllo, Goat Cheese
      Wrapped in, 90
  Pot Pie with Cheese Grits Crust,
    Barbecue, 163
  Tarts, Phyllo Potato, 89
Pineapple-Grapefruit Spritzers, 65
Pineapple Hot Sauce, Mango-, 190
Pistachio-Lime Vinaigrette, 225
Pizza
  Chicken-and-Bacon Pizza,
    Tex-Mex, 169
  Chicken Pizza, Barbecue, 169
  Chicken Pizza, Quick 'n' Easy
    Barbecue, 169
  Crusts, Quick-and-Easy Pizza, 143
  Individual Barbecue Pizzas, 159
  Onion Pizzas, Grilled, 144
  Pepper Pizza, Goat Cheese-and-
    Grilled, 142

Smoked Tofu and Roasted Red Peppers,
    Grilled Pizza with, 144
  Vegetable Pizza with Feta and Spinach,
    Grilled, 143
  Veggie Pizzas, Grilled, 145
Planking, 16–17
Pomegranate-Champagne Cocktail, 65
Pork. *See also* **Grilled/Pork;**
    Smoked/Pork.
  Barbecue, Beef and Pork, 174
  Chops
    Barbecue-Battered Pork Chops, 166
    Barbecue Pork Chops with Grilled
      Corn Salsa, 117
    Easy Barbecue Pork Chops, 175
    Glazed Barbecue Pork Chops and
      Peaches, Peach-, 116
    Tangy Barbecue Sauce, Pork Chops
      with, 111
  Deviled Eggs, Barbecue, 239
  Hash, Jim Gibson's Barbecue, 259
  Pot Pie with Cheese Grits Crust,
    Barbecue, 163
  Quesadillas, Barbecue, 163
  Ribs
    Baby Back Ribs, Beer-Smoked, 114
    Baby Back Ribs, Smoky
      Chipotle, 112
    Baby Back Ribs, So-Simple, 177
    Baby Back Ribs, Sweet-and-
      Sour, 113
    Barbecue Ribs, 159
    Country-Style Barbecue Ribs, 177
    Country-Style Ribs, Barbecued, 114
    Rub, Pork Ribs, 114
    Spareribs, Maple, 115
    Spicy-Sweet Ribs and Beans, 176
  Roasts
    Barbecue Pork, Tabb's, 110
    BBQ, Three-Alarm, 109
    Boston Butt, Smoked Teriyaki-
      Marinated, 107
    Brunswick Stew, 261
    Chipotle Barbecue Pork, Saucy, 174
    Mustard-Sauced Pork, Smoked, 108
    Sandwiches, Barbecue 'n'
      Slaw, 159
    Sandwiches, Debate Barbecue, 177
    Shoulder, Barbecue Pork, 109
    Shoulder, North Carolina Smoked
      Pork, 107
    Slow-Smoked Pork with Ranch-
      Barbecue Sauce, 110
    Smoked Pork with Texas Caviar,
      Mesquite-, 108
    3-Ingredient BBQ Pork, 174

Spaghetti, Barbecue, 163
Tenderloin
    Barbecued Pork Tenderloin,
      Fiery-, 111
    Hoagies, Barbecue Pork-and-
      Coleslaw, 160
    Molasses Barbecue Sauce and
      Mango Salsa, Pork Tenderloin
      with, 111
    Sandwiches, Asian Barbecue
      Pork, 162
    Sandwiches, Chipotle Pulled-Pork
      Barbecue, 161
    Sandwiches, Mini Pork, 87
Potatoes. *See also* **Salads and Salad**
    Dressings/Potato; Sweet
    Potatoes.
  Brisket and Potatoes, Saucy, 152
  Casserole, Potato-and-Gruyère, 257
  Hash, Hot Corned Beef-Potato, 258
  Hash, Potato-Smoked Sausage, 259
  Mashed
    Cheesy Mashed Potatoes, 256
    Simple Mashed Potatoes, 256
    Smoky Mashed Potato
      Bake, 257
  Scalloped Potatoes, Barbecue, 257
  Scalloped Potatoes, Out-of-This-
    World, 256
  Stuffed Barbecue Potatoes,
    Double-, 162
  Tarts, Phyllo Potato, 89
Poultry
  checking for doneness, 125
  handling safely, 125
  primer, 125
Puddings
  Banana Pudding, Best-Ever, 305
  Bread
    Almond-Cream Cheese Bread
      Pudding with Amaretto Cream
      Sauce, Layered, 308
    Blueberry Bread Pudding, 310
    Chocolate-Cherry Bread
      Pudding, 309
    Cinnamon-Raisin Bread
      Pudding, 307
    Whiskey Sauce, Bread Pudding
      with, 307
  Chocolate Pudding, 305
  Chocolate Pudding, Bittersweet, 305
  Corn Pudding, Sweet, 250
  Onion Pudding, Sweet, 249
  Peanut Butter-Banana Pudding, 307
  Rice Pudding, Creamy, 310
  Summer Pudding, 309

Quesadillas, Barbecue, 163
Quiches, Mini Mexican, 90
Quiches, Mini Spinach, 90

Raspberries
  Chicken, Raspberry-Barbecue, 129
  Lemonade, Fizzy Raspberry, 46
  Sauce, Raspberry Barbecue, 189
  Tartlets, Raspberry-Brie, 89
Relishes. *See also* **Salsas.**
  Chowchow, 205
  Corn and Tomato Relish, Sweet
      White, 204
  Hot Relish, 204
  Pepper-and-Onion Relish with Pine
      Nuts, Sweet, 205
  Pepper Relish, Grandma's, 204
  Pickle Relish, Sweet, 205
  Walnut-Cranberry Relish, 204
Rice Pudding, Creamy, 310
Rice, Red Beans and, 234
Rotisserie cooking, 16–17
Rubs
  Barbecue Rub, All-Purpose, 192
  Barbecue Rub, Sweet 'n' Spicy, 192
  Brisket Rub, 97
  Brisket Rub, Garlic-Pepper, 192
  Chicken Rub, Garlic, 125
  Chipotle Rub, 192
  Ginger Rub, 113
  primer, 192
  Ribs Rub, Pork, 114
  Spice Blend, Southwestern, 192

Salads and Salad Dressings
  Asparagus, Roasted Beet, and Goat
      Cheese Salad, 221
  Avocado Salad, 222
  Bacon-Mandarin Salad, 224
  Barbecue Dressing, 167
  Bibb Salad with Fried Green Tomatoes,
      Kentucky, 223
  Black Bean and Black-Eyed Pea
      Salad, 219
  Buttermilk-Chive Dressing, 218
  Caesar Dressing, Chipotle, 217
  Caesar Salad, Chipotle, 217
  Chicken Salad, Warm Barbecue, 167
  Cilantro Salad, Chopped, 216
  Cranberry-Strawberry-Jícama
      Salad, 226
  Cucumber Salad with Roasted Red Bell
      Pepper Dressing, 222
  Fried Okra Salad, 222

Fruit
  Congealed Salad, Layered Fruit, 300
  Honey-Pecan Dressing, Fruit Salad
      with, 226
  Spring Mix Salad, Fruity, 228
  Summer Fruit Salad with Blueberry
      Vinaigrette, 227
Green
  Cranberry-Gorgonzola Green
      Salad, 225
  Garden Salad with Buttermilk
      Dressing, 219
  Lettuce-Wedge Salad, 216
  Mixed Salad Greens with Warm
      Goat Cheese, 218
  Red Leaf Lettuce Salad with Sweet-
      and-Sour Dressing, 216
  Romaine Salad with Buttermilk-
      Chive Dressing, Grilled, 218
Honey-Pecan Dressing, 226
Lemon Dressing, Zesty, 219
Mozzarella-Tomato-Basil Salad,
      Fresh, 221
Orange-Walnut Salad, 224
Pea Salad, 219
Potato
  Bacon Potato Salad, 233
  Lemon-Basil Potato Salad, 233
  Southern-Style Potato Salad, 233
  Sweet Potato Salad with Rosemary-
      Honey Vinaigrette, 233
Roasted Red Bell Pepper Dressing, 222
Slaws
  Barbecue Slaw, 231
  Blue Cheese-Bacon Slaw, 229
  Broccoli Slaw, 229
  Broccoli-Squash Slaw, 229
  Buttermilk-Dressing Coleslaw, 231
  Chinese Cabbage Slaw, 231
  Cilantro Slaw, 229
  Marinated Coleslaw, Tangy, 230
  Memphis-Style Coleslaw, 231
  Overnight Slaw, Spectacular, 230
  Red Cabbage Coleslaw, Sweet-and-
      Tart, 230
Spinach Salad, Tossed, 219
Spinach Salad with Pistachio-Lime
      Vinaigrette, Cantaloupe-, 225
Strawberry Salad with Cinnamon
      Vinaigrette, 225
Sweet-and-Sour Dressing, 216, 224
Tomato Salad, Italian, 221
Vinaigrette
  Blueberry Vinaigrette, 227
  Cinnamon Vinaigrette, 225
  Pistachio-Lime Vinaigrette, 225

  Rose Vinaigrette, 223
  Sweet-Hot Vinaigrette, 228
  Watermelon-Prosciutto Salad, 226
Salmon
  Barbecue Roasted Salmon, 170
  Grilled Salmon, BBQ, 135
  Smoked Dilled Salmon, 135
  Smoked Rosemary-Scented
      Salmon, 136
  Smoked Salmon with Sweet-Hot
      Mustard and Dill, 135
Salsas. *See also* **Relishes; Sauces;**
      Toppings/Savory.
  Avocado-Feta Salsa, 77
  Avocado Salsa, Fresh, 77
  Black Bean Salsa, 76
  Corn Salsa, 76
  Corn Salsa, Grilled, 117
  Cranberry-Jalapeño Salsa, 207
  Green Tomato Salsa, Peachy, 207
  Mango Salsa, Fresh, 207
  Sweet-Heat Salsa and Cinnamon Crisps,
      South Seas Ice Cream with, 321
  Tomatillo Salsa, 77
  Tropical Salsa, 77
  Verde, Salsa, 207
Sandwiches
  Barbecue 'n' Slaw Sandwiches, 159
  Barbecue Sandwiches, Debate, 177
  Beef Sandwiches, Barbecue, 173
  Beefwiches, Barbecue, 149
  Brisket Sandwiches, Knife-and-Fork
      Barbecued, 173
  Brisket Sandwiches, Quickest, 150
  Brisket Sandwiches, Smoked, 99
  Chicken, Shredded Barbecue, 177
  Hoagies, Barbecue Pork-and-
      Coleslaw, 160
  Hot Browns, Baby, 87
  Meat Loaf Sandwiches, Barbecue, 157
  Open-Faced Sandwiches, Carolina
      Blond, 167
  Pork Sandwiches, Asian Barbecue, 162
  Pork Sandwiches, Mini, 87
  Pulled-Pork Barbecue Sandwiches,
      Chipotle, 161
  Roast, Barbecue, 149
  Roast Barbecue, Chuck, 172
  Turkey Sandwiches, Barbecue, 167
Sauces. *See also* **Relishes, Salsas,**
      Toppings.
  Apple Barbecue Sauce, 185
  Asian Barbecue Sauce, 188
  Big "D" Barbecue Sauce, 183
  Blueberry-Balsamic Barbecue
      Sauce, 189

Blueberry Barbecue Sauce, 189
Chili Sauce and Beer, Lone Star Brisket in, 152
Chipotle Barbecue Sauce, 186
Chipotle Sauce, Grilled Corn with Creamy, 137
Cider Vinegar Barbecue Sauce, 186
Citrus-Spiced Barbecue Sauce, 181
Cola Barbecue Sauce, 182
Cranberry Barbecue Sauce, Chicken with, 165
Cream Sauce, 257
Creole Sauce, 92
Dipping Sauce, Seared Chicken with Feisty Hot Barbecue, 164
Fiery-Sweet Barbecue Sauce, 183
Ginger-Hot Pepper Sauce, Fragrant, 190
Green Bell Pepper Sauce, 171
Herbed Lemon Barbecue Sauce, 190
Honey-Barbecue Sauce, 180
Honey-Mustard Barbecue Sauce, 187
Jalapeño Barbecue Sauce, Sweet, 125
Mango-Pineapple Hot Sauce, 190
Maple-Molasses Barbecue Sauce, 181
Mopping Sauce, Brisket, 97
Mustard Sauce, 93
Mustard Sauce, Spicy-Sweet, 187
Orange Sauce, Broccoli with, 244
Peach of the Old South Barbecue Sauce for Ribs, 185
Peppery Barbecue Sauce, 185
Ranch Barbecue Sauce, 186
Raspberry Barbecue Sauce, 189
Red Sauce, Brisket, 97
Roasted Red Pepper Rémoulade, 212
Smoky Barbecue Sauce, 96
Smoky Hot Sauce, 190
Smoky Sweet Barbecue Sauce, 181
Spiced Barbecue Sauce, 185
Sweet and Simple Barbecue Sauce, 180
Sweet-and-Sour 'Cue Sauce, 113
Sweet-and-Tangy Barbecue Sauce, 183
Swiss Cheese Cream Sauce, 254
Tangy Sorghum Barbecue Sauce, 184
Thick 'n' Sweet Barbecue Sauce, 180
Tomatillo Barbecue Sauce, 188
Tomatillo Sauce, 189
White Barbecue Sauce, 188
Zesty Barbecue Sauce, 187
Sausage
Andouille Grits, Grilled, 145
Balls, Sausage, 87
Smoked Sausage Hash, Potato-, 259
Scallops, Smoked Sea, 136

Seasonings
Marinades
Beer Marinade, 193
Browned Garlic and Burgundy Marinade, 193
Horseradish Marinade, 193
injection, 110
primer, 193
Red Wine-Mustard Marinade, 193
Oil, Rosemary, 141
Rubs
All-Purpose Barbecue Rub, 192
Brisket Rub, 97
Chipotle Rub, 192
Garlic Chicken Rub, 125
Garlic-Pepper Brisket Rub, 192
Ginger Rub, 113
Pork Ribs Rub, 114
primer, 192
Sweet 'n' Spicy Barbecue Rub, 192
Spice Blend, Southwestern, 192
Shrimp. *See also* **Grilled/Fish and Shellfish; Smoked/Fish and Shellfish.**
Barbecue Shrimp and Cornbread-Stuffed Peppers, 171
Cajun-Barbecue Shrimp, 171
Cocktail, Cinco de Mayo Shrimp, 84
Coconut Shrimp with Mustard Sauce, 93
Grilled Shrimp with Bacon and Jalapeños, 132
Grilled Zucchini-Wrapped Shrimp, 93
Hickory-Smoked Barbecue Shrimp, 132
Pickled Shrimp, 202
Smoked Shrimp, Citrus-Marinated, 133
Smoked Shrimp with Orange and Lime, Spicy, 133
Slow Cooker
Beans, Slow-Cooker Barbecue, 235
Main Dishes
Baby Back Ribs, So-Simple, 177
Beef and Pork Barbecue, 174
Beef Barbecue, Spiced, 174
Beef Brisket, Guinness-Braised, 173
Pork Chops, Easy Barbecue, 175
Pork, Saucy Chipotle Barbecue, 174
Pork, 3-Ingredient BBQ, 174
Ribs and Beans, Spicy-Sweet, 176
Ribs, Country-Style Barbecue, 177
Sandwiches
Barbecue Sandwiches, Debate, 177
Beef Sandwiches, Barbecue, 173
Brisket Sandwiches, Knife-and-Fork Barbecued, 173

Chicken, Shredded Barbecue, 177
Chuck Roast Barbecue, 172
Smoked, 16–17, 102. *See also* **Grilled.**
Beef
Brisket Sandwiches, Smoked, 99
Brisket, Texas-Smoked Beer-Marinated, 96
Brisket, Traditional Red-Sauced, 97
Eye of Round, Smoked Marinated, 102
Prime Rib, Smoked Garlic, 100
Prime Rib, Smoked Herbed, 100
Strip Steaks, Smoked, 102
Fish and Shellfish
Fish, Smoked, 134
King Crab Legs and Lobster Tails, Smoked, 136
Salmon, Smoked Dilled, 135
Salmon, Smoked Rosemary-Scented, 136
Salmon with Sweet-Hot Mustard and Dill, Smoked, 135
Sea Scallops, Smoked, 136
Shrimp, Citrus-Marinated Smoked, 133
Shrimp, Hickory-Smoked Barbecue, 132
Shrimp with Orange and Lime, Spicy Smoked, 133
Trout, Smoked, 134
Tuna, Smoked, 134
Pecans, Smoky, 80
Pork
Baby Back Ribs, Beer-Smoked, 114
Barbecue Pork, Tabb's, 110
BBQ, Three-Alarm, 109
Boston Butt, Smoked Teriyaki-Marinated, 107
Mesquite-Smoked Pork with Texas Caviar, 108
Mustard-Sauced Pork, Smoked, 108
Shoulder, Barbecue Pork, 109
Shoulder, North Carolina Smoked Pork, 107
Slow-Smoked Pork with Ranch-Barbecue Sauce, 110
Tenderloin with Molasses Barbecue Sauce and Mango Salsa, Pork, 111
Poultry
Chicken, Big "D" Smoked, 125
Chicken, Jerk Smoked, 122
Turkey Breast, Chili-Spiced Smoked, 131
Turkey Breast, Mesquite-Smoked, 131

Smoked, Poultry *(continued)*

    Turkey Breast, Spicy-Sweet
        Smoked, 131
    Turkey, Hickory-Smoked
        Bourbon, 130
    Turkey, Seasoned Smoked, 130
    turkey tip, smoked, 130
  Quail, Sage-Smoked Maple, 117
  Tofu and Roasted Red Peppers, Grilled
    Pizza with Smoked, 144

Soufflé, Spinach, 247

Spaghetti, Barbecue, 163

Spinach
  Florentine Artichoke Dip, 72
  Pizza with Feta and Spinach, Grilled
    Vegetable, 143
  Quiches, Mini Spinach, 90
  Salad, Tossed Spinach, 219
  Salad with Pistachio-Lime Vinaigrette,
    Cantaloupe-Spinach, 225
  Soufflé, Spinach, 247

Spreads. *See also* **Butter, Mayonnaise.**
  Artichoke and Cheese Spread, Pecan-
    Crusted, 75
  Chile-Cheese Spread, 76
  Horseradish Spread, 76
  Olive-Parsley Spread, Cream Cheese-
    and-Olive Biscuits with, 79
  Sun-Dried Tomato-and-Basil Spread,
    Layered, 74

Squash. *See also* **Zucchini.**
  Summer Squash, Grilled, 138
  Yellow
    Casserole, Crunchy Squash, 254
    Casserole, Two-Cheese Squash, 253
    Grilled Summer Squash and
      Tomatoes, 252
    Halves, Grilled Yellow Squash, 138
    Pickles, Refrigerator Squash, 195
    Slaw, Broccoli-Squash, 229

Stews
  Brunswick Stew, 261
  Brunswick Stew, Chicken, 261
  Burgoo, Classic Kentucky, 260
  Burgoo, Kentucky, 260

Strawberries
  Ice Cream, Low-Fat Strawberry
    Cheesecake, 317
  Ice-Cream Pie, Spiked Strawberry-
    Lime, 298
  Ice-Cream Pie, Strawberry-
    Lime, 298
  Ice-Cream Pie, Strawberry
    Smoothie, 298
  Ice Cream, Strawberry, 318

  Salad, Cranberry-Strawberry-
    Jícama, 226
  Salad with Cinnamon Vinaigrette,
    Strawberry, 225
  Trifle, Strawberry-Sugar Biscuit, 302

Succotash, Garden, 255

Sweet Potatoes
  Grilled Sweet Potatoes with Orange-
    Chipotle Glaze, 141
  Hash, Savory Sweet Potato, 259
  Mélange, Beef Brisket with Sweet
    Potato, 155
  Roasted Smashed Sweet Potatoes, 256
  Salad with Rosemary-Honey
    Vinaigrette, Sweet Potato, 233

Syrups
  Blackberry Syrup, 289
  Bourbon Syrup, 68
  Mint Sugar Syrup, Fresh, 52
  Mint Syrup, 65
  Sugar Syrup, 49

Tofu and Roasted Red Peppers, Grilled
  Pizza with Smoked, 144

Tomatillos
  Salsa, Tomatillo, 77
  Salsa Verde, 207
  Sauce, Tomatillo, 189
  Sauce, Tomatillo Barbecue, 188

Tomatoes
  Butterbeans, Bacon, and
    Tomatoes, 244
  Cherry Tomatoes, Rosemary-
    Roasted, 252
  Chutney, Tomato, 206
  Chutney, Tomato-Garlic, 206
  Dip, Tomato-Basil, 70
  Green
    Fried Green Tomatoes, Kentucky
      Bibb Salad with, 223
    Jam, Green Tomato-Blueberry, 208
    Marmalade, Green Tomato, 210
    Pickled Green Tomatoes, 195
    Pickles, Green Tomato, 195
    Salsa, Peachy Green Tomato, 207
  Grilled Tomatoes, 139
  Relish, Sweet White Corn and
    Tomato, 204
  Salad, Fresh Mozzarella-Tomato-
    Basil, 221
  Salad, Italian Tomato, 221
  Sun-Dried Tomato-and-Basil
    Spread, Layered, 74
  Sun-Dried Tomato Cheesecake, 82

Tools for grilling, 11

Toppings
  Savory
    Apricot and Green Peppercorn
      Glaze, Grilled Venison with, 120
    Horseradish Glaze, Carrots
      with, 245
    Ketchup, Sweet-Hot, 212
    Orange-Chipotle Glaze, Grilled
      Sweet Potatoes with, 141
    Parmesan Topping, Buttery, 254
    Pico de Gallo, 103
  Sweet
    Blackberry Syrup, 289
    Brown Sugar-Pecan Topping, 280
    Buttermilk Glaze, 285
    Chocolate Glaze, 294
    Praline Topping, 282
    Royal Icing, 264
    Sugared Almonds, 228

Tuna, Smoked, 134

Turkey
  Hot Browns, Baby, 87
  Sandwiches, Barbecue Turkey, 167
  Smoked
    Chili-Spiced Smoked Turkey
      Breast, 131
    Hickory-Smoked Bourbon
      Turkey, 130
    Mesquite-Smoked Turkey
      Breast, 131
    Seasoned Smoked Turkey, 130
    Spicy-Sweet Smoked Turkey
      Breast, 131

Turnip Casserole, Scalloped, 247

Turnips, Sweet Skillet, 247

Vanilla Ice Cream, No-Cook, 315

Vanilla Ice Cream, Old-Fashioned, 315

Vegetables. *See also* specific types.
  Brisket with Veggies, 153
  Burgoo, Classic Kentucky, 260
  Burgoo, Kentucky, 260
  Grilled Vegetables with Cilantro
    Butter, 141
  Pico de Gallo, 103
  Pizzas, Grilled Veggie, 145
  Pizza with Feta and Spinach, Grilled
    Vegetable, 143
  Relish, Hot, 204
  Relish, Sweet Pickle, 205
  Roasted Baby Vegetables, 254
  Succotash, Garden, 255

Zucchini-Wrapped Shrimp, Grilled, 93